ISLAM AND PUBLIC CO

Global Connections

Series Editor: Robert Holton, Trinity College, Dublin

Global Connections builds on the multi-dimensional and continuously expanding interest in Globalization. The main objective of the series is to focus on 'connectedness' and provide readable case studies across a broad range of areas such as social and cultural life, economic, political and technological activities.

The series aims to move beyond abstract generalities and stereotypes: 'Global' is considered in the broadest sense of the word, embracing connections between different nations, regions and localities, including activities that are trans-national, and trans-local in scope; 'Connections' refers to movements of people, ideas, resources, and all forms of communication as well as the opportunities and constraints faced in making, engaging with, and sometimes resisting globalization.

The series is interdisciplinary in focus and publishes monographs and collections of essays by new and established scholars. It fills a niche in the market for books that make the study of globalization more concrete and accessible.

Also published in this series:

Islam and Public Controversy in Europe

Edited by

NILÜFER GÖLE
École des Hautes Études en Sciences Sociales, France

Routledge
Taylor & Francis Group

LONDON AND NEW YORK

First published 2013 by Ashgate Publishing

2 Park Square, Milton Park, Abingdon, Oxon OX14 4RN
711 Third Avenue, New York, NY 10017, USA

Routledge is an imprint of the Taylor & Francis Group, an informa business

First issued in paperback 2016

British Library Cataloguing in Publication Data
A catalogue record for this book is available from the British Library

The Library of Congress has cataloged the printed edition as follows:
Göle, Nilüfer, 1953–
    Islam and public controversy in Europe / by Nilüfer Göle.
      pages cm. — (Global connections)
    Includes bibliographical references and index.
    ISBN 978-1-4724-1313-0 (hardback)
1. Multiculturalism–Europe. 2. Islam–Europe. 3. Muslims–Europe. I. Title.

    HM1271.G645 2013
    306.6'97094–dc23

                                                2013021072

ISBN 978-1-4724-1313-0 (hbk)
ISBN 978-1-138-27026-8 (pbk)

Contents

PART V   EUROPEAN GENEALOGIES OF ISLAM AND POLITICS OF MEMORY

Acknowledgments

This volume grew out of two international conferences that I organized in Paris within the framework of my research project "EuroPublicIslam: Islam in the Making of a European Public Sphere." The aim of this project is to explore the role of controversies around religious-cultural difference in shaping European public spheres. Rewarded by the Advanced Grant for exceptional established research leaders, EuroPublicIslam project has received funding by the European Research Council under the European Community's Seventh Framework Programme from the end of 2008 to March 2013. My special thanks go to the European Research Council for the financial support it provided.

The majority of the chapters comprising this volume were first presented at these two international conferences. In the first conference, "Public Controversies around Islam in Europe," which was held on 13–14 October 2011 in Paris, we explored the religious, gendered, artistic, juridical and spatial dimensions of Islamic visibility across European public spheres. The second conference, "Transnational Study of Public Controversies around Islam in Europe," which took place 31 May–2 June 2012 in Paris, was a continuation of the previous one and featured the participation of junior researchers and Ph.D. students working on Islamic difference in diverse public spaces. Out of the 27 papers presented at the conferences, we had to select 16 to be written as chapters for the edited volume. I would like to thank all the participants for their presentations and comments that enriched the discussions during these gatherings. Most of all, I wish to express my gratitude to the contributors of the present volume, who brought new insights and critiques to the notions of the public sphere and religious difference.

Special thanks are due to the managers and the personnel of the Columbia Global Centers/Europe in Paris, where both conferences took place, for their hospitality and for providing us with a unique setting for intellectual exchange and discussion.

I would like to express my appreciation of the École des Hautes Études en Sciences Sociales for providing assistance as the host institution in terms of management and accounting.

Last but not least, I am thankful to the EuroPublicIslam project team, which consists mainly of my current and former Ph.D. students, namely Warda Hadjab, Bochra Kammarti, Anahita Grisoni and Thibault Dhilly, for accompanying me through the organization of the two conferences. My special thanks go to Zehra Cunillera, without whose immense assistance for the editorial preparation of each chapter, this volume would not have been possible.

Notes on Contributors

Stefano Allievi is Professor of Sociology at the University of Padua, Italy. He specializes in migration issues, the sociology of religion and cultural change, with a particular focus on religious pluralism and the presence of Islam in Europe. His latest publications include: *Conflicts over Mosques in Europe: Policy Issues and Trends* (Alliance Publishing Trust/Network of European Foundations, 2009); *Mosques of Europe. Why a Solution Has Become a Problem* (editor, Alliance Publishing Trust/Network of European Foundations, 2010); and *Producing Islamic Knowledge: Transmission and Dissemination in Western Europe* (co-editor, with M. Van Bruinessen and S. Allievi, Routledge, 2011).

Schirin Amir-Moazami holds a Ph.D. from the Department of Social and Political Sciences of the European University Institute in Florence, Italy. Since 2009, she has held the position of Assistant Professor for Islam in Europe in the Department of Islamic Studies at the Free University of Berlin, Germany. She has published a book on the headscarf controversies in France and Germany (*Politisierte Religion. Der Kopftuchstreit in Deutschland und Frankreich*, Bielefeld, 2007) and numerous articles relating to the issues of secular orders and Muslims in both countries. Her research interests include Islamic movements in Europe, political theory, gender questions and the sociology of religion. She is currently working on a book entitled *Producing the Tolerable. On the Governmentalization of Gendered Islam in Germany*, in which she looks at micro-political practices triggered by the emergence of the "Muslim question" in Germany and the discursive apparatus upon which these are based.

Gil Anidjar is Associate Professor at the Department of Religion and the Department of Middle Eastern, South Asian, and African Studies at Columbia University in New York. He is the author, among other works, of *The Jew, the Arab: A History of the Enemy* (Stanford University Press, 2003) and *Semites: Race, Religion, Literature* (Stanford University Press, 2008). His next book, *Blood: A Critique of Christianity*, is due to be published by Columbia University Press.

Nebahat Avcıoğlu is Associate Professor at Hunter College, City University of New York. She received her BA in Architecture from the Istanbul Technical University and her Ph.D. from the Department of History of Art, University of Cambridge. She specializes in Islamic art and architecture with a particular emphasis on Ottoman and European cultural encounters. Her books include

Turquerie and the Politics of Representation, 1737–1876 (Ashgate Publishing, 2011), *Globalizing Cultures: Art and Mobility in the Eighteenth Century* (co-edited with Finbarr Barry Flood, *Ars Orientalis*, 39 (2011)) and *Architecture, Art and Identity in Venice and its Territories 1450–1750* (co-edited with Emma Jones, Ashgate Publishing, 2013). She is also the author of "Istanbul: The Palimpsest City in Search of its Architext," *RES*, 53/54 (2008) and "Form-as-Identity: The Mosque in the West," *Cultural Analysis*, 6 (2008), as well as other articles in *Art Bulletin* and *Muqarnas* dealing with the dissemination and transformation of forms and cultures, theories of artistic contact, and the sociopolitical aspects of the history of art and architecture.

Etienne Balibar is Professor Emeritus of Moral and Political Philosophy at the University of Paris, Nanterre and Distinguished Professor of Humanities at the University of California, Irvine. His work has been vastly influential on both sides of the Atlantic throughout the humanities and the social sciences, and focuses on political philosophy, critical theory, the epistemology of the social sciences, and ethics. His recent publications include *Saeculum. Culture, Religion, Idéologie* (Editions Galilée, 2012) and *We, the People of Europe? Reflections on Transnational Citizenship* (Princeton University Press, 2003).

Florence Bergeaud-Blackler holds a Ph.D. in Anthropology. She is currently Marie Curie Fellow at the Université Libre de Bruxelles, Belgium and Research Associate at IREMAM, the Institute of Research and Study on the Arab and Muslim World at Aix-Marseille Université, France. Her work focuses on the halal market, consumption, regulation and ethical issues in Europe, particularly those concerning industrial religious slaughter. She is the author of numerous publications on these issues, including *Comprendre le Halal* (Edipro, 2010).

Julie Billaud received her Ph.D. in Socio-Legal Studies from the University of Sussex and the École des Hautes Études en Sciences Sociales, Paris. Her thesis, based on ethnographic fieldwork conducted in Kabul in 2007, investigates the issue of Afghan women's public visibility in the "post-war/reconstruction" period. Her most recent research deals with European Islam and, more specifically, everyday uses and practices of Islamic justice in England. She is currently a postdoctoral researcher at the Max Planck Institute for Social Anthropology in Halle, Germany. Her current research interests lie within the field of legal anthropology and involve more specifically Islam, gender and human rights.

Jean-Philippe Bras is Professor of Public Law at the University of Rouen. He has taught and has conducted research at diverse public institutions in France (including the Institut International d'Administration Publique, 1974–87) and abroad (including the ENA, Tunis, 1976–78; ENA, Rabat 1987–89). From 1997 to 2003, he was Director of the Contemporary Maghreb Studies Institute in Tunis

(CNRS); then, from 2006 to 2010, he was the Director of IISMM (Institute for the Study of Islam and Muslim Societies) at the École des Hautes Études en Sciences Sociales in Paris. His research interests include the transformations of the public law and jurisprudence in the Muslim world as well as in Muslim communities across Europe.

Jocelyne Cesari is currently Visiting Professor of Government and Senior Research Fellow at the Berkley Center for Religion, Peace and World Affairs at Georgetown University, Washington DC. She also directs the International Research Program at Harvard University called "Islam in the West." In 2011 and 2012, she was the Minerva Chair at the Office of the Secretary of Defense, which was affiliated to the National Defense University in Washington DC to conduct a research on Islam and democratization in the context of the Arab Spring (the subject of an upcoming book, *Understanding the Arab Spring: Islam, Modernity and Democracy*, due to be published by Cambridge University Press). She is a political scientist with a French background, tenured at the French National Center for Scientific Research in Paris and specializing in contemporary Islamic societies, globalization and democratization. She has written numerous articles and books on Islam, globalization, democratization and secularism, including *Muslims in the West After 9/11: Religion, Politics and Law* (Routledge, 2010).

Nilüfer Göle is Professor of Sociology at the École des Hautes Études en Sciences Sociales in Paris. She works on Islamic visibility in European public spaces and the debates it engenders on religious and cultural difference. Her sociological approach aims to open up a new reading of modernity from a non-Western perspective and a broader critique of Eurocentrism in the definitions of secular modernity. She is the author of *Islam in Europe: The Lure of Fundamentalism and the Allure of Cosmopolitanism* (Markus Wiener Publishing, 2010) and *The Forbidden Modern: Civilization and Veiling* (University of Michigan Press, 1997). She is Director of the "EuroPublicIslam: Islam in the Making of a European Public Sphere" project funded by the European Research Council.

Charles Hirschkind is Associate Professor of Anthropology at the University of California, Berkeley. His research interests concern religious practice, media technologies and emergent forms of political community in the urban Middle East and Europe. In his book *The Ethical Soundscape: Cassette Sermons and Islamic Counterpublics* (Columbia University Press, 2006), he explores how a popular Islamic media form – the cassette sermon – has profoundly transformed the political geography of the Middle East over the last three decades. He is also the co-editor (with David Scott) of *Powers of the Secular Modern: Talal Asad and His Interlocutors* (Stanford University Press, 2005). His current project is based in southern Spain and explores some of the different ways in which Europe's Islamic past inhabits its present, unsettling contemporary efforts to secure Europe's

Christian civilizational identity. This project has been funded through an award from the Carnegie Corporation of New York.

Rachid Id Yassine is a postdoctoral fellow at the Centre for the Study of Religions of the Gaston Berger University, Senegal and has taught at the Department of Sociology of the University of Perpignan Via Domitia (UPVD) since 2007. He is also Research Associate at the Centre for Sociological Analysis and Intervention (École des Hautes Études en Sciences Sociales) and the Catalan Institute of Social Science Research (UPVD). His work currently focuses on Islam and regionalisms (both European and African). A graduate in sociology, anthropology, religious studies and Islamic studies, he is a consultant to international organizations and a member of various research groups. He has also contributed to numerous edited collections on the subject.

Jeanette S. Jouili is a postdoctoral fellow at the Women's Studies Program at Duke University. After obtaining her Ph.D. in 2007 in Sociology/Anthropology jointly from the École des Hautes Études en Sciences Sociales in Paris and the European University Viadrina in Frankfurt-Oder, Germany, she has held research positions at the University of Amsterdam and the International Institute for the Study of Islam in the Modern World in the Netherlands. In 2011–12, she was a fellow of the Society for the Humanities at Cornell University. Currently, she is conducting research on the Islamic cultural and artistic scene in the UK and in France. She has published in various journals including *Feminist Review*, *Social Anthropology* and *Muslim World*. She is also completing a book manuscript based on the material of her Ph.D dissertation provisionally titled *Pious Practice and Secular Constraints: Women in the Islamic Revival in France and Germany*. Her research and teaching interests include Islam in Europe, secularism, pluralism, popular culture, moral and aesthetic practices, and gender.

Sune Lægaard is Associate Professor in Philosophy at the Department of Culture and Identity at Roskilde University, Denmark. His research focuses on political philosophy, especially issues of multiculturalism and related topics such as toleration, recognition, free speech and secularism. He is co-editor of the political philosophy journal *Res Publica*.

Silvia Naef is Professor at the Arabic Studies Department of the University of Geneva. She taught as a visiting scholar in the University of Toronto's Visual and Performing Arts Department (2008–9), in Sassari (2012) and previously in Basel and Tübingen. Her main research interest is in modern art and visual culture in the Arabic and Islamic world. She is the author of *Y a-t-il une question de l'image en Islam?* (2004, German 2007, Italian 2011, Turkish 2013) and of *A la recherche d'une modernité arabe* (1996, Arabic 2008). She is also the leader of the three-year Sinergia research project *Other Modernities: Patrimony and Practices* *of Visual Expression outside the West,* which is funded by the Swiss National Science Foundation.

Simone Maddanu is Postdoctoral Fellow in Sociology at the University of Political Sciences, Cagliari, Italy. His research interests include day-to-day practices of young Muslims in Europe. He currently leads a research project entitled *The New Generations of Muslims in Europe,* which is funded by a European and Regional Grant. He was also part of the EuroPublicIslam project team as Postdoctoral Research Fellow (2009–10).

Olivier Remaud is Associate Professor of Philosophy at the École des Hautes Études en Sciences Sociales in Paris and Director of the Centre d'Études Sociologiques et Politiques Raymond-Aron. He was Senior Fellow at the Internationales Forschungszentrum Kulturwissenschaften in Vienna, Visiting Professor at the Free University of Berlin as well as at the Universities of Chicago and Oslo, and Fulbright Research Scholar at the State University of New York. His work focuses on the philosophy of social belief, epistemologies of history, political theory of culture and critical cosmopolitanisms. His recent publications include *Michelet. La Magistrature de l'histoire* (Michalon, 1998); *Les archives de l'humanité. Essai sur la philosophie de Vico* (Seuil, 2004); *L'épreuve de la nouveauté (Laboratoire italien. Politique et société)* (with M. Gaille-Nikodimov and P. Girard, 2005); *La nature et les Américains* (2006); *Civilisations. Retour sur les mots et les idées* (co-edited with C. Avlami, *Revue de synthèse,* Springer, 2008); *War and Peace. The Role of Science and Art* (co-edited with S. Nour, 010); *Faire des Sciences Sociales (II): Comparer* (co-edited with J.-F. Schaub and I. Thireau, 2012); and *Un monde étrange. Essai sur le point de vue cosmopolitique* (2013).

John V. Tolan works on the history of religious and cultural relations between the Arab and Latin worlds in the Middle Ages. He received a BA in Classics from Yale University, an MA and a Ph.D. in History from the University of Chicago and an *Habilitation à diriger des recherches* from the École des Hautes Études en Sciences Sociales in Paris. He has taught and lectured in universities in North America, Europe, Africa and the Middle East, and is currently Professor of History at the University of Nantes. He is the director of a major project funded by the European Research Council, *RELMIN: The Legal Status of Religious Minorities in the Euro-Mediterranean World (5th–15th Centuries).* He is also the author of numerous books and articles, including *Saracens: Islam in the Medieval European Imagination* (Columbia University Press, 2002); *Sons of Ishmael: Muslims through European Eyes in the Middle Ages* (University Press of Florida, 2008); and *Saint Francis and the Sultan: The Curious History of a Christian-Muslim Encounter* (Oxford University Press, 2009).

Halide Velioğlu was born into a Bosniak family that migrated to Turkey during the second half of the 1960s. After receiving her MA degree in Sociology at Boğaziçi

University, Istanbul, she obtained her PhD in Anthropology with the dissertation entitled "Bosniak Sentiments: Poetic and Mundane Life of Impossible Longings" from the University of Texas at Austin in 2011. She is currently lecturer at Boğaziçi and Bilgi Universities in Istanbul, teaching graduate and undergraduate courses. Her research interests include the ethnography of mundane, affect, public culture, political imaginaries, ethnopoetics, material culture, Bosnia, the Western Balkans and Turkish popular culture.

PART I
Controversies and Publics

Chapter 1

Introduction: Islamic Controversies in the Making of European Public Spheres

Nilüfer Göle

In this volume, we study some of the controversies surrounding visible practices of Islam that take place in different public spheres across Europe. We focus on controversies that break out over the issues raised by Muslims who practice their religion and want to be recognized publicly for their religious difference. The public nature of these controversies implies and concerns social actors from all walks of life, rather than being limited only to those who are pious Muslims. Around a particular theme of converse, diverse actors with different voices and positions in relation to Islam emerge, including secular Muslims as well as non-Muslims, but also those who define themselves critically as "ex-Muslims" or as anti-Islam, producing new alignments and oppositions. In this sense, the controversies surrounding Islam change the established frameworks of European publics. We investigate the diverse manifestations of Islamic difference in the current context with a shared problematic around the notion of the public sphere. On the one hand, there is the need to describe the particularity of the historical moment and, on the other, to establish a conceptual framework, with both being intimately connected. We seek to explore the modes of encountering, confronting and connecting that are staged in public. New conceptual tools are required to study Islam in this particular point in time in which the sociological paradigm of immigration falls short of grasping the new dynamics of integration.

All the chapters in this volume give priority to the post-migration period from the end of the 1980s to the present day. We can broadly distinguish three stages to account for social and cultural changes in the phenomenon of immigration (Leveau 1998; Cesari 2004). The first stage is marked by the figure of the immigrant, the solitary male worker, with a status of foreigner, temporary guest-worker, *gastarbeiter*. The second stage is characterized by the settlement of the immigrant worker with his family. The figure of the "Arab boy" in France, for instance, is an outcome of this stage, representing the second-generation youth, who have no intention to return to their country of origin, yet who have not yet acquired the social credentials for integration into the host country. The Arab boy is perceived as a potential trouble-maker, a deviant, with problems of education and unemployment (Guénif-Souilamas and Macé 2006). Whereas in the first stage, social problems inherent in the living conditions and the legal status of workers are addressed, in the second stage, language learning and children's education become the priority for the politics of integration. Only in the third stage does the issue of religion become predominant. The new figure of the "veiled Muslim girl" at schools illustrates this new turn (Göle 2005). The figure of the immigrant thus changes from the working-class male and the unemployed youth to young schoolgirls. Islam becomes an issue at this stage of post-immigration that links together categories of gender and religion. We situate our inquiry in this third stage at a moment where the "visibility" of Islam becomes of central importance as Muslims manifest their religious difference publicly.

To broach this third stage, I propose highlighting the notion of the public sphere and the different modes of visibility of Islam so as to define the field and the problem that will be the subject of our investigation. The notion of the public sphere enables us to study the dynamics of encounters and confrontation, leading us to question the interface between private and public, personal and intercultural. How do Muslim actors reinterpret their religious piety in secular European contexts? Who are the Muslim figures with access to public spheres? What are the symbols and practices that become visible, ostentatious, even disturbing in the eyes of the majority? How is this difference perceived publicly and what controversies does the visibility of Islam in the European public space trigger? The question of the arrival of "new actors" is not limited to their expression in public life; it also poses the question of their representation in the political system. Although the relationship between the public sphere and the political realm warrants further exploration, especially as the participation of Muslim citizens in political life is in progress, this volume is dedicated specifically to the study of Islam in the public domain.

How are we to define the public sphere through the prism of Islamic difference? We cannot reduce Islam's dominant place in public debates to a sheer consequence of the media coverage given to it – it does not arise simply from media distortion or focalization. Certainly, the media participates in shaping the public agenda with regard to Islam – it can reinforce stereotypes and seek to communicate the sensational, building up "the Muslim problem" and sowing "social panic" (Dayan 2003; Macé 2007, 2008). Unquestionably, Muslims today are in the media spotlight, yet we cannot explain the phenomenon of the appearance of Muslims in the public spheres solely as a result of media coverage. This would be to deny any capacity to express agency or public manifestation on the part of Muslims. The public sphere cannot be confused with the media space. The latter amplifies the way in which the public views a phenomenon, while the public sphere reflects the interplay between the public and personal, intimate spaces. The visibility of Muslims in public spheres concerns both self-presentation and the perception of the other. Public spheres are the places of this articulation – of face-to-face meetings, encounters and confrontations. There is never a perfect connection between the subjective meaning that actors ascribe to their own practices and the perception of it by others; misunderstanding is intrinsic to this communication. Some of the meaning is always lost in crossing from the subjective to the public – a loss that is inherent to this kind of translation.

The notion of visibility pinpoints a far more complex reality than typical media stereotyping is capable of capturing and conveying.

The public sphere also points to the private space, as it is where the actor crosses – even sometimes, as with Muslims, transgresses – the boundaries between public and private, between inside and outside. However, the departure of the individual from the private to the public sphere is always connected to the way in which we organize the intimate and the private: what we hide, and the parts of the body that we allow to be seen, but also the meanings we give to emotions, words and taboo subjects. Since the Renaissance, we find in Europe a *jeu d'etiquettes*, a play of propriety, which distinguishes between honorable and dishonorable body parts and calls to mind the need to conceal emotions, not to let certain parts of the face appear in a natural fashion, such as the mouth, through the use of coded signs, masks and make-up.[1] The Western feminist movement proposes alternative labels and advocates liberty through a different set of rules for the body: stop wearing corsets, loosen one's hair, wear men's pants and so on. The body becomes the platform on which women's identity politics knocks down former markers of decency and brings down sexual taboos, thereby enabling women to break free from the private domain.

The emergence of Muslim actors in Europe signifies another reorganization of the boundaries between the private and public domains, inside and outside, sacred and secular. The body parts to be concealed change, Islamic norms on modesty are raised, and sexuality remains the central marker of the boundaries between private and public, as well as between religious and secular. The case of young generations of Muslims participating in diverse youth associations in France and in Italy illustrates the centrality of the issues of Islamic gender regimes and romantic love for the construction of the pious self. The search for reconciling their commitment to Islamic norms and the desire to participate in mixed gender contexts compel these young Muslims to question both Islamic and liberal grammar of sexual encounters (Maddanu, Chapter 16, this volume).

Beyond the Paradigm of Identity

We can identify the moment at which we intervene in the field of study of Islam in Europe by three axes of simultaneous developments: the formation of new subjectivities and forms of Muslim piety; the emergence of the visibility of Islamic difference in European public spheres; and discord over the norms of communal life. For each of these axes, I have elaborated the conceptual tools for analyzing and understanding these developments based upon my research project on "the role of

---

1   In the hearings of the National Assembly on the burqa, Nadeije Laneyrie-Dagen (2009), Professor of the History of Modern Art at the Ecole Normale Supérieure, noted that while Western civilization believes in revealing the face, as the vector of the soul, heart and personality, in reality it always develops *jeux d'etiquettes* that veil it in other ways.

Islam in the making of the European public sphere." This volume is an outcome of two international conferences, which were conceptualized as an extension of my research project to different case studies and disciplinary approaches.

With regard to the formation of new religious subjectivities, it is important to go beyond the paradigm of identity which served as a fecund heuristic category for studying new social movements in the 1970s but which falls short in the task of studying contemporary public expressions of Islam in Europe. By focusing on the public and private domains, we observe a series of renegotiations between the exigencies of Islamic ethics and secular life in the construction of subjectivities and articulations between different modes of visibility concerning modesty and piety. Rather than having a fixed and solid identity experienced in a collective and political form, Muslims are in a state of continual pursuit of piety, which is not given but is acquired through constant self-training (Mahmood 2005). The realization of piety and the construction of a pious self requires a self-scrutiny and coded practices for disciplining the "*nafs*" (the soul and the body in Islamic thought). These meditative and disciplinary practices guide their conduct in both the personal and public domains. In other words, what we try to do is not to do away with the problematic of identity entirely, but to redefine it through its translation into the ethical behaviors and aesthetic forms of the religious mode of life. Living as a Muslim in a secular context means living in a state of constant reflexivity, in a perpetual coming-and-going between subjective piety, private life and day-to-day experiences. This pendular movement creates tensions, readjustments and renegotiations in various cultural, artistic and commercial domains.

It is the notion of "halal" that best crystallizes these tensions in the encounters and confrontation between Islamic ethics and secular life. Halal recasts the issue of knowing how to live up to the prescriptions of one's religion and keep up one's piety in a secular age. How can one maintain one's piety, discipline one's "*nafs*" and control one's urges and desires? How can one conform to Islamic ethics, when they are tested daily by liberal mores and secular laws? In the current European context, the notion of halal is revitalized through the particularity of Muslims' experiences. We witness the Europeanization of halal that no longer concerns only the consumption of meat. The nuances between the terms *halâl*, the original Arab version, and halal, the more recent Europeanized version, reflect contrasted meanings (Id Yassine, Chapter 14, this volume). The new European version of halal is understood as permission, a lawful extension into new areas of life and pleasure that Muslims seek to enjoy. Halal certification makes these areas compatible with Islamic prescriptions. This new Islamic certification under the label of halal enables European Muslims to penetrate and to appropriate secular realms of life and pleasure. It even becomes a tool for satisfying mimetic consumerist desires for European tastes and products, like champagne, foie gras and sausages. Indeed, halal certification is at the disposal of Muslims who want to enter into areas of life hitherto "off limits," thereby creating new commercial opportunities and markets.

We have a tendency to think of the public sphere as a pre-established entity, an abstract place for argumentation. However, there is also a physical, spatial dimension to this notion. Public space puts the emphasis on the physicality of the public sphere. The Islamic presence bring into focus spaces such as beaches, swimming pools, public gardens, art galleries and markets, as they become sites in which competing norms are disputed. We observe the entry of Muslims into unexpected domains of life that they were not hitherto permitted to enter. In addition to the visibility of the veil in schools, burqinis (the Islamic swimming suit, the term coined using a combination of "burka" and "bikini") in swimming pools and mosques in cities, Islam in public spaces also extends into areas of art, commerce and finance. Muslims in Europe today penetrate these distinct areas of life with a halal certification that allows them to observe their religious prescriptions. Such examples illustrate how Muslims take part in European life and reinterpret the norms and practices of their own religion through their interactions with European norms and practices.

In the same vein, "Halal art" seeks to promote a certain Islamic ethics of communication and presentation of the self on the theatrical stage (Jouili, Chapter 11, this volume). In this alternative art form, actors and spectators seek to create public modes of appearance and interaction, all the while remaining within the circle of licit, halal authorization. In their representations and repetitions, the actors of halal art seek an alternative "distribution of the sensible"[2] that conforms to the Muslim codes of modesty. The halal circle defines the norms of what is forbidden. However, these prohibitions are constantly rethought and rearticulated in a reflexive manner in every enactment, dramatization and theatrical experience of Muslims. The theater thus becomes the place for the inventive reformulation of Islamic mores.

The access of Muslims to new areas of life through halal certification has triggered tensions throughout European societies. This also creates intra-community tensions among Muslims, who are forced to reflect on their urge to enter European modes of life and simultaneously remain in obedience to Islamic prescriptions. On the one hand, there is the self-questioning by Muslims of their entry into these areas of life whilst bringing the tenets of Islamic ethics along with them. On the other hand, there is also the perception of this difference by others – the public at large. Studying public spheres and spaces enables us to bring together the two facets of the subjective religiosity of Muslims and its public perception, with both sides challenging each other and sometimes colliding into one another. We thus witness the appearance of a particular form of Islam in Europe that triggers the Europeanization of public debates blurring national distinctions in the co-opting of Muslims' claims for being recognized as equal citizens while keeping their religious distinctions. The debates over the introduction of Sharia councils in England

---

2   According to Jacques Rancière (2004), the notion of the "distribution of the sensible" signifies the intersection of aesthetic practices and politics. What is sensed and perceived is determined and regulated by the established social order. Social groups and artistic forms that do not have the same share of the "distribution of the sensible" can potentially question the established order and change it.

and in France are cases in point that show how two very distinct conceptions of
law become more similar in their modes of accommodating Islamic normativity
(Bras, Chapter 12, this volume). The differences between legal traditions seem to
weaken and converge together as they confront the challenge of regulating Islamic
normativity. New dynamics of Europeanization are in progress with regard to
responses to the issues raised by Islam.

From the Notion of Conflict to the Notion of Controversy

Studying controversies enables us to grasp the two sides of the same coin:
confrontation and interaction. Controversies attest to the fact that the European
publics are not indifferent to the appearance of Islamic difference. I favor here
an agonistic approach of the public sphere that is open to conflict and not merely
determined by consensus-making. The public sphere is not solely a receptacle
to which newcomers must themselves conform in order to gain access; it also
provides a democratic site where newcomers can argue over their places and their
norms. The appearance of *différend*[3] is characteristic of a democratic public sphere
and is not symptomatic of its dysfunction. Indeed, an agonistic notion of the public
space allows us to approach it as a site to which actors try to gain access in order to
manifest their difference and dispute the majority's norms for collective life. From
this perspective, the notion of controversy becomes a privileged methodological
tool for studying the discord that simultaneously confronts and binds the different
actors together.

What is the *dissensus* that divides European citizens over the question of
Islam today? What is the nature of this disagreement? What are the sociological
or philosophical languages that can help us render an account of this divide? The
notion of conflict is often used in sociological approaches that privilege the study
of social and economic inequalities, closely tied to an analysis of class struggle
in industrial societies. It has gained ground through Marxist thought and has
been taken up again in the literature of new social movements that contest the
established order. Instead of the notion of conflict, I think it is more useful to apply
the notion of controversy. The notion of conflict refers to modes of collective,
group action, while controversies include personal, individual voices and public

3   The notion of *différend*, developed by Lyotard (1993), is a conflict that cannot
be settled due to the absence of a ruling judgment applicable to both arguments under
consideration. When two expressions "in a heterogeneous system are not translatable the
one to the other, there is a *différend* between these expressions (or between the categories to
which they belong), because they are heterogeneous" (1993: 10). *Différend* applies not only
to verbal expressions but also to silences that function as negations, to *phrase-affects* (1993:
29). I use this notion, going beyond the discursive domain, to indicate all the practices,
forms and norms that seem to be untranslatable to European imaginaries and languages at
this precise moment in time and which thus provoke controversies.

figures that do not share common interests and opinions. Studying controversies allows us to see the sudden emergence of new actors in unexpected places, in contrast to the study of conflicts, which observes actors in already-existing spaces: the factory, the family and so on. In this volume, the focus is on the disruptive effects of Islamic differences in unprecedented spaces. Unlike conflicts between two well-defined parties (boss–worker, man–woman), controversies potentially concern all citizens, the public at large.

Controversies break away from common sense, from what is consensual in the public space. The public space brings together actors who arrive at consensus, but it also carries the promise of the possible appearance of the *différend* and *dissensus* (Lefort 1994). It is this agonistic aspect of the public space, which is receptive to the staging of disagreements and discord, that informs us about the nature of the emergence of Islamic difference in Europe. By emphasizing the integral agonistic aspect of the public sphere, we seek to establish an understanding of the modalities of the transformations in Europe's public cultures. A consensual approach to the public sphere risks placing the emphasis on legislation, on shared norms, before allowing time and space for exploration, for action and interaction between actors. In this volume, we focus on studying the interconnections and intersubjectivities in the process of confrontation and controversies.

The arrival of Muslims with their religious differences in European public life is a challenge for democratic pluralism. The Islamic difference is not easily framed within the established perspective of cultural pluralism, religious freedom or personal rights discourse. Neither multiculturalism nor liberalism provides an answer as to how Islamic difference should be accommodated. It is perceived and reacted to as an "aberration" to the extent that it breaks away from the prevalent consensual norms. If we consider the consensus to be "all generally accepted opinions at a given time in a given environment, contrary views appear as individual aberrations" to be corrected (Remaud, Chapter 2, this volume). Controversies compel us to go beyond the consensus in recognizing individual agonistic opinions, which are not necessarily aberrations in need of correction.

Islamic difference is not expressed merely in a discursive register; it is also staged in performative and visual manners, creating pictorial "aberrations," so to speak. Controversies about Islam have a visual dimension in that the staging of the body and of religious symbols that are perceived as nonconformist with the secular norms and understandings of Europe. In this sense, the use of the notion of controversy is most fecund in its contribution to an understanding of the nature of Islam's disruptive effects, which produce a whole range of emotions. Beyond the rational discourse of argumentation, there is a series of irrational reactions and affects that are mobilized around these controversies, which include feelings of insecurity, invasion, fear, phobia, injury, humiliation, resentment and anger. For instance, face-veiling as a religious bodily practice and strong marker of gender segregation in public transgresses embodied conventions about bodily orders and freedoms, and thus provokes strong reactions which often elicit an emotional response ranging from fear through open disgust to fascination (Amir-Moazami,

Chapter 7, this volume). Controversies about Islam therefore destabilize the functioning of the reason-based publicness, which is defined by secular boundaries. The possibility of a faith-based publicness and a public sphere ruled by religious norms trigger reactions of rejection.

The public sphere is not a disembodied and neutral space: it is shaped by actors and their range of actions and emotions. There is a materiality to public spheres that refers to very specific physical spaces: streets, gardens, passages, cafes and so on. Public spaces in which people gather together and urbanity – the architecture and organization of cities – are tightly linked. But apart from the spatial dimension, the public sphere also conveys an abstract meaning and entity, functioning as an ideal democratic space that is broader than the political space, bringing together citizens in a community of debate. Jürgen Habermas (1991), in his pioneering work, brought to light these two aspects of public sphere: the abstract and the concrete. Based on the study of literary cafes as concrete places where literate classes debate societal issues, he demonstrates the emergence of a public sphere that is linked in a wider sense to the democratic ideal. However, in spite of this promise of an "open space," accessible to all citizens, in reality, the public sphere has lines of inclusion and exclusion, with imposed norms, which can be altered by the terms of the debate (Calhoun 1993). In order to clarify these two strata, which are intrinsic to the notion, we can distinguish between the public sphere and the public space. Controversies take place in physical places, like the school, the mosque, the theater and the market. These places become sites visible to the public gaze insofar as Muslim actors dispute their boundaries and norms. It is this disruptive effect of religious difference that confers a public character on these places. Islam becomes controversial and part of a more general democratic debate occurring at the level of the public sphere. The latter is not limited to the national territories; the Islamic controversies circulate across the national frontiers of European public spheres. The national boundaries and the national language community that underpins the public sphere are transcended. Islamic controversies acquire a European feature, fostering a transversal public sphere. Actors, themes and symbols all circulate in different national contexts and are debated across European publics.

Controversies, while being sources of division, also place different actors in closer proximity to each other. In the debates, we see figures that are foreign to each other interacting over controversies, creating unprecedented public gatherings. It is in this sense that controversies contribute to creating new publics. Debates call forth new public spokespersons, produce cleavages, but also generate new alignments. Not only are the boundaries of inclusion and exclusion of the public sphere being redefined; its complete reorganization is also in progress. We are seeing new female figures of Muslim immigration emerge and secular Muslim voices are beginning to be heard. Sometimes surprising pairings form in the production of films or publications of books in criticism of Islam or Muslim immigrants. We can cite the film *Submission* (written by Ayaan Hirsi Ali and produced/directed by Theo Van Gogh, 2004), which brings together the controversial figure of the Dutch intellectual and the legendary symbol of the female "immigrant," who became a congresswoman, a feminist and a world-renowned atheist activist. In a similar vein, in Germany, the publication of the book *Germany is Abolishing Itself* created an alliance between its author, Thilo Sarrazin, a respected financial leader and member of the SPD party, and Necla Kelek, a feminist and secular spokeswoman of Turkish origin. The different life stories of "natives" and "immigrants"; representatives of their national culture and those seeking to establish new roots; men and women; Muslims and atheists all intersect, finding themselves connected in a "snapshot," around a controversy, sharing in the same story, sometimes even in the same tragedy (as in the case of the assassination of Theo Van Gogh after the release of the above-mentioned film in 2004). These encounters, alliances and confrontations, debates and acts of violence form a new European history. Controversies create collages and assemble diverse actors, cultures and spaces.

Studying public controversies enables us to anchor our study in a specific place but also in the present time. However, the notion of contemporary is problematic insofar as this contemporaneity is relative to power relations – power relations between traditional and modern, religious and secular, Muslim and "native." The master narrative of modernity consists in creating a sense of the contemporary through a specific cultural orientation, stemming from Western history. The anthropologist Johannes Fabian (1983) has revealed the hierarchical use of time in the narrative of modernity, noting how it accords contemporaneity to some and not others. There are different time constructions competing with each other. Controversies intensify this link to chronopolitics, disputing the right to contemporaneity.

Controversies take place in the present, but sometimes mobilize repressed memories, thereby triggering the re-emergence of ancient controversies. The Danish cartoons of the Prophet Muhammad refer to a contemporary controversy, but we also know that the image of the Prophet and its description has been a source of tension between Islamic and Western cultures since the Middle Ages (Tolan, Chapter 9, this volume). We need historical as well as theological perspectives in order to better understand the layered reality of controversies over the representation of Muhammad. The common and largely shared assumption about Islam being inherently hostile to images is questioned by Naef in Chapter 8 of this volume. Focusing on Islamic theological debates, she argues that rather than being rooted in a presumably unchanging Islamic essence, the figural representation becomes an issue with the advent of the print media, and the recent controversies over the "clash of images" are the result of new practices and readings introduced by modernity.

We also observe the kinds of controversies that are contagious and recurrent from one public sphere to the other, each time reviving the original "founding" controversy. For instance, although the Danish cartoons affair is now outdated, it still resonates as a reference point through other recent controversies over the images of the Prophet Muhammad. It is therefore important to revisit the cartoons controversy, which has generally been considered merely as an issue of free speech and regarded as a legal matter. In Chapter 10 of this volume, Laegaard focuses on the non-legal terms of this controversy and goes beyond the framing of the dispute in terms of freedom of expression and blasphemy. By putting the notion of "civility" at the center of his analysis, he questions the potential and the weaknesses of the existing public spheres.

The headscarf affairs and then the wearing of the full veil, the burqa, are controversies taking place on European soil. But they also refer to a history of Muslim secularization in Muslim countries, which are marked by the abandonment of the veil. In this context, we speak of its resurgence since the 1980s for some Muslim women in the "return of the veil" or "re-veiling" movements, which represents a break from the Islam of the 1920s in Muslim majority countries. The linguistic repertoire concerning this controversy is also influenced by the history of Christianity and Western feminism. We cannot understand the debates over the veil without taking a retrospective look at the beginnings of feminism and the struggle of Western women against religion and against the Church's hold over their lives and bodies. If in France the issue of veiling is central, in Scandinavia the big question triggering controversies over the Muslim presence is about homosexuality. We note how the counterculture of the 1960s determines the ways in which European countries react to Islam's relations to women's issues.

The notion of controversy incites us to integrate different rhetoric, grounded upon different historical experiences. Although controversies first appear to be current events in connection with the media – even sometimes disappearing, as ephemeral debates – they give us the keys to understanding a collective life in gestation. Contrary to studies that see controversies only through the magnifying glass of the media, here we seek to give them an anchoring and thickness that reflects the texture of collective life. Collective life is staged in the current events of controversies. Through their disruptive effects on the social order, controversies provoke debates, produce new actors and repertoires of action, and engender simultaneously synchronic and diachronic assemblages.

The emergence of the visibility of Islam and the manifestation of Muslim actors in European public life are often studied as a symptom of the failure of immigrants to integrate or as the absence of reforms in Islam. The emergence of Muslim actors and the manifestation of religious difference in the European public spheres are certainly disruptive signs for the established secular order, but are not necessarily reducible to pathological symptoms that can be linked to a religion or a phenomenon of immigration. On the contrary, in this work, these manifestations are studied as a mode of public agency and as an act of citizenship on the part of the actors. According to Hannah Arendt (1981), it is in staging their difference in public that actors perform a gesture of citizenry. It is through the courage to manifest their presence and difference in public that actors as "ordinary heroes" become citizens. In Arendt's approach, citizenry does not precede recognition; on the contrary, it is through manifesting our difference that we become citizens. The presence of Muslims in the public space must be understood as a mode of public agency. However, I am not attempting to argue that this agency arises from an Islamic political movement in the sense of a collective and organized action with a well-defined ideology; rather, I introduce a differentiation between the public and the political modes of agency. This mode of public action links the personal to the public and creates a disruptive effect in staging difference, bringing different topics into the public and changing social imaginaries.

Dissimilar Yet Peers

At a theoretical level, controversy is believed to unfold among peers, among those who are recognized for their scientific and literary authority and are thus able to formulate and discuss their views. At a sociological level, what is the status of peers in the controversies over Islam in Europe? In these debates, are Muslims recognized as peers, as legitimate interlocutors? Must "peers" be "similar"? It is this tension between peers and those dissimilar to them that creates new dynamics of confrontation in European democracy. In manifesting their presence and their difference in public spaces, Muslims become peers of European citizens, but they become peers by expressing their dissimilarity. Their difference is not a pre-established category, but is created in their public manifestation. Difference does not precede their action, but takes shape in their public emergence.

The public space is a place of encounter for a multiplicity of actors and views. It is the place for actors to stage the choreography of social life, which is in a constant dispute for the orientation and production of norms. Imagining the public space as neutral, ruled by predefined and fixed norms, signifies the negation of the actor's ability to improvise and the dismissal of the dimension of drama associated with renewal, new stories, new forms of action and new actors. The Islamic presence reminds us through different controversies that the public space is not neutral, but rather is based on the tacit norms of the majority. We see *dissensus* appear with each controversy. The public space maintains an important relationship to the political field. It is in the public space that the improbable in politics can emerge through discussions of taboo issues, consensual or simply taken-for-granted matters that are being raised in the public consciousness, usually through dissident voices, anachronistic practices and active minorities. In its democratic ideal, the public sphere enables the contradiction of hegemonic narratives, creating the *différend* through which we become aware of taboo, ideologized and unthought-of issues. However, this opening up of the public space, this invitation to debate is not without its limits. On the contrary, the public space has boundaries: there are those who are invited and those who are excluded. Some subjects are heard, while others are silenced. The image of Speakers' Corner in Hyde Park, where any passing person or resident of the city is allowed to speak, is too idyllic to be real.

Public spheres bear the stamp of state power, of its authorities and laws, with states seeking to control and regulate public spaces by putting in place measures of power to control the boundaries of inclusion and exclusion. Government methods seek to create citizens, in this case Muslim citizens who will conform to the host society. We see Muslim public figures appear, preferably secular Muslims or otherwise religious representative bodies, being invited to occupy the public space. In Germany, the Islamic Conference marks a turning point in the position of the state towards Muslims and Islam. In 2006, Wolfgang Schäuble, then Minister of the Interior, organized the first round table on Islam that sought to establish a dialogue between the state and the Muslim community in Germany. It brought together state representatives of the Länder and municipalities as well as Muslim associations and personalities (Amir-Moazami 2011). We see in this initiative, in the solicitation of potential Muslim spokespeople, the emergence of new voices and the creation of a new category as "secular Muslims" in public debates (Abay 2012). In France, we can cite the example of the Stasi Commission in the aftermath of the first headscarf affair in 1989. It was created in response to the demand for a reliable authority and was made up of intellectuals, historians and civil society actors who could give their "expert opinion" on the question of *laïcité*, which was supposedly under threat from Islam.[4] We see through these examples how public debate is initiated and organized by political power; how the selection of auditioned players operates; and how experts weigh in on the debates, providing an explanation and scientific legitimacy for legislation.

Muslim actors constitute themselves in the manifestation of their difference and challenge the established order, but they do not entirely escape being shaped and filtered by modes of governance and experts in power. We observe different layers of power at work, differentiated public circles with strategies for the visibility and invisibility of actors. The process of elaboration and negotiation of norms does not operate in a space of total liberty, but is crisscrossed by an arsenal of power relations, including the field of knowledge. Through controversies, new, ambivalent figures appear, namely secular Muslims, intellectuals, theologians and so on. We also observe the emergence of a new vocabulary containing Arabic terms such as hijab, fitna, Sharia, fatwa, etc. A differentiation between secular and observant Muslims emerges through these controversies. Therefore, the controversies are not simply vectors of opinions, but actually create a public domain through the arrival of new figures, new lexicons and new forms of action. At the level of actors, we see both autonomy and creativity, but also solicitation. It is in the process of interaction with the state power and larger society that actors of Islam are formed. It is thus through the interplay of social recognition and power relations that the visibility (and invisibility) of the Muslim actors finds its place in the public space.

---

4   During the societal debates on the wearing of the headscarf in public schools in 2003, a parliamentary commission was formed on July 3, 2003. The "Stasi Commission," named after the commission chair and then Minister of Education, Bernard Stasi, was set up to examine the application of the principle of secularism in France. Based on the Commission's report, the government issued a law on March 15, 2004 banning the Islamic headscarf, along with other religious signs, from public schools.

The Judeo-Christian Roots of European Identity

How can we define the eligibility of Muslim actors for fully-fledged citizenry? Under what conditions do the Muslims become the peers of their fellow citizens? Considering these questions in tandem with the age-old "Jewish Problem" can give us the keys to understanding the issue of religious difference in relation to European history. With the Enlightenment, it is in the name of the Universalist European modernity that the Jews progressively confined their religious identity to the private sphere and consequently made their Jewishness invisible (Arendt 1944; see also Raz-Krakotzin 2001). In the case of Arab Jews, the strategies of invisibility implicated a break from the Oriental origins to have access to Europeanness. And the definition of Europeannes implied a process of construction of the Jew as the internal and theological enemy on the one hand and the Arab as the external and political enemy on the other (Anidjar 2003). In a similar way, we note the power of this Universalist narrative of modernity to perpetuate and require autochthonous Muslims of Europe, namely the Bosniaks, to break with their "Oriental", namely Ottoman and Muslim roots (Velioğlu, Chapter 19, this volume) in order to be recognized as Europeans.

Controversies surrounding Islamic visibility in the public spheres led to a need to redefine the Europeanness and triggered a series of reactions that can be explained as the fear of the loss of Europe's particularity or being invaded by an emerging foreign religion. Especially controversies over mosque constructions reveal this anxiety. As Avcıoğlu (Chapter 5, this volume) argues, unlike other religious buildings that are seen as inherently or "naturally" European, the mosque is still read by those who oppose it as a marker of another, alien set of cultures and nationalities. And what lies behind this resistance to accept the mosque-form is the generic fear of seeing the European city, which is conceptualized and experienced as the opposite of the Oriental city, dissipate. In a similar vein, Allievi (Chapter 6, this volume) demonstrates how conflicts over the construction of mosques are connected to the symbolic appropriation of territory and its symbolic imprinting. For him, Islam is a transitional object which represents and signifies the pluralization of society. Very few of those opposing the presence of mosques or prayer halls would claim to want to prevent anyone from praying; rather, the issue is connected to the feeling of the loss of homogeneity or the hegemony of Judeo-Christian traditions. Whether or not there should be a reference to Judeo-Christian values in the European Constitution was the subject of intense debate among the Member States of the EU before it was refuted by the leadership of France. These examples enable us to depict the changing self-presentation of Europeans in their encounters with different facets of Islam. European self-presentation goes back to its civilizational roots, but the notion of civilization shifts from Universalistic tones towards European distinctiveness and exceptionalism. The growing visibility of Islamic difference and the controversies it prompts lay bare the unspoken tacit equation between Europe and its Christian heritage. The former Pope Benedict XVI, in his lecture in 2006 at the University of Regensburg, invited citizens to embrace their Christian heritage. In this controversial speech, the Pope claimed that, unlike Islam, the context of the tradition of Christian faith has the virtue of using reason and cherishing rational values – a tradition that stems in his view from the harmony and the "inner rapprochement between Biblical faith and Greek philosophical inquiry" (Benedict XVI 2006). A wide range of intellectuals from different fields also become more receptive of their religion and turned towards the defense of Christian values.

Furthermore, the debates on the Judeo-Christian roots of Europe bring forth Spain's Islamic past. The image of the Moorish Empire is considered either the proof that Islam is an inherently violent religion that invaded Spain in the eighth century or as a legacy of *Convivencia*, the practice of mutual tolerance and respect that characterized relations between the Muslims, Christians and Jews of al-Andalus. The debates on Europe's Judeo-Christian identity can contribute to current scholarly conversations on religious pluralism within Western societies, and particularly to debates on the place of Muslim minorities within Europe (Hirschkind, Chapter 18, this volume). On the other hand, the heritage of Andalusia as *the* locus of interreligious harmonious cohabitation is subject to criticism and various questions: can the Muslims do it again? Did they in fact do it? Can they coexist in and with Europe as they did – and *if* they did – in the Middle Ages? Can they now, perhaps for the first time, be integrated (Anidjar, Chapter 17, this volume)?

Apart from encouraging the revisiting of Judaism as one of the cultural roots of Europe, controversies surrounding the visibility of the Islamic difference increasingly interrogate European Jews. Regarding the similar issues such as halal and kosher, Sharia and Beth Din courts, and more recently the controversy in Germany regarding circumcision, Jews are increasingly called forth to participate, often against their will, to the debates over religious rights and practices in secular contexts. The French controversy over the ritual slaughtering in particular created a stir amongst the Jewish community, forcing rabbis to defend their long-gained rights to kosher food (Bergeaud-Blackler, Chapter 15, this volume).

Concluding Remarks: A New Public Culture?

How can the case studies in this book lead us to a new way for rethinking difference and pluralism in Europe? In relating the controversies to the discussions about "Public Culture," we aim to broaden our understanding of Islam and to provide a fresh look at the disturbances caused by the Islamic presence in Europe. Our objective is to go beyond the approaches brought forth by the sociology of immigration and integration, as well as by the normative discourses of multiculturalism, and observe at the ground level the emergence of a new social fabric in confrontation with Islam. There is an implicit intellectual engagement behind this project. I believe in the democratic potential of the public sphere as a site for mediating, confronting differences as well as exploring new pluralist imaginaries. We need to address the issue of democracy from the prism of sociological processes and seek out the possibilities of turning confrontation into a process of co-penetrations. Since the post-1968 period, our sociological perspective has been shaped by the politics of identity and multiculturalism, and we currently face new challenges, both intellectually and politically. We need to decipher the nature of confrontation, the disruptive effect of Islam in secular modernity and the conditions under which the confrontation does not lead to exclusionary dynamics but to mutual borrowings and creative metamorphoses. What are the conditions for interaction and communication that can turn confrontation into a process of cultural interpenetration? How can the public sphere be a site for linking culture and politics, fostering cultural innovation and political pluralism?

However, we should also ask the question whether the public sphere still functions as the locus of democracy. The ideal public sphere is conceptualized as a foyer of democratic and dialogical space (Habermas 1991). In modern times, communication technologies accelerate the global, transnational dynamics of the public sphere, whereas the political sphere remains national. The acceleration of communication brings different cultures and people into closer contact, but this process does not lead in a peaceful and linear way to democracy. How can we revisit the relationship between democratic politics and the dialogic public sphere? The political field is constrained by the nation, while the public sphere stretches easily to other levels and to different publics. Facilitated by communication technologies, controversies relating to Islam and their visual representations circulate at uncontrollable speeds, spreading to national, European and even global levels. Public spheres are open to stereotypical representations, to provocation, to violence and visceral, sensory politics that attempt to break down appeals to reason. By appealing to personal sentiments and eliciting the visceral and the emotional, the public sphere can turn into a place plagued by prejudices. We should remember that European democracies have emerged by making a distinction between opinion and truth, by advocating the use of reason in public debate. The current political populism threatens this European tradition of the "enlightened public." The public sphere is at risk of losing its role as the ideal expression of democracy and becoming a place of common sense, of the sacralization of public opinion and of the contagion of the sensational and scandalous.

Islamophobic movements find fertile ground in the promotion of the politics of fear. Anti-Islamic discourse is based on equating the public sphere with the nation. Such discourses tend to close off the public sphere. Through their multiple linguistic, cultural and religious belongings, the presence of Muslims defies the national boundaries of the public sphere. It is around the theme of Islamic visibility, in large part, that collective passions and public debates are mobilized today. The headscarf at school, the burqa in the street, the mosque in the city and the minarets in the landscape indicate the presence of Muslim actors in daily life, but also place the debate over the secular norms of common space on the public agenda. These questions put the public sphere to the test of democracy. The tendency towards a closed national public sphere, which has a level of appeal in some sections of

European societies that affirm their identity against Islam, threatens the freedom to debate and explore norms of collective life.

In this respect, can the notion of "cosmopolitan" help us to rethink politics beyond national boundaries? Can it be helpful to opening it toward a certain heterogeneity of belongings that surpasses national identities? At its core, the European project offers the possibility of politics beyond nation states. However, today we see a kind of exhaustion with the ideal of this union. The notion of "cosmopolitan" can give new life to the European project. But how can we transform the notion of cosmopolitan to the cosmopolitical, giving it political force (Balibar, Chapter 3, this volume)? We often reproach cosmopolitanism for being too neat, for lacking depth, for often carrying an element of nostalgia and for being the monopoly of the privileged classes. Consequently, the notion seems politically weak. We can decentralize our regard and examine the experience of Bosnia to see whether cosmopolitanism always corresponds to the secular and Christian world. In current debates, we see an equating of cosmopolitanism and secularism, and indeed even of global liberalism. And yet, from the viewpoint of the Ottoman Empire, it is the reverse: it was the process of national secularization that put an end to Ottoman cosmopolitanism. We must introduce into the debates on cosmopolitanism the heritage of the Eastern world and the figure of the Jew, the Armenian and the Greek, as well as the new figures of cosmopolitan Muslims. It remains to be seen whether we can escape the nationalist closing down of the public sphere by introducing the notion of "cosmopolitics."

One thing is certain: we should reconsider the tenets of European secularism in the light of emerging religious pluralism that the visibility of Islamic difference crystallizes at this point in time. As Cesari (Chapter 4, this volume) argues, most of the controversies surrounding the presence of Muslims in European public spaces relate in fact to the opposition of private convictions versus public behaviors, a distinction which is the result of the Western secularization process. As the concept of good political order and social virtues was disconnected from Christian ethics and the world became divided between the immanent and the transcendent, a believer in the transcendent is expected to keep it to himself and not let belief influence the political or social practices in which he engages. Within this European secular framework, Muslims are seen either as non-compliant with the principle of secularism or as privileging collective rights over individual rights. In this regard, the debates over the introduction of some parts of Sharia law to the British legal system can provide the potential for understanding individual agency in the light of growing religious pluralism in Europe, as well as opening up the notion of justice to debate. Billaud (Chapter 13, this volume) gives an empirically grounded account of everyday interactions in various British Sharia councils and studies the ways in which Islamic agency asserts itself through ethical disciplining. Muslims making use of Sharia councils seek to cultivate an ethical self by actively engaging with the values, norms and codes of conduct they perceive as essential to the nurturing of their faith. They provide an alternative understanding of justice and struggle to define alternative conceptions of "the good." The various dimensions of

Islamic legal practices point to the Muslims' quest for keeping a balance between religiously licit acts while remaining within the boundaries imposed by the "law of the land," the legal system of their host countries.

It is imperative to acknowledge that we are no longer living in one-language community societies with monocultural idioms. We need cultural translations, shifts between different language codes and moral norms, providing a new set of vocabulary and concepts to better grasp in-between practices and subjectivities. In putting the notion of the public sphere at the center of the analyses, I intend to go beyond the politics of identity and multiculturalism, and stress the process of encounter, interaction and confrontation among actors in search of shared practices and values. From this perspective, the definition of the public sphere needs to distance itself from the national community and open up to the multiplicity of perspectives. Arendt's (1983) notion of the public sphere can be heuristically fruitful in terms of adopting an approach that privileges the multiplicity of views, horizontal ties between actors and the visibility of differences. A public sphere inclusive of cultural differences means complexity and the existence of diverse layers of meanings. We need to broaden our approach to agency and include different forms of visibility, signs and symbols, cultural and artistic performances, subversion and humor. As much as we need the public sphere for communicative democracy, we need alternative spaces, where, retreating from the mainstream hegemonic public spheres, we can turn confrontation of differences into cultural criticism, playful action and social creativity through reflexivity and humor.

References

Abay, F. 2012. "Secular Muslims: New Actors in the Debates on Islam in Germany," paper presented at the international colloquium *Transnational Study of Public Controversies around Islam in Europe*, May 31–June 2, 2012, Paris.

Amir-Moazami, S. 2011. "Pitfalls of Consensus-Oriented Dialogue: The German Islam Conference (Deutsche Islam Konferenz)," *Approaching Religion*, 1, 2–15.

Anidjar G. 2003. *The Jew, the Arab: History of the Enemy*. Stanford, CA: Stanford University Press.

Arendt, H. 1944. "The Jew as Pariah: A Hidden Tradition," *Jewish Social Studies*," 6–2, 99–122.

Arendt, H. 1981. *The Life of the Mind*, vols 1 and 2. New York: Mariner Books.

Arendt, H. 1983. *Condition de l'homme moderne*. Paris: Pocket.

Benedict XVI. 2006. "Papal Address at the University of Regensburg," *Zenit: The World Seen from Rome*, September 12, http://www.zenit.org/article-16955?l=english.

Calhoun, C. (ed.) 1993. *Habermas and the Public Sphere*. Cambridge, MA: MIT Press.

Cesari, J. 2004. *When Islam and Democracy Meet: Muslims in Europe and in the United States*. New York: Palgrave Macmillan.

Dayan, D. 2003. "Téléviser des monstres en Méditerranée." *La Pensée de Midi*, 9, 57–68.

Fabian, J. 1983. *Time and the Other: How Anthropology Makes its Object*. New York: Columbia University Press.

Göle, N. 2005. *Interpénétrations, L'Islam et l'Europe*. Paris: Galaade.

Guénif-Souilamas, N. and Macé, E. 2006. *Les féministes et le garçon arabe*. Paris: Éditions de l'Aube.

Habermas, J. 1991. *The Structural Transformation of the Public Sphere: An Inquiry into a Category of Bourgeois Society*. Cambridge, MA: MIT Press.

Habermas, J. 1997. *L'espace public: archéologie de la publicité comme dimension constitutive de la société bourgeoise*. Paris: Payot.

Laneyrie-Dagen, N. 2009. Speech at *Mission d'information sur la pratique du port du voile intégral sur le territoire national*, December 8, Séance 4.30, Compte rendu no. 16.

Lefort, C. 1994. *L'invention démocratique, les limites de la domination totalitaire*. Paris: Fayard.

Leveau, R. (ed.) 1998. *Islam(s) en Europe: Approches d'un nouveau pluralisme culturel européen*. Berlin: Centre Marc Bloch.

Lyotard, J-F. 1983. *Le différend*. Paris: Editions de Minuit.

Macé, E. 2007. "Des 'minorités visibles' aux néo-stéréotypes: Les enjeux des régimes de monstration télévisuelle des différences ethno-raciales." *Journal des Anthropologues*, Hors-série, Identité nationales de l'Etat, 2–11.

Macé, E. 2008. *As Seen on TV: Les imaginaires médiatiques, une sociologie postcritique des médias*. Paris: Edition Amsterdam.

Mahmood, S. 2005. *Politics of Piety: Islamic Revival and the Feminist Subject*. Princeton, NJ: Princeton University Press.

Rancière, J. 2004. *Aesthetics of Politics: The Distribution of the Sensible*. London and New York: Continuum.

Raz-Krakotzin, A. 2001. "Binationalism and Jewish Identity: Hannah Arendt and the Question of Palestine," in S. Aschheim (ed.), *Hannah Arendt in Jerusalem*, Berkeley: University of California Press, 165–80.

Chapter 2

How Do You Become Contemporary? On Controversies and Common Sense

Olivier Remaud

What are the most obvious features of a controversy? At first glance, we all admit that a controversy is founded on an insistent divergence of opinions. At least two parties are brought together at a given moment. Several pieces of contradictory discourse are put forth and presented in an alternating and ordered way. A confrontation is organized in the form of an arena. The parties are likely to confront each other in a face-to-face encounter, a tribunal, an amphitheater, a public space in general, or indirectly via various media supports. They can also converse across eras. In this case, a given controversy may recall a previous controversy. Such is the case in Galileo's famous trial with the Holy Office, where we see, at the beginning of the seventeenth century, discussions of heliocentrism and geocentrism which reproduce, via Copernicus and Kepler, some of Heraclides' convictions which were themselves contested by classical tradition.[1] In each case, it is important to note that none of the arguments exchanged agree with each other, making it difficult, if not impossible, to find an applicable rule of judgment which authorizes the reciprocity of a conversation in equal parts.

A controversy generally brings together pairs. At least initially, it occurs among a group of like-minded people. The differences between controversy and crisis have been mentioned on several occasions (Dobry 1986; Chateauraynaud and Torny 1999). While the former remains in the milieu in which it arose, the latter quickly surpasses its original space and invades the public sphere. While the actors in a controversy appeal to an audience largely composed of individuals who are sociologically similar to them, those in a crisis atmosphere are confronted by the multiple and often imponderable reactions of public opinion and journalistic circles. In both cases, the interplay of contradictions does not follow the same codes. It is not expressed in the same spirit. In a controversy, it is still possible to maintain respect for the norms that drive the exchange of arguments. Each party is capable of controlling its reputation, measuring its fluctuations in popularity according to its own free will. Each party better assesses the consequences of its words because it sees their immediate effects on its interlocutors. Rumors are

---

1 Koestler (1959) recalls this feature by attaching it to a philosophy of scientific discovery that compares actors in these controversies to "schizophrenic" creators, "sleepwalkers" who are as blind as they are clairvoyant.

relatively ineffective in a controversy that does not develop into a crisis. In the case of a crisis, no one controls the tools of argumentative civility in the same way. Often, an individual no longer recognizes himself in the position assigned to him, his image is suddenly given a somewhat autonomous existence by the sole effect of the public's murmurs and he is obliged to speak up in order to distance himself from it. In the maelstrom of social appearances, the quest for celebrity and the paths of its destruction often converge to an absurd degree. This is when rumors work their magic. Finally, in a controversy, arguments are divided up and weighed with caution. In addition to this calibration, it is possible for individuals to exercise contradiction more or less masterfully. In a crisis, the individual who wishes to benefit does not initially aim for precision or mastery in a debate. He is concerned above all with giving the impression that all is lost and that he alone offers an effective way out.

This last point also helps explain why a crisis is almost always solved through mediation or even through an imperative decision. In order to resolve a crisis, intercession or external arbitrage proves necessary. It is the same in a polemic. In contrast, the debaters in a controversy rarely need mediation. Instead of resorting to an auxiliary third party, they settle things in such a way that the controversy is normalized. The normalization of a controversy does not indicate that it ends up as a "normal" discussion. Instead, it signifies that it is tamed, that the arguments put forth by the parties are laid out and that the concerned people apply themselves to clearly distributing roles. Peers often find ways of responding to the changes that the controversy has produced. Controversies are distinguished from many other forms of debate by the supreme competency of peers to themselves solve the conflicts of opinion that occur within a community. This way of concluding a controversy can be seen as a "skimmed-through conception" of a scholarly debate. The levels of conflict are measured with respect to different public constituencies as varying "degrees of publicity" or "confinement." At times, individuals appeal to each other through private correspondence, while at others they exchange thoughts behind the scenes, and sometimes social actors in a controversy present themselves on a more exposed stage (Lemieux 2007: 191–212).[2]

Yet what distinguishes a controversy from a scholarly quarrel, which also takes place among a more or less closed audience? Just like controversy, the rhetoric of a scholarly quarrel puts into play, and opposes, unities of discourse under heterogeneous regimes. But in the medieval *disputatio*, the formal dialogism of an exchange between *pro* and *contra* arguments was preferred in order to arrive at a definition of the truth. This definition of the truth in a given problem is closely related to the ability to defend to the very end the position put forth. It was not only the result of an interest in the rational treatment of an object; it also signified a true passion for verbal sparring. The scholastic system of the "disputed question"

2 When the controversy is not resolved in an internal manner, according to the agreed-upon norms of *inter pares*, a judiciary logic appears in which authorities announce a "verdict": see Lilti 2007: 25–7.

contained a search for truth as well as a playful philosophy.[3] Controversy can certainly employ the dialectical tactics of a game of wits. Furthermore, the debaters who present their arguments do not consider *a priori* a truthful outcome, or even an examination of the various protocols of different paradoxes. *In a controversy, we seek neither discord, nor reconciliation, nor speculative entertainment. Above all, we try to organize a conflict of opinions and tame anomic passions. We do not attempt to stir debate in order to resolve it from an objective (or playful) standpoint, but rather to find in it the social grammar.* Through the opinions he expresses and the mode of intervention he favors, each speaker in a controversy reveals his social status. He also contributes to the constitution of the controversy as a common object. In short, controversy creates an argumentative community by thematizing differences of opinion and considering the social diversity of the debaters involved. It structures a civility that appears to be antagonistic in content and temperate in form. On the contrary, in a polemic, a quarrel and *a fortiori* an affair, posturing, presentation and the style of attack or revenge are encouraged – even if they are tied to a quest for truth. Finally, the lifecycle of a controversy is not exactly the same as that of a scholarly quarrel: like the latter, the former takes place in a limited space, develops and ends there, but in the meantime will often leave it and change the nature of the public sphere by bringing social actors face to face with other modes of discursive conflict before returning to its original milieu.

Here we can raise an objection: how does a controversy among peers come to modify the general outline of the public sphere and create a new order, as though it were a polemic or a crisis? The answer is that a constituent, and destabilizing, power is apparent in moments of intellectual ferment caused by controversies. What is the nature of this power? *The constituent power in a controversy, which creates a before and after in the public sphere, arises from an ambivalence which places the controversy around polemics and crises without, however, conflating them.* Controversies retain precise motivations and their sources are almost always apparent. Often, it is obvious why controversies occur. Still, they remain surrounded by vagueness and characterized by ambiguity. This ambivalence explains why public opinion regularly confuses these terms. It results from a certain usage of the notion of contemporaneity. In order to clearly understand and explain the ambivalence in question, we must first briefly recall the standard morphology of controversies.

Let us then state that numerous controversies are characterized by varying degrees of at least four features:

---

3   On these educational arguments supervised by a teacher, which were one of the characteristics of Paris – unlike Oxford, known for its technique of *disputatio in parviso* (on the porch of a church and without a teacher) – see Glorieux 1968. The adversaries of scholastic reasoning also insist on its playful nature in order to remind us that the numerous techniques for skill applied to trivial subjects were more significant than the notion of truth. We see this criticism, taken to its extreme, in Molière's *Le Malade imaginaire* (1673): Diafoirus is an incompetent doctor who hides his ignorance behind incomprehensible jargon.

a. a doctrinaire state of knowledge or a previous history of discussions which have already shaped the range of responses that debaters in the public sphere can draw upon in order to analyze related problems;

b. a strong dose of uncertainty along with a sometimes interminable longevity as no one is capable of predicting the exact conditions for resolving a controversy, especially as it penetrates the public sphere and takes on the features of a crisis;

c. relatively restricted objects inasmuch as a controversy is formed and often resolved among peers but in a field of exercise that can surpass it and can mobilize other social actors;

d. a status deemed exceptional because even when a present controversy repeats aspects of a past controversy; this iteration does not cancel out the *coefficient of contemporaneity* of the topic discussed in the turmoil *hic* and *nunc*, which is modified in the collective order of things.

I would now like to insist upon the idea of contemporaneity because it is a less visible, and less analyzed, feature of controversy. On closer inspection, it seems that a controversy provides an occasion to define anew the relationship to contemporaneity and to outline the ways in which those who speak can become contemporaries of their time.

What drives us in controversy to become one another's contemporaries? There is a simple answer, already mentioned above: a controversy can be seen as an *eruption of history*, a sudden protrusion of the past in the present. You become the contemporary of your times in virtue of a kind of boomerang effect that controversy echoes and through which the past is "wrench[ed] ... destructively from its context" and resurfaces in the present.[4] But what then is the criterion that distinguishes a controversy from a polemic or any other form of antithetical discussion? Should we associate it with discussions between peers, or historical events that blur the line between the components of the private sphere from those of the public sphere, institutional upheavals, or even longer series of political or social consequences? We find these aspects, for example, in current debates concerning the different colonial legacies of European empires. However, we need to push further toward a more specific notion of contemporary in order to explain why all controversy must additionally, and perhaps especially, be seen as *an intrusion of contemporaneity in the present*.

We can distinguish, as does Vincent Descombes, two conceptions of contemporaneity. The first is provided by the philosophy of history: the contemporary represents the most modern part of modernity, the most recent present. That which is contemporary belongs to our time both at its most precise and active – a definition from which the expression "contemporary art" derives. In this characterization, we often see the part as the whole. We look for the

---

4   Like the quotation whose function, according to Walter Benjamin, is to "wrench ... it [the word] destructively from its context": see Benjamin 1999.

common features of different historical phenomena in a given time. We are thus contemporaries just as we are compatriots. Some features of a time fit together, take shape, form an era and prove to us that we live in the same present. This is the "epochal" conception of contemporaneity. The second conception is provided by reflecting on the notion of time and on the way in which changes occur. The contemporary in this conception is a "competition between several current changes" and we share not so much a present as a current moment. If we separate it from its journalistic meaning (as is happening today), the notion of the "current" has the advantage of being a modal concept. It designates what is really happening (and not what is possible or probable). This is what truly affects us, even if newspapers do not mention it (Descombes 2007: 139–41). This is the "modal" conception of contemporaneity. On the one hand, a chronology defines a neutral contemporaneity: two activities happen at the same time. On the other hand, there is an "historical current" which produces a series of actions and reactions. From this perspective, "contemporaneity initially appears as a set of activities which, because they occur at the same time, contradict or reinforce each other" (Descombes 2007: 151, my translation). On one hand simultaneity and on the other contemporaneity.

It is possible to illustrate -Descombes' distinction by comparing it to the historian's craft. Methodologically, historians consider at least two different orders: a cognitive-descriptive order, which takes into account the risk of retrospective illusion, and a cognitive-emotional order, which considers systems of experience. Simultaneity thus designates the global landscape which the historian reconfigures when he attempts to extract an articulated narrative from the contingency of events. Consider the luminous portrait of the autumnal Middle Ages that Johan Huizinga presents in his 1919 book *Herfsttij der middeleeuwen*. Contrastingly, contemporaneity is what the individual, pushed by historical current events, experiences when he urgently forges a conviction. Here again – Huizinga provides an interesting example, but here as the author who, some years later in 1935, entitled his work *In de schaduwen van morgen* in condemnation of the crepuscular horror of a totalitarian age (Huizinga 1997).

We can also find a more ordinary yet otherwise evocative example. If we pay close attention, the distinction between simultaneity and contemporaneity is present in Alfred Hitchcock's thriller film *North by Northwest* (1959). We see it in the dialogue between Eve Kandall (Eva Marie Saint) and the police inspector who questions her in her train compartment about her encounter with the suspected runaway assassin Roger Thornhill (Cary Grant), who is hiding in the bed just above them. When the officer tells her that a waiter saw them leave the dining car together, Eve replies simply, hiding her emotions: "We might have happened to leave [the dining car] at the same time but not together." The inspector deduces from this that Eve and Roger are strangers, even if they passed each other as they left the dining car. The fact that they occupied a similar present does not cause him to question his seemingly innocent interlocutor's account. He does not suspect any collusion between the distinguished lady and the suspect individual the police are looking for. For him, these two people were only contemporaries in the sense of simultaneity. If he were to suspect any complicity between them, he would have to change his analytical lens and envision a current regime between them, suspecting that Eve and Roger are contemporaries in the modal sense. He would have to adopt the view of the spectator, who understands something very different in Eve's answer: he knows that the two protagonists are "together" and contemporary to one another, all the more so as they are experiencing in this scene an important moment of mutual seduction.

How does all this help us distinguish a controversy from other types of conflicting discussions? I will call *the scandal of synchronicity* the way in which a controversy asserts itself. I take this expression from Hans-Magnus Enzensberger, who uses it to refer to the paradox of the coexistence of disparate elements in the same era, the culture of assembling, and the alliance between the sacred, the profane and the trivial, a certain art of montage which characterizes the Weimar period and the rise of totalitarianism. Totalitarian societies never abolish the piecing together of daily life and the residue of normality. In this way, they prevent individuals from hierarchizing levels of importance and using their capacity for political judgment in an era where an indiscernible eclecticism reigns. This is what Enzensberger means by the "scandal of synchronicity" (Enzensberger 2009). For the purposes of my study, I detach this expression from such a precise context in order to propose a general condition for the appearance of controversies and determine their type of constituent power beyond the ambiguity which distinguishes them from polemics, scholarly quarrels or crises. Regardless of the historical moment that Enzensberger considers, I share a similar political intuition: while being contemporary indicates the capacity of inferring the meaning of the infinitesimal temporal parameters in which we live and knowing what action is preferable, not being contemporary means considering surface elements and becoming ignorant of the new details which constitute the backdrop to the modern-day landscape, running the risk of not choosing one's actions oneself. I will return to this point in my conclusion. First, what is the general condition mentioned above?

Take the example of the famous controversy surrounding "romanticism" in which Stendhal is a central figure. On one side is the party linked to the *Académie*, defined as "classicist," which advocates the respect for the two unities of place and time in theatrical performances. On the other side is a writer who questions not only the constraints of this rule, but who reveals the sophism inherent in it which emblazons the national image: "I claim that respect for the unities of place and time is a French habit, a deeply rooted habit from which it will be difficult to free ourselves, because Paris is the salon of Europe and sets the tone; but I maintain that these unities are in no way necessary for producing deep emotion and a true dramatic effect" (Sidnell 1994: 250). The problem is that no spectator has this rule in mind as he watches a given performance. Stendhal even affirms that this beneficial illusion, which allows the spectator to ignore any considerations linked to the notion of chronology codified by a genre and which creates real emotion, is more often found in Shakespeare's tragedies, which do not observe the rule of two unities, than in those of Racine. Choosing between, on the one hand, the tradition of performances with powdered wigs, or the imitative technique, and, on the other hand, the feeling of the sublime awoken in one's own heart, or the art of imagination, is central to the dilemma between classicism and romanticism. Hence Stendhal's next point: "Romanticism is the art of presenting to nations the literary works which, in the present state of their habits and beliefs, are likely to give them the greatest possible amount of pleasure. Classicism, on the contrary, offers them the type of literature which gave the greatest possible pleasure to their great-grandfathers" (Sidnell 1994: 251).

The terms of the controversy are presented clearly: you are either in favor of the past or the present. Yet it is worth noting that the vocabulary he uses here does not mention the opposition between "Ancients" and "Moderns." Stendhal is more interested in ways of thinking and acting than in the fixed categories that do not account for the diversity of different lifestyles. The opposition between classicism and romanticism contains a conditional clause: *we must also admit that each author could have been the romantic of his time.* Not only did he say of Racine: "I do not hesitate to say that Racine was a romantic. He gave the *marquis* of the court of Louis XIV a portrayal of the passions tempered by the *extreme formalism* then in style, which was such that a duke of 1670, even in the most tender effusions of paternal love, never failed to call his son *Monsieur*," but also of Shakespeare: "Shakespeare was romantic because he presented to the English of 1590, first, the bloody catastrophes brought on by the civil wars and then, by way of relief from those sad spectacles, a wealth of exact portrayals of the emotions and the delicate nuances of feelings" (Stendhal 1962: 38–9).

What misunderstanding fuels the controversy in question? This misunderstanding comes from the fact that the classicist confuses the *modernized* and the *current*: he modernizes so as not to upset habit. In this way, he limits himself to imitation by adopting the manners of yesterday and neglecting to consider the elements which make up the essence of his time. The romantic, however, studies the world in which he lives. He speaks to his contemporaries' prevailing passions. He conveys these passions without trying to associate them with a pre-existing model, and does not submit them to any formal test which would lend them the mark of authenticity sanctioned by the ancestors of the contemporaries or contemporary intellectuals. On the contrary, he considers them as the primary matter of today's theater arts. Thus, "Molière was a romantic in 1670, because at that time the court was full of Orontes, and provincial châteaux were full of very discontented Alcestes. Rightly viewed, all great authors were romantic in their time. A century after their death, it is the writers who copy them, rather than opening their eyes and imitating nature, who are the classics" (Sidnell 1994: 253). It is essential not to reuse an attitude that conforms to the codes of yesterday's society, but to succeed in ascertaining today's manners, "studying the world we live in" and, like Shakespeare, in "giving our contemporaries precisely the kind of tragedy they need but do not have the boldness to demand, because they are so terrified by the reputation of the great Racine" (Stendhal 1962: 133). In order to achieve this, the artist need not affirm his originality or show signs of inimitable genius. Instead, he must forge the best representation of the state of man's collective soul, favoring creative "boldness" over imitative "prudence," and striving to understand the "nature" that manifests itself in existing social mores.

In this way, Claude Lefort believes that Stendhal perfectly understood how "the author has a different relationship to time than the sycophant: he must uncover the nature of the here and now. Nothing is more precious than this work of exploration and expression required by invention" (Lefort 2007: 700). The "historical sense" is the product of an acute awareness of differences in time, not the blind praise of past centuries, and literature is its privileged sphere of development. This is why literature has an "imperative of non-repetition" (Lefort 2007: 701, my translation). In this sense, Baudelaire resembles Stendhal when, several years later, he affirms that romanticism is the "way he [the artist] feels" and expresses "a view of art analogous to the moral attitudes of the age" (Baudelaire 1981: 52). In order to decipher the uncertainties of his age, the artist must examine it at work in himself, in the movable totality of his own details, and above all not compare it to previous ages. The romantic is a contemporary because he possesses this awareness of signs.

What then is the scandal of synchronicity? It is the combination of two enigmas:

a. The first enigma has to do with the coexistence of contradictory opinions when common sense requires shared evidence. It does not exactly concern the plurality of opinions because in a controversy, there is no attempt at resolution through consensus – which is the objective of all discussions, even contradictory ones, on pluralism. In a controversy, we aim first at *justifying our own astonishment, even our concerns, about the non-coincidence of opposing opinions*. The problem is not the (natural) difficulty of establishing the proper rules for discussion, but the recognition that everyone does not agree on a subject that affects the common sphere. Let us here recall André Lalande's definition of common sense: "common sense is the sum of generally accepted opinions in a given era and place, *so that contrary opinions are seen as individual aberrations* which cannot be seriously refuted and instead should be mocked, if they are trivial, or treated, if they become serious" (Lalande 2006: 972, my translation, emphasis added). When a controversy suddenly occurs, before we can even consider the degree of disagreement and its possible repercussions in the public sphere, we are surprised by the difference of opinions in this supposedly common world. We notice that everyone does not believe the same thing and that there are other judgments which are not only different but also legitimate. Controversy provides the occasion for a basic discovery: that there is individual opinion in our societies, that this opinion is not necessarily an "aberration" and that living alongside one another in the public sphere neither guarantees unanimity nor sets in motion a communalization of perspectives on a given topic. Traditionally common sense has two meanings: *bon sens* and community sense, which indicates a pooling of differentiated logics of understanding and action (Rescher 2005). *In a controversy, we discover that the premise of the community sense is unfounded* a priori *or, better still, that community sense is a premise awaiting confirmation, despite repeatedly proving to be invalid. We rediscover the impossibility of remaining indifferent to anything which resists our assumption of bon sens, or spontaneous consensus.*

b. As previously mentioned, in a controversy we can distinguish what separates one era from another; we hear something like an untimely tone of current times. We try to determine what is the most contemporary, to define what is part of our present and what is not, and what changes in the present under the effects of controversy – in short, what becomes current. The emotions that cause or accompany controversy play this role. Stendhal's indignation, like his anger, must be understood in this sense. His indignation and anger point out the arguments of those who address their contemporaries as though they were speaking to their ancestors. They give their adversaries a specific tone that ties them to a chronological whole. Stendhal's indignation and anger are emotions that make up a shared attitude toward the present. In a controversy, there is often a division between individuals from a similar time according to their symbolic belonging or non-belonging to it, up or down, before or after, in or out. People strive to *justify their system of accusations of anachronism*. What then is the precise meaning of allegations of anachronism in a controversy?

It is not clear whether the two conceptions of contemporaneity mentioned above are easily distinguishable from one another. The error, writes Descombes, "is not in believing that there are many commonalities between historical actors, but in believing that these commonalities can constitute their modernity." In other words, these actors have no "common essence" (Descombes 2007: 153). He adds that the other error is to believe that people are central when in fact activities produce the crucial changes. It seems to me that the general form of a controversy reveals the "modal" character of contemporaneity: in a controversy, we are influenced by what is done or, more commonly, by what is said. I stress that the "epochal" conception of contemporaneity is no less influential. Far from disappearing, it seems quite strategic. In the combination of activities that define the notion of contemporaneity, there are those which serve to point out non-contemporaries so that a division is created at the heart of simultaneity between contemporaries and non-contemporaries: while a certain individual lives beside me in the same society, he is not really with me because he has chosen values which are ideograms from another time. In many controversies, the "epochal" conception and the "modal" conception blend together. Individuals end up using the former for their own purposes. Controversies provide debaters with occasions to influence each other and to become each other's contemporaries *by assigning positions in the present according to perceived relationships with the current* and by declaring their interlocutors non-contemporaries.

How then do we understand the term "non-contemporary"? Do controversies provide unique occasions to infinitely redefine the traditional opposition between Ancients and Moderns? In his work, Descombes relativizes the analytic impact of this distinction, showing that it is always contextual. Its boundaries are vague: who was really an "Ancient" during the Renaissance when "Moderns" themselves promoted a return to Antiquity? Moreover, the division of ancient from modern assumes that nothing remains. Yet there is always a "remainder," something which came before the ancient (the "archaic") or from another place (the "exotic"). Finally, no one in present society is "a person of the past" or "a person of the future," but only "a person of today": "The two parties that face off are, by this very fact, contemporaries. It is the historian of the present who ultimately decides that among these contemporary parties there are those whose presence is anachronistic: the party of those who, like Don Quixote, are in the wrong era" (Descombes 2007: 148–9). It is apparent that everyone living in the present is, in a certain manner, a "Modern." But situations of controversy change this observation: we rarely react to them according to Stendhal and Baudelaire's precepts because we do not believe that everyone is, or was, "a person of today" (or modern in that sense). In a controversy, there are always people who, while they are each other's contemporaries, consider each other simultaneous and anachronistic. It is no longer the historian of the present who divides them but the different debaters and social actors in the controversy. This is why the division between ancient and modern is not really appropriate here. We must newly re-examine the accusation of anachronism in the arguments made in many controversies.

By adapting it to the specific context of a controversy, another of Descombes' formulations helps us establish the difference between modernity's "chronological sense" and its "ideological sense." In the former, "modernity corresponds to modern times. We belong by definition to the most recent phase of modern times (the contemporary era)." In the latter, "it is up to he who uses the adjective 'modern' to tell us which feelings and ideas are typical of modern man in contrast to those typical of an ancient (or generally and more significantly, in contrast to those of the members of a 'traditional' society, whether this traditional society belongs to our past or to another cultural arena)" (Descombes 2008: 247). Here we clearly see how the above-mentioned distinction between the two concepts of contemporaneity, which is not mentioned in this passage, is supposed to play out within the chronological sense of modernity. In the contemporary era, there are various ways of being contemporary, one "epochal" or doubly "chronological" and the other "modal." The "ideological sense" of modernity adds the aspect of temporal sharing as it happens, between Ancients and Moderns.

Needless to say, in many controversies, actors use the *notion of an era as an exclusionary tool* – although the recognition of simultaneity might cause it to be seen more as an inclusionary tool in the sense that, according to the chronological conception of time, we supposedly live in a common time. Yet declaring who is modern and who is ancient is not the point. *In a controversy, it is essential to identify the non-contemporary among all those who observe each other simultaneously.*

In this way, the non-contemporary is not initially an "Ancient." He is someone who cannot or does not choose to be the contemporary of his own time in the way that Stendhal mentioned, someone who always confuses the modernized with the current. This individual will not aim to decipher the particularities of his era. This is the second enigma. It characterizes the constituent power of a controversy by reflecting the ways in which each individual assesses the relationships of others to the current from which it deduces what is changing in the present. In order to do this, debaters in a controversy tacitly exploit the two conceptions of contemporaneity. They create *the "ideological" sense of contemporaneity (no longer simply that of modernity).* In this way, they expose the deep faultlines in a social time seen as unbroken and reveal the dissimilar in a public considered similar. As Sophia Rosenfeld put it clearly: "claims about common sense are, in public life, almost always polemical: statements about consensus and certainty used to particular, partisan, and destabilizing effect" (Rosenfeld 2011: 15).

The debaters in a polemic or a crisis more often turn to the contrast between "Ancients" and "Moderns." By using these categories, they suspend their interlocutor's opinions. The opposition between these two camps, while neither questions the respective attributes of the eras they reference, allows them to assign a fixed position to their adversaries on an unmovable intellectual map and situate them in a philosophy of history characterized by its lateness (everything deemed "less modern" is then considered "ancient"). In a controversy, the characterization of the relationship to the current moment is central. Among individuals who live alongside each other, there are those who are not deemed contemporary in the modal sense. Here certain blindness to current circumstances and morals in society is contested. *Considered in light of the modal conception of contemporaneity, the "ideological sense" in a controversy proves that the agonistic use of the idea of the times does not reinforce the opposition between Ancients and Moderns, but is used to reveal the interlocutor's unawareness of the details of what is changing in society.*

Many controversies surrounding cosmopolitanism, to cite one more example, have experienced a similar situation. One of the major figures on the international stage on this topic, Ulrich Beck, proposes linking "methodological nationalism" to a past "first modernity" and instead imagining "cosmopolitan democracy" as "concerned with comprehending social and political conditions at the beginning the twenty-first century" as a category of contemporaneity in the modal sense (Beck 2006: 56).[5] In a very different context, as Arnold Ruge, during his Parisian exile at Karl Marx's side as the co-editor of *Deutsch-Französischen Jahrbücher*, declared provocatively in 1844: "*Wer ist noch patriotisch? Die Reaktion. Wer ist es nicht mehr? Die Freiheit*" ("What is patriotism now? Reaction. What is it no longer? Liberty"). Liberty is here a vehicle for unity between France and Germany, the first step toward internationalism and a new way of formulating the

---

5   On the apparent and underlying arguments which inform the numerous contradictory debates on the notion of cosmopolitanism, see Remaud 2012; 2012a.

idea of humanity. For Ruge, patriotism reduced to the vow of national unity is "Reaction." It represents a negative sense of self from another time and a mistrust of foreigners. The division of attitudes in the present, expressed by the "*nicht mehr*," designates a way of being contemporary which poorly accommodates simultaneous situations. Neither "Moderns" nor "Ancients," "cosmopolitans" or friends of liberty, and "patriots" or advocates of withdrawing into nationalism, live together with increasing difficulty, according to Ruge. Yet, only the former are capable of foreseeing future forms. No longer being a patriot in the reactionary sense means opting for liberty and changing not so much the times as the perception of what is current in order to attempt to achieve what is the "most difficult": "humanizing society" (Ruge 1968: 74, my translation).

Let us now turn to the types of conflict that characterize controversies. As we mentioned, controversies force debaters and social actors to adopt a point of view of contemporaneity in the multiple senses previously enumerated. Controversies force people to recognize the link between the conflict and individual opinion. In a controversy, the disagreement first concerns the enigma of the simultaneity of diverging personal opinions. It is this simultaneity which is not accepted, beyond the difference of the arguments. We are surprised to discover that common sense is not common to all. *The contemporary is he who is shocked by the foreignness of a present that contains so many incommensurable opinions.* He is jarred not by the difficulty in building consensus but by the surprising fragility of the common sense that he took for granted. Conversely, he understands that *sensus communis* always requires presupposing *communis sensus*.

This is actually the premise of the hermeneutic obedience of pluralism that controversies attack (without organizing a systemic critique of it). In fact, pluralism raises the justified agreement to the status of an endpoint. This means two things: that all *dissensus* rests on a fundamental *consensus*, an agreement about language that represents the absolute starting point; and that all *dissensus* is clarified in a final *consensus* and that this explication resides in language itself. But in a controversy, the objective is not to restate plurality in terms of a convergence of opinions that has finally been called into question, including on the basis of an initial disagreement that exists only thanks to the language that everyone solicits and uses.

If the disagreement in a controversy is not resolved by an ordinary agreement (either conditional or final), it also differs from the "*différend.*" In an appeal to a court, Jean-François Lyotard explains that "a case of différend between two parties takes place when the 'regulation' of the conflict that opposes them is done in the idiom of one of the parties while the wrong suffered by the other is not signified in that idiom." The second party, "the one who is a victim ... is reduced to silence" (Lyotard 1988: 9–10). This situation is not a controversy. A controversy is not an impossible agreement in the center of language. It in no way resembles the kind of misunderstanding that comes from the impossible reunification of heterogeneous kinds of speech which creates a relationship based on legal inequality. In a controversy, each side remains able to argue, even if one type of argument tends to win over the others.

Nor is a controversy situation related to a disagreement in the sense of a "*mésentente*." Jacques Rancière describes an "extreme form of disagreement ... where X cannot see the common object Y is presenting because X cannot comprehend that the sounds uttered by Y form words and chains of words similar to X's own." For him, the *dissensus* is not foreign to the idea of community – it is the same tool of common belonging, of the creation of a certain sense of reciprocity: "A political community is not the realization of a common essence or the essence of the common. It is the sharing of what is given as not being incommon: between the visible and the invisible, the near and the far, the present and the absent. This sharing assumes the construction of ties that bind the given to what is not given, the common to the private, what belongs and what does not belong. It is in this construction that common humanity argues for itself, reveals itself, and has an effect" (Rancière 1999: 12, 186–7). The desire to build a common horizon is unthinkable because the "wrong" – in other words, everything that interrupts the work of identity and egalitarian logic – is located in the foundation of societies, in place of "rights." The "wrong" shows that a political group never precedes *de facto* what it presupposes, in other words, community sense. The difficulty nevertheless derives from the fact that social actors often believe the contrary, in a sense *de jure*, and they often adopt this belief in daily life without trying to construct the "ties" in question. Moreover, it is not apparent that controversy manifests a "common humanity," unless we again suppose that language and argumentation serve to unify conditions as though they were spheres of speech. It remains to be seen how this same humanity, in a controversy, assumes that it is common, yet discovers in misunderstanding and the contradictory uses of speech the absence of commonality. The "wrong" reveals the existence of the "partyless," those who are outside social mechanisms for distributing goods and rights. I want to show that controversy creates another kind of distribution system where *it is essential neither to know who is "lacking," nor to identify who is "modern," or not, but to designate who understands the singularities of his time and who understands them poorly, or not at all.*

In summary, in a controversy, we recognize the surprising evidence of incompatible judgments and the unexpected disappearance of the two traditional meanings of common sense (*bon sens* and community sense) – unexpected because we always assume *a priori* their presence. The condition of disagreement is not in the language that provides the common stage with a more fundamental agreement. From a hermeneutic or even a pluralistic standpoint, the most radical disagreement always relies on the premise of language. In a controversy, words reveal not only *dissonance as a primary element of social interaction* but also *the untimely lack of community sense.* And our surprise at this absence launches *the battle of our regimes of inscribing ourselves in time. This is the initially political sense of controversy: the goal is to decipher the specific properties of the times to which we belong and to discern the social attitudes that distinguish them.* Reflecting on common sense requires unraveling the tangle of simultaneity, or synchronicity, according to a certain understanding of contemporaneity and stripping it of its veil of illusions: no simultaneity naturally produces community sense at a given moment. Multiple incompatibilities are hidden in simultaneity. The analysis of controversies is in this way different from the epistemological paradigm of homogenization which plagues numerous theories of collective consciousness. It does not speculate that *sensus communis* is common.

In my approach to this question, the aims of a controversy are inseparable from views on the particular forms of the contemporary. When simultaneity is no longer the guarantor of common sense, we struggle to hierarchize and choose among the mass of opposing arguments. Often, we attempt to describe the temporal regimes of social affiliations of individuals who surround it. Controversy situations make this reflex more radical: *each individual assigns positions in the present to others based on his estimations of their relationship to the current.* These estimations remain entirely subjective. They are also "ideological" in the previously mentioned sense of the word. Thus, we can explain the ambivalence, or the vagueness, of the constituent power in a controversy. In this way, we see how difficult it is for individuals to assess their own relationship to the age they live in, as their perceptions of what is current in the present are caught in a web of opposing judgments.

References

Baudelaire, C. 1981, "Salon de 1846," in *Baudelaire: Selected Writings on Art and Artists*, trans. P.E. Charvet. Cambridge: Cambridge University Press.

Beck, U. 2006. *Cosmopolitan Vision*, trans. C. Cronin. Cambridge: Polity Press.

Benjamin, W. 1999. "Karl Kraus," in M. Jennings (ed.), *Walter Benjamin: Selected Writings*. Cambridge, MA: Harvard University Press.

Chateauraynaud, F. and Torny, D. 1999. *Les sombres précurseurs. Une sociologie pragmatique de l'alerte et du risque* Paris: éditions de l'EHESS.

Descombes, V. 2007. "Le présent, l'actuel, le simultané et le contemporain," in *Le raisonnement de l'ours*. Paris: Seuil.

Descombes, V. 2008. *Philosophie du jugement politique. Débat avec Vincent Descombes*. Paris: Points-Seuil.

Dobry, M. 1986. *Sociologie des crises politiques*. Paris: Presses de la Fondation Nationale des Sciences Politiques.

Enzensberger, H.-M. 2009. *The silences of Hammerstein*, trans. M. Chalmers. Calcutta: Seagull Books.

Glorieux, P. 1968. "L'enseignement au Moyen Age. Techniques et méthodes en usage à la faculté de théologie de l'université de Paris au XIIIe siècle," *Archives d'histoire doctrinale et littéraire du Moyen Age*, 35, 65–186.

Huizinga, J. 1936. *In the Shadow of Tomorrow*, trans. J.-H. Huizinga. New York: W.W. Norton & Company.

Huizinga, J. 1997. *The Autumn of the Middle-Ages*, trans. R.J. Payton and U. Mammitzsch. Chicago, IL: University of Chicago Press.

Koestler, A. 1959. *The Sleepwalkers. A History of Man's Changing Vision of the Universe*. London: Penguin.

Lalande, A. 2006. *Vocabulaire technique et critique de la philosophie*. Paris: Presses Universitaires de France.

Lefort, C. 2007. "Le sens historique. Stendhal et Nietzsche," in *Le temps présent. Ecrits 1945–2005*. Paris: Belin.

Lemieux, C. 2007. "À quoi sert l'analyse des controverses?" *Mil neuf cent. Revue d'histoire intellectuelle*, 25(1), 191–212.

Lilti, A. 2007. "Querelles et controverses. Les formes du désaccord intellectuel à l'époque moderne," *Mil neuf cent. Revue d'histoire intellectuelle*, 25(1), 25–7.

Lyotard, J.-F. 1988. *Différend*, trans. G. van den Abbeele. Minneapolis: University of Minnesota Press.

Rancière, J. 1999. *Disagreement: Politics and Philosophy*, trans. J. Rose. Minneapolis: University of Minnesota Press.

Remaud, O. 2012. "Les antinomies de la raison cosmopolitique," in P. Haag and C. Lemieux (eds), *Faire des Sciences Sociales: Critiquer*. Paris: École des Hautes Études en Sciences Sociales, vol. I, 87–117.

Remaud, O. 2012a. "On Vernacular Cosmopolitanisms, Multiple Modernities and the Task of Comparative Thought," in M. Freeden and A. Vincent (eds), *Comparative Political Thought: Theorizing Practices*. New York: Routledge, 155–71.

Rescher, N. 2005. *Common Sense. A New Look at an Old Philosophical Tradition*. Milwaukee: Marquette University Press.

Rosenfeld, S. 2011. *Common Sense. A Political History*. Cambridge, MA: Harvard University Press.

Ruge, A. 1968. *Der Patriotismus*. Frankfurt am Main: Hrsg. von P. Wende.

Sidnell, Michael J. (ed.). 1994. *Sources of Dramatic Theory, Vol. 2: Voltaire to Hugo*. Cambridge: Cambridge University Press.

Stendhal. 1962. *Racine and Shakespeare*, trans. G. Daniels. New York: Cromwell-Collier Press.

Chapter 3

Secularism and/or Cosmopolitanism[1]

Etienne Balibar

Like so many progressive intellectuals (ranging from Liberalism to Marxism), I have long considered that "Secularism" and "Cosmopolitanism" are complementary notions and that we should try to build – or rebuild – a discourse combining a definition of secularism, even a secularist perspective, with a cosmopolitan perspective. In my view these are positive notions and values, which form part of a civic and democratic understanding of the political. More recently, I have become aware that their combination is profoundly contradictory, and I went as far as becoming convinced that each of these two notions, in the contemporary situation, essentially undermines, destructs or deconstructs the meaning and stability of the other and puts its validity into question. At the very least, there is no such thing as a "natural" possibility to combine them.

For example, suppose that, in the conditions of contemporary politics, no "cosmopolitan project" can acquire meaning without involving a "secular" dimension, so that no such thing as a "religious cosmopolitanism" is thinkable; why is it then that, initially at least, a secular understanding of the construction of the cosmopolis adds difficulties and contradictions to those already contained in the classical idea of instituting citizenship at a transnational level or granting it with a new transnational dimension? And, conversely, suppose that – at least in some regions of the world, or perhaps in all of them, albeit each time in a singular way – there no longer exists any possibility to ground and implement a secular agenda in politics, to vindicate secularism in the regulation of social conflicts or the development of such public services as education, healthcare, urbanism, etc., without referring to a "cosmopolitan" way of defining the political; why is it that such a formula does not so much remove obstacles as create them?

Since these considerations are very abstract, allow me to illustrate with a concrete example the kind of situation and debate that lead me to rethinking the contradictory articulation of cosmopolitanism and secularism. This episode, known as the legal and political controversy about the wearing of the so-called "Islamic veil" or hijab by young Muslim girls in schools and its prohibition by the

---

1 A preliminary version of this chapter was given as the Anis Makdisi Memorial Lecture, 2009/10, American University of Beirut, November 12, 2009, and subsequently published both by the Anis Makdisi Program in Literature at the American University of Beirut and the journal *Grey Room 44* (Summer 2011). A revised and enlarged version appears in French as *Saeculum. Culture, Religion, Idéologie*. Paris: Editions Galilée, 2012.

state authority in the name of constitutional secularism, has been widely discussed outside France, perhaps at the cost of some simplifications, and the fact that it produces such echoes, even in the form of a widespread critique of the rationale and the effects of the law which banned the veil from schools, is itself part of the cosmo-political meaning of the event.

It will be argued here by some that again the terminology is misleading, because it is not possible to purely identify what the French official discourse calls *laïcité* and what the English language and culture (on both sides of the Atlantic) calls "secularism." The two terms are not completely equivalent, but also not totally external to one another. The aspect of secularism that *laïcité* pushes to the extreme is not the equal right of religious denominations in the public realm, but the separation of church – more generally religions – and state or state functions, including education. This specific emphasis certainly does not represent the only possible form of secularism or its mainstream realization – far from it. But the variation again is part of the problem rather than an extrinsic element. We should not be surprised to discover that, while the kind of "extremism" involved in the discourse and practice of *laïcité* distorts many of the issues involved in the secularizing process within Western societies, it also reveals some of the deepest contradictions that are at stake in a discussion of "secularism" in general.

I have strongly disagreed and I continue to strongly disagree with the French law, in spite of its apparent peaceful implementation, which has in fact been greatly helped by the global conjuncture. Independently of other circumstances, I deny that an injunction, directed at individuals who are supposed to be the victims of religious and/or patriarchic oppression, to abide by the law or leave the public school can have the least emancipatory effect or educative function, since it denies to the subjects themselves every possibility of expression, self-determination and negotiation (or it treats them precisely as subjects, in the old sense referring to subjection, not as virtual citizens). In fact, this conspicuous constraint was destined to give satisfaction and grant legitimacy to the racist components of French society as much as to impose secular obedience on Muslim girls. Accordingly, this seems to be a very clear case of the situation described by Gayatri Spivak (1985) as the scenario of "white men liberating brown women from the oppression of brown men," which testifies eloquently for the continuation of colonial relations and perceptions in the post-colonial era.

But things are less simple because there also exists a counter-scenario whose exact practical importance has to be carefully assessed but cannot be entirely denied, that of "brown men protecting brown women from being liberated by white men." This was clearly illustrated when street demonstrations were staged by some Muslim associations, where girls wearing veils, sometimes mockingly colored like the Republican flag, protested and marched against the ban under the close custody of male Islamic militants who prevented any access to or conversation with them. This image can be seen on the cover of Joan W. Scott's recent book *Politics of the Veil* (2007), which discusses the French controversy and its historical roots, where she mainly describes the continuity in the representation of the "indigenous woman" (especially the Muslim woman) which was an integral part of the colonial "orientalist" imaginary, and now becomes protracted in the dominant view of gender relations among migrant populations in post-colonial France. This is hardly disputable. But in the same analysis, she apparently endorses a discourse of the opposition between the traditional "modesty" of women as a cultural trait of the Muslim world, which would allow them to resist the brutal exploitation of the female body and its image in Western modernity, as illustrated by commercials and advertisements. And she combines in a single critical concept of "abstract universalism" the capitalist mass-consumption, of which the sex industry and gender oppression form part, with the typical neutralization, that is, the denial of anthropological differences (be they sexual, cultural or religious) in French republicanism. The result, in my view, is not to allow for a more concrete investigation of the contradictions; rather, it is to render this definition of "abstract universalism" itself completely abstract and ahistorical.

In fact, what I find more satisfactory than referring back to antithetic notions of resistance to cultural imperialism or liberation from culturally oppressive traditions is to describe a double-bind situation. The fact is that, in precise episodes of the conflict over the acceptance or rejection of hijab-wearing girls in French schools, these female subjects found themselves caught between the coercive agencies of two rival phallocratic groups (which can indeed include many women): one speaking the language of religious traditions and religious freedom, and the other speaking the language of secular education and the emancipation of women, each of them in fact targeting their body and making it the stake of their will to power, the reproduction of their domination, however unequal politically these forces remain and however heterogeneous the social realms in which they are exercising their power.

The first provisional conclusion that I draw is that such seemingly local, even parochial conflicts are always already cosmopolitical. They involve the whole world, or crystallize elements arising from world history and world geography within a specific national microcosm, which by definition is open and unstable. The more you try to enclose it, the more you destabilize it. This is clearly the case with social and institutional tensions taking place in the middle of what (with Saskia Sassen) we may call global cities (with their global "banlieues," sometimes also located in the inner cities), where migrations and diasporas have increasingly "normalized" the heterogeneity of cultures and religions, sometimes their clashes but always their huge inequalities of power and institutional legitimacy. This is even more the case because, generally speaking, the interaction between local and diasporic cultures is a post-colonial phenomenon in a double sense. It continues the colony, but also it transposes or "translates" it, therefore it transforms it, and sometimes it reverses it. The process of globalization, which has been in progress for several centuries, was not simply "capitalist" in the abstract sense of the term, a mere process of commodification and accumulation. It was capitalist in the concrete political form of colonization. This is already to say that what is cosmopolitical must also be cosmopolitical in the sense in which the "political" is inseparable from historical and social "conflict." But our example shows more if we draw attention to the necessary intervention of religious discourses, or discourses labeled religious, and the "counter-discourse" of *laïcité* and state secularism, which clearly has a symmetric tendency itself to become sacralized, i.e. to appropriate some of the most typical characteristics of the "religious."

My tentative formula would be, and I want to insist on this as strongly as possible, that there is no such thing as a purely "religious conflict": a conflict that pits religious representations and allegiances against one another, or against their "secular" antithesis, is always already entirely political. Perhaps that was always the case, but the modalities have changed, especially since the relativization of national boundaries and sovereignties, and the increasing importance of migrations made it impossible to assign the religious discourses to the place of the particular, or "particularism," whereas the secular discourse of "public reason" would occupy the place of the universal. In fact, we always have to deal with conflictual universalities, which may explain why it proves increasingly difficult to project a dichotomy of the private and the public realms on the distinction of religious membership and legal citizenship. A "public" discourse and institution that derives its legitimacy from a national (and nationalist) tradition is not more universal or universalistic than a transnational religious discourse. In any case, its greater degree of universality cannot be asserted *a priori*. It has to be proved and experienced, especially in terms of its emancipatory power. Whenever the religious difference becomes conflictual, this conflict is virtually a cosmopolitical one.

This leads me to a second conclusion, which is still provisional. Among the varieties of "cosmopolitanism" that seemed likely to be implemented at the institutional level, there was something called "multiculturalism." It is (or was) both a very important and a very ambiguous idea. Indeed – and this is crucial in my view – this term was never taken in the same sense on all sides. And it should be said that, among the modern, post-colonial nations, the receptions of one or another of these conceptions of "multiculturalism" have been extremely diverse themselves, depending in particular on the historical imaginary of their nationalism and their exceptionalism. France was certainly one of the least receptive places, regardless of the measure. But, generally speaking, it would seem that the so-called "return of the religious" has produced the dissociation and, in fact, the crisis of the idea of a "multicultural" cosmopolitical agenda, or cosmopolitanism as multiculturalism. I am not thinking here – or not only – of nationalist, or exclusivist, xenophobic discourses, which – contrary to every historical lesson – declare the homogeneity of culture within certain sovereign boundaries to be the condition for the survival of any existing political community. Rather, I am thinking of discourses which explain to us that the agenda of a "multicultural constitution" grossly underestimates the violence of potential conflicts between religious allegiances, precisely because they are not conflicts among particularisms, but conflicts between rival universalities. The lesson to be drawn should be, we are told, that the multicultural project tries in vain to relocate on the "cultural" terrain what should be treated primarily, if not in theological terms, at least in terms of a civic *différend* among religious discourses, therefore not so much in the anthropological language of cultures than in the moral and political language of "tolerance" or "interfaith dialogue."

I am aware of the fact that, in a very powerful way, some contemporary anthropological discourses will reverse the pattern and invoke the "return of the religious" as an argument against the very use of the category "religion." There are different versions of this argument. One was proposed in a cautious manner, which was almost entirely negative or deconstructive, by Jacques Derrida (2001) when he submitted that the term "religion," with its Roman and Christian background, is strictly speaking untranslatable and therefore imposes a Christian stamp on the very claims of recognition that are raised by non-Christian faiths, such as Judaism and Islam, when they ask to become recognized as "equals" in the "religious" realm. Another formulation, which has quite different sources and intentions, was put forward by Talal Asad (2003) when he argued in famous essays on the *Genealogies of Religion* and *Formations of the Secular* that "religion" is a purely Christian category used to impose the domination of the church over practices and creeds which, by themselves, are not "religious." To this he added that the dominant notions of secularism have inherited this theological notion. I think that this argument ought to be taken very seriously, if only because it stresses the fact that there is no process of recognition without an institutional pattern of representation, and there is no representation without a code of representation, which is either dominant or dominated. The "secular," or rather the antithesis between the secular and the religious, is precisely one such code, a dominant code in certain societies where it is both institutionally organized and intellectually elaborated, in particular through the discipline called the "history of religions."

If we take seriously the idea of alternative conceptions of cosmopolitanism, based on a deconstruction or internal critique of what has been institutionalized as secularism in the national framework and as an element of its sovereignty, we will have to consider another problem, which is the problem of the regime of translation, in which the collective historical subjects (re)present themselves to one another (and for one another). The critique of the "religious secular code," inherited from Christianity, suggested by Asad and others, is certainly useful here, but is it sufficient? Is it consistent? In fact, I cannot help but wonder if it is not aporetic as well, because it almost inevitably ends with a recourse to the alternative "anthropological" category of culture. Indeed, the category of "culture," as that of "society," or "politics," is no less Eurocentric and "Western," if you want to go that way, than the categories of religion and secularism.

So, are we in a complete circle which can produce only skepticism? I see an alternative possibility, which is not based on a choice between the language of "culture" and the language of "religion," or a reduction of one term to the other, but a critical use of the conceptual duality itself, in order to identify certain differences, which are elusive but crucial, at stake in the political conflicts with either "cultural" or "religious" content. This, I must admit, is also on my part a way to reintroduce or rehabilitate an old-fashioned category: that of ideology, as a formal and heuristic instrument; not to reduce everything to ideology and disqualify it, but to complicate the "semantic demarcation" of "culture" and "religion" and also to displace it. I want to see which clarification of debates involving "religion" and "culture" could arise from their being considered opposite "poles" of the ideological processes. Formally speaking, I would suggest that such a duality is not only a logical construction but also a dynamic pattern: "cultural processes" of generalization, routinization and hybridization alter and even destroy religious models of life, subjectivity and community in the long run, just as "religious symbols" associated with rituals, beliefs, imperatives, revelations, myths and dogmas crystallize cultural differences. They limit the flexibility of cultures, or in some cases ignite their internal tensions and transform them into forms of political opposition. Cultural habits and imaginaries travel only with people, whereas religious rituals and symbolisms can become adopted out of their place of origin. You can convert to a belief, not to a culture, only adapt to it more or less completely, or adopt it. We are not certain of the exact meaning of the categories "culture" and "religion," but, paradoxically, even if the terms of the opposition are not really clear and possibly refer to practices and processes which materially are "the same," we are in increasing need of a formal, differential polarity of the "religious" and the "cultural." It should work as a critical instrument to problematize irreducible notions of "community," of the incorporation of individuals/subjects into communities, establish reciprocities, frame collective destinies (social or asocial) in situations which are always singular. A distinction of the "religious" and the "cultural" dimensions of ideology in this sense is in my view an instrument against the indiscriminate use of the category "community," which plagues debates about communitarianism and universalism. The "community" as such is probably neither religious nor cultural; it takes shape against others in a historical process that is essentially political, even cosmopolitical, through a combination of cultural and religious determinations plus X, the "material" processes of economy and power relations.

To emphasize this methodological distinction does not preclude that cultural or religious determinations undoubtedly have a common "object" or rule upon a common "materiality." However, it is so elusive that they take it or construct it in opposite ways. What is this common "disjunctive" object? We could say simply that it is "the human" – I try to avoid the tautology looming behind this indeterminate reference by saying that it is the "anthropological difference" as such, a category that I coined some years ago to indicate differences that are at the same time unavoidable (impossible to deny) and impossible to locate in a univocal or "final" manner, differences whose exact location and content remains, for this reason, problematic. The sexual difference (the masculine and the feminine as pure opposition, preceding the attribution of gender roles and functions in the family, whatever its social content, which is always arbitrary) is an obvious example of such a difference. It is primordial. It is tempting to suggest that, as such "differences" require at the same time fixation and displacement, normalization and perturbation, it is "culture" which normalizes or "routinizes" them, as Weber would say, and "religion" which destabilizes and sublimates them in a revolutionary or mystical way.

However, this is still a rather mechanistic division of labor and therefore only an allegoric indication that the opposite tasks cannot be performed by the same "ideological" systems. Thus, while trying to keep something from the idea of an essential polarity of the "religious" and the "cultural," my tendency is to push the opposition toward a complete (ideal) antagonism in this respect, with cultural evolutions, transformations and "inventions of traditions" on one side, and religious processes or moments of "reform" and "revolution" on the other side. This is suggested for political reasons, in particular because I want to emphasize the role of religious symbols in "radicalizing" or pushing to the extremes the anthropological differences and the corresponding distributions of roles and practices, whose normalization is the essential function of "culture"; pushing to the extremes, that is, sacralizing, absolutizing, idealizing, sublimating or, on the contrary, "in-defining" or "deconstructing" through mythical representations or mystical notions of transcendence. But this is also because I want to suggest that it is crucial (and will be crucial) for us in the future to observe the coming of religious revolutions (in the sense of revolutionary transformations of the religious traditions themselves, which indeed cannot remain without political effects: the "Liberation theology" is an example of this; "Islamic feminism" could be another equally important example if it concentrates on its core objective of challenging from the inside the cultural structures of domination which, since the original revelation or shortly after, were fused with the theological premises of Koranic monotheism. And it will be crucial to observe the emergence and the development of new religions, which indeed will be "religious" in a new sense of the term. They might emerge, precisely, out of the new "culture" created by capitalist globalization and the extremities that it reveals or reactivates. And the hypothesis of "new religions" quite naturally leads to hypothesizing a new "secularism." However, whereas the first remains a conjecture, the second is also in my view a political and philosophical imperative, whose means of realization call for urgent discussion and elaboration, in the form of a denationalized and de-sacralized secularism, or a secularization of secularism itself, to borrow a felicitous expression from Bruce Robbins in his contribution to the recent Said-Derrida conference. I call for philosophers and citizens of the world to try and invent its language in the perspective of what Derrida once called "the New Enlightenment."

References

Asad, T. 2003. *Formations of the Secular: Christianity, Islam, Modernity*. Stanford, CA: Stanford University Press.
Asad, T. 1993. *Genealogies of Religion: Disciplinces and Reasons of Power in Christianity and Islam,* Baltimore, MD: The Johns Hopkins University Press.
Derrida, J. 2001. *Acts of Religion,* Gil Anidjar (ed.). New York: Routledge.
Scott, J-W. 2007. *The Politics of the Veil*. Princeton, NJ: Princeton University Press.
Spivak, G. 1985. "Can the Subaltern Speak? Speculations on Widow Sacrifice," *Wedge,* 7–8, 120–130.

PART II
Public Islam, Piety and Secularity

PART II

Chapter 4

Self, Islam and Secular Public Spaces

Jocelyne Cesari

Islamic voices appear to violate secular principles of Western democracy, or so goes the dominant consensus in Europe and increasingly in the US. We have seen this strong consensus emerge during the controversies surrounding the hijab, the niqab, the minaret and Danish cartoons. As tempting as it can be for pundits and politicians to put "Islam" in opposition to secularism, it is crucial to differentiate what among Islamic practices and activities is at odds with the Western understandings of secularity.

Interestingly, most of the controversies surrounding the presence of Muslims in European public spaces relate to the opposition of private convictions versus public behaviors. This distinction is the result of what Charles Taylor calls the second mutation of the Western secularization process. The first mutation happened during the Renaissance period, when states started to assert their political sovereignty over the church. This redistribution of political power required a new social status for the church. Because people kept on believing in God, the churches were seen as an essential element of social cohesion. However, their roles were increasingly understood exclusively in terms of "worldly" goals and values (peace, prosperity, growth, flourishing, etc.) (Taylor 2012).

This shift led to two major changes: first, the concept of good political order and social virtues was disconnected from Christian ethics; and second, the world became divided between the immanent and the transcendent. This divide was the invention of Latin Christendom and, incidentally, Christendom's contribution to the secularization process (Taylor 2012). The new understanding of the secular builds on this separation. It affirms, in effect, that the "lower" (immanent or secular) order is all that there is and that the "higher," or transcendent, is not to regulate the "lower." So a believer in the transcendent is expected to keep it to himself and not let belief influence the political or social practices in which he engages. This is the foundational principle of the difference between private convictions and public behaviors (Taylor 2012).

In this light, Muslims are seen either as non-compliant with the principle of secular justification or privileging collective rights over individual rights.

Private versus Public Behaviors

To accommodate the possibility of religious voices, John Rawls and Jürgen Habermas define public space as split into two parts. For Rawls, it is split between a constitutional and a broader public, whilst for Habermas, it is divided between a formal and informal public sphere. In other words, both recognize a broad public sphere, where every contribution – even if couched in religious terms – is legitimate, and a more restricted institutional realm where binding decisions are made (parliaments, courts, governmental agencies, etc.) and where religious arguments are excluded. Between these two realms, there must be a filter that lets only secular contents and arguments pass through. The problem lies in determining where exactly this filter has to be metaphorically located and what it should block (Ferrara 2009). Some are directly geared toward the constitutional domain and the restriction of freedom of expression in the name of religious conviction, such as Sharia law and the Danish cartoons, respectively. Others – like the controversy over the hijab and other dress codes – are taking place in the broader public sphere.

But even this distinction – between the restricted sphere and the larger public sphere – is not fixed, depending on the nature of each domain and being specific to each country. For example, France stands apart as the country in which religious voices in the broader domain are the most limited. In contrast, Islamic voices can be expressed more freely in the UK or the US.

Moreover, within each society, the location of the threshold evolves according to political and cultural changes. Since the eighteenth century, the general tendency across Europe has been to push most religious customs and rituals outside the area of civil legality. In most countries, such an evolution has affected the presence of religious voices in the broader public space. For example, we have seen a continuous decline in the religious identity of citizens. Most Europeans assert that they are not religious, do not belong to religious groups and claim that God is not important in their lives (Colas 1997). Even when they identify themselves as believers, citizens participate less and less in the broader public space in the name of religious beliefs. The debate on Christian crosses in public spaces in Italy and Germany provides a good example of this seemingly inexorable trend.

The consequence is a reification of what is public and what is private (assuming that religions generally belong to the private space), even for those citizens who express religious beliefs. Collective views have evolved to the point that any claim or expression in public space resulting from religious beliefs is seen as illegitimate. Unlike other religious believers in Europe, most Muslims have not gone through this identity transformation. They do not regard their Islamic religion as part of a private space and conceive beliefs and practices as closely connected. In other words, they cannot believe without performing certain practices, and some practices without beliefs are meaningless.

Some of these practices have a social dimension. For example, the debate over dress codes or recognition of dietary rules in public spaces, among others, illustrates how impossible it is completely disconnect beliefs from practices that "spill over" in social relations. In this regard, "embodied practices" of Islam such as dress codes, dietary rules in social life and prayer space in the workplace seem to violate the neutrality of public spaces where most religious practices have been removed or "naturalized" as elements of the mainstream culture.

Another dimension of the tension between Islamic claims and secular norms lies in the challenge of translation imposed on religious citizens when they want to voice opinions in public spaces – a problem that Muslims, at least in terms of religious leadership, do not systematically address. An example is the assumption that Muslims are intolerant toward homosexuality, especially because, shortly before 9/11, a Moroccan-born imam clearly condemned the sexual orientation during a TV program and described it as a "sin."

As noted by Habermas, the liberal vision of the secular public space places a special burden on the shoulders of religious citizens. Taken to the extreme, it implies that many would not be able to undertake such an artificial division – that between their religious beliefs and their civic participation – within their own minds without destabilizing their existence as pious persons.

Our surveys show that actually most Muslims have accepted this division.[1] However, this is not the case for some religious authorities who do not automatically translate their viewpoints into secular terms, therefore breaking the principle of secular justification. As such, arguing protection against blasphemy in countries where such laws do not exist cannot be legitimate.[2]

In short, according to liberal theories, expressions of religious citizens would be acceptable in public spaces as long as they do not influence formal law-making and as long as they are expressed in an acceptable public venue. The political reality is actually more complex and reveals a narrowing or even a complete disappearance of room for Islamic religious expressions in European public spaces. In other words, even when Muslims abide by these principles (and the vast majority in Europe does), their claim can remain illegitimate.

A case in point would be the protest against the cartoons in the Danish newspaper based on the argument that it is forbidden to depict the image of the Prophet Muhammad (Klausen 2009). In this context, the cartoons crisis reveals the arbitrary limits of universal approach to secular public space, which in this particular event was not an open space for all, even when they conform to the principle of secular justification. Talal Asad explains this contradiction by engaging in a Foucauldian deconstruction of the public space. Unlike liberal theoreticians like John Rawls and Charles Taylor, Asad does not see the secular space as a "neutrally" shared space composed of different voices that accept and abide by the same principles or ethics of citizenship. Instead, he defines the private/public divide and secularism in general as a heterogeneous landscape of power. From the beginning, he argues that the "liberal public sphere" excluded certain types of people: women throughout the nineteenth and twentieth centuries, the poor classes, immigrants, religious groups and others. The tension between civil authority and

---

1   See my forthcoming book on *Naked Public Spaces: The Challenge of Islam to Western Secularism* (to be published by Palgrave Macmillan).

2   British Muslims incidentally used this reasoning during the Salman Rushdie affair, when some leaders asked for protection by the law against blasphemy, which has since been abolished in 2006 (following the Danish cartoons crisis).

the particular cultural and religious norms of minority communities is the crucial issue at the heart of the debate over the definition of "secularism." In twenty-first century Europe, it is important to understand the public sphere as not only a disembodied voice, but also a product of the media and state-mediated discourses.

From such a perspective, it is easy to see that the same issue of tension between civil authority and Islamic communities is a crucial driving topic of the current debate in Europe. As mentioned when discussing the cartoons crisis, along with the voices of Muslims that were protesting against blasphemy, several were using more secular arguments that could have been received in the public space, but were rejected because of the particular balance of power between European establishments and the growing and increasingly assertive Muslim minority. Some, for example, utilized arguments similar to those concerning the prevention of hate speech (as it is guaranteed by most European states), Holocaust denial and political acts which can incite violence. Still, perceptions of political expression by individuals who are Muslim vary greatly. Interestingly, previously conceived perceptions of Muslims that are based on extremism often prevent rational consideration of expressions that are legitimate within existing legal systems.

Individual versus Collective Rights: The Sharia Debate

Another example of the tension between civil order and the Islamic community concerns the recognition of Islamic law within existing legal systems. In this specific context, contrary to Asad's interpretation, secularism is not simply a politics of hegemony in the sense that it is an attempt to foster equality and tolerance. Rather, the way in which equality and tolerance can be achieved is never certain or defined in one fixed process. In the Western world, where there is democratic constitutionalism, the debate does not stem from constitutional issues. Contrary to the widespread belief that Muslims in the West seek the inclusion of Sharia in the constitutions of European countries, most surveys show that Muslims are quite satisfied with the secular nature of European societies. When Muslims agitate for change, they engage in politics and the democratic process, utilizing mainstream parties and institutions.[3] At the same time, their acceptance of secular practices does not mean that they renounce Islamic principles and legal rules to guide or structure their daily life. We clearly observed this tendency in the focus group discussions undertaken in Europe and in the US in 2007 and 2008 when many Muslims expressed strong attachment to religious, rather than civil, marriage and divorce.[4]

---

3   See "Muslims in Europe: Basis for Greater Understanding Already Exists," Gallup Polling, 30 April 2007. Available at: http://www.gallup.com/poll/27409/Muslims-Europe-Basis-Greater-Understanding-Already-Exists.aspx.

4   This research was conducted among Muslims of different genders, ethnicities, nationalities, generations and levels of education. It took place throughout Europe (in Paris,

An important question raised by the Muslim presence in Europe is how the protection of specific subcultures can promote, rather than stifle, individual emancipation. Will Kymlicka provides us with a possible way to reconcile the two conflicting forces: "If we simplify to an extreme, we can state that minority rights are compatible with cultural liberalism when a) individual freedom is protected within the group, and b) they promote equality, and not domination, between groups within the different European societies" (Kymlicka 1995: 153). Sometimes, however, Islamic groups collectively request rights that limit individual freedom. The Rushdie affair was an illustration of such a dilemma, as British Muslims claimed the right of Islam to be protected by the law against blasphemy that traditionally applies only to Anglicanism.

Within the Sharia debate, Kymlicka's two conditions are under intense scrutiny. Individual freedom is perceived as being threatened by forced marriage, polygamy and inequality between husband and wife in divorce proceedings. Tensions may thus occur between the dominant civil laws and the prescriptions of Islamic religion concerning the family. However, our research shows that there can be a great deal of adaptation when it comes to issues of potential conflict between Sharia and civil laws. The second condition is also problematic, since Islam as a religion and culture is still perceived as alien and external to Europe. Promoting equality between cultures involves redefining public culture and the status of Islam within the public space at the level of both nation states and the European Union. In the post-9/11 context, some of the Muslim claims champion the European conception of human rights by arguing, for example, that laws banning religious symbols from French public schools are contradictory to the European notion of fundamental rights. This second part of the debate on Islam and secular principles is more relevant to the US than Europe, where participation in organized religion remains high.

There is no clear desire among European Muslims to change the secular nature of their states of residence, but that does not preclude tension between Islamic prescriptions and the provisions of secular law. Islamic traditions of marriage, divorce and child custody most often cause friction between devout Muslims and European civil law. In legal practice, the question of whether to take Muslim family law into account in the regulation of daily life is bound to the condition that these laws meet the criteria prescribed by human rights and fundamental liberties. Therefore, due to inequalities between men and women, personal status appears problematic in the process of integrating Muslims, to the point that some compare the situation to a conflict of civilizations (Mercier 1972; Deprez 1988). However, even though the silent majority of European

London, Amsterdam and Berlin) to obtain results that are as representative as possible. We conducted 12 focus groups in which over 500 Muslims participated. There were at least two "control" groups in each town to discuss the same topics with non-Muslim immigrants. The research was funded by the European Commission, 2005–9. See CEPS, *Securitization of Islam in Europe*, October 2009. See also Cesari 2004; 2009; and Cesari and McLoughlin 2005.

Muslims already accept Islam's compatibility with the basic precepts of human rights, there exist fringes of the Muslim population across Europe that reject this paradigm and act violently in ways that strongly prejudice Europe's perception of Islam and Muslims.

We examined the literature and jurisprudence of several key European countries in order to ascertain the arguments used by the courts and by Muslims when conflicts arise. The plethora of national laws in Europe and the diversity among Muslim groups makes comparison difficult, but we found a general trend of recognizing foreign law. In countries like France, Belgium, Italy and Spain, the law distinguishes between national and foreign jurisprudence, resulting in residents acting under their national laws. In this case, the country of residence may apply a discriminatory foreign law. For Muslims, Islamic laws on marriage, divorce and custody may differ according to their school of thought (Hanafi, Shafi'i, Maliki, Hanbali, etc.) or country of origin (Pakistan, Algeria, Morocco, etc.). Furthermore, in some countries like Tunisia, Turkey and Morocco, family law has been secularized and respects, in theory, the principle of equality between men and women. However, it does not prevent the continuation of customs that can be discriminatory toward women and can be presented as "Islamic." One example is the recent case of the divorce of a Moroccan couple before the French courts; the husband wanted a divorce because his wife was not a virgin at the time of the marriage.

Because of these complex circumstances, we find different and sometimes contradictory attitudes among Muslims toward European secular laws. As mentioned previously, complete rejection of secular law is rare, except for elements of French secularism. But the complete acceptance of European civil law is also rare.

In short, the majority of European Muslims acknowledge the compatibility of Islam with the basic tenets of human rights, although there are still parts of the Muslim population in Europe that reject this paradigm. For example, a group that emerged in the fall of 2009 in the UK demands the enforcement of Sharia. It is also significant that Islamic parties have recently emerged on the political scene in Germany and the Netherlands.

Surprisingly, this reconciliation of the acceptance or rejection of secularism has often been conducted in an indirect way through decisions by European judges rather than Islamic legal experts or Muslim theologians.[5] Consequently, a slow and "invisible" form of personal Islamic law is being constructed and adapted to Western secular laws. Of course, European judges do not claim Islamic authority, but the fact that Muslim theologians do not contest their decisions, and sometimes even endorse them (King 1995), illustrates the law's adaptation.

---

5   This is not without certain dangers, given that in many cases the judge does not know Islamic law: Halima Boumidienne cites the example of a judge who did not understand that ordinary or definitive repudiation can lead, in Islamic law, to an abrogation of the wife's rights (Boumidienne 1995).

Conclusion

Islam is disturbing because Muslims claim or show by their embodied practices that modern and religious individualism are not synonymous. By covering, distinguishing and separating, they inconveniently remind us that the individual and especially his or her body are not absolutely powerful. In the current phase of modernity or, in Ulrich Beck's terms, Phase 3 of modernity (Beck 2008), the body has become the primary vehicle for individual expression in the public sphere. Individuality is expressed not only through ownership of the body (including upholding legal rights), but also through choices regarding gender and sexuality. In other words, in a modern and consumer-driven capitalist world, individual persons may even choose to change their physical bodies – from make-up and beauty salons to plastic surgery and gender reconstruction.

At the same time, this greater emphasis on corporality leads to conflict and tension. The body has become increasingly visible in the modern, public sphere and, as a result, there has been a recovered sense of sensuality in the mainstream culture that goes against the dominant intellectualization highlighted above that was so central in the initial stages of modernization. However, the cognitive dimension remains. These two perceptions of the body – the sensuous-oriented and the cognitive-oriented – can be seen throughout contemporary societies. The cognitive realm is manifested in popular obsessions with diet, health and medical discourses that were already central to the Protestant Reformation. With the Enlightenment and its central critique of Christianity, reason and intellect were prioritized over emotions and ecstasy, especially in Protestant forms of religiosity. Eventually, almost all forms of religion were influenced by this more intellectual worldview and gave priority to reason and logic over the ecstatic. In this sense, the Enlightenment period engendered a fundamental shift in the relationship between the body and mind. As new theories of agency, responsibility and individuality emerged, the body became an object controlled by the mind of the individual.

In the postmodern era, the cognitive focus from the Enlightenment is in tension with a body-focused consumerism. The modern individual exercises personal body rights with the new tools of advanced science and medicine, including procedures such as cloning, gender changes and fertility treatments. In contrast to a more medieval and ascetic perspective, consumerist culture emphasizes the right to body control and the right to pleasure. Hedonistic images dominate mainstream culture, most clearly in advertising and popular entertainment. Predictably, these new corporally focused forms of individualization seep into contemporary forms of religiosity.

The change in perspectives on the body has affected religiosity to the point that modern individualism is often equated with religious individualism. Such a conflation, which is very much influenced by Protestantism, is reflected in the way in which religion has largely been understood by Western scholarship. The dominant scholarship on religion emphasizes ideas and beliefs, values that are central to the Protestant Reformation, over behavior and functions of the body.

As Asad argues, such a focus leads in turn to the construction of religion as a transhistorical/ideational object of study removed from social contexts or groups (Asad 1993). This perspective leads to the dominant topos that religious modernity is synonymous with religious individualism. But, in all religious traditions, including Islam, there is a concept of the individual (personal responsibility of the believer *vis-à-vis* God, obligations of the believers, etc.), but it is far from being similar to the modern individual. Thus, the idea that religious modernity is equal to religious individualism is questionable. The religious individual is restricted by the ideas of discipline, restraint and asceticism, and thus cannot follow through on all personal motives or desires. On the other hand, the modern individual is defined by the absence of limits in the pursuit of its desires. Therefore, the so-called irresistible progression of the individualization of beliefs is a staple of the Western narrative, but does not reflect the historical tension between the autonomy of the subject as a believer and the modern individual.

In this sense, the current discourses and concerns of Muslim believers *vis-à-vis* the body reflect these tensions, but are not specific to the Islamic religion.

References

Asad, T. 1993. *Genealogies of Religion: Disciplinces and Reasons of Power in Christianity and Islam*. Baltimore, MD: Johns Hopkins University Press.

Beck, U. 2008. *World at Risk*. Cambridge: Polity Press.

Boumidienne, H. 1995. "African Muslim Women in France," in Michael King (ed.), *God's Law versus State Law: The Construction of an Islamic Identity in Western Europe*. London: Grey Seal, 49–61.

Cesari, J. 2004. *When Islam and Democracy Meet: Muslims in Europe and in the United States*. New York: Palgrave Macmillan.

Cesari, J. (ed.) 2009. *Muslims in the West after 9 / 11: Religion, Law and Politics*. New York: Routledge.

Cesari, J. 2013. *Why the West Fears Islam: Exploration of Muslims in Liberal Democracies*. New York: Palgrave Macmillan.

Cesari, J. and McLoughlin S. (eds) 2005. *European Muslims and the Secular State*. Aldershot: Ashgate.

Colas, D. 1997 [1st French edn 1992]. *Civil Society and Fanaticism: Conjoined Histories*. Translated by Amy Jacobs. Stanford, CA: Stanford University Press.

Deprez, J. 1988. "Droit international privé et conflit de civilisations. Aspects méthodologiques. Les relations entre systèmes d'Europe Occidentale et systèmes islamiques en matière de statut personnel," *Recueil des Cours de l'Académie de la Haye*, 211(4), 9–372.

Ferrara, A. 2009. "The Separation of Religion and Politics in a Post-secular Society," *Philosophy & Social Criticism*, 35(1–2), 77–91.

King, M. (ed.) 1995. *God's Law versus State Law: the Construction of an Islamic Identity in Western Europe*. London: Grey Seal.

Klausen, J. 2009. *The Cartoons that Shook the World*. New Haven, CT: Yale University Press.

Kymlicka, W. 1995. *Multicultural Citizenship: A Liberal Theory of Minority Rights*. Oxford: Clarendon Press.

Mercier, P. 1972. *Conflits de civilisation et droit international privé: polygamie et répudiation*. Geneva: Librairie Droz.

Taylor, C. 2012. "Rethinking Secularism: Western Secularity," *The Immanent Frame*, http://blogs.ssrc.org/tif/2011/08/10/western-secularity/.

Chapter 5

The Mosque and the European City

Nebahat Avcıoğlu

Today many cities in Europe, from Russia to England, possess purpose-built mosques, big and small, constructed in a variety of styles and locations (Avcıoğlu 2013). Ever since its first appearance in the late nineteenth century, the mosque in Europe has evolved as a continuous social and cultural effort to make Islam visible on the continent and to give agency to Muslim citizens. Scholars have already shown that the history and significance of this needs to be assessed against a rather complex background, entangled as that history is in a heavy past of colonial domination and forced economic migrations as well as the current trends of globalization.[1] Encouraged by Europe's boastful claim to pluralism, Muslims continue to exert their right to the city, and their claim to public space, within the boundaries of secularist legislations (Göle 2005). However, the process has been uneasy, slow and often politically acrimonious. Unlike other religious buildings seen as inherently or "naturally" European, the mosque is still read by those who oppose it as a marker of another, alien set of cultures and nationalities. Jocelyn Cesari succinctly sums up this uphill struggle thus: "From being invisible, Islam goes to being unwanted … [And only] through a process of [long and arduous] negotiation [does] the mosque's incorporation into the urban space" become possible (Cesari 2005: 1018). The desire for visibility, then, underlines the political nature of mosque architecture in European cities (Crinson 2002; Khan 2002; Avcıoğlu 2008; Erkoçu and Buğdacı 2009; Roose 2009a). Consequently, the rejection or incorporation of certain architectural features associated with Islamic traditions (such as domes and minarets) often defines the agenda and assumes central importance in negotiations between European Muslim and non-Muslim citizens (Avcıoğlu 2008; Khalidi 1998; Verkaaik 2012). This focus on iconography is symptomatic of tendencies that essentialize (e.g. Muslim otherness) or naturalize (e.g. Europe) what are in fact contingent and historically conditioned forms and identities. A minaret, for instance, quickly becomes the frozen signifier of an alleged eternal otherness of Islam in front of an equally fantasized immutable European identity.[2] My object in

---

1   The literature addressing some of these issues is too vast to be listed here, but notable works include Metcalf 1996; Cesari 2006; Allievi 2009; Maussen 2009.

2   More often than not reduced to its Christian heritage, as for instance in Nicolas Sarkozy's repeated rally slogan in the last French presidential election: "Voyez le long manteau d'églises et de cathédrales qui recouvre notre pays." See http://lelab.europe1.fr/t/ quand-nicolas-sarkozy-cite-nicolas-sarkozy-820.

this chapter, however, is not so much the role of architecture in defining Muslim identity, but rather the tension that the mosque reveals in the European city. I will argue that the reasons for this tension, although manifold, are as much to do with history and resistance to Islam as with a more generic fear of seeing the European city dissipate. The latter is a polemic that has been around since the beginning of the twentieth century, parallel to the overall Western malaise that has been framed by a variety of discourses from Freud to Adorno to postmodernism and, in the field of architecture, by critiques of modernism, industrialization and urbanization. In his critical history of modern architecture, Kenneth Frampton writes that:

> Increasingly subject to the imperatives of a continuously expanding consumer economy, the city has largely lost its capacity to maintain its significance as a whole. That it has been dissipated by forces lying beyond its control … as a consequence of the combined effect of the freeway, the suburb and the supermarket. (Frampton 1985: 9)

This anxiety, packed with all the disillusions of late modernity (about secularism, technology or multiculturalism), is today somehow reactivated around the familiar foreignness of the mosque-form. My aim is to show how the mosque, a byproduct of European imperialism and economic expansion, is seen both a symptom and a burden of such dissipation of the city, as well as a means for its regeneration. As such, it is a perfect entry point for understanding the ongoing, often troubled redefinition of the European city that lies behind the public controversies around Islam's presence in Europe.

*   *   *

Since the eighteenth century, the city has been seen as a place of contrasts defined by the heterogeneous practices taking place within it. Given that the City of Man is no longer thought of as the flawed copy of the City of God, the dialectics between order and chaos, form and force, immutability and open-endedness have begun to be negotiated not only in the vertical dualism of religious transcendence but also in a new set of discourses (the Nation, the Empire, the Republic, the Global World, etc.) that require a more lateral topography (Mumford 1938; Sennett 1977; Habermas 1989; Lefebvre 1991). This new dialectics, reformulating the links between modern and traditional, universal and singular, religious and secular, came to permeate all of Western culture. Generally, the European city has become the concrete ground on which (for better or worse) this tension is played out, while at the same time constituting a key topos of its reflexivity: from Fritz Lang's *Metropolis* to today's thriving urban studies, artists and thinkers have thought about the city and through the city. But architecture, or rather specific building types, by virtue of being both concrete and topographical, is often entrusted with the task of embodying the various negotiations at work in the city as process. The Louvre Pyramid in Paris is seen as an example of a smooth handling of heterogeneous temporalities, while the Gherkin in London has become a symbol of the city's contemporary global standing.

The mosque adds to this constant reformulation of identity a spatial dimension (the East, meaning a non-European dimension), while complicating Europe's relation to its past, as it is reminiscent of colonialism. With the contemporary mosque, the existential debate that the European city represents is no longer solipsistic. Other forms, other creeds, other practices – other lives – are here to be reckoned with. The secularism invented during the Enlightenment, and embodied by the city, is also put to the test. Focusing on the institutional mechanisms and discourses that bring Muslim citizens and political authorities together around the construction of mosques, sociologists and anthropologists have already considered the issues of Islam's visibility as a process that fosters new forms (both diasporic and local simultaneously) of cultural identity in Europe, as well as fashioning and refashioning Islam itself (Göle 2005: 24–5; Powel and Rishbeth 2011). In doing so, they have drawn attention to issues of urbanization – to the conflicts, challenges and contradictions inherent in the planning and settlement of rapidly growing cities (Eade 1996; Gale 2004; Cesari 2006). Yet this has further shown that the anxiety, if not outright hysteria at times, around the mosque is not just about secularism per se.

The tension between the European city and the mosque started as early as the first mosques, which were imperial monuments steeped in the traditional styles of the colonies, such as those erected in St Petersburg and Paris in the early twentieth century, and later in London (the mosque in London, though conceived in 1910, was only completed in 1977 due to shifting politics). It may surprise the reader to learn that these mosques were constructed as landmarks in their respective cities. They aimed at establishing European empires as symbolic protectors of Islam, since at the time Russia, France and Britain declared themselves to be "great Musulman powers" (Dimnet 1926: 250). A 1942 editorial in *The Times* reports: "His Majesty indeed has more Muslims than Christian subjects" (Tibawi 1981: 193–208). The imperialistic ambitions behind these edifices impelled them to be located on prime sites befitting their exuberant style and monumental size. For example, the Executive Committee of the London Mosque Fund was quite categorical at its second meeting on 20 March 1911 that "the site must be in the center of Empire," meaning "at Westminster."[3] The decision was clearly not based on necessity, as there were hardly any practicing Muslims living in Westminster at the time, and we know that even "by 1961 there were only 7 mosques in Britain" (Peach and Gale 2003: 477). Eventually, although not at Westminster, the Committee secured a site adjacent to Regent's Park in 1942 for the first mosque to be erected in central London (Tibawi 1981: 202–3). It is striking that the St Petersburg Mosque and the Great Mosque of Paris are also erected in monarchical gardens, the former in Alexander Park and the latter on the edge of the *Jardin des Plantes* (formerly the *Jardin du Roi*). This was not a coincidence. In 1911, the London Mosque

3 Proceedings of the Mosque Committee, *Camden Fifth Series*, 38 (2011), 81–288.

Committee suggested that an "enquiry might be made from the Russian Embassy as to the exact [location and] area of the mosque at St. Petersburg" before embarking on a specific site in London.[4]

Symbolizing imperial prowess (and with the architects in full awareness of the plans of the others), then, these mosques had to be built in prestigious locations. This is clearly a far cry from the industrial, derelict or suburban sites that are now home to minority places of worship in and around European cities. It is worth citing here the observation of Peach and Gale to underscore the contrast between then and now, who write:

> Exotic religious buildings, some of exquisite beauty, have been built on unlikely inner-city sites. The Shri Swaminarayan Mandir, handcrafted in the Gujarat in India from white Romanian marble, was shipped to England and assembled into an astonishingly beautiful temple off London's North Circular ring road – opposite an IKEA furniture store. The elegant Dawoodi Bohra Shi'a Masjid in Northolt is hidden away in a London industrial estate. The largest Sikh gurdwara in the Western world has been built almost under the flight path of Heathrow Airport in suburban Southall. (Peach and Gale 2003: 469–70)

Yet, although they were exceptional constructs both in their architecture and location, to say that the imperial mosques were embraced by the city would be an exaggeration. Built at a time when the idea of the European city was very much on the minds of contemporaries, particularly during the planning of modern colonial cities, these Orientalist mosques located at the heart of the metropolis were nonetheless set apart from it. If their oriental looks gave them a distinctive appearance, their location next to botanical gardens and zoos was no less ambiguous. Presented as part of a natural environment, and showcased thus, they were the product of both the eighteenth-century relativistic spirit (when exhibitions and ornamental mosques first appeared in gardens such as at Kew and Potsdam) and the nineteenth-century colonial *Universal Exposition* mindset (where exotic things brought back from the East were displayed in their so-called natural environment for maximum reality effect). Consequently, their garden locations in effect prevented even the landmark mosques from being legible as urban objects in their own right.

From the beginning, the mosque has been part of the ambivalence and fantasies of the European city. While the idea of tolerance, an imperial building block, classified the mosque as an urban curiosity, the assimilationist ideologies of decolonialization sought a more "passive" presence of Islam in the city. Functioning within modern secular imperatives, local authorities chose to grant planning permission for converting a variety of old and unused buildings such as stately homes, libraries, churches, and synagogues into mosques rather than allow for new constructions to be erected. Although operating within the homogenizing

---

4   Ibid., 82.

tendencies of modernist and assimilationist ideologies, the recycled structures both rendered the Muslim presence implicit and prevented major transformation of the "traditional" European city. The real challenge began when later-generation European Muslims reacted against these homogenizing tendencies, which they read as erasure of their identities and that of their parents, and demanded larger mosques built in what they conceived to be traditional Islamic forms and archetypes. Authorities conceded to this by restricting their erection to the peripheries of the city, in contrast to the concomitant rise in Muslim migration to urban centers. Often located in the middle of nowhere, these structures were called, in unconscious irony, cultural *centers* rather than mosques – becoming centers of their own. Banishing mosques to the city limits or suburbs perpetuated an imagined identity of the European city without mosques. Faced with democratic pluralism and multiculturalism, current governments, seemingly impartial to matters of faith, whether secularist or not, still keep a tight control over decisions about the location and style of religious buildings.

It was in the 1960s that social engineering schemes characteristic of the utopian new town movement, originating in the British concept of the garden city and practiced from Finland to France, turned to places of worship to animate new suburbs. The housing projects surrounding the shopping mall, the train station and the church constituted the dreamscape of modern life for the underclass. The best-known example of the French version of this movement is Evry, in the southeast of Paris, planned in the 1970s with an "Agora," forming "the most important multipurpose cultural and leisure centre in France" (Merlin 1980: 84). Right from its inception, the town was to contain a number of *lieux de culte*, including a pagoda, a cathedral, a synagogue and a mosque, to showcase liberty of conscience as enshrined in the French conception of *laïcité* (Brisacier 1990: 108–11). However, embroiled in public and legal controversies, because of the 1905 law of separation between state and religion, the realization of these places of worship took more than 20 years, with the mosque and the cathedral finally being completed as late as 1995. Aesthetically, they were conceived with a formal rationality to maintain modernist harmony with their surroundings. The vernacular thus embodied in the invented towns (eight in total for the Paris region) more importantly allowed the bourgeois city to keep the immigrants out of their midst. In effect, these new metropolitan centers merely exemplified the erratic nature of the modern project itself.

The 1990s saw the alternative to conversion or suburban mosque in the form of the out-of-sight multipurpose Islamic cultural centers built in the international style. The Great Mosque of Rome is a case in point (see Figure 5.1 in the color plate section). Though monumental in size and striking in its somewhat postmodern design, it is very hard to get to without a car. Located on one of the main arteries that connect the city to the green suburbs, the mosque and its huge courtyard with palm trees face the road but are separated from it by a painted green wrought iron fence. Designed by Sami Mousawi and Paolo Portoghesi and opened in 1995, it is one of many purpose-built mosques that give visible proof to the Muslim presence in Europe. And yet, like many others, it remains empty for the most part. The arrangement is clearly made to maintain a culturally and socially as well as ideally intact Rome, sending out a subliminal message that is not so much "There is a mosque but you can't get there," but rather "There is a mosque but this is Vatican City." Similarly, the banning of minarets in Switzerland in 2009, though largely interpreted as racism and Islamophobia, is clearly also about iconophobia and the preservation of the traditional cityscape, as the ludicrous poster showing the country invaded by dark pencil-shaped minarets and a giant niqab-wearing woman demonstrates.

More recently, the unprecedented concentration of Muslims in urban centers and the general features of globalization, such as geographical and social mobility, diversification, image-making and consumption, make it hard for Europe to keep mosques at bay. At the same time, new proposals are considered not as individual structures but only if they form part of comprehensive urban schemes. Nevertheless, some of these projects are uncompromising in their Muslim, sectarian or national identities as regards their formal characteristics. But, at the same time, conscious of their urban context, they also react to the essentializing rhetoric of the East/West divide. Among them I isolate three kinds of reformulations: the urban-mosque, the open-mosque and the mega-mosque. All of these are in a way a rethinking of earlier practices, radically transformed to reach out to the city and some even conceived as little cities themselves.

The best example of an urban mosque is the Westermoskee in Amsterdam, which is in progress (see Figure 5.2 in the color plate section). It is designed as part of an urban rehabilitation of a 1930s neighborhood. The Hagia Sophia look-a-like structure stands in the middle of an irregular piazza surrounded by 118 units of housing and shops regenerated by the same project. The mosque is not only part of the same planning scheme but is also built with the similar redbrick and decorated with white stripes, which creates a vernacular atmosphere despite the Ottoman character of the mosque. By sharing the same masonry with the neighboring buildings, the building is not objectified but somehow camouflaged, which helps diffuse its urban impact, whereby the typology (sacred building) rather than style (oriental) expresses the hierarchical status of the building. Yet it differs from the converted buildings for it aims to speak of European pluralism and not only of Muslim assimilation.

If visual compatibility with the surroundings is a condition for the central urban mosque, then the precept for the open-mosque is literally to reveal itself to the city. The much-debated Cologne mosque currently in progress (designed by the architect Paul Bohm and, with its 1,200-worshipper capacity, set to be one of the largest mosques in Europe) is a case in point (see Figure 5.3 in the color plate section). Its central location in the city near a famous cathedral attracted heated adverse reactions, which led to the idea of a "transparent, open mosque" supported in particular by local authorities (Connolly 2012). After grueling negotiations, the architect came up with a modern design that is both distinctive and engaged with the city. The rigid and uniform hemispherical dome shell covering the prayer hall, which approximated the building to the traditional cascading Ottoman domes, is cut through by vertical openings to facilitate a dialogue with the city. Laid out on an open square, the complex lacks a protective fence, which is clearly intended to give direct access, both visual and physical, to the mosque from the city. The local imam enthusiastically interpreted the design and the setting as part of the multicultural rhetoric, saying: "The new mosque would put Islam in plain sight ... [And show that] Our hearts are open, our doors are open, our mosque is open" (Lander 2007). The paradox is that, having tried to push Islam out of the city, European authorities now exploit it as an instrument of urban dialogue, but once again the burden is placed on architecture and on Muslim communities to develop and refine the new conditions. The proclamatory potential of the "transparent, open mosque" is also evident in other recent proposals: in the Netherlands, for instance, where many architects encourage mosques to be built of glass (Roose 2009b: 14; Verkaaik 2012: 168).

Perhaps the most radical response to the idea of an urban mosque is the project designed by Mangera Yvars Architects, winners of an international competition held in 2005, for a so-called mega-mosque in East London next to the site of the 2012 Olympic Games. Like the Westermoskee, it was conceived as an urban redevelopment project, but with multifunctional facilities created entirely anew together with a prayer hall of extraordinary capacity (40,000 worshippers). The design is based on movement patterns and activities rather than emphasizing the mosque per se. A high-tech roof stretches over multifunctional spaces and public walkways. Based on modern technology and ecological programming, the futuristic complex resembled an organic city with distinct sociocultural characteristics in favour of Muslim citizens (DeHanas and Pieri 2011: 798–814). Although initially welcomed, the project has become controversial and was ultimately halted because of its urban scale which is seen as a device to proselytize Islam in Britain. It seems that as soon as Muslim communities comply with the new requirements but propose a superior or better-conceived version of them, at least architecturally speaking, the rules of the game change.

The resentment *vis-à-vis* urban mosques is finally the same against both visually distinct mosques and discrete places of worship. This is indicative of the European city's inability to come to terms with the idea of having a mosque in its midst. When it becomes impossible to avoid it, the lines of reasoning put forward seem even more perplexing. In Créteil, a satellite city of Paris, the mosque is erected "where everyone can see it" in order to "eliminate underground sites and extremist ways" (Moore 2007). The central location that was chosen for the building was not, therefore, for its religious or cultural merit, but rather for its utility as a way to survey Muslims. Another recent trend in suburbia is to insist on a "landmark building" through which municipalities seek to energize their expanding city. For instance, in the new town of Almere near Amsterdam (founded in the 1960s, now the sixth largest city in the Netherlands), "the municipality wants a minaret" while the users of the mosque do not. Such insistence is no less dogmatic and prescriptive. Indeed, Muslims no longer want to be judged according to certain iconic features broadly defined as Islamic. For them, the importance of the urban aspect of a mosque is not about acknowledging Islam; rather, as one commentator puts it, it is about the "acknowledgement of the city towards its citizens" (Moore 2007).

The Islamic versus the European City

These recent attempts are clearly geared toward both bringing the mosque back to the city and to undermining its exceptional status. They try to replace the unitary approach to its construction with urbanistic thinking. And yet, rather than the city openly embracing them, mosques still carry the burden of reaching out to the city. This turns the city (not the mosque) into a very particular kind of political space both for Muslims and non-Muslims, one that is not intolerant of Islam per se but that struggles to define itself through the instrumentalization of the mosque. As most projects remain unrealized, plagued by controversies often revolving around Islam versus modernity and the cathedral versus the mosque, the definition of the European city itself is performatively reproduced. With each mosque, appearing over time – be it orientalist, recycled, suburban, diasporic or mega-mosque – discursive strategies operate either in maintaining or (very rarely) dismantling the distinction between European and Islamic identities. It is this struggle in effect that forms the basis of the constantly negotiated architectural styles of the mosques. The contemporary version of this ongoing dilemma seems to be the struggle around the redefinition of the city, between its conscious evolution as postmodern melting pot on the one hand and eradication of its fundamental characteristics on the other. Consequently, the battles fought between "visionary" architects and "traditional" urban planners of the modern period are now replaced by battles between the myriad communities that make up the metropolis and refuse to be subsumed under a single identity. This cannot be properly understood without an analysis of the ways in which distinctions between the "Islamic" and the "European" city have been constructed, played out and reiterated through the erection of mosques across the continent.

It is important to remember that as the quintessential Islamic space, the mosque has been crucial in drawing distinctions between *the* Islamic and *the* European city – notions that were forged as binary opposites in early twentieth-century Orientalist discourse, with one (the European city or modernity itself) being the hierarchically superior model and the other (the Islamic city or Islam in general) being merely derivative.[5] However, this claim was not only flawed in substance but was also laden with contradictions from the outset. The European city that was contrasted with the Islamic city was not the Greek *polis*, with the agora (intellectual and commercial space) as its core, but the medieval city where the

---

5 The literature on this topic is vast, but a full discussion of it is beyond the scope of this chapter. For one of the best treatments of the subject, see Raymond 1994.

cathedral constituted the urban heart and fulfilled both religious and non-religious functions. Even though the medieval city and the Islamic city were structured around a sacred core, thus sharing characteristics, the mosque, unlike the church, was never seen as purely religious in nature. The mosque, seen as dictating the social, political and cultural life of the city, is portrayed as incapable of autonomy in the separation between the sacred and the secular, unlike the church, which demonstrated this capacity with the dawn of modernism.[6] As recently as 2005, while reacting to the construction of the Cologne mosque, the German writer Ralph Giordano reiterated this prejudice by claiming: "[a] mosque is more than a church or a synagogue. It is a political statement" (Lander 2007). Though his point might be about the importance of secularism in society, to assume that religion became obsolete or impolitic in European cities is the myth of modernism, which came to play a significant role in the distinction between Islam and modernity. While Islam continues to be seen as intrinsically alien to Europe, modernity is regarded not as a fact of life in the East but as an exceptional phenomenon of the "Islamic city." Speaking of a contemporary art event in Turkey, *The Economist* writes: "The Istanbul Biennale is a celebration of culture's fundamental unity. It is a reminder also that this city of mosques is a place of modernity" (*The Economist* 2001: 79). These seemingly innocuous utterances show just how stubborn binary oppositions in European discourses are and how the mosque (as religion and culture) plays a central role in them.

Indeed, the Orientalist invention of the notion of Islamic city was not fortuitous. The argument proved particularly helpful in the European strategy of self-definition as it deflected attention away from the inherent contradictions between European universalism and its imperial practices as well as those belonging to the process of modernization itself. While orientalist claims about city types were formulated, Europeans were carrying out modernist and rational urban planning projects in the Muslim colonies, often fully embraced by the locals, creating public squares and laying out streets on geometrical patterns and erecting uniform building facades (Raymond 1994). This happened either through a total destruction of the existing urban fabric (as in Algeria) or through the construction of a new city adjacent to the old, where a sense of contrast between traditional and modern (i.e. "Islamic" and "European") was forever engrained (as in Tunisia). The preservation of "*la medina*" helped demonstrate the irregular, labyrinthine streets sprawling around the mosque as a timeless fixture of an eternal Islamic city (i.e. both archaic and scenic). As the late André Raymond reminds us, during the colonial period, the Muslim natives living in these cities were called "Muslims" in official documents, not Algerians or Tunisian, let alone French.[7] Claimed by Orientalists to fulfill most functions of the city, the mosque was seen to stand in

---

6 For the evolving role of the mosque as public space in the Muslim world, see Rabbat 2012: 1–9.

7 Raymond argued that "the classic concept of the Muslim is very much a French affair" (Raymond 1994: 3).

the way of modernism and political progress. To curb this image, post-colonial secular-nationalist governments, exhilarated by their newfound independence, readily destroyed them to make room for new roads, railways and public parks, or converted them into museums to mark their indisputable modernity, thereby acting out an internalized self-orientalism. However, the adoption of modern urban layouts, forms, functions and ideals has done surprisingly little to lift the stigma around the mosques constructed in Europe. Perhaps the biggest challenge for Europe was to see the monumental, celebratory mosques erected in the hearts of Paris, London and St Petersburg. At least it was in this context that, by the 1950s, Gustav von Grunebaum formulated the doctrine of the Islamic city in which the mosque not only defined the city but was also categorically precluded from the European city. Tellingly, von Grunebaum claims that: "Constantinople would not have tolerated a mosque on its soil" (von Grunebaum 1961: 181).[8] But, as recent research has shown, in this he was wrong. Constantinople contained not only a few Muslim spaces but also a purpose-built mosque for diplomatic use long before the Ottoman arrival (Anderson 2009: 87). Such an acknowledgement not only unsettles the key Orientalist principle but also signals the gradual erosion of the distinction between the European and the Islamic city, or rather European and Muslim identities, which were from the start tenuous constructs.

Reactions to current mosque projects in effect carry forward or (more rarely) repudiate the distinction between the Islamic and the European city made by Orientalists in the early twentieth century. Through these reactions, the status of Muslims as imperial subjects, permanent immigrants and eventually citizens is also negotiated. The political, social and demographic changes occurring over time affect the settlements and development of cities amid deepening national consciousness. Thus, the issue of having a mosque in a European city is closely bound to questions of where and how they should be built.

None of these conflicts distorts the reality of the tension between the sacred and the city, nor is such tension specific to Europe. Modern Turkish architects design and build mosques with flat roofs and without minarets in an attempt to reform Islam but also in order to challenge the image of the "Islamic city." When Islam regained political currency in Cairo in the early 1990s, the illegal *shanty towns* were protected from the government bulldozers by a mosque built almost overnight to block road access (Al-Sayyad 1995: 18). Whether in aesthetic, political or social terms, religious architecture invites us to reckon with the city. It has a remarkable ability to adapt to new urban conditions based on the intrinsic relationship between the sacred and the city. Since the early twentieth century, this tension has often played out in the evolution of the architecture of mosques and the debates about their location.

---

8   For his theories of the Islamic city, see von Grunebaum 1961.

References

Al-Sayyad, N. 1995. "From Vernacularism to Globalism: The Temporal Reality of Traditional Settlements," *Traditional Dwellings & Settlements Review*, 7(1), 13–25.

Allievi, S. 2009. *Conflicts over Mosques in Europe: Policy Issues and Trends*. London: NEF/Alliance Publishing Trust.

Anderson, G-D. 2009. "Islamic Spaces and Diplomacy in Constantinople (Tenth to Thirteenth Centuries C.E.)," *Medieval Encounters*, 15, 86–113.

Avcıoğlu, N. 2008. "Form-as-Identity: The Mosque in the West," with response by Nasser Rabbat, *Cultural Analysis*, 6, 91–112.

Avcıoğlu, N. 2013. "Towards a New Typology of Modern and Contemporary Mosque in Europe including Russia and Turkey," in Richard Etlin (ed.), *Cambridge World History of Religious Architecture*. Cambridge: Cambridge University Press, forthcoming.

Brisacier, M. 1990. "Une cathedral pour Evry," *Vingtieme Siecle. Revue d'histoire*, 25, 108–11.

Cesari, J. (ed.) 2005. "Mosque Conflicts in European Cities," Special issue of *Journal of Ethnic and Migration Studies*, 31(6), 1015–24.

Connolly, K. 2012. "Row Threatens Cologne's Mega Mosque," *The Guardian*, March 5.

Crinson, M. 2002. "The Mosque and the Metropolis," in Jill Beaulieu and Mary Roberts (eds), *Orientalism's Interlocutors: Painting, Architecture, Photography*. Durham, NC: Duke University Press.

DeHanas, D-N. and Pieri, P.Z. 2011. "Olympic Proportions: The Expanding Scalar Politics of the London 'Olympics Mega-Mosque' Controversy," *Sociology*, 45(5), 798–814.

Dimnet, E. 1926. "The Paris Mosque," *Saturday Review of Politics, Literature, Science and Art* 142(3697), September 4, 250.

Eade, J. 1996. "Nationalism, Community and the Islamisation of Space in London," in B.D. Metcalf (ed.), *Making Muslim Space in North America and Europe*. Berkeley: University of California Press.

The Economist. 2001. "Mosques and Modernity," *The Economist*, 361(8245), October 27, 79–80.

Erkoçu, E. and Buğdacı C. (eds) 2009. *The Mosque: Political, Architectural and Social Transformations*. Amsterdam: Nai Publishers.

Frampton, K. 1985. *Modern Architecture: A Critical History*. London: Thames & Hudson.

Gale, R. 2004. "The Multicultural City and the Politics of Religious Architecture: Urban Planning, Mosques and Meaning-making in Birmingham, UK," *Built Environment*, 30(1), 30–44.

Göle, N. 2005. *Interpenetrations: L'Islam et l'Europe*. Paris: Galaade.

Habermas, J. 1989. *The Structural Transformation of the Public Sphere*. Cambridge: Polity Press.

Khan, H-U. 2002. "An Overview of Contemporary Mosques," in Martin Frishman and Hasan-Uddin Khan (eds), *The Mosque*. London: Thames & Hudson.

Khalidi, O. 1998. "Approaches to Mosque Design in North America," in Yvonne Yazbeck Haddad and John L. Esposito (eds), *Muslims on the Americanization Path?* Oxford: Oxford University Press.

Lander, M. 2007. "Germans Split over a Mosque and the Role of Islam," *New York Times*, July 5.

Lefebvre, H. 1991. *The Production of Space*. Oxford: Blackwell.

Maussen, M. 2009. "Constructing Mosques: The Governance of Islam in France and the Netherlands," PhD dissertation, University of Amsterdam.

Merlin, P. 1980. "The New Town Movement in Europe," *Annals, AAPSS*, 451, 76–85.

Metcalf, B.-D. (ed.) 1996. *Making Muslim Space in North America and Europe*. Berkeley: University of California Press.

Moore, M. 2007. "In a Europe Torn over Mosques, a City Offers Accommodation," *Washington Post*, December 9.

Mumford, L. 1938. *The Culture of Cities*. New York: Harcourt, Brace and Company.

Peach, C. and Gale, R. 2003. "Muslims, Hindus, and Sikhs in the New Religious Landscapes of England," *Geographical Review*, 93(4), 469–90.

Powel, M. and Rishbeth, C. 2011. "Flexibility in Place and Meanings of Place by First Generation Migrants," *Tijdschrift voor Economische en Sociale Geografie*, 103(1), 69–84.

Rabbat, N. 2012. "The Arab Revolution Takes Back the Public Space," *Critical Inquiry*, January, 1–9.

Raymond, A. 1994. "Islamic City, Arab City: Orientalist Myths and Recent Views," *British Journal of Middle Eastern Studies*, 2(1), 3–18.

Roose, E. 2009a. *The Architectural Representation of Islam: Muslim-Commissioned Mosque Design in the Netherlands*. Amsterdam: Amsterdam University Press.

Roose, E. 2009b. "The Architectural Representation of Islam," in E. Erkoçu and C. Buğdacı (eds), *The Mosque: Political, Architectural and Social Transformations*. Amsterdam: Nai Publishers.

Sennett, R. 1977. *The Fall of Public Man*. New York: Knopf.

Tibawi, A.L. 1981. "History of the London Central Mosque and the Islamic Cultural Centre 1910–1980," *Die Welt des Islams*, 21, 1/4, 193–208.

Verkaaik, O. 2012. "Designing the 'Anti-mosque': Identity, Religion and Affect in Contemporary European Mosque Design," *Social Anthropology/Anthropologie Sociale*, 20, 161–76.

Von Grunebaum, G. 1961. "The Structure of the Muslim Town," in *Islam, Essays in the Nature and Growth of a Cultural Tradition*. London: Routledge & Kegan Paul, 141–58.

Von Grunebaum, G. 1964. *Medieval Islam*. Chicago, IL: University of Chicago Press.

Chapter 6

Conflicts over Mosques in Europe: Between Symbolism and Territory

Stefano Allievi

Controversy over mosques is today probably the most significant example of public debate concerning Islam in Europe. Far from being solely an example of religious conflict, this controversy explicitly and implicitly "contains" several different types of conflict. Very few of those opposing the presence of mosques or prayer halls would claim to want to prevent anyone from praying. The line of reasoning is always more complex, linked, among other things, to the symbolic appropriation of territory, which has to do with history and its reconstruction but also with deep sociocultural dynamics – with Islam itself and its presence in Europe.

Controversies around mosques represent conflicts that are debated not only *within* society but are *about* society itself. This point seems even more crucial in light of the focus of these controversies on control over the territory and its symbolic imprinting. The fact that these conflicts also emerge in countries where Islam is more or less well and peacefully established makes them an ideal type to analyze in order to understand the deeper implications of these issues (Allievi 2009; 2010).[1]

The problem of mosques (I use this word to signify any Muslim prayer room) is not actually a quantitative one. If we attempt an initial statistical approximation, we obtain the following figures: there are around 16,790,000 Muslims in Europe (most significant countries included) and a total of almost 11,000 mosques. If we eliminate from our statistical approximation the Muslims and mosques of Bosnia and Thrace, in which Muslims constitute a historically stable and institutionalized presence, we obtain the figures of 15,170,000 Muslims and 8,822 prayer halls, which corresponds to one prayer hall per 1,720 potential Muslims.

These figures are probably comparable to those for the places of worship of all major religions in many nations, both Christian and Muslim, and are sufficient to confirm that in principle and in general there is not a problem of religious freedom or freedom of worship for Muslims in Europe. Indeed, in many European countries, the number of mosques is currently in a phase of consolidation,

---

1   The issue of conflicts over mosques has become the object of European comparative research, from which the following data and several considerations originate. For an extended bibliography on mosques in Europe, see also the free downloads of both publications at www.nef-europe.org and www.stefanoallievi.it.

stabilization and even augmentation, as well as a phase of investment in their internal structures and enlargement of their spaces and functions. But a closer analysis of the situation within various countries offers further significant material for analysis, with conflicts emerging as a frequent and quite interesting qualitative issue that is essential in order to arrive at an understanding of the dynamics of, and opposition to, Islam in Europe.

Between Symbolism and Territory: Mosques as a Visible Dimension

Mosques are a way for Islam to leave the private sphere and officially enter the public sphere, where it becomes qualified as an interlocutor with society and institutions. They are good barometers of the level of organization of various ethnic and religious communities. They are also a feature of growth, often within conflictual dynamics, of Islamic leadership, or sometimes a demonstration of its immaturity. Finally, they are an indicator of the integration of Islam within a new context, its ability to transform that context and give it an Islamic slant.

It is interesting to note, from a European perspective, that even some non-Islamic local authorities are beginning to view the presence of mosques as a sign of cultural openness and "globalization." It must be stressed, however, that this is not the response to small, local neighborhood mosques, called *mosquées de proximité* in the French debate, or for the large mosques (*mosquées cathédrales*) visited by important foreign guests, trade delegations, institutional representatives and ambassadors, and which thus play a symbolic, cultural and even diplomatic role. Most strikingly, mosques – like any form of construction that is proposed in an area where previously it was not present – constitute a form of symbolic ownership of the land. Similarly, opposition to them is a very concrete and material sign of dominance and power over the territory. It is clear, therefore, that the conflict over mosques is, above all, a conflict of power. Several different variables come into play in this sphere: the actors deemed legitimate and their increasing strength, the resistance of social actors already present (their "culture," as it is often called), and each group's respective forms of legitimization and expression of their own beliefs.

A first observation is self-evident: not all buildings, even those that are novel in form and function, produce this kind of conflict. Rarely does a public or commercial building produce such protest. A new hospital, bank, supermarket or multiplex cinema may be the subject of criticism, but such criticism is rarely expressed in cultural terms. Appraisals may be made regarding the appropriateness of its placement in terms of other, potentially compromised, interests; for instance, a supermarket with reference to the threat that it poses to small shops in the surrounding area or, in addition, a building's aesthetic qualities such as size and shape, for example, when a high-rise building is constructed in an area of low-rise development. But, although common, such conflicts rarely induce an identity reflex and an "us/them" dynamic, as is found in response to mosques. Even when this kind of dynamic manifests itself in other select instances, such as in response to a neighborhood enclave of new residents or when people move from cities into rural areas to dramatic effect for local communities, only rarely do such instances generate actual conflicts; again, even in the rare event of such conflicts, it is unusual to encounter reflexes of collective identity. In contrast, mosques produce these very frequently, in mild or radical form, in many parts of Europe, at least at this moment in history. Meanwhile, churches, synagogues or temples of other non-dominant confessions in any given European nation do not – although it would be historically inaccurate to say that this has not happened to other religious groups in Europe in the past. In this sense, there is a real "mosque issue" in Europe today.

Some forms of conflict pertaining to mosques could actually be interpreted using the tools not of anthropology and sociology and, still less, of urban planning, but instead of ethology and sociobiology – specifically for the interpretation of forms of imprinting on an area such as the spreading of pig urine or the placing of pigs' heads or blood in the area where a mosque is planned. Cases of this kind have occurred widely, from Sweden to Italy to Spain to the Czech Republic, and are in themselves a phenomenon worthy of study.[2] These cases are worth mentioning because of the use of primitive proprietary dynamics of privatization, passing through the logic of sacralization and desacralization of space. If we were discussing relations between animals, we would say that it was simply an appropriation of space by means of unpleasant or aggressive signs and smells – claims of exclusivity to the territory and an assertion of aggressive competitiveness toward other possible contenders. Regarding the more general question of mosques, we should note the spread of a vocabulary that refers to contamination, pollution and precautionary measures, which is used explicitly in reference to mosques by various anti-Islamic groups, as well as the return of categories of purity and contagion in cultural and political debate. Given the historical precedents and the concerns that these raise, further reflection is needed on the use of such vocabulary in response to mosques.

Architecture, Symbolism, Space

Returning to the symbolism attached to space, it is a fact that architecture is a particularly assertive form of expression: it is highly visible and therefore conducive to the expression of ideology. The use of architectural logic and monuments by totalitarian regimes, such as the Nazi, Fascist and Soviet regimes, and by fundamentalists, notably in the destruction of the religious symbols of others (the most recent and resounding example of which was the destruction

---

2   Cases also involve raising pigs' heads on spikes planted in the ground where the construction of a mosque is planned, throwing pigs' intestines and pieces of pork onto the future sites of mosques, strolling with a pig in front of TV cameras on land where the erection of a mosque is planned, public roast-pork eat-ins, etc.

of the Bamiyan Buddhas in Afghanistan) is a never-ending story, which over history has involved hundreds of churches and mosques. In secular terms, there is an ideological dimension, albeit less explicitly pronounced, in the progressive replacement in many city centers of symbols of religious or civic power (town halls and cathedrals) with symbols of economic and financial power (banks and shops) or with places of entertainment (cinemas, theatres, and bars). In regard to mosques, many different factors come into play. From the Islamic side, we should emphasize the role of great Islamic centers, especially in capital cities, in the definition of symbolic space. Their presence constitutes a contractual form of "visibilization"; for instance, it is no accident that the inauguration of the great mosque in Rome in 1995 – the first purpose-built mosque in the capital of Christendom – represented a near-realization of the famous *hadith*, which states that first Constantinople will open to Islam, then Rome. This fact was widely quoted at the time and enjoyed exceptional media coverage in Arab countries.

Elsewhere, the function of being ostentatious is clearly apparent. For example, in Britain, we can point to the mosques of Bradford and Birmingham, placed on high ground or in highly visible sites; or the project, which has attracted much criticism, to create a "mega-mosque" in the London borough of Newham; to the construction of a mosque in the Arab quarter of Albaicin in Granada – a return to the glorious times of Muslim Andalusia, with all its associations; or to the small, perfectly useless as no Muslims live there but crucially located mosque in Gibraltar on the strip of European land closest to the Muslim coastline, from which point it is easier than anywhere else in Europe to look to Islam and hope for its "return." Finally, there are a variety of projects, often oversized compared to the needs they address and not always economically sustainable by their respective communities, in almost every European country, from Germany and France to the Netherlands and Italy. Opponents of the announced but not-yet-built mosque in Athens worry that it would be the first thing that a visitor would see from the plane when arriving in Greece, given its location close to the airport. Visibility is part of the logic of institutionalization, acceptance and even symbolic integration. The day that such visibility no longer raises any problems will be the day that the integration of Islam in the European public sphere is complete.

In Europe, with the exception of Islamic centers in some capital cities and a few others, there is often the symmetric and contrary logic of "peripheralization" and marginalization in the suburbs, in and around degraded areas. A rationale that is often used implicitly by the authorities and even more frequently adopted independently by Muslims themselves aims not so much to solve the problem of visibility and its consequences in terms of predictable conflict, but rather to avoid having to face these issues. This generates the principle of "architectural mimicry," which proposes that a mosque is fine as long as it is not overly recognizable as such. We will tackle the symbolism of conflicts over minarets more explicitly later, but this principle can be seen in countless cases of conflict, leading to decisions to build in a style not too dissimilar from a nearby church or simply to eliminate domes, minarets and crescent moons. Another approach is to adopt a "modern" style of construction rather than the architectural orientalism found in the nostalgia mosques (the so-called *heimweemoskee* in the Dutch debate) so dear to earlier generations who brought to their adoptive countries the styles of construction typical of their country of origin (such as the round double minaret on the sides of the dome found in Turkish mosques or the square minaret favored by Moroccans). Still others go strongly in the direction of architectural futurism, a style advocated in particular by second-generation architects.[3] Most often, however, architectural mimicry manifests itself not when new mosques are constructed, but when existing buildings are adapted into mosques; in the event of the latter, modifications may be made to the interior, but none or almost none are made to the exterior – to such an extent that sometimes not even a sign or plaque indicating the building's function as a prayer hall is made visible. This can be attributed to the fact that the acceptance or rejection of a presence of a prayer hall within a community may depend on its architecture, as is clearly shown by the public controversy over visibility and, in particular, minarets.

Minarets as Missiles? Battles over a Contested Symbol

Many conflicts over mosques in Europe raise, either primarily or marginally, the question of the minaret in terms of either its height or its very existence. The minaret appears to have become a symbol par excellence of the conflict over Islam, or rather the conflict over its visibility in the public eye, even more than, for example, the hijab. The politics of identity, as manifested in connection with mosques, has ended up confining itself to a repertoire of forms. And, paradoxically, the minaret has ultimately become "a structural metonym of Muslim identity" (Avcıoğlu 2008), in spite of the fact that there are mosques in Muslim countries with no minarets and that this feature does not actually belong to the original history of Islam.

The minaret, like skyscrapers and the Tower of Babel, is a symbol that rises up into the sky, a symbol of power, size and strength. Even without making too much of its obviously phallic aspect – a symbol of domination, which is not incompatible with the ethological perspective that we have already introduced – it can be demonstrated historically that towers have always been a sign of power and domination. It is no coincidence that in the long history of medieval Italian municipalities, the victory of a family or a city over another resulted in the destruction of the towers of the defeated family or city. The broken towers found in many cities still testify to this. During the recent war in the former Yugoslavia, there was a race to destroy minarets and church towers (the principal symbolic and architectural targets of the war) in order to establish dominance. A similar

---

3   In this regard, we should note that architects responsible for "nostalgia" projects are often natives and non-Muslims who have simply chosen to interpret in this manner desires that their clients have not always clearly expressed.

competition is visible in the present-day race between large companies and big cities, particularly between contending economic and financial powerhouses, to build the highest skyscraper in the world as a visible symbol of power.

Disputes about minarets are thus, perhaps especially, conflicts of power. Minarets represent attempts by Muslims to introduce a symbol with high visibility and with a function of ostentation – at least interpreted as such by local populations. And, indeed, they are also often perceived as such as part of the Muslim imaginary about them. As a consequence, a sort of marked "political visibility" is achieved, which may also include other symbols. Interpretation plays a major role. For Muslims, it is often more a question of nostalgia, of doing things as they would "at home," because, after all, even if, as we have noted, there is often also a hidden intention of visibility, "a mosque should look like a mosque," as an Islamic exponent in Rotterdam succinctly put it (Maussen 2009). But for non-Muslim residents, it is often interpreted as a matter of being invaded, almost as if a foreign body has been forced upon them. It is not by chance that the promoters of the Swiss referendum depicted the minarets in their propaganda as missiles menacing the Confederation. And the issue does not stop at architecture (where concern is often justified): the residents of many cities that have tolerated without any resistance all sorts of, architecturally speaking, foreign bodies (residential or administrative buildings, shopping malls or leisure facilities, convention centers or sports infrastructures, strange churches of the majority confession, even the temples of other religious minorities) perceive the minaret as having another meaning, an offensive element of what we call Islamic exceptionalism,[4] so much so that in many cases, the minaret had to be cut down to a height below that of the local cathedral or of the nearest church and sometimes even eliminated completely. Often, elimination of the minaret takes place without any particular reaction from the Muslim community, revealing the extent to which the minaret has a nostalgic function rather than a fundamental identifying purpose. At times, the Muslim community has been content with drawing a minaret on the entrance door, as in many non-purpose-built mosques.

In some countries, the minaret issue has triggered anti-Islamic legislation. In 2008, Carinthia, one of the Austrian regions with the lowest Islamic presence but with a xenophobic party led by Jörg Haider that was in power at the time, was the first to approve (along with Vorarlberg, a region that has a higher percentage of Muslims, nearly double the national average) a law banning minarets. Requests for copies of these regional laws then came from other regions of Austria, such

---

4   The idea that Islam must be considered a religion that is different from all others and not treated the same way but instead requiring specific norms and rules, as is visible in the specific representative bodies invented for Muslims and specific to them in many countries, to the politics of intervention of local and national powers (from opposition to specific customs that sometimes are not so specific, but become important as soon as any customs labeled as Islamic become important for the existence of anti-Muslim groups and political parties).

as from the German-speaking regions of Switzerland, where a referendum on the issue was held in 2009 (see below) and from certain German *Länder*. Yet it was also in Austria, in 1979, that the Islamic center of Vienna was inaugurated with its minaret – with no reaction. It is the Swiss referendum against minarets that has been a sensational demonstration of how important the minaret issue has become.

The Swiss Paradox

Conflicts over the building of mosques and the visibility of prayer rooms in Europe have been a significant characteristic and a real issue in the debate over Islam. The referendum against minarets was held in 22 of the 26 cantons of Switzerland on 29 November 2009, passing with 57.5 percent of the votes in favor of a ban. However, the most sensational thing about the Swiss referendum was not its results, but the fact that it was completely unexpected: no one had realized what was happening, what was brewing within public opinion and the effects it would have. It took not only the political classes but also internal and external observers, from academics to journalists, by surprise.[5]

Yet this issue is not only an internal Swiss question, as most observers like to imagine. In fact, it is probable that in other areas of Europe, similar referendums would have the same results. The problem is that in terms of the constitution of many countries, Switzerland included, issues of this kind should never have even been put to the vote, because such legislation is completely illegitimate: one of the pillars of democracy is precisely that majorities cannot decide the basic rights of minorities and that the universal rights of individual groups cannot be put in question.

The Swiss referendum made apparent a significant and paradoxical element on the cultural and social plane, which merits further reflection. Few people have noticed the (only seemingly contradictory) fact that in three of the four cities where minarets and their corresponding mosques actually exist and have existed for a long time and where the Islamic presence is greatest, the referendum was unsuccessful: Zurich, where the minaret of the local Ahmadiyya mosque dates back to 1963; Geneva, where the authorities had insisted that the minaret built in 1978 should be *only* 22 meters high; Winterthur, whose minaret was built in 2005 in an Albanese Islamic center; and Wangen bei Olten, north of Bern, where a little minaret of only six meters was inaugurated in 2009.[6] Meanwhile, the highest

---

5   One month before the referendum, the first poll commissioned by Swiss Radio gave a majority against the referendum to ban minarets: 53 percent against, 37 percent in favor of the ban. Non-believers and persons with an income above 11,000 Swiss francs were the categories of those most against the referendum.

6   It was precisely the request in 2006 to build minarets in many towns belonging to German-speaking cantons that triggered the national debate over minarets that then led to the referendum. Wangen, not by chance a little village with fewer than 5,000 inhabitants

percentage of votes (71 percent) in favor of the ban on minarets was obtained in internal Appenzell, where the Muslim presence is insignificant if not non-existent – the same canton, which, after rejecting the referendum to extend the vote to women three times (1973, 1982 and 1990), was finally forced to concede to it only through the direct intervention of the Federal Tribunal. It seems fair to interpret this historical fact as a sign of general, and not just specifically as regards minarets, close-mindedness.

Deliberately stating this double tendency in extreme terms, we can interpret the evidence as follows: where there are no minarets, and possibly even no Muslims, fear forces people to banish first and then be scared; where Muslims already exist and are visible, there is much less fear. This does not necessarily mean that the more you know Muslims, the more you must like them (or at least not fear them), but it does mean that where there are natural dynamics of encounter and confrontation, long-term trends of integration as well as concrete intercultural policies are set in motion, which have their effects. This fact is a good indicator of the difference between the dynamics of presence, which is not so much a problem, and the processes of visibilization, which are the real problems, of Islam in the European public space.

The Confederation is still coming to terms with the results of the referendum. The analysis of the "official" vote of Vox, published by the research institute gfs.bern in January 2012, gives more information, but nothing that was not already known. Among the reasons given of the persons in favor, the most common was the intention to deliver a symbolic blow against the expansion of Islam. Many also added that minarets have nothing to do with religious practice. About one favorable person in six justified their decision as a reaction to the discrimination against Christian churches in Muslim countries. Significantly, indicating a vote that was experienced more on the symbolic than the practical level, only 15 percent of those in favor gave a concrete criticism of Muslim residents in Switzerland as a reason for their decision. Only seemingly paradoxical in light of our analysis, the most significant figures in this sense are that even those who have an elevated sense of tolerance supported the referendum with 49 percent, and, lastly, that 64 percent of all voters, favorable or not, remain convinced that the Swiss way of life and the principles of Islam are completely compatible. For the adversaries of the referendum, the restriction to the fundamental rights of freedom of religion and non-discrimination guaranteed by the Swiss Constitution were the main reasons for their vote against the campaign.

However, Switzerland and Austria are not isolated cases. What would have happened in other European countries if they had found themselves faced with a similar situation? Following the Swiss referendum, many surveys have tried to simulate the outcomes, with significant results. Apparently, few countries could sustain a referendum like the Swiss one. 78 percent of Czechs, 70 percent of

---

and not an urban canton like the other three, was the only place with a mosque and a minaret where the referendum passed, with 61 percent in favor.

Slovaks and 43 percent of the French would vote to ban minarets. According to a survey published by *Le Soir*, 59.3 percent of Belgians would vote against minarets. In Denmark, according to a Megafon opinion poll, 51 percent of the Danes would support a minaret ban, while only 34 percent would allow minarets. A total of 46 percent of Italians would vote against minarets, especially among supporters of the right-wing parties then in power (60 percent), the more elderly and those with lower levels of schooling. However, many countries continue to insist that they would vote differently, rejecting the referendum in spite of extremely significant percentages of their populations in fact being in favor of such a ban. It must be remembered that one month before the referendum, the Swiss also declared themselves to be as a majority against the ban, and we saw what happened in the secrecy of the voting booth.

How do we explain all this? It is above all a sign that a problem with the Islamic presence in Europe really exists and, in addition, that where there are no conflicts (and there nonetheless remains a very advanced level of formal and institutional integration of Islam), problems can still emerge, and emerge strongly, as is happening to some extent across Europe.

We cannot leave the issue of the referendum on minarets without mentioning its intrinsic bureaucratic stupidity (similar to the law banning religious symbols in schools in France, which is hard to take seriously given how difficult it is to define exactly when, why and on who a symbol becomes ostentatious) and the interpretative contradictions to which the referendum lends itself when we descend from the heavens of principles to the practical level. If Muslims asked a local authority to build a minaret in the exact shape of the nearest church steeple but smaller, what would or could be the answer, and what contradictions would it introduce? What arguments could be used to oppose it? Or, again, what if the minaret was built horizontally rather than vertically, next to the mosque or in the neighboring field, or as a decorative element in the car park? Or painted on the front of a building? An interesting example of contradiction has already emerged in the non-opposition in Switzerland to a minaret because it was built not as part of a mosque but rather as a provocation by a non-Muslim on his own roof after the results of the referendum. Meanwhile, Muslims in the Swiss Confederation have also proposed an amiable architectural provocation: a request to build a minaret of 10 centimeters on the roof of an Albanian prayer room at Frauenfeld. And at Langenthal (one of the places where the request for a mosque, going back to 2006, triggered the process that led to the referendum), Muslims have opposed calling the minaret a "tower," underlining that "no legally clear and comprehensible definition of a minaret" exists, which is a perfectly true and valid point.

Finally, there is a more general contradiction within many of the discussions over mosques. Muslims have often been criticized or feared for their places of worship being invisible – in some way (even if involuntarily) concealed, not easily accessible, closed. Gradually, as their pursuit of visibilization has increased, and they have carried out projects that have brought their prayer rooms more and more into the daylight, instead of invisibility, it is now their visibility that is receiving criticism. It is time for European countries to start thinking about how to get out of this impasse, and what guidelines and what (reasoned and reasonable) criteria they should apply to the issue.

Some Observations on Conflicts over Mosques

We cannot here go into detail in our analysis of the conflicts over mosques in Europe regarding their similarities and differences by country and national legislative traditions as well as by time (conflicts were different in their content and "style" 20 years ago in comparison to today). Such an indepth analysis is available in the research that has been conducted in the different countries and in the synthesis report that is mentioned at the beginning of this chapter. Instead, I will simply make some quick references to the main social actors and dynamics.

Conflicts about mosques always involve people in the surrounding areas, either directly (public protests, demonstrations, collection of signatures, petitions, local committees) or indirectly (political groups and the media, acting or professing to act on behalf of the citizens themselves). Citizens' reasons for protesting can be attributed to the following:

a. "Real" or presumed reasons, such as: a fall in the value of property, fear of increased traffic, loss of peace and quiet, parking problems, fears of increased crime and the increased presence of unwelcome persons, fears of violence and incidents associated with Islamic fundamentalism, fears of occupation of public spaces (courtyards, pavements, parks and playgrounds) on Fridays and other Islamic holidays;
b. "Cultural" reasons: the foreignness of Islam to "our" culture, the defense of women's rights, reciprocity, the "non-integrability" and/or incompatibility of Islam with Western/European/Christian values.

While the first order of reasons may be (but are often not) empirically based and may be constructed discursively as such, the second serves only to justify a *Kulturkampf* whose objective is no longer the mosque as such – which becomes a symbol to be targeted – but Islam itself as a different, foreign religion, "alien" and incompatible with democracy, the West, liberalism, Christianity or "our traditions," depending on the context.

These dynamics lead local authorities to become involved in the conflicts, often assuming an unusual and even abnormal role. In fact, with reference to Islam, citizens and authorities feel entitled, in cases of conflict, to interfere heavily in the internal affairs of Muslim communities – in ways they never would with any other religious group – regarding not only urban planning and architectural choices (the location and the presence or absence of external signs such as minarets), but also organizational aspects (the type of board, language used in celebrations, modes of prayer or the call to prayer, separate entrances and facilities for women, etc.).

In the local context, various factors are involved. First of all, national events play a part, including legislative and political changes and attitudes toward Islam. A locally important element is the existence of a cooperative or, alternatively, conflictual approach to Islam. Often, when the controversies explode, it is the second that prevails: the municipality raises objections and obstacles rather than acting as a promoter of Islamic places of worship. Elsewhere, the local authorities may declare themselves "agnostic" – neither for nor against the mosque or the minaret, but rather following the line of the mobilized population.

The intervention of political entrepreneurs of Islamophobia is gradually becoming more pervasive and widespread, tending to become stronger because, as shown in the European elections of 2009 (and the national elections in the following years), their power is increasing. At a local level, if they do not already have them, these parties often take advantage of conflict to find local roots for themselves. The anti-Islamic parties are strongly linked at the European level: one can speak of a truly "international" show of Islamophobia, connecting the Vlaams Belang of Belgium, the FPÖ of Austria, the BNP of the UK, the Lega Nord of Italy and many others through their respective conferences and events "against the Islamization of Europe." The slogans are also similar: the call of a West in danger, the defense of Christianity in Europe, the systematic use of stereotypes and anti-Islamic prejudices, and references to "our" identity, to "our" roots or simply to "our" city. On their websites, a medium that allows anonymity and thus sees the use of very extreme and aggressive language, one can download flyers, stickers, posters and facsimiles of banners.

These campaigns are not simply rhetorical references without consequences. They are often accompanied by demonstrative acts, not necessarily perpetrated by members of these parties, but which are part and parcel of the same cultural and political climate.[7] Arson attacks were recorded in countries ranging from Italy to Sweden, and from Spain to the Czech Republic. Both after 9/11 and at the time of "hot" debates on Islam, France and the UK also experienced a series of anti-Muslim attacks, albeit of a more local nature, with only a minority of them being reported to the authorities. The same forces are sponsors of referenda, or threatened referenda, when local governments make themselves available to consider the project for a mosque, activating a very strong blackmail mechanism, even when it remains only a threat.

---

7   It is impossible not to mention, even if it requires a much more comprehensive analysis than is possible here, the massacre in Oslo and Utoya on 22 July 2011. Of course, it cannot be considered a direct effect of this climate, just as the acts committed by individual radical Muslims cannot be considered a direct consequence of the climate among European Muslim communities. But it was an unavoidable turning point – a no-return reference point – in discussion; see Allievi 2011.

The anti-Islamic movements – even when these movements come from outside – thus end up affecting internal local contexts too. In fact, conflict has the effect of drawing attention to such movements. Islamophobic movements, once aware of a case of controversy, operate in the territory with their slogans and also with their means of struggle (more visible than, for example, many citizen initiatives), causing a shift in the controversy from local issues of a practical nature to ideological and "civilizational" conflicts, making solutions for the actual conflict more difficult to devise. They therefore play a role as amplifiers of the conflict and obstacles to its solution. The political parties that take Islamophobia as the central platform of their program, and at the same time as an efficient method of gaining consensus, are expanding strongly in most European countries. And they systematically use the controversies over mosques that are initiated by them or in which they intervene even when they are not present locally as a means of visibilization – a strategy through which they are obtaining notable success. The main problem with their intrusion into the conflicts (aside from the serious cultural fallout, particularly for civil cohabitation, which sooner or later Europeans will have to deal with) is that they have a strong interest in stoking up the conflict, but none in finding a solution to it. Their political success proceeds and increases as long as the conflict remains open; the moment the conflict is in some way resolved, and the tension and attention disappear, the political entrepreneurs of Islamophobia lose their centrality, their visibility and their consensus. It is for this reason that they are the worst enemies of any attempt to find a solution to the conflict: they simply have no interest in that. This makes their role problematic for society as a whole, not only for Muslims. Society has no interest in protracting the conflicts, which are socially, culturally, politically and also economically costly, and which, in the long run, produce secondary effects that are strongly negative for the processes of integration and for the actors themselves involved in the conflict.

The media interlink with political action not only in their reflection of it but because the two reciprocally support each other. But the media and politics need another fundamental support: intellectual legitimization. This is offered by a number of key players who enjoy a substantial monopoly in the public debate: intellectuals, artists, journalists, academics, theologians, orientalists, priests and pastors, etc. It is often through their opinions and stances that political forces have been able to strengthen their anti-mosque campaigns, which the media in turn have made more visible.

In an analysis of the conflict over mosques, we can make some generalizations on at least the following points:

- Conflict is less intense and less frequent where Muslims enjoy more rights and are more frequently citizens, and where Islam has greater institutionalization at the national level.
- Conflict is more intense and more frequent where political entrepreneurs of Islamophobia are present. And the general trend is toward their increasing influence and presence, even in areas where they were not

active at the national level in the past. Their success at this stage seems to be growing.

- The "T factor" ("T" as in time) plays an important role. As the processes of integration move forward and one generation succeeds another, Islam is gradually being perceived as less alien and less of an enemy. However, these processes are going through important reactive phases, and it is by no means a foregone conclusion that an older Muslim presence necessarily means less conflict.

Conclusion

Minarets, mosques, as well as veils and burqas all begin to seem, when we analyze them in more depth, to be false problems. The real problem that these pseudo-problems reveal is greater than all this: on the one hand, it is the relationship of Europe with Islam and, on the other, the relationship that Muslims have with Europe and the West – that which they have and that which we imagine they have.

Mosques and minarets end up looking more like a discursive substitute – a transitional object, to put it in psychoanalytic terms. Mosques are the symptom: the illness is Islam or, rather, the West's imaginary of Islam, which, like the Islamic imaginary of the West, appears more and more conflictual.

But this is only the most immediate, the first half of the argument. The second half is that Islam is in its turn a transitional object which represents and signifies the pluralization of society and, in particular, religious pluralism. Islam has become the discursive substitute for important changes in society, which are not tied generically to religious pluralism as such. In concrete terms, they are called gender roles, clothing codes, family models, parental authority and notions of modesty, purity and sacredness. As far as the relationship between religion and politics goes, it has to do with changes in the relationship between religion and democracy, religion and state, and religion and gender. These are all subjects that in secularized societies have become more difficult to discuss in religious terms and yet have been brought into the limelight by cultural and religious pluralism.

Islam, perhaps rightly or wrongly, has thus become the most extreme example of otherness and the changes that otherness brings to European societies. The problem is much more profound, the change even more traumatic and the issues to face even more decisive because it does not involve only Islam and Muslims, but European societies themselves. However, Islam, because of its symbolic overload and the problematic history that joins it to Europe, because of the striking and formidable aspect of some of its contemporary manifestations (including, obviously, the emergence of transnational Islamic fundamentalism and terrorism), and because of the significant statistical dimension of its presence in Europe, is inevitably at the center of the political and social debate in Europe. And it will remain there for a long time.

References

Allievi, S. 2009. *Conflicts over Mosques in Europe. Policy Issues and Trends.* London: NEF/Alliance Publishing Trust.
Allievi, S. (ed.) 2010. *Mosques in Europe. Why a Solution Has Become a Problem.* London: NEF/Alliance Publishing Trust.
Allievi, S. 2011. "Europe: The Time Has Come to Reflect," *Reset Dialogues on Civilizations*, http://www.resetdoc.org/story/00000021694.
Avcıoğlu, N. 2008. "Form-as-Identity: The Mosque in the West," *Cultural Analysis*, 6, 91–112.
Maussen, M. 2009. "Constructing Mosques: The Governance of Islam in France and the Netherlands," Ph.D. dissertation, University of Amsterdam.

Chapter 7

The Secular Embodiments of Face-Veil Controversies across Europe

Schirin Amir-Moazami

In spring 2012, I attended a conference at Heidelberg University on "gender equality and religious freedom – conflicting norms and unresolved conflicts." Unsurprisingly, discussions quickly turned to forms of Islamic female coverings as symbolic markers of such conflicting norms. The recent debates across Europe on the face veil and its prohibition did not pass unnoticed. The legal scholars in the conference room vividly discussed whether full coverings in Europe transgressed legal norms either by symbolizing a repressive gender regime, something which was incompatible with the liberal constitutional order, or by disrespecting the more general prohibition of face coverings and rules of being identifiable in public. After having extensively exchanged arguments and legal tenets for and against banning the face veil, one professor of constitutional law stepped in and voiced his take on the issue. He said that in this type of legal uncertainty cases, it was always worthwhile for him to use the "daughter test": asking himself how he would react if his daughter decided to wear a "burqa,"[1] he responded that he would definitely be very displeased. This test, in other words, his own personal aversion to fully covering the female body, led him to the conclusion that one should continue the discussions not by focusing on the question of whether to allow or prohibit the "burqa," but rather on the question of how we could "avoid" it altogether, explaining his concern with the formula "not to forbid but to get rid of" the face veil. There was a tangible sense of relief among most of the participants in the room as this professor spelled out what the majority of people probably thought but were unable to voice: that veiling provokes reactions and touches on a number of embodied emotions that can hardly be addressed by legal rules. The law professor's personal turn at the Heidelberg conference can thus be understood as a symptomatic displacement of the (un)lawfulness of this bodily practice to the level of civic pedagogy.

In this chapter, I will try to make sense of such conversations by situating them within recent controversies around bans on the face veil across Europe.[2] It is my view that the discussions in the conference room in Heidelberg mirrored the recurrent navigations between the (il)legality of veiling and the (il)legality of bans through interventions into codified individual freedoms. This navigation

---

1   This was the term he used for the face veil.
2   For an overview of these discussions, see Sivestri (2012).

can hardly be captured on the grounds of legal dogmatism, nor are these even legal issues in the first place. Rather, these controversies center on unloaded and consensualized aversions to the public display of specific religious bodily practices which have currently reached legal dimensions.

I therefore claim that veiling in general, and face veiling in particular, as religious bodily practices and strong markers of gender segregation in public transgress embodied conventions about bodily orders and freedoms, and thus provoke strong reactions which often, if not always, elicit an emotional repertoire ranging from fear through open disgust to fascination. If this assumption is correct, we should understand the emotional repertoire running through discussions of the face veil as more than spontaneous expressions of unmediated feelings and instead situate them within what Sara Ahmed calls "affective economies" (Ahmed 2004a; 2004b). In other words, it is important to analyze the functionality and productivity of the emotions running through many controversies on Muslims in Europe. My sense is that the emotional politics *vis-à-vis* this Islamic practice – in this case, aversion, distaste, fear and sometimes open disgust – is shared across Europe and reflects what I would like to call a "secular matrix," despite different and sometimes divergent arrangements of the church, the state and the nation.

As I will more thoroughly argue, by the secular I mean two things: first, a set of regulative practices, closely tied to the institutions and practices of a nation state, which guide the borders between the religious and the secular in public and thereby necessarily also in private, and which form and shape citizens (Asad 2003; 2006); and, second, a more tacit and often unmarked set of secular affects prevalent in the social practices of secular societies on various levels. I call these "secular embodiments" and will argue that the controversies around the face veil in Europe revealingly bring together these two dimensions in a more tangible manner than those on other forms of veiling, like the headscarf.

The "Affective Economies" of Face-Veil Controversies

In her account of controversies on the face veil in the Netherlands, Annelies Moors (2009) observes that the arguments raised both for and against banning this bodily practice in public commonly displayed a strong emotional dimension both in the media and in parliamentary discussions. Additionally, those who distanced themselves from banning the face veil, Moors shows, evoked its "high undesirability" and underlined their "feelings of discomfort" (2009: 400).[3]

---

3 We can indeed see this reasoning in much earlier debates. For example, in Britain, where a ban on any kind of covering has never been on the political agenda, I find Jack Straw's comments quite revealing: he argued that the question was by no means about legally banning head coverings, but that it nonetheless concerned the wellbeing of women and that the social order that this religious practice was somewhat disturbing (Kilic 2008; Meer, Dwyer and Modood 2010: 89). Such a stance reveals a largely paralegal kind of interventionist

A similar mood of aversion can be observed in the French controversies on the so-called "voile intégrale." Here, common statements like "it is shocking for our occidental values" (Joffrin and Pierre-Brossolette 2009) or "it is an offense, an aggression against the dignity of the woman" are mild expressions of this emotional repertoire running through French public controversies.[4]

Already, the debates on the headscarf across Europe have conjured up strong passions and affective vocabularies on which political authorities have drawn when discussing and regulating this religious practice in state educational institutions (Asad 2006: 500; Motha 2007).[5] The main rationale in most headscarf controversies has been primarily anchored in "rescue narratives" (Amir-Moazami 2007; Bracke 2012) and is coupled with sentiments of pity and, at times, sympathy. However, the face veil controversies have openly displaced victimization onto those who feel threatened by this religious practice, considering fully covered bodies an attack on their own bodies. This becomes obvious in the recurrent slippage of the humiliated fully covered female body that humiliates the secular order. The affective vocabulary, already salient during public controversies on the headscarf, has thus gained an additional dimension in controversies on the face veil: the personal aversion of politicians and other agents involved in the process of gathering information and making decisions not only produced a sense of national belonging, but also turned the speakers into victims of their aversions.

While Annelies Moors and Stewart Motha (2007) highlight affect as a central feature of veiling controversies in Europe from very different perspectives,[6] they both only marginally elaborate on the functionalities and productivity involved in these politics of emotion and their relatedness to a broader set of discursive formations. I therefore want to first locate the controversies on the face veil in Europe in what Sara Ahmed calls "affective economies" (2004a). In her contributions to the politics of emotion, Ahmed is especially interested in the question of how emotions move between bodies. She argues that emotions play a crucial role in

---

politics *vis-à-vis* veiling and can be considered characteristic of other European countries, which have recently developed new modes of pushing Muslims towards "integration" (Peter 2008; Amir-Moazami 2011). In the British case, this is closely related to a backlash against institutionalized forms of multiculturalism (Modood 2010; Lentin and Titley 2011).

4   In France, the face veil has officially been banned since 11 October 2010.

5   In France, Asad reminds us that, for example, through recurrent elements like "free will" or "desire," in the official justification of the headscarf ban in state schools, the French state referred to a quasi-psychological repertoire, strongly anchored in the understanding of a hidden mindset of covered women, and thereby brought the private to the attention and examination of the state authorities.

6   Moors undertakes a close reading of the controversies in the Netherlands and critically discusses the main arguments against the face veil, such as security, women's subordination and the refusal of communication. Motha argues from a more theoretical political/legal point of view and locates affect mainly in the realm of expressions of piety inherent in veiling practices, which are troublesome for notions of the autonomous subject that is central to both feminism and secularism.

the surfacing of individual and collective signs. She thereby wants to challenge assumptions that emotions are a private matter expressed by and belonging to the individual. Instead, she claims that "emotions are not simply within or without but that they *create* the very effect of the surfaces or the boundaries of bodies and worlds" (2004a: 118, emphasis added).

Seeing acts of hate speech and fear of terrorism in the British context as characteristic not only of an aversion articulated against someone but also as an act of alliance with those who consider themselves threatened by the presence and invasion of others, Ahmed contends:

> It is the emotional reading of hate that works to bind the imagined white subject and nation together … The passion of these negative attachments to others is redefined simultaneously as a positive attachment to the imagined subjects brought together through the repetition of the signifier, "white". It is the love of the white, or those recognizable as white, that supposedly explains this shared "communal" visceral response of hate. Together we hate, and this hate is what makes us together. (2004a: 118)

Ahmed thus reminds us about the interpersonal or social dimension of emotions – affect does not reside positively in the sign or in the person, but moves and is shared. Borrowing from Marxist approaches, she underlines the productivity of emotions *through* their circulation through bodies. Emotions are productive in separating the hated, disgusted objects from oneself as much as their productivity consists in binding together those who articulate common feelings. Publicly displayed and staged emotions in particular, Ahmed contends, should therefore not be understood in any linear sense as moving from the individual to the collective and thereby becoming public; rather, the circularity consists in an anticipated collective which makes the circulation and (re)production of emotions possible and acceptable.

Reading controversies on the face veil along these lines, I think one should start by taking much more seriously the affectivity already evident in the terminology. In other words, even if emotions are not always directly stated, they are present in the articulation, arrangement and order of certain concepts and speech acts. To begin with, the very labeling of full veils or face veils as "burqas," which is then transformed in the vernacular into "burqa-debates" and "burqa-bans," is far from innocent. The burqa, the Afghan style of veiling, suggests the mandatory imposition of covering as a form of male authority and control over women's bodies, provoking an image which literally transfers the face veil to a different space and externalizes the bodies concerned. This terminology evokes feelings of fear *vis-à-vis* an invasionary religious practice that has now reached European borders. While it literally prevents women who live within European borders from sharing the same space, it simultaneously produces feelings of uneasiness, as it suggests that these external forms of veiling along with a whole set of unwanted gender norms and practices have now entered European spaces. The French case makes this clear. During the hearings in the French Parliamentary Commission charged with the promulgation of anti-burqa law to study full veiling, a set of emotions were mobilized and pointed in this double direction: first, the spatial externalization of the fully covered women; and, second, their relation to a gender regime that is found wanting because it does not share the patterns of individual freedoms that French society presumes to follow. The face veil is thus not accidentally labeled "burqa," as it stands for something broader: an anticipated process of transgression by the Other within Europe. I suggest that this terminology should be looked at in its productive form as well: as evoking particular kinds of emotions and thereby contributing to the decontextualization of a religious practice which supposedly belongs to a different spatial and normative order while at the same time suggesting that this order is moving closer.

Relating her theories of the politics of emotions to the specific emotion of disgust, Ahmed furthermore makes explicit the idea of the intercorporality of affective economies:

> Disgust is clearly dependent upon contact: it involves a relationship of touch and proximity between the surfaces of bodies and objects. That contact is felt as an unpleasant intensity: it is not that the object, apart from the body, has the quality of "being offensive", but the proximity of the object to the body that is felt offensive. The object must get close enough to make us feel disgust. (2004b: 85)

With regard to discussions on the face veil in Europe, this raises the immediate question of how we can understand contact and intercorporality between the small number of women who wear the face veil and the overwhelmingly large number of political authorities, public intellectuals, feminist activists, etc. involved in the controversies who felt compelled to articulate their aversion and, not infrequently, disgust against this bodily practice. The proximity of disgusted bodies, to which Ahmed refers, in this case consists in the ascribed symbolism attached to a particular kind of Muslim other moving closer, as already expressed through the terminology mentioned above.

There are two important aspects which I would like to capture from Ahmed's analyses with regard to the controversies on face-veil bans. First, there is an emotional repertoire which is unloaded and consensualized *through* the controversy, or the *productivity* of these shared emotions which Ahmed alludes to. Rather than being the expression of a sudden distaste of individual political authorities or other actors who articulated aversions, the emotional repertoire has, indeed, been produced in and through the emergence of the controversy itself. Many scholars and commentators have mentioned the small number of women who wear the face veil in the various national contexts in which the controversies emerged (Moors 2009; Brems et al. 2012; Silvestri 2012). Through their production and circulation of affects of aversion, distaste, unease, discomfort or disgust, these controversies thus have to be understood by this productivity and by their largely performative way of functioning. They produce what they pronounce: a community of civilized citizens who are bound together by their aversion to non-civilized subjects who reveal a divergent gender regime, expressed through a kind of bodily practice that contradicts the norms of visibility, gender relations and the norms of discreet displays of religiosity in public.

If we take Ahmed's assumptions seriously, we therefore have to understand the emotional *structures* running through controversies surrounding the face-veil bans as more than simple expressions of spontaneous feelings of uneasiness, but rather as tied to a broader "economy" in and through which an emotional repertoire is mobilized not only because it binds participants through shared emotions ("We feel offended," "it shocks us"), but also through a set of norms connected to these emotions, and which connect the bodies that share them: "it shocks *us* because it questions *our* established norms of gender equality" (Joffrin and Pierre-Brossolette 2009, emphasis added).

Second, Ahmed's elaboration on economies of emotions generally, and on the sense of disgust in particular, draws our attention to the centrality of power relations prevalent in these affective economies. Ahmed claims that power becomes particularly important "when we consider the spatiality of disgust reactions, and their role in the hierarchizing of spaces as well as bodies" (Ahmed 2004b: 88). Quoting William Ian Miller, Ahmed claims that "disgust reactions are not only about objects that seem to threaten the boundary lines of subjects, they are also about objects that seem 'lower' than or below the subject, or even beneath the subject" (2004b: 89). The power of emotions, she contends, consists in the first place in their success in binding certain bodies together, in making them "stick" together, as she puts it (2004b: 89–92). It is the "stickiness" of certain emotions with regard to certain bodies, in other words, that is dependent on embodiment, on something that has already been shaped and formed. I find Ahmed's reflections very helpful as they push us to understand the productivity of emotions as strongly tied to both broader discursive structures and in their embeddedness in relations and techniques of power.

It is thus important to connect the emotional repertoire running through these as well as other controversies to something prior, which makes circulation and "stickiness" possible in the first place. This leads us to a crucial question, to which Ahmed constantly alludes, about the *historicity* of emotions. The sharedness of emotions, in other words, is dependent on something which makes sharedness possible at all.

It is important to take into account the historicity of the aversions mobilized against covered women in general, and women with veiled faces in particular, as both victims of oppression and at the same time evidence of a troubling bodily order of femininity that gives them a suspicious kind of agency. Rather than an unmediated aversion to the imagined spread of fully covered women articulated in various public settings, the publicly orchestrated distaste for veiling thus needs to be embedded in a longer trajectory prior to post-migration.

It is useful in this regard to recall Meyda Yeğenoğlu's (1999) interesting analysis of the politics of unveiling in her book *Colonial Fantasies*. One way of historicizing the European obsession with various forms of veiling and its conversion into a discourse is to understand the colonizer's obsession with transparency, which Yeğenoğlu embeds in the proliferation of modern techniques of control. Looking at the political practices of unveiling in the colonial context, she traces these back to epistemological trajectories, evoking Bentham's panopticon and Lacan's gaze.

Yeğenolğu's work helps us to understand the interventionist practices into the female body and the various politics of unveiling not just as recent attempts to control the growing visibility of Islamic religious practices in public or as post-9/11 responses and processes of securitization, but as practices with a much longer political *and* epistemological history. The recurrent aversion to various forms of veiling (and face veiling in particular) in European public spaces could accordingly be interpreted as the expression of difficulty surrounding the loss of control of bodies in public, as spelled out in the often-iterated argument that fully veiled faces disturb not just commonly shared modes of interaction and communication but also the identifiability of the veiled person. The fact that the fully covered woman can see without being seen gives her a disturbing kind of agency. It reverses the panoptical logic to control and examine all bodies through tacit modern technologies of power. Although it would definitely be problematic to draw a linear causality between the "colonial desire" to lift the veil for the purpose of bodily control in the colonies and the recent controversies around face coverings in European public spaces, I suggest that these accounts help us historicize the emotional repertoire, mobilized in new ways in current post-colonial configurations.[7]

In what follows, I would, however, like to move from this broader trajectory of control, visibility and surveillance to something more specific, which I find salient in the affective economies of face-veil controversies. I suggest locating this historicity within the "secular" as the underlying matrix of the mobilized affects prevalent in the controversies under scrutiny. I suggest that the secular architecture which mediates the structures of emotions undergirding the face-veil debates not only filters what can be said, thought and articulated in public and what remains unheard; it also largely depends on these kinds of iterations in order to remain vital.

Secular Embodiments

> In our occidental societies the face is the part of the body which carries the heart of the individual, the soul, the reason, the personality. For us this is a cultural secular heritage. (Laneyrie-Dagen 2009)

---

7   For very productive attempts to locate current narratives about Muslims in France in post-colonial reconfigurations of *laïcité* and French national identity, see in particular the works by Paul Silverstein (2004) and Ruth Mas (2006).

Much has recently been written on secularism – its crisis, its disappearance, its prevalence or simply its current reconfiguration in light of the global revival of religious movements and religious sensibilities (e.g. Casanova 1994; Connolly 1999; Asad 2003; 2006; Taylor 2007; Habermas 2008). While a number of scholars have tried to unveil secularism's "ideology" while safeguarding some of its intrinsic features (e.g. Casanova 1994; Modood 2011), others have attempted to revise some of its anti-religious orientation in order to move to what Habermas (2008) calls "post-secular" rearrangements of liberal-democratic societies. All these attempts challenge linear narratives of secularization and articulate two main objections. First, by countering the secularization thesis from an empirical point of view, a number of scholars have indicated that the religious revival worldwide contradicts the assumption of a gradual disappearance of religion from the public and societal as well as the political sphere, and also questions the idea of a globally tamed Christianity.[8] Second, from a more normative perspective, a number of authors have criticized the prescriptive presuppositions underlying the secularization thesis itself and its teleological and imperial impetus.[9] For my study, this most notably raises the question of the extent to which this "ideology" has been used as a foil to measure or qualify the stage of secularization of other, non-European, non-Christian societies or movements.

Although I largely agree with these approaches, they tend to dismiss some important components of secularism which I would call, along with Talal Asad and other scholars (Asad 2003; 2006; Agrama 2010; Hirschkind 2011; Mahmood 2011), the potency and productivity of the secular, or its anchorage in modern technologies of power. Emphasizing the productivity of secularism in particular in the self-understanding of European liberal democracies, I furthermore suggest that this potency of the secular has gained new momentum in the spread of controversies surrounding the Muslim question in European public spheres, in which those concerning veiling are paradigmatic.[10] In other words, I do not start from the assumption that secularism is a myth or an ideology because both terms suggest that there was a path to overcome the mythical or ideological baggage in order to rescue a purer version of secularity.

---

8   A phenomenon which José Casanova (1994) called the "deprivatization" of religion. See also Habermas (2008; 2009).

9   Casanova, for example, posed the interesting question as to whether the observation of a supposed gradual disappearance of religion from the public and political stage itself has not turned into an ideology in the sense of becoming prescriptive. Apart from his problematic attempt to safeguard the functional differentiation inherent in processes of secularization, Casanova convincingly unpacks the ideological character of scholars like Weber and Durkheim and reminds us of the extent to which these early sociologists of religion also produced what they observed on an empirical level.

10   I am thus not making the claim that the secularization paradigm is right or wrong; rather, I think we should focus on the functions of its constant reiteration and the question of how it enacts specific ways of dealing with the religious in political and public life.

Borrowing from these Asadian approaches to the secular, by "potency" and "productivity," I mean two things: first, the emphasis on the regulative stance of liberal nation states with regard to the management of the borders between the religious and the political; and, second, the "emotional structures of modern individual freedoms" (Asad 2006) upon which these regulations are based. This aspect of the secular refers to a large degree to its unmarked, tacit and not easily discernible character. I will call these "secular embodiments."

Along with Asad and others, I thus suggest moving beyond an understanding of secularism in terms of a formal legal division between church and state or religion and politics. Secularism is rather to be conceived as a mode of regulating these separations, historically tied to the emergence and implementation of the modern nation state in charge of regulating the religious realm. As Asad makes clear, the modes of state regulation of religion are deeply indebted to the post-Westphalian order of *cuius regio, eius religio* through which the state became the "transcendent as well as a representative agent" of the spatial organization and regulation of religion (Asad 2006: 499).

Accordingly, it is not so much the commitment to or interdiction of particular religious practices through state institutions that is most significant, but rather the establishment of the nation state as the main source of authority in charge of the worldly cares of its population, regardless of their concrete beliefs and forms of religiosity (Asad 2006). As many scholars have pointed out, a number of contradictions inherent in the secular structures of liberal nation states have emerged from here. Amongst the most salient for my study is the fact that while the modern secular nation state formally assigns itself a position of neutrality and distance on religious matters, its authority is dependent on its capacity to determine which kinds of religious expressions and practices are legitimate in public and which are not. Likewise, according to Asad, the debates and political measures surrounding the ban on the headscarf in France are less based on the formally strong separation between the state and the church (even if this provided the legal grounds for the ban in state schools); rather, they concern political freedoms, which the modern constitutional state simultaneously guarantees *and* governs. It is through this mandate that the state is authorized, and even compelled, to judge the contents and limits of religious practices like wearing the headscarf in public institutions. Again, dismantling such contradictions does not imply conceiving secularism as a myth or claiming that on closer inspection, the boundaries between the religious and the political are more blurred in European societies than is commonly acknowledged. Instead, it means looking more closely at the concrete practices through which these boundaries are governed and thereby also at the formation of religious and non-religious subjects by modern technologies of power closely tied to the nation state.

The strongest example of the inherent contradictions in the secular architecture of the modern nation state is definitely the French Republican state, which has been torn since its inception between, on the one hand, non-intervention into religious realms (including abstaining from defining the content of religious signs and symbols) and, on the other, its mandate and practice of regulating religious life according to normative scripts of liberal freedoms (Asad 2006: 504; see also Baubérot 2004). The principle of *laïcité* is thus anchored in something which is currently reflected and re-enacted in the management of religious practices, like veiling, which potentially reveal a different understanding of selfhood than that of the normative notions of individual autonomy (see also Scott 2007).

Regulations of the boundaries between the religious and the political thus always rely on specific understandings about the ways in which citizens in a society should act, about which forms of religious expression are legitimate in public and thereby also in private, and which are not permissible according to socially embedded conventions of citizenship, gender and sexuality norms and, more generally, notions and conventions of freedom.

Likewise, Asad also claims that the differentiation between public and private spaces, central to the regulation of religion and the boundaries between the political and religious, is strongly connected with and regulated by political powers, instead of being a fixed mode of separation or connection. Current developments in the regulations of religiosity in public spaces in France as well as in many other parts of Western Europe succinctly corroborate Asad's argument about the constant rearrangement of these boundaries through state authority and institutions. Indeed, the regulation of public spaces in the case of a particular style of face veiling shows that the notion of public space has shifted again since the *Commission Stasi* and the 2004 law banning headscarves in state schools. What had before been limited to the sanctity of the secular school has now been extended to basically any space outside the home – potentially monitored, managed and policed. The measures surrounding the face-veil ban reveal a striking extension of state control of public space and a further shift in the conception of the public sphere as a place for free circulation and communication, detached from various forms of political authority. The consequences of such forms of control of the public and their long-term effects in regard to the self-understanding of liberal-democratic orders definitely merit further study.

There is, however, another aspect which I would like to examine more closely with regard to the emotional structures undergirding institutionalized secular practices and related individual freedoms. Looking at the emotional vocabulary employed by political authorities and experts in the *Commission Stasi*, Asad reminds us of the extent to which the presumably rational-critical language of political and legal authorities addressing common concerns reveals embodied life, which is typically assumed to reside in the private, affective and expressive. Again, it is especially this dimension of the secular which largely surpasses ideology (at least if located in the mind) as it touches upon largely unmarked conventions.

I find it important to take these unmarked presuppositions very seriously in order to understand the public, and at times very violent, outcry against veiled faces and bodies in European public spaces. In an article on the politics of visibility of Islamic bodily practices in Europe, Nilüfer Göle (2006) succinctly reflects on this by taking up Bourdieu's notion of "doxa." Drawing on the performative character of Islamic bodily practices in European public spaces, Göle notes that veiled bodies unmask the power structures inherent in the relations between Western models of modernity and Muslim religious practices:

> To the extent that social actors perceive the world through a hegemonic normative framework, they take it for granted, and the social world appears to their eye as ordinary and natural, as a "doxa." A doxic experience is one in which members of a society share a common opinion, a common sense that is transmitted by a series of implicit assumptions and values that appear as a matter of fact, as truth. Consequently such common sense perception of the social world masks social and symbolic relations of domination. (Göle 2006: 23)

The idea of the secular as a habitualized, largely implicit and often unreflected set of conventions, behaviors, bodily practices and unwritten rules of communication mainly points to what Asad sees as lying at the heart of the secular architecture of modern secular nation states: the formation and shaping of secular citizens, who are educated and learn religion's assigned place and who share a consensus on conventions of bodily practices and techniques of communication along the lines of liberal secular orders.

This point leads me to the rhetorical question that Charles Hirschkind (2011) recently posed: "Is there a secular body?" Hirschkind himself emphasizes the peculiarity of this question, especially if we conceive of the secular in its contingency and dependency on the religious. While the question of whether or not there is a secular body is too direct, since "the secular is water we swim in" (Hirschkind 2011: 634), I still find it a challenging and, for my present study, helpful one. It encourages us to focus more seriously on secular embodiment as learned, inscribed and often unconscious bodily dispositions, practices and affects, which are difficult to recognize as such because of their embodied nature. Precisely because it is strange to consider a secular body, if we follow Asad's assumption that the secular is not a stage that is easily denotable and detachable from the religious, the secular body consists of largely unmarked and inconspicuous forms of embodiment. In the present case, secular embodiment concerns shared conventions of gender mixing, exposing parts of the body (in particular the face) in public while hiding others, notions of gender and sexual freedom, gendered conventions of visibility and, more generally, habitualized forms of communication in public. Hirschkind would probably caution against such a reading, since his analysis of the secular "directs us less to a determinant set of embodied dispositions than to a *distinct mode of power*, one that mobilizes the productive tension between religious and secular to generate new practices through a process of internal self-differentiation" (2011: 643, emphasis added).

I conceive of the secular embodiments at stake in the controversies over the face veil not as unmediated, but rather as anchored in such modes of power as much as they depend on their constant iterations. As I have tried to argue, it is important to constantly look at the intertwinement between contingent, indeterminate embodied dispositions and this distinct mode of power which mobilizes and attempts to stabilize them. Some of Hirschkind's arguments, indeed, bring us back to the beginning of this chapter and Ahmed's elaborations on affective economies and the stickiness of certain emotions binding certain bodies together at the expense of others. Drawing on William Connolly, Hirschkind argues on a theoretical level that "the practice of articulating and defending secular political claims ... serves to mold and deepen the affective attachments that passionally bind one to the secular life those claims uphold" (2011: 636).

I suggest that face-veil controversies can be read as somehow materializing Connolly's (1999) rather philosophical inquiry and as a foil to see secular embodiments at work on a microscopic scale. It is namely only through such religiously connoted transgressions that the secular body can be revealed and simultaneously stabilized. If the secular is to be conceived of as relational, these practices and conventions can be discursively marked and valorized as secular only because they are constituted through engagement with practices that are considered religious in a particular way, in this case, displaying religiosity illegitimately and ostentatiously in public. In other words, we are only able to realize what kind of water we swim in when a foreign substance is introduced. In this sense, one could argue that the appearance of the face veil – real or imagined – in European public spaces simultaneously bounds and triggers embodied secular emotions.

Hirschkind also poses the interesting yet again rather rhetorical question of why so few scholars of religion and secularism have not systematically analyzed the techniques of ritual practices, *self*-cultivation and *self*-disciplinary techniques through which the secular body is formed and enabled to a similar extent as they have studied its formation through religious rituals. I agree with Hirschkind that it is difficult and problematic to discern the secular through the same methodologies as those used by critics of secularism like Asad, who look at religious embodiments (through rituals, symbols and disciplinary self-practices), namely because self-differentiation works on an entirely different register. I suggest, however, that one could also conceive of such self-techniques in terms of passionally unloaded discursive practices, which are based on habitualized ones, and hence as a kind of constant self-cultivation through self-assurance about the contours of what constitutes the secular order and its bodies in public.

The statement quoted above by the art historian Nadeije Laneyrie-Dagen during the hearings in the French controversies on the face veil can be seen as paradigmatic for my point here. Laneyrie-Dagan hints exactly at the disruption and simultaneous reiteration of secular conventions and embodiments, articulated in particular religious expressions. In her statement, Laneyrie-Dagen highlights the face as the noblest part of the body and the means of dissimilating the person's emotions and thus her individuality, while tracing this triumph of the individual back to a linear trajectory from Antiquity through Christianity to secularized Europe, characterized by a tamed Christianity. One could definitely analyze this grand narrative of the "Western" body more thoroughly, as it discards the numerous tensions, nuances and contradictions at work in the revealing of the face as the marker of the inside, the soul. However, I used this quotation primarily in order to highlight one of many examples of what we could understand as both "doxa" *and* as a practice of the self-cultivation of secular dispositions. The depiction of the face and the gestures through which the "soul" of the individual and his "reason" are revealed are definitely part of the social imaginary and unmarked presuppositions to which Göle refers. Yet in this linear narrative, it is also first and foremost part of the self-reassurance of one's own bodily order, articulated against a spatially and normatively remote and yet approximating Other.

Conclusions

By looking at the face-veil controversies throughout Europe in their productive force, in producing and circulating emotions and thereby binding certain bodies together while excluding others, I have suggested that we should understand these controversies as largely performative practices. As I tried to argue, it is not so much the neutralized, disembodied language of the law that ultimately calls for banning the religious practice of face veiling, which I consider powerful in this case, but rather the act of pronouncing and proclaiming sanctions and controlling public life. More generally, the interventionist character lies in the very fact that a non-issue has turned into a matter of public controversy, in which speakers are bound together on the basis of their public expressions of disturbance, discomfort, unease or disgust for the present or imagined covered bodies. This and other controversies relating to forms of Muslim social life and religious practices in Europe thus reveal a kind of "speaker's benefit" (Foucault 1978: 6).

Thinking about the "speaker's benefit" brings us to ask the following questions: whose speech acts and emotional vocabularies are enabled and authorized, whose are silenced, and what techniques of power enable or incite some to speak and prohibit others from doing so through related implicit or explicit mechanisms of silencing? In other words, power structures and techniques are crucial both in the circulation of embodied emotions and the discursive matrixes underpinning these affective economies and enabling them at all.

I thus understand the publicly articulated aversion to the face veil in Europe as part and parcel of a broader process of creating discourse around the "Muslim question," in which Muslims have become both an object of analysis and a target of intervention. I suggest that the matrix, which binds the articulation of speech acts and evoked emotions, can be identified as secular in two intertwined ways: while the secular is characterized by a set of institutionalized practices and state regulations of the borders between the religious and the political, when it intervenes with various techniques into the bodies of not-yet or not-any-longer secular citizens, it also consists of conventions and unmarked presuppositions.

The face-veil controversies in my interpretation namely bring to the fore some of these unmarked presuppositions inscribed in liberal principles, institutionalized through various techniques of power, including inscriptions in bodily acts and conventions of communication.

The widely shared view that the face veil constitutes a transgression of legitimate forms of religious practices in public life is thus based on the fact that it challenges an inscribed, embodied and therefore largely unmarked secular consensus by bringing non-conformist and suspicious forms of religiosity into the public and legal discourse. Rather than being a fixed and determined set of conventions, this secular consensus, I argued, is fragile, contingent and dependent on iterative practices. In my view, the functionality of the face-veil controversies consists exactly in this double move: on the one hand, pointing to the limits of individual freedoms and revealing the boundaries of (il)legitimate religious practices in public life and, on the other, re-establishing these boundaries by reasserting the secular order as secular. This, as I have tried to show, is largely based on the effectiveness and mobilizing forces of a set of affects which are *inscribed* in a variety of ways into this order.

From a normative political theoretical point of view, one could, of course, object that my critical account of the emotional vocabulary characterizing the discussions on and interventions into the practice of face-veiling raises the issue of whether emotions should be discarded from the political scene in the interest of a solely rational deliberation. Unpacking the emotional structures of liberal secular orders, however, does not imply a call for rational debate, but rather an argument against the assumption of an emotion-free, disembodied zone of rational deliberation and individual freedoms (see Warner 2005; Mouffe 2008). My critique of the emotional economies salient in the controversies around the face veil should thus not be misunderstood as a suggestion to "go back" to a conception of liberal deliberation in order to return to a purer version of liberal-secular ideals. I have tried to make clear that I do not understand the unloading of emotions as accidental deviations from the liberal theory, which temporarily disguise the "real" nature of liberal neutrality. Rather, my aim was to start in a very preliminary way unpacking the emotional structures inscribed into liberal-secular orders.[11]

---

11   In a recent article on headscarf bans in France and Germany, Christian Joppke (2007) suggests, for example, that a return to liberal politics, "real" state neutrality, constitutional rights, etc. as opposed to "multiculturalist alternatives" would remedy the shortcomings of the present system, such as "illiberal" headscarf bans. Indeed, the interpretation of measures such as legally codified headscarf bans as purely accidental fails to account for the entrenchment of liberalism in illiberal governance (see especially Hindess 2001) and, more generally, its productivity in conceptions and formations of liberal subjects (Rose 1999).

References

Agrama, H. 2010. "Secularism, Sovereignty, Indeterminacy: Is Egypt a Secular or a Religious State?" *Comparative Studies in Society and History*, 52(3), 1–29.

Ahmed, S. 2004a. "Affective Economies," *Social Text*, 22(2), 117–39.

Ahmed, S. 2004b. *The Cultural Politics of Emotion*. Edinburgh: Edinburgh University Press.

Amir-Moazami, S. 2007. *Politisierte Religion. Der Kopftuchstreit in Deutschland und Frankreich*. Bielefeld: Transcript.

Amir-Moazami, S. 2011. "Dialogue as a Governmental Technique: Managing Gendered Islam in Germany. *Feminist Review*, 98, 9–27.

Asad, T. 2003. *Formations of the Secular: Christianity, Islam, and Modernity*. Stanford, CA: Stanford University Press.

Asad, T. 2006. "Trying to Understand French Secularism," in H. de Vries et al. (eds), *Political Theologies: Public Religion in a Post-Secular World*. New York: Fordham University Press, 494–526.

Baubérot, J. 2004. *Laïcité 1905–2005, entre passion et raison* [*Secularization of French Ssociety 1905–2005. Between Passion and Reason*]. Paris: Seuil.

Bracke, S. 2012. "From 'Saving Women' to 'Saving Gays': Rescue Narratives and their Dis/continuities," *European Journal of Women's Studies*, 19(2), 237–52.

Brems, E. et al. 2012. "Wearing the Face Veil in Belgium: Views and Experiences of 27 Women Living in Belgium Concerning the Islamic Full Face Veil and the Belgian Ban on Face Covering," Human Rights Centre, Ghent University, available at http://www.ugent.be/re/publiekrecht/en/research/human-rights/faceveil.pdf.

Casanova, J. 1994. *Public Religions in the Modern World*. Chicago, IL: Chicago University Press.

Connolly, W. 1999. *Why I am not a Secularist*. Minneapolis: University of Minnesota Press.

Foucault, M. 1978. *History of Sexuality, Volume 1*. New York: Pantheon.

Göle, N. 2006. "Islamic Visibilities and Public Sphere," in N. Göle and L. Ammann (eds), *Islam in Public: Turkey, Iran and Europe*. Istanbul: Bilgi University Press.

Habermas, J. 2008. "Notes on Post-Secular Society," *New Perspectives Quarterly*, 25(4), 17–29.

Habermas, J. 2009. *Zwischen Naturalismus und Religion. Philosophische Aufsätze*, Frankfurt am Main: Suhrkamp.

Hindess, B. 2001. "The Liberal Government of Unfreedom," *Alternatives: Global, Local, Political*, 26(2), 93–111.

Hirschkind, C. 2011. "Is There a Secular Body?" *Cultural Anthropology*, 26(4), 633–47.

Joffrin, L. and Pierre-Brossolette, S. 2009. "Une loi anti-burqa: républicain ou démago?" *Libération*, June 19. Available at http://www.liberation.fr/politiques/06011042-une-loi-anti-burqa-republicain-ou-demago.

Joppke, C. 2007. "State Neutrality and Islamic Headscarf Laws in France and Germany," *Theory and Society*, 36(4), 313–43.

Kilic, S. 2008. "The British Veil Wars," *International Studies in Gender, State and Society*, 15(4), 433–54.

Laneyrie-Dagen, N. 2009. Speech at Mission d'information sur la pratique du port du voile intégral sur le territoire national, December 8, Séance 4.30, Compte rendu n 16.

Lentin, A. and Titley, G. 2011. *The Crisis of Multiculturalism. Racism in a Neoliberal Age*. London: Zed Books.

Mahmood, S. 2011. "Religious Reason and Secular Affect. An Incommensurable divide?" *Critical Inquiry*, 35, 836–62.

Mas, R. 2006. "Compelling the Muslim Subject. Memory as Post-colonial Violence and the Public Performativity of 'Secular and Cultural Islam'," *The Muslim World*, 96(4), 585–616.

Meer, N., Dwyer, C. and Modood, T. 2010. "Embodying Nationhood? Conceptions of British National Identity, Citizenship and Gender in the Veil Affair," *Sociological Review*, 58(1), 84–111.

Modood, T. 2010. *Still Not Easy Being British: Struggles for a Multicultural Citizenship*. London: Trentham Books.

Modood, T. 2011. "2011 Paul Hanly Furfey Lecture: Is There a Crisis of Secularism in Western Europe?" *Sociology of Religion*, 73(2), 1–20.

Moors, A. 2009. "The Dutch and the Face-Veil: The Politics of Discomfort," *Social Anthropology/Anthropologie Sociale*, 17(4), 393–408.

Motha, S. 2007. "Veiled Women and the Affect of Religion in Democracy," *Journal of Law and Society*, 34(1), 139–62.

Mouffe, C. 2008. *Über das Politische. Wider die kosmopolitische Illusion*. Frankfurt am Main: Suhrkamp.

Peter, F. 2008. "Political Rationalities, Counter-Terrorism and Policies on Islam in the United Kingdom and France," in J. Eckert (ed.), *The Social Life of Anti-Terrorism Laws*. Bielefeld: Transcript, 79–108.

Rose, N. 1999. *The Powers of Freedom: Reframing Political Thought*. Cambridge: Cambridge University Press.

Scott, J.W. 2007. *Politics of the Veil*. Princeton, NJ: Princeton University Press.

Silverstein, P. 2004. *Algeria in France: Transpolitics, Race and Nation*. Bloomington: Indiana University Press.

Silvestri, S. 2012. "Comparing Burqa Debates in Europe: Sartorial Styles, Religious Prescriptions and Political Ideologies," in S. Ferrari and S. Pastorelli (eds), *Religion in Public Spaces: A European Perspective*. Farnham: Ashgate, 275–82.

Taylor, C. 2007. *A Secular Age*. Cambridge, MA: Harvard University Press.

Warner, M. 2005. *Publics and Counterpublics*. Brooklyn: Zone Books.

Yeğenoğlu, M. 1999. *Colonial Fantasies: Towards a Feminist Reading of Orientalism*. Cambridge: Cambridge University Press.

PART III
Islam, Art and the
European Imaginary

Chapter 8

Representing Prophets and Saints in Islam: From Classical Positions to Present-Day Reactions

Silvia Naef

Alongside older controversial themes, like the wearing of the "veil" and the construction of mosques and minarets, images depicting religious themes have crystallized as a major source of controversy between Muslims and non-Muslims since the destruction of the Buddhas of Bamiyan by the Taliban in 2001 and the Danish cartoons affair in 2005–6. Other "minor" or rather local incidents were subsequently reported by the media, such as the Muhammad-teddy bear trial in the Sudan in 2007 in which the British teacher Gillian Gibbons was found guilty of "insulting religion" or, in the same year, when the Swedish artist Lars Vilks represented the Prophet of Islam in the shape of a dog.[1]

The Muhammad cartoons affair seemingly changed the "clash of civilizations" into a "clash on images," where defenders of freedom of speech opposed those whose primary concern was freedom of belief. Especially in Europe (the North American media were more cautious) (Klausen 2009: 8), there seemed to be no conciliation possible between what was deemed to be an unbridgeable, "civilizational" difference of values. This was the main theme. The subtext, the supposed Islamic "hostility" toward images, was reiterated by many Muslim organizations as well as by the Western media. The common and largely shared assumption was that "Islam" is, in its founding texts, hostile to images of any kind and in any context. This idea precedes the cartoons crisis: following the destruction of the Bamiyan Buddhas, even an excellent scholar like Jack Goody could write in the preface to the French translation of his book *Representations and Contradictions* that Islam forbids *any* kind of images (Goody 2003: 5).

The thesis put forward in this chapter is that such an inherent hostility is a construction rather than a necessary result of what the Islamic tradition – in text and practice – has produced. In order to discuss this, we will first give an overview of Islamic positions developed in classical times and will then present modern reformulations by Muslim 'ulamas of such positions. In the conclusion, we will try to see why images have become such a controversial theme.

---

1   Vilks has since been the victim of several acts of aggression.

Doctrinal Positions

Before we touch upon this question, it is important to underline that the images that pose a problem in Islam are those that depict beings endowed with the breath of life (*ruh*), i.e. humans and animals; plants and minerals are not part of the issue.

The Koran does not mention images in the proper sense: its priority is to fight idolatry. The verse that is sometimes advocated in order to condemn images is 5:90: "O you who believe! Intoxicants and gambling, (dedication of) stones [*ansab*], and (divination) by arrows are an abomination – of Satan's handwork – eschew such (abomination), that you may prosper."[2] The Arabic term *ansab* (the plural of *nasb*), translated here by "stones," means literally those "erected stones" that were used in ancient Arabia in order to embody deities.[3]

The hadiths make two points against images:

1. The first results from comparison with pre-Islamic polytheist practices: images (for which the texts employ different terms without differentiating between their meanings) are impure because they are assimilated to idols. Several hadith texts mention that, for this reason, angels will not enter a room where there are images. Ritual purity being a condition for the legal validity of the religious duty of prayer, the common interpretation of these texts was that images consequently had to be banned from the spaces where it was performed.

2. The second has a linguistic origin: *musawwir*, the Arabic word for painter, comes from *sawwara*, meaning "to shape, to give form, to create," one of God's prerogatives, which is repeatedly mentioned in the Koran. This understanding turned painters (*musawwir*) into competitors with God, the only *Musawwir* (creator of shapes); for that, God would punish them harshly in the afterlife, keeping them in the flames of Hell until they would be able to breathe life into his creatures. However, this applies only to animated beings, those endowed with the breath of life; plants and stones may be depicted in paintings, as other hadiths concede.

In spite of varying narratives and the reference to other authorities – Shiite traditions go back not only to the Prophet but also to the 12 Imams – there is no significant difference between the Sunni and Shiite texts. It might be added that no mention is made in either tradition of the representation of Muhammad or other holy persons.

The hadiths express an attitude that developed in the very beginning of the Islamic era and that is reflected by the two first religious buildings erected by

---

2   Translation by Abdullah Yusuf Ali.

3   On sculptural representations in pre-Islamic Arabia, see the catalog of the groundbreaking exhibition Routes d'Arabie, Archéologie et histoire du Royaume d'Arabie Saoudite, Paris, Musée du Louvre, 2010.

Islamic rulers: the Dome of the Rock in Jerusalem (built in 694–5) and the Umayyad Mosque in Damascus (706–14/15), where no representations of humans or animals are to be found, in contrast to the profane decorations of the Desert Castles (namely Qusayr 'Amr, Qasr al-Hayr al-Gharbi, or Khirbat al-Mafjar) built by the same master builders only a few decades later. This leads to an important conclusion: images were banned from the religious space and from official ritual practices. Figural objects of art and representations did, however, exist since the very dawn of Islam in almost all regions of the Islamic world, but the production of figurative images became a profane activity throughout most of Islamic history. As a consequence of this subdivision, Islam had no major iconoclast crises like Christianity, although iconoclasm was practiced throughout the ages in specific contexts, at times stemming out of individual initiatives and at others being performed as an act of power by new rulers, as Finbarr Barry Flood has convincingly shown (Flood 2002). To Islamic scholars, images were not really an issue, as the absence of treatises on the topic shows. They are only episodically condemned by theologians. And even in such cases, images are mentioned only in passing in relation to other topics considered to be more relevant.

Representing Holy Persons

In such a conception, images of holy persons could not have a ritual function, at least in the official performance of religious duties. Nevertheless, a representational tradition developed in later ages; in the earliest centuries, there is no material evidence that such images could have existed, although some texts mention them and Islamic art historians such as Oleg Grabar and Priscilla Soucek have given accounts of them (Grabar and Natif 2004: 19–37; Soucek 1988: 193–209). Grabar underlines that in spite of the mention of images of Muhammad in texts, there is no way to prove that they really existed. The narratives are mostly about conversions to Islam that such images should have induced outside the realm of Islam, in China or in Byzantium; it is not clear why such narratives appeared. In the first part of her 1988 article on the illustrated lives of the Prophet, Priscilla Soucek also mentions textual sources reporting the existence of such representations. Writing in the ninth century of the Common Era, the scholar Dinawari described portraits of Muhammad, who had supposedly been seen in Constantinople by a messenger of Caliph Abu Bakr (who ruled 632–4). They were believed to belong to the Byzantine Emperor, but had reportedly been executed for Alexander the Great of Macedon. Other Koranic prophets like Adam, Noah, Abraham, Moses, David, Solomon and Jesus were also represented. The historian al-Mas'udi (d. 956) mentions a portrait that belonged to the Emperor of China representing Muhammad on a camel. Another source evokes a picture of Muhammad that could have been in Abraham's possession, with Abu Bakr on his right and Ali on his left (Soucek 1988: 193).

The first figural representations of Muhammad of which we know go back to the thirteenth century (Soucek 1988: 194) and show him with his successors, the four right guided caliphs Abu Bakr, 'Umar, 'Uthman and 'Ali. At the end of the thirteenth and the beginning of the fourteenth centuries, depictions of scenes of the life of the Prophet (or of other prophets mentioned in the Koran) begin to appear in some Iranian manuscripts, as for instance in Rashid al-Din's *Universal Chronicle* (*Jami' al-tawarikh*).[4] Three illustrated manuscripts of this chronicle are known today: one is in Edinburgh,[5] another is in Istanbul[6] and the best-known copy, published as a facsimile by Sheila Blair in 1995 and shown in recent exhibitions, belongs to the collector Nasir D. Khalili and is dated 1314 (Blair 1995).[7] The Edinburgh manuscript illustrates episodes of the Meccan period of the Prophet's life, while the other two show the Medinean period (Soucek 1988: 199).

These first representations of episodes of Muhammad's life appear in chronicles and illustrate historical events from his biography; they take sides in the Sunni–Shiite controversy about the legitimacy of power, as Soucek has shown. Although the oldest representation of the Prophet's Journey to Heaven (*mi'raj*) can be found in the Edinburgh copy of Rashid al-Din's *Universal Chronicle* (Soucek 1988: 203–4), this religious episode from his biography became quite popular later on. Such illustrations could be found in poetry albums, historical texts or in accounts of his Journey to Heaven (*mi'raj-nameh*). The earliest manuscripts have full-face representations of Muhammad or other prophets; in later paintings, the prophets' faces are almost always covered by a veil. This has been explained as an intention to lessen the humanity of the represented person by depriving him of a face, or otherwise as a mystical attitude, since many of these images were found in texts inspired by Sufi practices. Figural representations of such subjects could also have, in specific circumstances such as Il-Khanid Iran, the function of promoting Islam in a context of religious instability, as Christiane Gruber has proved (Gruber 2010: 30–31).[8] In this sense, they could be compared to the literary evocations of miraculous images that induced conversion.

The Multiplication of Images and Scholarly Reactions

Since the nineteenth century, there has been a multiplication of images in the Islamic world. With the spread of the press, the introduction of lithography, then of photography, cinema, television and, later on, digital images, the production

---

4   The other two manuscripts examined by Soucek are: Bal'ami's Persian translation of Tabari's Ta'rikh al-rusul wa-l-muluk [History of Prophets and Kings] (late thirteenth/ early fourteenth century) and Biruni's Athar al-Baqiya [Chronology of Ancient Nations], dated 1307.

5   Edinburgh University Library, MS Arab 20.

6   Topkapı Sarayı Library, Hazine 1653.

7   It belonged formerly to the Royal Asiatic Society in London.

8   On religious representations in Islam, see also Cuomo 2011.

and reproduction of images became much cheaper and their popularity steadily increased (Heyberger and Naef 2003). This occurred in the general context of modernization and of partial secularization. All over the Islamic world, images conquered public and private spaces to an extent they never had before. This meant that religious scholars had to take a position on a question that had not previously been central in religious thought: that of the place of images and of the ways of dealing with them.

The liberal Egyptian reformer and scholar Muhammad 'Abduh (1849–1905) was impressed, during a trip he made to Sicily in 1903, by the concern its inhabitants showed for their pictorial heritage. He thus re-examined the founding Islamic texts condemning figural representations and concluded that the concern that was at their origin was that of a return to paganism. However, he pointed out, it was difficult to believe that after so many centuries of Islamization, people could seriously consider going back to the cult of idols. Therefore, 'Abduh said, Islam should not renounce such a useful means of spreading knowledge. But he also considered the esthetic value of visual arts: for him, painting was like a form of poetry addressing the eyes, while poetry could be seen as a form of painting addressing the ears. Comparing painting to the highest valued form of art, namely poetry, conferred new prestige upon it ('Abduh 1972). His disciple Muhammad Rashid Rida (1865–1935) was more restrictive: in the reformist periodical *Al-Manar*, he pointed out in 1917 that *rasm* – an Arabic term that can mean drawing as well as painting (and which had been already used by his teacher 'Abduh) – should only be allowed when useful for the Islamic community, for instance, in scientific publications, for military purposes or in dictionaries in order to explain the differences between the numerous varieties of animals and plants (Rida 1970–1971). Rida was totally opposed to three-dimensional images, like the statues that the new Turkish President Mustafa Kemal started to erect in public spaces in Turkey in the 1920s (Rida 1986: 137, 139–41).

In his 1917 text, Rida considered only handmade images, i.e. paintings and drawings; a sort of consensus has been established between scholars that photography was licit, because it was taken by a device and did not result from a human will to create what God had not created. They compared photography to an image reflected in the mirror. This attitude can still be found among present-day religious leaders such as Yusuf al-Qaradawi. Al-Qaradawi considers that only images created by man are problematic, by virtue of the *musawwir* principle formulated in the hadiths. However, in some cases, if there is no morally dubious content, they could be accepted. Three-dimensional images are to be rejected without exception. Photography, since there is no human intervention, is not problematic, unlike paintings: "The late Sheikh Muhammad Bakhit, the Egyptian jurist, ruled that since the photograph merely captures the image of a real object through a camera, there is no reason for prohibition in this case. Prohibited pictures are those whose object is not present and which are originated by the artist, whose intention is to imitate Allah's animal creation, and this does not apply to taking photographs with a camera" (al-Qaradawi 2001: 98–116).

However, some hardliners, as evidenced in a fatwa collection published in Saudi Arabia in 1988 – and still found on several Salafi websites – condemn any kind of images, including photography. Even family pictures are illicit because "the representation (*taswir*) of any being provided of breath of life (*ruh*) … is forbidden … conforming to what is stated in a majority of hadiths" (Al-Shamma'i 1988: 306–7). But even these hardliners are obliged to allow certain exceptions: in case of necessity (*darura*) – a principle of Islamic law – photographs are allowed for IDs and, interestingly, banknotes! This can only be explained by the fact that images of the rulers are found on Saudi bills, and that the government-sponsored mufti did not dare say that this should be (in the logic of the law he wanted to apply) forbidden (Al-Shamma'i 1988: 299, 310)!

By analogy to photography, cinema and television are lawful, since the images are mechanically produced; they reproduce God's universe and are not competing with it through man-made intervention. If they are condemned, it is not because of the nature of the media, but because its content does not respect morality.

Representing Prophets and Saints in Modern Times

In his book *The Lawful and the Prohibited in Islam (Al halal wa-l-haram fi-l-islam)*, first published in Arabic in 1960, and subsequently republished, translated into several languages and posted on his website, Yusuf al-Qaradawi stated that it is forbidden to make images of prophets, angels or saints like those of the Christians, even if some innovators of Islam have already imitated them by making images of 'Ali, Fatima and others: "It is prohibited to make or to acquire portraits of individuals who are either revered in a religion or respected for their worldly status. Examples of the first category are representations of prophets such as Abraham, Isaac, David, and Jesus; of angels such as Jibril and Mika'eel (Michael); and of saints and righteous individuals such as Maryam (Mary) and the like. This is a Jewish [sic!9] or Christian custom. Unfortunately, some Muslims, making innovations in religion and imitating the People of the Book, have begun to make and to acquire portraits of 'Ali, Fatimah, and others" (al-Qaradawi 2001). He reiterated this view in the 2007 documentary *Bloody Cartoons*, when he declared in the context of the discussion on the Danish cartoons that there is "a consensus (*ijma*') of Sunni 'ulama that prophets should not be represented" (Kjaer 2007).

As we saw, representations of prophets were not unusual in manuscripts. Their production ceased with the introduction of the printing press and the adoption of art in its Western – mimetic – modality since the end of the nineteenth century (Naef 1996; Shaw 2011). Modernization also prompted deep reflection on the reasons for the decline of the Islamic civilization, a decline that was often explained by the new forms and practices introduced by later generations that supposedly estranged Islam from its original sources that gave it its strength.

---

9   This seems to be a (wrong) addition to the English translation available on the Web.

A return to the example of the first generations of Muslims, who were believed to have practiced their religion in an unaltered form in opposition to their followers, was therefore required. This is a view shared not only by the strict Wahhabis but also by more liberal religious scholars. Muhammad 'Abduh, for instance, who spoke in favour of painting, considered later Islamic ages as being in decline. As figural representations of religious personages appeared only in later centuries, as we have seen, it is likely that they started to be considered as deviations from the "real" Islam of the forefathers. Therefore, religious representations disappeared from artistic production and survived only in popular art, as prints sold in bazaars and on the streets. In addition, it could be argued that the mimetic pretension of the newly adopted Western art made it difficult to represent prophets whose shapes could not easily be imagined.

The collection of modern popular prints belonging to the Swiss ethnologists Pierre and Micheline Centlivres provides evidence that prophets other than Muhammad were represented in the 1960s and 1970s (Centlivres and Centlivres-Demont 1997; Stocchi 1988). Nowadays, Buraq, the steed on which Muhammad is said to have ascended to heaven, is still a popular theme. However, her rider who was, in the representational tradition of miniature painting, mostly shown, has disappeared. In popular prints, Muhammad is represented only symbolically, through the shape of his footstep, his tomb in Medina or his calligraphied name (Centlivres and Centlivres-Demont 1998: 139–70). Shiite Islam experienced an opposite movement: since the nineteenth century, a tradition of holy images developed, first dedicated to the imams and, since the 1990s, representing Muhammad himself (Centlivres and Centlivres-Demont 2006; Zadeh 2008). This production is tolerated, although only rarely explicitly approved by Shiite 'ulama, whose scriptural sources are as strict as those of the Sunnis on this theme. These images, called *shamayel* in Iran, can even have a religious function in Sufi practices (Amir-Moezzi 2006). Recently, a high Shiite authority like Sistani authorized, on his website, the representation of prophets. To a believer who asked him about the lawfulness of this type of imagery, he answered that: "If due reference and respect is observed, and the scene does not contain anything that would detract from their holy pictures in the minds [of the viewers], there is no problem."[10]

Exceptions to the strict Sunni attitude do, however, exist. In 1997, Taha Jaber al-Alwani, who is Sunni, and Azharite as Qaradawi, declared, in a fatwa that he issued concerning the image of Muhammad which, since 1935, can be found on the frieze of the US Supreme Court in Washington, DC: "What I have seen in the Supreme Courtroom deserves nothing but appreciation and gratitude from American Muslims. This is a positive gesture toward Islam made by the architect and other architectural decision-makers of the highest Court in America. God willing, it will help ameliorate some of the unfortunate misinformation that has surrounded Islam and Muslims in this country. For this reason, I would like to express my gratitude and appreciation to the early twentieth-century architect and

---

10   www.sistani.org, March 11, 2012. The fatwa is not dated.

his associates who brought, in their own way, the essence of what the Prophet symbolized, namely law with justice, to the attention of the American people" (al-Alwani 2000/2001: 27–8). Although al-Alwani expressed a positive attitude toward images throughout his text, this decision needs to be contextualized: al-Alwani was trying to answer a question posed by the Council of American-Islamic Relations (CAIR). Noticing the representation of Muhammad on the frieze, a Muslim addressed the CAIR, which asked al-Alwani, Chairman of the Fiqh Council of North America, for a legal response, a fatwa. Al-Alwani's concern was to preserve a peaceful cohabitation between Muslims and non-Muslims: although recognizing that Islamic texts are hostile, generally, to representation, he speaks in favor of a conciliating interpretation of these texts. This can be better understood if we know that his prevailing concern was the pacific coexistence of different religious communities in the US (al-Alwani 2000/2001: 2). In order to achieve this priority goal, some (secondary) principles concerning images, could, in al-Alwani's reading, be relativized.

The representation of prophets became an issue in another popular medium: cinema. In 1926, the Egyptian actor Yusuf Wahbi had been chosen to play the role of Muhammad in a movie directed by Wedad Orfi, a Turkish director. A press campaign was started against the author and al-Azhar issued a fatwa saying that the representation of Muhammad and of his family and companions was prohibited. The then king of Egypt, Fu'ad, threatened to revoke the actor's Egyptian nationality and deport him: the actor finally renounced the role and the movie was not produced (Wassef 1995: 21). In 1947, Egyptian censorship law was reinforced: the cinematographic representation of the Prophet, his family, the first four caliphs Abu Bakr, 'Umar, 'Uthman and 'Ali, as well as the prophet's nearest companions, even in a symbolic way through a shadow, was outlawed (Bergmann 1993: 71–2).

In the 1970s, another attempt was made to show the life of the Prophet Muhammad. *Al-Risala (The Message)*, shot in 1976–7 by the Syrian-American movie director Mustafa al-'Aqqad and partially financed by Libya, respects the criteria enounced in 1947 by the Egyptian censorship law. The film shows neither Muhammad nor any of his close companions, nor can we hear their voices.[11] This was not a free choice by the movie's director, but was due to the negative reaction that the project provoked internationally at the instigation of religious leaders and institutions. In 1970, the Islamic World League, close to Saudi Arabia, condemned the movie script, whose preliminary version had the roles of Muhammad and his main companions performed by actors. From Morocco to Lebanon's Shiites, the protests went global. Finally, the film was shot with the above-mentioned precautions and two versions were made: an Arabic one, released in 1976, and an international one, starring Anthony Quinn and Irène Papas, in 1977. In spite of these precautions, the movie was not shown in Egyptian theaters and in 1977, a dissident group of Black Muslims took 140 hostages in a cinema in Washington, DC, demanding that the screening be suspended (Ende 1981: 32–52).

---

11   http://www.youtube.com/watch?v=-sY3dkXx0iE&feature=related.

In 1994, the film *The Emigrant* (*Al-Muhajir*) by Youssef Chahine, illustrating the life of the Koranic prophet Joseph, was temporarily forbidden in Egypt because "it embodied prophet Joseph, against a fatwa of 1983." However, this decision was overturned by a court decision.[12] In an interview with the Arab daily *Al-Hayat*, the movie's director Chahine considered that this had been an attack against Egyptian cinema as a whole.[13]

More recently, there has been a Sunni–Shiite dispute about representations of holy persons on TV screens. In the serial directed by the Syrian 'Abd al-Bari Abu al-Khayr first called *Al-Asbat* ("the tribes," a reference to a Koranic word designating the Hebrews), Hasan and Husayn were supposed to be represented. While some Sunnis expressed concern about the representation of these two holy men, Shiites were worried about the possibility that Sunnis would the wrong idea about them. The serial was finally shown during Ramadan 2011 with the title *Hasan, Husayn and Mu'awiya*, and received the approval of several religious authorities around the Arab world, among them Yusuf Qaradawi, Salman al-'Awdeh and Hani al-Jubayr, judge at the Court in Mecca; Hasan and Husayn were not embodied by actors (Gonzales-Quijano 2009; 2012).

"Islam" and Controversial Images

Although opinions may differ, representations of prophets have become a controversial issue, be it in the confrontation between the West and Islam or in inter-Islamic debates between Shia and Sunni. Thus, a Sunni salafi blog in French, created by a non-identified Abu Mohamed, quoting and commenting Sistani's fatwa on the permissibility of representing the Prophet, qualified him as a Madjusi, or Zoroastrian, i.e. a "Persian," a typical offense directed at Shiites by Sunni radicals, and defined the fatwa as "vile" (*immonde*).[14] A similar controversy broke out in March 2012 in Najaf around the wax statues of Shiite religious personalities like Ayatollah Muhammad Sadiq al-Sadr or the Lebanese leader Muhammad Husayn Fadlallah that were exhibited in one of the city's museums. To Sunnis – as to some Shiites – these seemed to be unlawful and constituted proof of the lack of respect of Islamic law by the Shiites.[15]

The representation of prophets, which was fairly widespread between the thirteenth and the early nineteenth centuries, has mostly disappeared in the modern age in the Sunni realm. A new sensitivity developed, often tied to specific events and circumstances. Thus, in the Abu Dhabi and Paris exhibitions *The Arts of Islam*,

---

12   Le Monde, 31 December 1994, 9; and Le Monde, 31 March 1995, 32.

13   Al Hayat, 4 February 1995, 19.

14   http://mondearabe.discuforum.info/t429-Le-chiite-Sistani-permet-la-representation-du-prophete-saws.htm.

15   AP, "Wax Statues in Shiite Holy City Prompt Awe by Fans, Cries of Heresy by Critics," Washington Post, March 21, 2012, http://www.kerkuk.net/eng/?p=5219.

showcasing the already-mentioned Islamic art collection of Nasser D. Khalili, who owns one of the discussed manuscripts of Rashid al-Din's *Universal Chronicle*, the images illustrating Muhammad's life were not exhibited, nor were they published in either catalog. However, images of other Koranic prophets, such as Noah or Joseph, were displayed,[16] which proves that this choice had not been dictated by "Islamic considerations," since, otherwise, representations of any prophet or holy person would have been avoided. It can be assumed that after the cartoons crisis, the curators of the exhibition preferred to renounce the public exhibition of images of Muhammad in order to avoid controversy. Thus, we might say that although resulting from the offensive character of the Danish cartoons rather than from a religious attitude toward images, as Stephan Rosiny has convincingly shown (Rosiny 2007: 107–9), the crisis not only had political implications, but also repercussions on the public display of representations produced by Muslims in past times.

From the preceding examples, it should, however, be clear that it would be difficult to understand recent controversies about images solely as stemming from a century-old Islamic tradition of hostility toward figural representations. In the past, images of prophets were not used in religious practice, but appeared as illustrations in manuscripts in the late thirteenth century in Il-Khanid Iran and spread to other regions. This habit disappeared through the technical and cultural changes introduced in the nineteenth century. Therefore, rather than being rooted in a presumably unchanging Islamic "essence," such controversies are the result of new practices and readings introduced by modernity.

References

'Abduh, M. 1972. "Al-suwar wa-l-tamathil, wa-fawa'iduha, wa-hukmuha" ["Paintings and Sculptures: Their Usefulness and Ruling"], in *Al-a'mal al-kamila li-l-imam Muhammad 'Abduh*, vol. 2. Beirut: Al-mu'assasa al-'arabiyya li-l-dirasat wa-l-nashr, 204–8.

al-Alwani, T-J. 2000–2001. "Fatwa Concerning the United States Supreme Courtroom Frieze," *Journal of Law and Religion*, 15(1/2), 1–28.

Amir-Moezzi, M-Ali. 2006. "Icône et contemplation: entre l'art populaire et le soufisme dans le shi'isme imamite," *Bulletin of the Asia Institute*, 20, 1–12.

Bergmann, K. 1993. *Filmkultur und Filmindustrie in Ägypten*. Darmstadt: Wissenschaftliche Buchgesellschaft.

Blair, S. (ed.) 1995. *A Compendium of Chronicles, Rashid al-Din's Illustrated History of the World*. London: Nour Foundation and Azimuth Ed./Oxford: Oxford University Press.

16   Emirates Palace Hotel, Abu Dhabi, January22–April 22, 2008. Catalog: The Arts of Islam, Treasures From the Nasser D. Khalili Collection, Abu Dhabi, Tourism Development and Investment Company (TDIC), 2008; Institut du Monde Arabe, Paris. Catalog: Arts de l'Islam. Chefs-d'oeuvres de la collection Khalili, Paris, Hazan, 2009.

Centlivres, P. and Centlivres-Demont, M. 1997. *Imageries populaires en Islam*, exhibition catalog. Geneva: Georg Editeur.

Centlivres, P. and Centlivres-Demont, M. 1998. "Une présence absente: symboles et images populaires du prophète Mahomet," *Derrière les images*, Neuchâtel, Musée d'Ethnographie, 139–70.

Centlivres, P. and Centlivres-Demont, M. 2006. "The Story of a Picture. Shiite Depiction of Muhammad," *ISIM Review*, 17, 18–19.

Cuomo, C. 2011. "Images sacrées et représentations dans les traditions islamiques," Ph.D. thesis, Université Lumière Lyon 2/Università di Napoli L Orientale.

Ende, W. 1981. "Mustafa al-'Aqqads 'Muhammad'-Film und seine Kritiker," in H.R. Römer and A. Noth (eds), *Studien zur Geschichte und Kultur des Vorderen Orients, Festschrift für B. Spuler*. Leiden: Brill.

Flood, F.B. 2002. "Between Cult and Culture: Bamiyan, Islamic Iconoclasm, and the Museum," *The Art Bulletin*, 84(4), 641–59.

Gonzales-Quijano, Y. 2009. "Le 'croissant chiite' et la guerre des images saintes," April 14, http://cpa.hypotheses.org/880.

Gonzales-Quijano, Y. 2012. "idjaztu'l qaradawiyya..." March 25, http://www.alarabiya.net/save_print.php?print=1&cont_id=155439.

Goody, J. 2003. *La peur des représentations. L'ambivalence à l'égard des images, du théâtre, de la fiction, des reliques et de la sexualité*. Paris: La Découverte. Translated by P.-E. Dauzat as *Representations and Contradictions, Ambivalence Towards Images, Theatre, Fiction, Relics, and Sexuality*. Oxford: Blackwell, 1997.

Grabar, O. and Natif, M. 2004. "The Story of Portraits of the Prophet Muhammad," *Studia Islamica*, 96, 19–37.

Gruber, C. 2010. *The Ilkhanid Book of Ascension, A Persian-Sunni Devotional Tale*. London/New York: I.B. Tauris.

Heyberger, B. and Naef, S. (eds) 2003. *La multiplication des images en pays d'Islam, De l'estampe à la télévision (17e–21e siècle)*. Istanbul/Würzburg: Ergon Verlag.

Kjaer, K. 2007. *Bloody Cartoons*, Freeport Media and Steps International for BBC.

Klausen, J. 2009. *The Cartoons that Shook the World*. New Haven: Yale University Press.

Naef, S. 1996. *A la recherche d'une modernité arabe, L'évolution des arts plastiques en Egypte, au Liban et en Irak*. Geneva: Slatkine.

al-Qaradawi, Y. 2001. *The Lawful and Prohibited in Islam*. Cairo: Al-Falah Foundation, available at: http://www.2muslims.com/directory/Detailed/226100.shtml#The%20Subject%20Matter%20of%20Photographs,

Rida, M-R. 1970–1971. "Hukm al-taswir wa-san' al-suwar wa-l-tamathil wa-ittikhadiha" ["Ruling and Position on Representations and the Making of Images and Statues"], in S. al-Munajjid and Y. Khuri (eds), *Fatawa al-imam Muhammad Rashid Rida*, 4 vols. Beirut: Dar al-Kitab al-Jadid, 4, 1392–418.

Rida, M-R. 1986. *Le califat ou l'imamat suprême*, translated by Henri Laoust. Paris: A. Maisonneuve.

Rosiny, S. 2007. "Der beleidigte Prophet. Religiöse und politische Hintergründe des Karikaturenstreits," in B. Debatin (ed.), *The Cartoon Debate and the Freedom of the Press, Conflicting Norms and Values in the Global Media Culture.* Berlin: LIT Verlag.

Sergio, S. 1988. *L'islam nelle stampe/Islam in Prints.* Milan: Be-Ma Editrice.

al-Shamma'i, Q. (ed.) 1988. *Fatawa islamiyya li-majmu'a min al-'ulama'.* Beirut: Dar al-Qalam.

Shaw, W-M-K. 2011. *Ottoman Painting, Reflections of Western Art from the Ottoman Empire to the Turkish Republic.* London: I.B. Tauris.

Soucek, P. 1988. "The Life of the Prophet: Illustrated Versions," in P. Soucek (ed.), *Content and Context of Visual Arts in the Islamic World.* University Park: Pennsylvania State University Press.

Stocchi, S. 1988. *L'islam nelle stampe/Islam in Prints.* Milan: Be-Ma Editrice.

Wassef, M. 1995. *Égypte, 100 ans de cinéma.* Paris: Institut du Monde Arabe.

Zadeh, M-M. 2008. "L'iconographie chiite dans l'Iran des Qâdjârs: émergence, sources et développement," Ph.D. thesis, University of Geneva/Ecole Pratique de Hautes Etudes, Paris.

Chapter 9

Islam in the Mirror of Our Phantasms

John V. Tolan

Looking at the European media, one might think that Islam has only been at the heart of European controversies for a few decades. Headscarves and halal meat in France, minarets in Switzerland, forced marriages in Denmark: all these conflicts have less to do with questioning Islam itself than with the exploiting of Islam (or the symbols associated with it) in debates about national politics. Yet Islam has been a subject of much debate in Europe since at least the twelfth century, and the symbol most often at the center of these controversies is the Prophet Muhammad.

In order to more thoroughly discredit Islam, Geert Wilders, a Member of Parliament from the Partij voor de Vrijheid (the Dutch far-right Party for Freedom), has attacked its prophet, calling him a terrorist, a pedophile and a psychopath (Wilders 2011). Wilders is hardly the first person to exploit Muhammad in European controversies. In order to put these polemics surrounding the Prophet (and, through him, Islam) into historical perspective, I will examine the role he has been assigned in European controversies from the twelfth to the twenty-first centuries. As we will see, discourse about the Prophet is often, though not always, hostile. I will begin with the Middle Ages, when Muhammad was seen as a threat to Christian European authors, especially because he represented a rival religion and civilization that was both triumphant and attractive. However, in some circumstances, the Prophet assumed a very different function: at the end of the Middle Ages, he was cited as a supporter of the Immaculate Conception. During the French Wars of Religion, he became a point on a spectrum of error: Luther or the Pope (according to the point of view of the writer) was seen in a far worse light than Muhammad. In eighteenth-century controversies concerning the power of the Catholic Church, the figure of the Prophet was used to combat religious superstition, either by portraying him as a violent fanatic (in order to denounce religious figures en bloc) or, on the contrary, as a reformer who fought superstition and the power of clerics (Tolan 2010).

Let's begin in the era that, since the thirteenth century, has been known as the time of the Crusades, when the disputes generally centered on the sacralization of war (Flori 2006). In the early Church, pilgrims went to Jerusalem (or to Rome, or elsewhere), often in order to perform penance, humbly and peacefully. But the Crusades were given the status of "armed" pilgrimages, and chroniclers often bestowed the title of "martyr" on fallen Christian soldiers. In order to justify and glorify these wars, the "Saracen" adversary had to be demonized either as a pagan idolater or as a heretic.

In *The Song of Roland* (dating from the end of the eleventh or the beginning of the twelfth centuries), "Saracens" worshipped idols of their three gods: Apollo, Tervagant and Mahomet (Tolan 2002; Akbari 2009). After a bitter defeat, they shatter a statue of Muhammad; at the end of the epic, Charlemagne's victorious troops enter the captured city of Saragossa and use axes to shatter the idols they find in "*sinagoges*" and "*mahumeries.*" This is not unique to *The Song of Roland*. A number of chroniclers, poets and polemists depict the Saracens as adepts of a polytheistic and idolatrous religion whose primary god is Mahomet or Mahon. This includes chroniclers of the First Crusade (1096–99) or the anonymous author of *The Song of Antioch*, which combines accounts of authentic battles from the First Crusade with wholly imaginary scenes, some of which concern the daily life of the enemy Saracens. Of course, these images are the product of profound ignorance of (or a total lack of interest in) Islam. Authors (especially clerics) immersed in Latin culture (including ancient poetry) imagine that the cult of Saracen "infidels" is exactly like those depicted in pagan Antiquity. This may seem a bit ironic, since it was Christians who filled their churches with statues of saints, crucifixes, etc. to such an extent that Muslims (and Jews) accused them in return of idolatry.

Of course, once Europeans were better acquainted with Islam, they realized that "Saracens" were anything but idolaters. Thus, a slightly less unsophisticated yet no less hostile caricature developed: Islam was a heresy (a deviant and illegitimate form of Christianity) and Muhammad, its founder, a heretic. We find this idea in eastern Christianity beginning in the eighth century, in Spain in the ninth century and elsewhere in Europe by the twelfth century. In fact, in the twelfth century, a black legend about the Prophet circulated, which we can find in a number of texts in Latin (and, beginning in the thirteenth century, in French) (Tolan 2002: Chapter 6; 2006). Mahomet, a young merchant educated by a heretical monk, pretends to be a Prophet in order to seize power. He trains a dove to eat seeds from his ear and then explains to the stunned crowds that it is the Archangel Gabriel who has come to deliver his revelation. He announces that God will send a new holy book through an unexpected intermediary; then a bull, which Mahomet had also trained, arrives, carrying on his horns the book that Mahomet had himself written. This new law authorizes polygamy and incest, and promises a Heaven full of sexual debauchery, which succeeds in winning over the crowds. According to some of these tales, upon his death, Muhammad was put in an iron coffin and laid in a temple in Mecca whose ceiling was covered with magnets. As a result, the coffin floated in mid-air, proving to the pilgrims that he was indeed a great Prophet of God. We find portraits of Muhammad based upon these texts in a number of medieval manuscripts: truly, Danish caricatures before their time. Figure 9.1 in the color plate section is a fifteenth-century illumination combining a number of these legends which portrays Muhammad as an impostor and a charlatan.

To put this scene into context, we must remember that in the twelfth century, the Muslim world was more powerful, better educated and richer than Latin Christendom: Latin clerics tried to explain the manifest success of this rival civilization and religion whilst reassuring their readers of the superiority of the Christian religion. Yet this position is clearly ambiguous: Islam and its prophet fascinate and repulse.

It is unsurprising that these caricatures of Muhammad played a role in the larger context of an ideological and military confrontation with Islam. But the Islamic prophet surprisingly appears at the center of another controversy: the one that for a good part of the Middle Ages and up to the nineteenth century surrounds the doctrine of the Immaculate Conception. This doctrine, which was not officially adopted by the Catholic Church until 1854, was the object of bitter debate during the Middle Ages and the sixteenth and seventeenth centuries. It stipulates that the Virgin Mary was born without the stain of original sin: this makes her the first (and, besides her son, the only) person to avoid this curse ever since God chased Adam and Eve out of his earthly paradise. Our goal here is not to enter into the complexities of this abstruse debate, but to highlight the role assigned to the Islamic prophet as a supporter of this doctrine.

The hadiths of Bukhari (ninth century) cite the Prophet affirming: "There is none born among the off-spring of Adam, but Satan touches it … except Mary and her child' (Houdas and Marçais 1977: 278). This is one of the traditions that show the special status accorded to Jesus and his mother in the Muslim religion. In what context or "controversy" can we situate this Hadith's writings in Abbasid Khwarezm? Perhaps Bukhari sought to emphasize the harmony that should exist among those who respect Mary and her son, and the universalism of the monotheistic message brought by the two prophets Jesus and Muhammad.

In any case, this text resurfaces in a very different context five centuries later, when the Franciscan Marquard von Lindau inserted into a chapter on the Immaculate Conception a Latin translation of this Hadith, alongside quotations from the Koran praising Mary. From this point on, Muhammad is portrayed as a partisan of the doctrine and is quoted as a supporter of the dogma by his fellow partisans (who often confuse the Hadith and the Koran) (Gay-Canton 2010). Of course, neither the Koran nor the Hadith contains the doctrine of the Immaculate Conception, which is linked to the notion of original sin, a concept entirely foreign to Islam. But this is beside the point: what we are interested in is the role assigned to the Prophet in an entirely European debate.

Perhaps the most astonishing aspect of this astonishing story is that Muhammad is even depicted in a number of altarpieces which, from the sixteenth to the eighteenth centuries, illustrate the dispute concerning the Immaculate Conception. A 1727 altarpiece by Michele Luposignoli, based on a model by Nikola Bralič (1518), shows the Virgin in a lecture hall, surrounded by a number of doctors of the Church holding parchments containing their scholarship affirming this doctrine. In the bottom-right corner we can discern the figure of Muhammad carrying a scroll with the text: "No one descended from Adam has not been touched by Satan, except Mary and her son: Muhammad in the Koran." Even Muhammad and Luther (the second person from the bottom) support the doctrine of the Immaculate Conception. Of course, they are relegated to the bottom of the painting, but they are nonetheless supporters. This is even more surprising when we consider that this painting was intended as a decoration for the altar of a church.

At this time, the great controversy tearing apart Europe, of course, pitted Catholics against Protestants. In it, Islam and its Prophet are a point on a spectrum of error. For many Protestant polemists, Catholics were far worse than Muslims. According to Luther: "The Pope's devil is bigger than the Turk's." Elsewhere, Luther describes the Muslims' ceremonial fast and their diligence in both fasting and prayer in order to conclude that they are better Catholics than the Pope himself (Francisco 2007).

Catholics too used this effective tool of grouping the great heretics (Muhammad, Luther and Calvin) together.

In an almanac, published in Paris in 1687, Muhammad and Calvin are shown in Hell (see Figure 9.2 in the color plate section). In anger, Muslims and Calvinists, whose leaders had promised they would go to Heaven, take revenge against their leaders. Note that a Muslim tramples on "The Alcoran of Mahomet," while the Calvinist who is grabbing his victim by the goatee brandishes a copy of *Constitutions de Calvin* (*Calvin's fundamental laws*). A demon watches them, laughing (Carnoy-Torab 2006: 440–41).

Let's turn to another great European controversy, this one in the eighteenth century, pitting philosophers and deists on the one hand and religious figures on the other. In it, the Prophet was used in attacks by philosophers against religion (and, in particular, against the Catholic Church). First, let's take the example of the *Traité des trois imposteurs* (*Treatise of the Three Impostors*) from 1719.[1] According to its anonymous author, religion had been a way for elites to manipulate the masses since the earliest priests of pagan Antiquity. But the worst charlatans are the three great impostors: Moses, Jesus and Muhammad. They devised false miracles and revelations in order to glorify themselves and fool their followers. Moses, a magician trained in Egypt, was a despot and an impostor. Jesus was hardly any better: he made a group of fools believe that his mother was a virgin and his father the Holy Spirit. The same went for Muhammad, whose portrait here resembles the one sketched by medieval authors. The difference here is that the anonymous author treated Moses and Jesus in the same way as the Islamic prophet. His strategy was to compare the three, attributing the role of charlatan and impostor, so often given to Muhammad, to Moses and Jesus as well.

But in this war of ideas, the opposite strategy was used as well: Islam and its prophet were praised in order to criticize the Church. Henri, the Count of Boulainvilliers, provides an example of this in his *Vie de Mahomed* (*Life of Muhammad*, published posthumously in 1730). According to him, Muhammad

---

1   The first edition was published under the title *La vie et l'esprit de Mr. Benoit de Spinosa* (Amsterdam: Charles le Vier, 1719); it was next published under the title *Le traité des trois imposteurs* and was republished many times during the eighteenth century. For the English translation of the 1777 edition, see Anderson 1997; Berti, Charles-Daubert and Popkin 1996.

was a divinely inspired messenger sent by God to confound quarrelsome eastern Christians, liberate the Orient from the despotic rule of the Romans and Persians, and spread the knowledge of the unity of God from India to Spain. Muhammad, says Boulainvilliers, adopted the best aspects of Christianity and abolished its abuses: the cult of relics and icons and the power accorded to ignorant priests and monks. Boulainvilliers protests against Christian authors who, in their hatred of a rival religion, insult the Prophet:

> Since if the fortune of this personage was not the effect of natural means, the success could be only from God; whom the impious will accuse of having led half the world into an error, and destroy'd violently by his own revelation. (Boulainvilliers 1730: 179)

For Boulainvilliers, the impious are not Muslims; they are Christians who refuse to recognize that Muhammad was divinely inspired and guided. This text has been presented as a striking example of the spirit of tolerance that characterized the Enlightenment era. But this flattering portrait of Muhammad is above all an implicit criticism of the Catholic Church: his Muhammad is an enlightened deist who fights superstition and the abuse of power by clerics. Muhammad is again used in this controversy as a point on a spectrum: the frankly positive presentation of the Prophet allows Boulainvilliers to underscore the abject state of the Church.

Some Enlightenment authors hesitated: should the Prophet be portrayed as a reformer or a fanatic? Voltaire first attacks Muhammad as a fanatical figure in his play *Mahomet ou le Fanatisme* (1742). Here, "Mahomet" is a deceitful impostor who schemes, lies and murders to get what he wants: power, a young woman he desires and the title of "prophet." But through the figure of the fanatical and manipulative prophet, Voltaire is targeting the Catholic Church and, in effect, the strong reactions engendered by this play show that he touches a nerve (Cornoy-Torab 2006: 468–71). Voltaire's depiction of the Prophet is quite different in his historical work *Essai sur les Mœurs*, in which he paints Muhammad as Boulainvilliers did: a wise man, great legislator and leader of a proud and valiant people. Is it possible that Voltaire changed his mind in the 14 years that separate these texts; did he become more tolerant of Islam and its prophet? Perhaps. But, more than that, he adopted a strategy suited to his chronicle, where the image of medieval Islam as a tolerant and enlightened religion and an erudite and sophisticated civilization contrasts with the fanatical, barbarous and ignorant Europe of the Crusades. Muhammad the fanatic or Muhammad the legislator? Voltaire is ready to adopt either stance in order to attack the Church.

It is Muhammad the legislator that we find in Emmanuel Pastoret's 1787 book *Zoroaster, Confucius and Mahomet*, in which he recounts the lives of these "great men," "the best legislators in the universe," and compares their careers as reformers and legislators (Pastoret 1787). Pastoret explains that in the Koran, the Prophet provides "the most sublime truths of cult and morals" (p. 234); the Koran defines the unity of God with "admirable concision" (p. 236). The accusations of the Prophet's immorality are unfounded: on the contrary, his law encourages sobriety, generosity and compassion. Undoubtedly, the "legislator of Arabia" was a "great man" (p. 1).

The image of Muhammad the "great man" was so widespread that another "great man," Napoleon Bonaparte, took him as a role model. During his Egyptian campaign, he claimed to defend Arabs and Islam from their two enemies: the papacy and the "Mamluks" (the Ottomans). In December 1798, he went so far as to declare:

> All human powers are helpless against me. My expedition from the Occident to the shores of the Nile has been foretold in the Koran. One day, all men will be convinced of it. (Napoleon I 1998: 167)

Was this the cynical affirmation of a man searching for any argument that justified his power? Undoubtedly, yes. The next year, before leaving Egypt, he warned his administrators: "we must convince the Muslims that we respect the Koran and venerate their prophet; any small error might undo years of work" (p. 275).

But years later, writing his memoirs in exile on the island of Saint Helena, Napoleon expands upon the portrait of the Prophet as a great legislator and conqueror:

> Muhammad was a prince; he rallied his compatriots around him. In a few years, his Muslims conquered half the world. They plucked more souls from false gods, knocked down more idols, razed more pagan temples in fifteen years than the followers of Moses and Jesus Christ did in fifteen centuries. Muhammad was a great man. (Napoleon I 1998: 140–141)

A brilliant general and charismatic leader, Muhammad succeeded where Napoleon, condemned to end his days on a windswept island in the southern Atlantic, failed. Of course, admitted Napoleon, Muhammad told his troops that beautiful virgins awaited them in heaven, but it was in order to motivate them. And he was right to do so: his military successes prove it. The former emperor was even ready to defend polygamy as a means of combating racism (since the children of women from different backgrounds and races would grow up as brothers under one roof) and to recommend its use to eradicate racism in the French colonies and promote the liberty of black subjects (1998: 153).

Adolf A. Weinman, an American sculptor born in Germany, provided a visual expression of Muhammad as a legislator in the frieze he sculpted in 1935 for the US Supreme Court's courtroom. The Prophet appears among the 18 great legislators honored, ranging from Hammurabi to John Marshall, a Supreme Court judge, and including Moses, Confucius and Napoleon. Muhammad holds an open Koran in his left hand and a sword in his right (as do many other legislators in the frieze).

There are a number of examples of nineteenth- and twentieth-century portraits of Muhammad as a great legislator and statesman. They were used to pay homage to the man and to those who venerated him, all the while avoiding the central question: the religious role of the Prophet. This would change in the twentieth century.

In the twentieth century, the Prophet appeared in another debate dividing the Catholic Church, concerning the universality of the Christian message and the proper attitude to adopt towards adherents to other faiths. While this issue raises a number of questions, the most important concerns the role of the Savior in the Christian religion: are only Catholics destined for Heaven or can others be saved? Certainly, this debate was not new: in the sixteenth century, some Christians affirmed that good Muslims and Jews could go to Heaven by following their own faith (Schwartz 2008; Tolan 2012). This subject assumed a particular intensity after the Holocaust, leading the Catholic Church to reflect on the right attitude to adopt towards other religions. On October 28, 1965, Pope Paul VI announced the *Nostra aetate*, a declaration of the Church's relationships with non-Christian religions (Vatican 1965). While the Pope mostly focused on Judaism, he also mentioned Hinduism and Buddhism as well as Islam. "The Church regards Muslims with esteem," the Pope affirmed, listing the points of commonality in doctrine, practice and morality between the two religions. Yet there was no mention of Muhammad, a discreet but problematic omission.

Yet this subject could not be avoided in the respectful dialogue that the Pope hoped to have with Muslims. Louis Massignon (1883–1962), a professor at the Collège de France, was a brilliant Arabist and a fervent Catholic. He respected and was fascinated by Islam, in particular its mystical currents. For him, Muhammad was sincere, divinely inspired, preached the truth and led his people to belief in one supreme God. But while he was not a false prophet, he was a "negative prophet" who was unable to arrive at the supreme truth of Christianity (Waardenburg 1969: 141–8).

Other Catholic authors go further, calling Muhammad a prophet and demanding that Christians recognize him as such. William Montgomery Watt, the author of an important scholarly biography of the Prophet, affirms that Christians who want to engage in dialogue with Muslims "should reject the distortions of the medieval image of Islam and should develop a positive appreciation of its values. This involves accepting Muhammad as a religious leader through whom God has worked, and that is tantamount to holding that he is in some sense a prophet" (Watt 1991: 148).

The Swiss Catholic theologian Hans Küng is responsible for the most developed theological argument in favor of the recognition of Muhammad as a Prophet by the Church. Küng shows how the Church's doctrine concerning the salvation of non-Christians has evolved over the centuries. The Council of Florence (1441) had declared that no one outside the Catholic Church could be saved and that infidels would burn in hell. But in 1962, the Second Vatican Council stated that "the plan of salvation also includes those who acknowledge the Creator, in the first place amongst whom are the Muslims; these profess to hold the faith of Abraham, and together with us they adore the one, merciful God, mankind's judge on the last day" (Vatican 1962). Those outside the Church, and among them Muslims,

could attain eternal salvation. But Küng expressed regret at the fact that Vatican
II, despite its respect for Islam and Muslims, did not mention Muhammad by
name. He compares the Islamic prophet to those in the Old Testament: like them,
Muhammad draws his authority not from his role as a statesman, but via his special
relationship to God. Like the Jewish prophets, he announces God's message to his
people and asks that they submit to his divine will. In short, he resembles these
past prophets. He concludes:

> In truth, Muhammad was and is for persons in the Arabian world, and for many
> others, *the* religious reformer, lawgiver, and leader; the prophet *per se*. Basically
> Muhammad, who never claimed to be anything more than a human being, is
> more to those who follow him than a prophet is to us: he is a model for the mode
> of life that Islam strives to be. If the Catholic Church, according to the Vatican II
> "Declaration on Non-Christian Religions," "regards with esteem the Muslims,"
> then the same church must also respect the one whose name is embarrassingly
> absent from the same declaration, although he and he alone led the Muslims
> to pray to this one God, for through him this God "has spoken to humanity":
> Muhammad the prophet. (Küng 1992: 167, emphasis in original)

In this brief study, which shows how the Prophet Muhammad has been exploited
in European controversies, we may notice that the historian's work (or, in the
contemporary era, the sociologist's) consists not in applauding those who appear
to be "tolerant" and chastising those who do not, but in deconstructing images
in order to reveal their rhetorical strategies and understand what is at stake.
Islam, seen from Europe, often appears as a *frère ennemi*: a neighbor and rival
with roots in a common heritage of Greco-Roman-Persian Antiquity and Jewish
monotheism. When European Christians reflect on Islam as a religion, they
often focus on the figure of the Prophet, considering him either the embodiment
of error or a symbol of religious freedom and tolerance. European discourse
concerning Muhammad can be seen as a deforming mirror: it tells us more about
the hopes and fears of Europeans than about this elusive character from seventh-
century Arabia.

References

Akbari, S-C. 2009. *Idols in the East: European Representations of Islam and the
    Orient, 1100–1450*. Ithaca, NY: Cornell University Press.
Anderson, A. 1997. *The Treatise of the Three Imposters and the Problem of the
    Enlightenment*. Lanham, MD: Rowman & Littlefield.
Berti, S., Charles-Daubert, F. and Popkin, R. (eds) 1996. *Heterodoxy, Spinozism,
    and Free Thought in Early-Eighteenth-Century Europe: Studies on the "Traité
    des trois imposteurs"*. Dordrecht: Kluwer Academic Publishers.
Boulainvilliers, H. 1730. *La vie de Mahomed*. Amsterdam: P. Humbert.

Carnoy-Torab, D. 2006. "Regards sur l'islam, de l'âge classique aux Lumières," in M. Arkoun (ed.), *L'Histoire de l'islam et des musulmans en France*. Paris: Albin Michel, 436–74.

Flori, J. 2006. "Les croisades et leur signification idéologique," in M. Arkoun (ed.), *L'Histoire de l'islam et des musulmans en France*. Paris: Albin Michel, 96–117.

Francisco, A. 2007. *Martin Luther and Islam: A Study in Sixteenth-Century Polemics and Apologetics*. Leiden: Brill.

Gay-Canton, R. 2010. "Lorsque Muḥammad orne les autels. Sur l'utilisation de la théologie islamique dans la controverse autour de l'Immaculée Conception de la fin du XIVe au début du XVIIIe siècle," *Revue des Sciences Philosophiques et Théologiques*, 2(94), 201–48.

Houdas, O. and Marçais, W. 1977. *Les traditions islamiques*, vol. 3. Paris: J. Maisonneuve.

Küng, H. 1992. "Christianity and World Religions: Dialogue with Islam," in L. Swidler (ed.), *Muslims in Dialogue: The Evolution of A Dialogue*. Lewiston, NY: Edwin Mellen Press, 161–75.

Napoleon I. 1998. *Campagnes d'Egypte et de Syrie*. Paris: Imprimerie Nationale.

Pastoret, E. 1787. *Zoroastre, Confucius et Mahomet, comparés comme sectaires, législateurs, et moralistes; avec le tableau de leurs dogmes, de leurs lois et de leur morale*. Paris: Buisson.

Schwartz, S. 2008. *All Can Be Saved: Religious Tolerance and Salvation in the Iberian Atlantic World*. New Haven, CT: Yale University Press.

Tolan, J. 2002. *Saracens: Islam in the Medieval European Imagination*. New York: Columbia University Press.

Tolan, J. 2006. "Les récits de vie de Mahomet," in M. Arkoun (ed.), *L'Histoire de l'islam et des musulmans en France*. Paris: Albin Michel, 156–77.

Tolan, J. 2010. "European Accounts of Muhammad's Life," in J. Brockopp (ed.), *Cambridge Companion to Muhammad*. Cambridge: Cambridge University Press, 226–50.

Tolan, J. 2012. "Tra il diavolo di Rustico e il ninferno d'Alibech: Muslims and Jews in Boccaccio's Decameron," in A. Eisenbeiß et L. Saurma-Jeltsch (eds), *Images of Otherness in Medieval and Early Modern Times: Exclusion, Inclusion and Assimilation*. Berlin and Munich: Deutscher Kunstverlag, 133–41.

Vatican. 1962. "*Lumen Gentium*," http://www.vatican.va/archive/hist_councils/ii_vatican_council/documents/vat-ii_const_19641121_lumen-gentium_fr.html.

Vatican. 1965. "*Nostra Aetate*," October 28. http://www.vatican.va/archive/hist_councils/ii_vatican_council/documents/vat-ii_decl_19651028_nostra-aetate_fr.html.

Waardenburg, J-J. 1969. *Islam dans le miroir de l'Occident; comment quelques orientalistes occidentaux se sont penchés sur l'Islam et se sont formé une image de cette religion*. Paris: Mouton.

Watt, W-M. 1991. *Muslim-Christian Encounters: Perceptions and Misperceptions.* London: Routledge.

Wilders, G. 2011. "Geert Wilders Weblog," March 30, http://www.geertwilders. nl/index.php/component/content/article/80-geertwildersnl/1741-time-to-unmask-muhammad-by-geert-wilders.

Chapter 10

The Case of the Danish Cartoons Controversy: The Paradox of Civility

Sune Lægaard

The Plurality of Controversies

It is common to talk of "the Danish cartoons controversy" (Klausen 2009; Lindekilde, Mouritsen and Zapata-Barrero 2009). However, it is important to note that the chain of events usually referred to under this label, which was set in motion by the publication of 12 drawings under the title "the face of Muhammad" by the Danish daily *Jyllands-Posten* in September 2005, and the disagreements and issues debated in this context, in fact comprised *several* controversies. At least, this is the case if one describes and individuates controversies on the basis of what they are *about*, what their *occasion* is and *among whom* they take place. If one looks at public controversies in these terms, the Danish cartoons controversy fragments into several distinct, albeit overlapping and mutually reinforcing, controversies.

The label "cartoons controversy" is misleading, since much of the debate usually subsumed under this label did not mainly concern the Muhammad cartoons or their *publication*. In Denmark, most of the debate centered on something else entirely, namely Muslim *reactions* to the publication of the cartoons. Many Muslims found the cartoons controversial and wanted to discuss their publication. But as events unfolded in Denmark, it was not the publication that became the main issue in the ensuing debates, but the actual or perceived reactions to it by Muslims.

Thus, we already have two different agendas generating different perspectives on the controversy. In the narrow Danish national perspective, the main focus was on Muslim reactions. Most people in Denmark – especially, but not only, defenders of *Jyllands-Posten* – did not refer to the controversy as "the cartoons controversy," but as "the Muhammad crisis." This choice of label implies that the problem was with the Muslims and the way they venerate their prophet, not the publication of the cartoons. In a broader perspective, however, most non-Danish observers saw the controversy as centering on the publication and deliberate republication of the cartoons across Europe.

Therefore, not only do we have different controversies depending on what the *object* of controversy is, we also have different *scopes* of controversy. One might distinguish between the national scope, in which participants were members of the Danish public, and the transnational scope, in which different individuals, groups, organizations and states constituted a transnational public in relation to a controversy that neither respected national borders nor agendas set by national authorities or opinion makers.

In this chapter, I mainly focus on the narrower controversy within Denmark. This is not because the broader controversy is not interesting (Lægaard 2010), but because I want to draw attention to a third distinction between different *terms* of the controversy, which emerges clearly in the national perspective. Yet, once identified, this aspect of the controversy is arguably also relevant in a transnational perspective.

By the "terms" of the controversy, I am referring to the way in which the object of debate was framed and what was understood to be at stake; for example, the discussion of whether the publication of the cartoons was acceptable or not. This question can be understood in different ways. One way in which it was interpreted both by some critics and some defenders of the publication was as an issue of free speech, which in turn was taken to be a legal issue concerning the coercively enforceable limits of public utterances; in other words, it became a question of what was to be permitted by the law, and hence also what should be criminalized and punishable by the state.

Many defenders of *Jyllands-Posten*'s right to publish the cartoons took this legal framing for granted. This provided them with a classical liberal platform for rejecting all criticism of the publication, since these were understood – sometimes correctly – as demands for legal restrictions of free speech. This understanding was to some extent reflected on the side of the critics. Some Danish Muslims and sympathizers reported the newspaper to the police for having violated the clauses in the Danish penal code which criminalize speech that publicly mocks or degrades the religious beliefs or worship of legal religious communities, or threatens, insults or degrades a group of persons due to their faith (Lægaard 2007a: 485–6). In effect, this made the controversy a matter of whether the newspaper should be legally sanctioned for the publication. In the end, the Director of Public Prosecutions rejected the claim that the publication was in breach of Danish hate speech and blasphemy provisions, so the publication was never tried in court on these counts. *Jyllands-Posten* was subsequently tried for breach of individual defamation provisions and was found not guilty, since the cartoons were not found to defame specific individual Muslims.

This legal framing of the controversy persisted and was reinforced when various transnational Islamic actors demanded that Denmark and other European states enforce stricter limits on free speech. This campaign continued through the infamous process leading up to the Durban II UN World Conference Against Racism in Geneva in 2009, during which the Organisation of the Islamic Conference demanded the introduction and enforcement of bans on blasphemy. Against this background, the legal framing of the issues at stake in the cartoons controversy remained dominant.

My point is that even though the controversy over legal limits on free speech was real and important, it was not the only and was perhaps not the most important or interesting aspect of the cartoons controversy. The legal framing tended to displace other ways of understanding what was at stake in the controversy and led to a widespread misunderstanding and misrepresentation of some of the criticisms of the publication of the cartoons. I therefore want to draw attention to a third distinction: just as there are different controversies depending on what we take as the object and scope, there are also different controversies depending on whether the ensuing disagreements and confrontations are framed in legal or non-legal terms.

Here, I focus on the non-legal terms of the cartoons controversy and consider in more detail how one might understand what was at stake in the controversy thus framed. I propose that an important part of the non-legal controversy can be understood by interpreting it in terms of the concept of "civility." I sketch an understanding of civility as a social-theoretical concept and an analytical category. Since the concept thus employed is analytical, a theoretical interpretation of the controversy in terms of civility still leaves the normative issues open. The concept of civility thus provides a conceptual framework for understanding the controversy and for placing different views represented in it rather than a normative position in the debate. My claim is that the introduction of this analytical perspective gives a more complete picture of what was actually at stake in the cartoons controversy, which exemplifies a more general theoretical point relevant to the understanding of other public controversies.

I further suggest that the introduction of the concept of civility makes visible how some views and interventions in the controversy were displaced or misrepresented, giving defenders of *Jyllands-Posten* a rhetorical advantage that allowed them to dominate the controversy, at least in Denmark. But the introduction of the concept of civility is not a way of redeeming or siding with the critics who are thus displaced or misrepresented. Indeed, I want to further suggest that the very framing of the debate in terms of civility, even if not displaced or misrepresented, leads to a problem due to the discursive logic of civility claims. This is what I call "the paradox of civility." The paradox (which might not be a paradox in the strict philosophical sense) is a practical problem facing any attempt by minority groups to raise issues of civility. I suggest that the paradox, besides being in itself an interesting discursive phenomenon, might have empirical explanatory significance, since the logic of claims of civility might explain some of the dynamics in the cartoons controversy and perhaps other public controversies about Islam in Europe as well.[1]

---

1   The concept of civility is here introduced as an analytical category for the interpretation of controversies viewed in a *discursive* perspective, i.e. with a focus on the claims staked and the arguments and positions formulated as part of the controversy. This discursive perspective differs from other perspectives one might adopt, e.g. the social movements perspective adopted by Klausen (2009). These and other perspectives need not be incompatible or competitive; in fact, they may arguably complement each other. One reason for focusing on a discursive perspective in relation to the cartoons controversy is that the cartoons were themselves discursive acts with a performative function and meaning. Thus, even if a discursive perspective is not exhaustive, it is arguably indispensable in a case like this.

The Concept of Civility

One way to approach the concept of civility is by contrasting it with other types of relationships and the attitudes characteristic hereof. In a very crude and simplistic conceptualization of the types of relationships in which citizens of modern states stand, there is a distinction between "vertical" relations between citizens and political institutions, and "horizontal" relations among citizens. Both are regulated by legal rights and duties; the relations between citizens and state by public law and the relations between citizens by private law. But these legal incidents do not exhaust the relations in question. In addition to the legal rights and duties of citizens in relation to their state, they might also relate to the state in terms of loyalty and support (or mistrust and opposition). And citizens do not approach each other only in terms of rights claims, but also interact in social spaces which are either carved out by the legal framework in a way that leaves the participants discretion in terms of how they choose to interact, or in which the invocation of legal rights and duties is considered either irrelevant or inappropriate.

"Civility" has been proposed as a label for the non-legal, horizontal type of relationship between members of a society, or as the attitude required in or appropriate to this relationship, which may even be elevated to the status of a civic virtue. Benjamin Barber, for instance, used the concept to denote the virtue characteristic of common activity and engagement in a republican ideal of "strong democracy," in which citizens associate and cooperate in a spirit of reciprocal empathy and respect (1984: 223). Barber contrasted civility as a style of social interaction with, on the one hand, the totalitarian demand for full unity between citizens and, on the other, a form of purely instrumental and residual democracy in which citizens can in principle completely disengage from each other and only interact though institutions. Whatever one may think of these different conceptions of democracy, the concept of civility can be abstracted from Barber's particular vision. One can then derive the idea that civility is the mode of interaction characteristic of a social space in which people are strangers rather than intimates, but in which they need to interact, engage and cooperate with one another.

There is accordingly a close connection between the notions of civility and civil society as distinct both from the family and the state (Pérez-Díaz 2009). Civil society is usually defined as the sum of certain types of non-state institutions where strangers interact, and as such, it is an arena for civility, understood as non-legalized forms of interaction. But the relationship between civil society and civility may in fact be more intimate than this characterization supposes. It might be more appropriate to define civil society in terms of certain types of relations characterized by participants with specific social orientations rather than in contrast to the state and family understood as independently existing institutions (Akman 2012). Civil society is then defined as the set of relations where participants adopt what I will call a "civility stance" toward each other, meaning that they understand their relationship in civility terms, i.e. as a relation appropriately regulated on the basis of non-legal interpersonal norms. They accordingly form expectations of each other and assess one another's actions on the basis of an understanding of what is required or permitted by such norms. Civil society is then constituted by civility, rather than the former merely being the contingent arena where the latter is displayed.

Therefore, civility is both a way of highlighting the space in which the relationship takes place – which is neither intimate, as in family or personal associations, nor a fictional space of complete independence and disconnection – and of indicating the type of non-legally enforceable attitudes required for or appropriate in this type of relationship (Lægaard 2011: 86). On the most general level, being civil means engaging in social interactions with strangers in a non-violent way that is regulated by non-legislated and non-enforceable standards of conduct that facilitate cooperation. "Civility" may then denote this type of social relationship, the standards of conduct which govern it, or even the attitudes and dispositions of people engaging in civil interaction according to such standards.

It is crucial to appreciate the distinction between two different notions of civility: first, as a social-theoretical concept and analytical category used to conceptualize a certain type or mode of social interaction characterized by difference as well as a degree of mutual adjustment in order to facilitate necessary cooperation; and, second, what I will call specific *norms* of civility, that is, the concrete, although often inexplicit and unwritten, expectations and standards of social conduct that people take for granted in civil interactions or that they invoke in cases where they do not perceive the actual conduct to be sufficiently civil. My suggestion is that civility as an analytical category is helpful, since it provides us with an interpretative perspective in which we can identify and investigate a specific type of social coordination and the types of conflicts that arise within this type of relationship. These conflicts can then be understood as disagreements over the appropriate norms of civility in the case. Civility in the first sense is a *social-theoretical category*, whereas civility in the second sense denotes particular *normative views* about how this type or mode of social interaction should proceed.

These two senses of civility are often conflated or collapsed. To take one example, Karen Tracy criticizes the attempt to "refashion civility" as a communicative ideal according to which people should express opinions with self-restraint and sensitivity, and recognize that, in some circumstances, it is better to say nothing than to express a critical opinion. She argues that such communicative norms do not take seriously the fact that expressions of anger and outrage are essential to and legitimate in public life. Instead of civility, she proposes a communicative norm of "reasonable hostility," according to which "uncivil" expressions of emotion and anger are judged reasonable if they match the perceived wrong to which they respond (Tracy 2010: 203). My point is that Tracy is arguing against particular substantive norms of civility (which equate good communication with "niceness") rather than against the more general category of civility; in fact, her proposed norm of reasonable hostility is itself a specific candidate for what the appropriate norms of civility should be in specific cases.

The distinction between the analytical concept and specific norms of civility means that the former is not normative or evaluative. For this reason, although I agree with Akman's social orientation perspective, I think one should not load evaluative content into the notion of civility when considering it as a social-theoretical category. This is arguably what Akman does when he defines civility as "social actors' willingness for non-repressive engagement with others" (2012: 334). This is because "repression" can arguably only be distinguished from other sorts of social regulation on the basis of normative criteria. But in that case, the very designation of something as a civil mode of interaction becomes a positive evaluation of it. This is problematic, since there is bound to be disagreement over what the appropriate norms of civility are. It would be strange to say that a relationship is not one of civility because one disagrees with the norm of civility on which the participants rely; one would then bar oneself from using the analytical category in understanding the relationship and from raising the normative question as to whether this is an acceptable or justifiable norm of civility. Therefore, my proposal is to distinguish between two descriptive questions: first, is a relationship one of civility, which is a matter of the social orientation or "stance" of participants?; and, second, what are the norms of civility in the relationship on which participants rely or which they invoke? Furthermore, these two descriptive questions must in turn be kept distinct from a third, normative question: is the relationship acceptable when considered as a relationship of civility, which is a matter of the justifiability of the norm of civility relative to those involved in or affected by the relationship?[2]

The Cartoons Controversy: The Struggle over Norms of Civility

Given this concept of civility, I now suggest that an important aspect of the cartoons controversy concerned civility. As I previously mentioned, there was a legal aspect to this controversy. However, as I suggested, this was not its only, and perhaps not its major, theme.

Initially, many Danish Muslims were irritated and hurt by the publication of the cartoons and perhaps especially by the general debate about Muslims in Danish society; the cartoons became an important element in this debate, and reinforced and further polarized the positions of those involved. The first response by Danish Muslims and their sympathizers was a mixture of outrage, resignation and public protest, as evidenced in the large, peaceful demonstration in the City Hall Square

---

2   Here I merely note the normative question, which raises broader issues. Many theorists discuss civility not just as a practical necessity for social interaction, but also as a way of showing respect (Lægaard 2011: 86). Civility has, for instance, been advocated as a natural and necessary extension of liberal egalitarian citizenship, since the equality required by liberal egalitarianism cannot be secured by purely institutional and legally enforceable mechanisms, but also requires the inculcation of civility as a social virtue among citizens (Spinner 1994: Chapter 3; Kymlicka 1998: 188–9).

in Copenhagen shortly after the publication of the cartoons. Many people primarily thought of the cartoons as inappropriate, not just because of the precise nature of the drawings, but mainly because of the motives ascribed to *Jyllands-Posten*: even though the editor responsible for commissioning the cartoons, Flemming Rose, explicitly justified the publication in terms of concerns about free speech and what he called "self-censorship" out of fear of Muslim extremists, many Muslims and critics of the publication did not take this public justification very seriously (Klausen 2009: 17).

Jyllands-Posten has a history of support for restrictive immigration and integration policies, and is perceived by many of its opponents as conservative, provincial, nationalist and even xenophobic. Many of its critics therefore did not give much credence to the fact that Rose's arguments for publication were framed in distinctively liberal terms. Despite his statement that causing offense was not the publication's ultimate aim or even desire (quoted in Lindekilde, Mouritsen and Zapata-Barrero 2009: 291), it was interpreted by many as emanating from a wish to mock, ridicule and hurt Muslims. Much of the disapproval and dissatisfaction generated by the publication of the cartoons was due to such perceived attitudes. Thus, at least a part of the problem with the publication was that it was experienced as a symptom of a defective social relationship between *Jyllands-Posten*, serving as a representative or proxy for a broader segment of Danish society, including the government and the anti-multiculturalist parliamentary majority, and Danish Muslims.

Even though some radical or merely confused Danish Muslims went further in their objections and in the means they thought legitimate to right the perceived wrong, the vast majority of Danish Muslims was mainly concerned with and offended by the cartoons because of this perceived failure of civility by *Jyllands-Posten* and a significant part of Danish society toward Muslims. The main response from many Danish Muslims was to demand an apology from *Jyllands-Posten* (Klausen 2009: 33). This can be seen as an expression of the view that the problem was about mending a broken social relationship. Reporting the publication to the police for breaching the statutes criminalizing blasphemy and hate speech can also be seen, at least in part, as an attempt to gain recognition of this perceived incivility.

The main criticism of the publication from non-Muslim quarters in Denmark also focused on civility: the center-left progressive newspaper *Politiken* took the lead in criticizing the publication and framed the problem as a matter of "the tone" of the debate. Here, the controversy was explicitly not understood as a matter of legally enforceable limits on free speech, but as a concern that all responsible citizens should be polite, should restrain themselves and should consider the feelings of others, including Muslims.

Therefore, my claim is that an important aspect of the criticism of the publication of the cartoons concerned the lack of civility it was thought to both instantiate and represent. This means two things: first, one of the main aspects of this controversy concerned whether the kinds of views associated with the cartoons should be socially acceptable in Danish public debates, not whether they should be legal; and, second, to the extent that critics and defenders of the publication agreed on this framing of the controversy, they furthermore had different standards of civility about what should be socially acceptable in Danish public debates.

The interpretation of the cartoons controversy as partly a matter of civility differs from other interpretations, such as the claim that it was a "struggle for recognition" (Henkel 2010). The perspective of recognition is broader and often also involves the official stance of public authorities toward minorities struggling for recognition. Talk of recognition is often both unclear about whether the subject supposed to offer recognition is the state or some non-state actor, and what form of recognition is in question (Lægaard 2007b). The focus on civility is more precise, since it makes clear that the terms of the controversy concern non-legislated norms regulating social relations. Controversies over civility can of course be seen as part of broader struggles for recognition – but then civility is the immediate medium and point of contention, and (some form of) recognition the possible mediate aim of the minority engaging in the controversy.

Although there are some parallels, my distinction between the perspectives of legality and civility on the cartoons controversy is also different from the subsequently very popular and dominant distinction between censorship and self-censorship launched by Flemming Rose in the text that accompanied the cartoons. Censorship is of course a legal relationship and self-censorship is non-legal, but the differences are more important: whereas both legality and civility are analytical categories, "censorship" as well as "self-censorship" are *moralized* concepts. In a liberal Western context where concerns about free speech have a high prominence, censorship is considered inherently illiberal, oppressive and (all other things being equal) wrong. The use of the derived term "self-censorship" to describe forms of discursive self-restraint is therefore an implicit moral condemnation of the fact that people thus described withhold or refrain from making certain utterances.[3] Rose's conceptualization of the cartoons controversy in terms of "self-censorship" is not a neutral description, but a way of stacking the deck against proponents of self-restraint. An interpretation of the controversy in terms of civility does not engage in a similar covert *a priori* valuation, but simply provides a conceptual space for understanding that an aspect of the controversy concerned the applicable norms of civility. My theoretical interpretation in terms of civility leaves it open as to whether Rose or his critics were right, but provides a more transparent conceptual space to further discuss this normative issue.

The understanding of the controversy as (at least partly) a matter of civility was, however, to a large extent either misrepresented or displaced from the mainstream public debate. One reason for this was that Flemming Rose's initial framing of the

---

3   John Horton (2011) proposes a more fine-grained analysis, according to which the moral valence of self-censorship depends on how one understands the reference to the "self." Here, I am not engaging with this more abstract and general conceptual analysis. I merely say that at the discursive level, the use of the notion of "self-censorship" in the cartoons controversy seems to be moralized in the sense noted in the text.

publication as a matter of free speech was very successful and was reinforced by the filing of legal complaints. It was further supported by Prime Minister Anders Fogh Rasmussen's response to the request by 11 ambassadors from predominantly Muslim countries for a meeting to discuss what they considered "an on-going smear campaign in Danish public circles and media against Islam and Muslims," in which the cartoons were one of the examples to be discussed (Klausen 2009: 65). The Prime Minister refused to meet with the ambassadors, justifying his decision on the basis of the broad scope of the Danish freedom of expression, stating that as Prime Minister, he had no means of influencing the press. Whether or not this was the correct interpretation of the ambassadors' complaint, his response effectively froze the interpretation of the controversy as being about the legal limits of free speech.

This dominant understanding of the controversy gave the defenders of the cartoons a rhetorical advantage over Muslim demands for an apology and the concerns about the "tone" of the debate, such as that made by *Politiken*. These criticisms were represented as implying legal restrictions on free speech, which was now both elevated as an absolute liberal principle and a non-negotiable "Danish value." Thus, the dominant framing of the debate made it possible, on the one hand, to unite liberals and nationalists against Muslims and critics of *Jyllands-Posten*, and, on the other hand, to ignore the substance of an important part of the criticism of the publication.

In this way, the civility agenda, which was arguably a significant motivation for critics of the publication, was effectively either misrepresented or simply ignored in most of the Danish debate.[4] The introduction of the concept of civility as an interpretative framework makes it possible to see this dynamic of the controversy, which I think is interesting, both as a discursive phenomenon, as an expression of the interpretative power of different actors involved in the controversy and as a partial explanation of why some Muslims sought to enlist support from powerful Muslim allies abroad. But the focus on civility also makes more substantial issues salient about the normative content of civility, to which I now turn.

---

4 Note that this diagnosis of the cartoons controversy is distinct from, and does not presuppose the truth of, common claims about "the displacement of civility." There are two prominent understandings of what this means: 1) the increasing legalization of formerly legally unregulated relations, which has given rise to concerns about an extensive focus on rights instead of duties, as well as about the role of courts in society; 2) conservative laments over "the decline of civility" understood as a loss of earlier notions of obligation and responsibility which were allegedly tied to a society where everyone occupied specific and fixed social positions. Even though my diagnosis shares certain features with the former understanding of displacement, there is an important difference – I propose an *analytical* category which is meant to capture a *discursive* reality. Therefore, my analysis is silent on what the law actually says, or on what the law should say something about. And the second, conservative, notion of displacement is simply a specific (arguably both historically and normatively implausible) normative view about what the norms of civility should be, whereas my diagnosis is not normative in itself.

The Paradox of Civility?

If one adopts the interpretative perspective of civility and focuses on the aspects of the controversy that can be understood as contestations in terms of civility, it is clear that different norms of civility were in play. Some Muslims apparently held the view that Islam should be completely raised above criticism or ridicule. What is more interesting, from the point of view of civility, is that other Muslims and many of their non-Muslim sympathizers thought that people should in general be considerate and show respect for other members of society by not unnecessarily hurting their feelings, which, in this case, happened to be the feelings of members of a minority defined in religious terms. This is a conception of civility reminiscent of well-known notions of good manners and etiquette. In many social contexts, it is simply impolite, inappropriate and irrelevant to make religion an issue. Both a concern with respect for others as equal members of society and a more pragmatic need to facilitate social cooperation require people to restrain themselves and continue social interaction without making an issue of contentious and potentially hurtful subjects such as religion. If someone nevertheless insists on making religion an issue and even on mocking the religious beliefs of someone else, this is impolite, and an apology is usually appropriate in order to get the social relationship back on track.

Given this understanding of the objection to the publication, one might think that the opposite view – that the publication was not wrong or that it was even a good thing – would be a form of "civility nihilism," that is, a position which rejects the relevance or applicability of concerns about civility. But given my distinction between the general concept of civility and specific norms of civility, this conclusion is imprecise. In fact, the defenders of the publication also assumed certain norms of civility – they just happened to be different.[5]

If an important part of Danish Muslims' criticisms of the publication were attempts to make it an issue of incivility, the interesting thing is that this reaction was itself taken to be *un*civil by many Danes and defenders of the cartoons and the newspaper's right to publish them. Thus, two discursive changes took place during the cartoons controversy: first, the *object* of the debate was shifted from the publication of the cartoons to Muslim reactions to it; and, second, while many Muslims wanted to publicly thematize and question the civility of the publication, the fact that they did this in turn exposed *disagreements* about the applicable norms of civility. These two changes together shifted the issue from being one of social regulation and reconciliation *within* a social group assumed to be united by norms of civility (i.e. the Danish public) to one where Danish Muslims were represented

---

5   Elsewhere (Lægaard 2011), I have discussed a distinction between public and private civility: the former concerns political debates and the latter ordinary social interactions, the point being that different norms of civility are appropriate in each type of context. This philosophical distinction is different from, but might be partially mapped onto, the more discursive dynamics of civility that I discuss in the present chapter.

as uncivil because of their criticisms and as outside the Danish consensus on norms of civility.

This discursive shift is in itself interesting and might contribute to a fuller understanding and explanation of how the controversy developed. But the shift can itself be understood and explained as an effect of what I will call the discursive logic of civility claims. I will use this case to briefly sketch a broader picture of how civility claims function and how this logic was at play in the cartoons controversy.

Norms of civility are omnipresent and inevitable in any social context. Such norms serve as a means of fixing expectations and as recourse for social coordination, regulation and sanction; if unacceptable behavior takes place, norms of civility can be invoked to point this out and to get the interaction back on track. This sort of social coordination requires that participants adopt the "civility stance" I introduced earlier. This means that they view social coordination in terms of civility, as something amenable to social regulation on the basis of applicable norms of civility, form expectations and assess the actions of others on the basis of an understanding of what is required or permitted by such norms, and are willing to comply with applicable norms. But in order for this to work, one of three things must occur: either there has to be agreement (often implicit, informal and even tacit) on the applicable norms of civility, in which case social regulation is relatively easy and automatic; if this is not the case, social regulation can be achieved if one group of people has the interpretative authority and social power to determine which norm should be in force and enforce it against dissenters, for example, by social pressure and the marginalization of non-compliers; alternatively, the achievement of social coordination can be made the aim of a social process of negotiation. This requires that people are willing to enter into a negotiation in relation to appropriate norms of civility, which then have to be made explicit and thematized, and to accept some compromise that results from this negotiation.

The cartoons controversy seen in the perspective of civility might have begun, at least for some critics of the publication, as a simple case of trying to draw attention to a perceived incivility and as a request for an appropriate social sanction of the uncivil behavior. The criticisms then started out in the first of the three scenarios sketched above. However, it quickly became apparent that in fact there was no agreement on the applicable norms of civility or their interpretation. The exposure of this normative disagreement led to a debate in Danish society over the applicable norms of civility. But this was not a debate oriented toward achieving an inclusive consensus and compromise, as in the third scenario sketched above. What transpired was instead a classical exclusionary "us versus them" exercise, where being Danish was equated with the wholehearted acceptance of a radical and absolute value of free speech, and Muslims were represented as un-Danish because of their failure to accept this non-negotiable national value (for a discussion of how liberal values such as free speech can be invoked in an exclusionary manner, see Lægaard 2007c). So, rather than highlighting *Jyllands-Posten*'s publication of the cartoons as a case of incivility, the reactions by Muslims and their sympathizers had a completely different effect: instead of managing to invoke a shared norm of civility to sanction the newspaper, Muslims, by their very attempt to do this, placed themselves outside the apparent consensus on norms of civility among influential sections of Danish society. Their very objection to the publication was widely seen as an act whereby they positioned themselves outside the Danish social consensus.

The paradox of this dynamic is that norms of civility are first of all integrative, both in their ordinary function and in terms of the aims of people adopting a civility stance: by being civil to one another, we both facilitate social cooperation and express a more general respect for each other as equal members of society. The act of appealing to a norm of civility in some social relationship expresses a drive for inclusion and a wish to be a part of a common scheme of social cooperation. When one adopts a civility stance in relation to some act or interaction, this assumes that there exists a shared social relationship governed by some norm of civility to which it is possible to appeal. The fact that I adopt a civility stance toward an act signals my belief that there is a common scheme of social cooperation between me and the agent performing the act in question, and that the basis for agreeing on a civil resolution is thereby already present in our scheme of cooperation. The civility interpretation of the cartoons controversy accordingly highlights that an important aspect of the controversy in Denmark centered on the terms of social integration, not in the sense of the legal requirements on immigrants to integrate, for example, by learning the language, passing tests and getting a job, but in the sense of what it should mean to be a member of the Danish public in a broad social sense. And to the extent that the civility interpretation captures the objections of Danish Muslims to the publication, the cartoons controversy can be understood as a contestation over the terms of social integration which signals a drive for social inclusion on the part of at least some Danish Muslims and a belief that they are part of Danish society. But as it turned out, this contestation did not take the form of a negotiation aimed at mutual understanding and consensus; rather, the questioning of the civility of the cartoons was met with an uncompromising attitude that rejected any accommodation or negotiation and served as an occasion for conjuring up a reified idea of hitherto unknown "Danish values" defined in a way that left Muslims with the equally unpalatable options of complete acceptance or symbolic exclusion.[6]

Accordingly, the discursive logic of civility claims shows how the drive for inclusion can be turned into exclusion: because any contestation of an act as an incivility has to take place in a social space which is itself governed by norms of civility, the attempt by some minority group, such as Muslims, to challenge an

---

6 My claim that Muslims were to some extent excluded from the Danish public in virtue of their contestation of the norms of civility is only about symbolic exclusion. I am not implying anything about whether further effects followed from this – in fact, it seems that the cartoons controversy did not lead to significant increases in discrimination against Muslims in Denmark. But even if this is so, one may still find symbolic exclusion problematic in itself.

act in terms of civility always runs the risk of exposing the challenging group rather than the act they seek to challenge if its civility claim runs counter to the reigning conception of civility or can be effectively represented as such. In that case, making a given act an issue of civility does not succeed as a reconciliatory gesture that supports or mends social cooperation or signals a drive for inclusion, but rather appears as a revolutionary rupture signaling the rejection of the existing scheme of social cooperation – in effect, the most uncivil form of behavior.

Conclusion

In this chapter, I have proposed that adopting a civility perspective is a fruitful way to approach the cartoons controversy. I have explained the concept of civility and have illustrated how aspects of this controversy involved contestations over civility, and how an important part of the dynamics of the controversy concerned the displacement or misrepresentation of the civility aspect. This exemplifies what I believe to be a more general point about public controversies, namely that an important element, and often the most important element, of any controversy is a meta-controversy over what the *terms* of the controversy are; public controversies are often centrally about what it is that is controversial and how it should be framed and debated. This feature of controversies makes a civility perspective especially interesting because it exposes the logic of civility claims: the very norms of civility that are contested will often make the act of contestation problematic. But one can only appreciate this important aspect by availing oneself of a theoretical framework that can conceptualize different framings of controversies. The civility perspective is one such analytical and interpretative category which I have argued is useful in this way in relation to the cartoons controversy.

References

Akman, A. 2012. "Beyond the Objectivist Conception of Civil Society: Social Actors, Civility and Self-limitation," *Political Studies*, 60(2), 321–40.

Barber, B.R. 1984. *Strong Democracy: Participatory Politics for a New Age*. Berkeley: University of California Press.

Henkel, H. 2010. "Contesting Danish Civility: The Cartoon Crisis as Transitional Drama," in K.F. Olwig and K. Paerregaard (eds), *The Question of Integration*. Newcastle: Cambridge Scholars Publishing, 129–48.

Horton, J. 2011. "Self-censorship," *Res Publica*, 17(1), 91–106.

Klausen, J. 2009. *The Cartoons that Shook the World*. New Haven, CT: Yale University Press.

Kymlicka, W. 1998. "Ethnic Associations and Democratic Citizenship," in A. Gutmann (ed.), *Freedom of Association*. Princeton, NJ: Princeton University Press, 177–213.

Lægaard, S. 2007a. "The Cartoon Controversy: Offence, Identity, Oppression?" *Political Studies*, 55(3), 481–98.

Lægaard, S. 2007b. "The Cartoon Controversy as a Case of Multicultural Recognition," *Contemporary Politics*, 13(2), 147–64.

Lægaard, S. 2007c. "Liberal Nationalism and the Nationalisation of Liberal Values," *Nations and Nationalism*, 13(1), 37–55.

Lægaard, S. 2010. "Normative Significance of Transnationalism? The Case of the Danish Cartoons Controversy," *Ethics & Global Politics*, 3(2), 101–21, available at: http://www.ethicsandglobalpolitics.net/index.php/egp/article/view/1977.

Lægaard, S. 2011. "A Multicultural Social Ethos: Tolerance, Respect, or Civility?" in G. Calder and E. Ceva (eds), *Diversity in Europe: Dilemmas of Differential Treatment in Theory and Practice*. Abingdon: Routledge, 81–96.

Lindekilde, L., Mouritsen, P. and Zapata-Barrero, R. (eds) 2009. *The Muhammad Cartoons Controversy in Comparative Perspective*, special issue of *Ethnicities*, 9(3).

Pérez-Díaz, V. 2009. "Markets as Conversations: Markets' Contributions to Civility, the Public Sphere and Civil Society at Large," in V. Pérez-Díaz (ed.), *Markets and Civil Society: The European Experience in Contemporary Perspective*. New York: Berghahn Books, 27–76.

Spinner, J. 1994. *The Boundaries of Citizenship: Race, Ethnicity, and Nationality in the Liberal State*. Baltimore, MD: Johns Hopkins University Press.

Tracy, K. 2010. *Challenges of Ordinary Democracy: A Case Study in Deliberation and Dissent*. University Park: University of Pennsylvania Press.

COLOR PLATES

Figure 5.1 Sami Mousavi and Paulo Porteghesi, the Cultural Centre of Rome, Italy, 1995 @ photo Nebahat Avcioglu

Figure 5.2 Breitman and Breitman, The Westermoskee, Amsterdam, Netherlands, 2010 @ Architects Breitman and Breitman

Figure 5.3   Paul Böhm The Cologne Mosque, Cologne, Germany, 2010 @ photo DITIB

Figure 9.1   French translation of Boccacio, De casibus, BNF MS Français
226, f. 243 (XVe s.)

Figure 9.2   Mahomet, the impostor, and Calvin, Hell's seducer, in an almanac. Recueil. Collection Michel Hennin. Estampes relatives à l'Histoire de France. Tome 63, Pièces 5542-5601, période : 1687

Chapter 11

Halal Arts: Censorship or Creative Ethical Practice?

Jeanette S. Jouili

The idea that Islam, and in particular Islamic movements, have a vexed relationship with cultural heritage, artistic creativity, irony and laughter has been discussed in media outlets in Europe and North America since at least the 1990s. Starting with Khomeini's fatwa against Salman Rushdie's novel *The Satanic Verses*, the rate of these types of public affairs has accelerated since 2001: the destruction of the Buddha statues in Bamiyan by the Taliban, the Danish cartoons affair of 2006 and the most recent violence caused by a YouTube film about Islam's Prophet, to name just a few, have bolstered ideas about the incompatibility of Islamism and creative freedom. Those protesting against Salman Rushdie, the cartoons or the YouTube film are often placed outside modernity, in line with a modernist teleological narrative that equates arts and artistic freedom with progress and modernity.

The emergence of an Islamic cultural and artistic scene has therefore been welcomed by activists and public servants as an opportunity to show a "different," "moderate" and thus more "modern" face of Islam.[1] For scholars, too, the increasingly cultural orientation of Islamic movements and the subsequent important transformations of contemporary Islamic (and Muslim) cultural practices have become an attractive topic.[2] At times, however, scholarship cannot fully escape readings that reiterate the teleological progress narrative of the arts, modernity and freedom, in which Islamic modernity takes a stance in endorsing culture and arts.[3] My take in this chapter is slightly different: I try to understand what exactly is at stake for pious practitioners and their audiences

---

1 Not only religious Islamic art productions, but artistic and cultural expressions from the "Muslim world" have been exposed, curated and staged increasingly after 9/11 in order to enrich the Western understanding of Islam (e.g. Swedenburg 2004; Flood 2007; Winegar 2008b).

2 See notably Boubekeur 2007; LeVine 2008; van Nieuwkerk 2008; 2011; Winegar 2008a; El-Asri 2010.

3 These positions occur notably when working within the framework of "post-Islamism," as formulated by Olivier Roy (2004) or Patrick Haenni (2002). For these scholars, post-Islamism delineates a "liberalization" of Islamic movements. This notion, which equally reflects a normative (teleological) understanding of modernity, implies practices which increasingly follow the logic of liberal consumer capitalism, as well a general individualization and privatization of religion.

in the project of building a space for artistic expression in line with Islamic ethics (hence the term halal arts). I ask the following question: what kinds of negotiations, reflections and forms of discipline accompany this project? The emergence of halal arts is a critical reaction to omnipresent secular mass culture deemed to be destructive to the cultivation of a pious self, but which at the same time has shaped the understanding of younger generations of Muslims of the role of culture. Rather than dismissing mass culture altogether, its proponents intend halal arts to be an alternative to secular arts and entertainment. Whether explicitly addressing pious subjects or not, this Islamically correct art seeks to provide permissible entertainment, notably by avoiding vulgarity, illegitimate content and conduct. But because the halal–*haram* boundary is not so clearly defined as it may seem, pious artists often need to reflect and negotiate where precisely the boundaries of the licit lie. In this endeavor, not only is the authorization by religious scholars crucial, but so too is the audience's reaction.[4] This attentiveness to the sensibilities of the Muslim audience puts the artist in an interesting position in relation to his audience. Because pious Muslim artists openly acknowledge that they do not want to transgress limits and taboos, halal arts are at times perceived by secular art practitioners or observers as a form of "artistic censorship" and are therefore compared to the other forms of anti-arts mentioned above and are consequently seen as being at odds with the ideal of the "autonomy of the arts."

How then can we answer these questions, how can we grasp the normativity of this artistic project without reading it through the binary opposition of freedom versus censorship? In order to tackle these issues, I discuss some of my findings from my research on the Islamic performing arts and music scene in European urban contexts (notably in France and the UK).[5] In most cases, those involved in halal arts are lay artists, who form an underground scene known only within Muslim circles. While this small "scene" is nonetheless highly diverse and in many ways fragmented,[6] I focus here on some of its common features, mainly with regard to its emphasis on the necessity to find legitimate Islamic artistic expression in terms of content, form and the aspects surrounding its performance. The second part of the chapter challenges prevalent modern understandings of aesthetic autonomy and shows how the Muslim art practitioners I work with offer a different account of aesthetics, one intrinsically linked to ethics. This, I argue, is

---

4   Many artists' webpages long contained links to religious scholars who endorse the possibility of artistic expression, which are licit from an Islamic perspective.

5   In this research I have looked at traditional and modernized nasheed singers and bands, Islamic pop and hip-hop bands, spoken poetry, theater and stand-up comedy.

6   The artists were affiliated with a range of different Islamic groups or movements, Sunni and Shi'a, Sufi or orthodox, more assertive political or explicitly non-political piety movements. They are equally fragmented around ethnicity and race. In France, they are mainly Muslims of Maghrebi origin, while in the UK, next to a South Asian majority, Afro-Caribbean and white converts are also strongly represented in this scene.

a central notion, which allows us to grasp the significance of halal arts for many young pious Muslims today.[7]

Artistic Expressions and Normativity

When talking to these pious practitioners of art, the concern for producing a form of music or performance that respects Islamic standards in content, form and performance is always present. Artists constantly reflect on how to best bring Islamic norms and ethics into their artistic expression, and this effort is reflected in wide-ranging ways and on many levels in their artistic choices.

One of the most basic conditions that the artists mention is that their arts must convey appropriate content: the content or "the message," as they put it, is the very reason for doing what they do. All artists insist in similar ways that the message is the core of their work; consequently, the particular genre through which the message is conveyed is often described by the artists as a mere "tool" – albeit an important one, as it has to guarantee an adequate and successful transmission of that message, and should neither distract from nor contradict the message, as I discuss below. In regard to the specific content, Islamic artistic projects cover a wide range of issues. The artists generally emphasize the importance of promoting ethical messages, from piety and God-consciousness to morality and sincerity in human relations, to social and political justice. Many of the artistic activities I studied engage in explicitly "pious" arts, like singers who perform -*nasheed* songs that praise God and the Prophet (whether in a traditional or pop music form) or Islamic theater groups that perform plays with a clearly pious Islamic message. The concern for the political state of the global *umma* is another valuable message that defines the artistic projects I studied. Frequently evoked topics are connected to the plight of the Muslim community worldwide, whether in Bosnia, Palestine or Iraq, but also stigmatized Muslim minorities in the West. Many other cultural and artistic productions comprise a civil education for the Muslim community, which the artists consider as plagued by social ills such as drug consumption, criminality and extremism, but also practices that are often denounced in the media, such as forced marriages or so-called honor killings. These societal ills are often explained as a consequence of social marginalization and/or the lack of a sound knowledge of religion. The lyrics and narratives seek to raise awareness of "authentic" Islam and encourage Muslims to find their place as citizens in society without abandoning their identity and religious practice, to fight racism and Islamophobia, and to become politically and socially active. At times, these messages are articulated in a way that is not explicitly Islamic, but reflects a broader social or political concern.

---

7   While many pious artists use the term "halal," others do not, or stopped at one point labeling their artistic activity with this term. However, all the pious Muslim artists I worked with do insist on aspiring to produce an artistic expression that respects Islamic standards of normativity.

If many of the messages of halal arts are therefore inherently serious, not all are, as one can see notably in certain stand-up comedy shows that are merely entertaining, albeit with the minimum limit of not including insults, blasphemy or vulgarity.

Whereas the legitimacy of the content can be identified relatively easily, it appears that, for the artist, the question of form is much more challenging as it is the form rather than the message that is most often contested. The form demands the most reflection, discussion, negotiation and correction: what is the proper artistic form that can confer the status of "halal" on a play or song? And, consequently, what are the forms that fail to live up to this standard? For each genre, these questions are approached and resolved in a variety of ways. When it comes to music, this question is most often posed in regard to musical instruments. Given the strong concern within Islamic scholarly traditions for human subjectivity, the nature of music and notably of musical instruments was passionately disputed (and continues to be so today).[8] However, all agree on one thing: they attribute a clear prerogative to the human voice and the word. As a consequence, much of the debate among the musicians I have talked to is centered on whether or not to use musical instruments. Many groups that perform traditional devotional music (*nasheed*) perform a cappella or limit themselves to the hand drum (*duff*), the instrument most approved of among classical scholars. For musicians in more contemporary popular genres of music, this question is often more complicated.

Let me here use the example of Islamic hip hop in the UK as an interesting case in point. More than many other genres of music associated with an un-Islamic lifestyle, the Islamic hip-hop scene in the UK struggles to find a way to bring the tradition of hip hop into line with Islamic normativity, molding it to correspond to certain Islamic traditions of ethical listening and musical practices (which are, again, neither uniform nor unanimously accepted, but rather internally contested). In the UK, religious figures as well as lay Muslims often reproach hip hop as fundamentally un-Islamic and therefore incapable of being "Islamized." It is also accused of fostering an illegitimate lifestyle because of its rhythmic style, which is clearly geared toward danceability. The sensual dance style associated with hip

---

8 Music has been seen as potentially producing sensual pleasure and extreme emotional excitement by Muslim scholars throughout the ages, who have been concerned by its capacity to hinder the exercise of reason and self-mastery as well as with its promises of spiritual benefit. In general, those who have opposed listening to music are fearful that its force arouses worldly passions which distract from the remembrance of God, whereas those favorable to music – generally speaking, thinkers and practitioners from Islamic mystical traditions – highlight music's capacity to impel the believer to seek the spiritual world while simultaneously being attentive to its potential dangers. On these two sides, there is a wide range of theological positions, from those that prohibit any kind of music or singing (considering Koran and poetry recitation not as a form of music) and all musical instruments, to those that allow singing and certain musical instruments (i.e. drums are permitted, while instruments that are stroked are not), to those who allow for all kinds of musical expression (as long as specific moral conditions are fulfilled). For valuable information on this question, see, for instance, Al-Faruqi 1985; Nelson 1982; Shiloah 1995; During 1997.

hop is achieved through amplified bass and repetitive beats that often drown out the vocals. However, British Muslim hip-hop artists emphasize that it is not so much the beat but the art of spoken word that connects hip hop to the sonic-linguistic practices of Islam's own pronounced oral tradition. A minority of rappers adhere to a specific Islamic interpretation, according to which musical instruments are forbidden, and therefore use no instruments, but only human voices as background music. Nonetheless, the vast majority of pious Muslim hip-hop artists I talked to do use instruments. Yet, a fine line seems to exist where beats turn into "nightclub" sounds. While neither clearly defined nor necessarily articulated by the artists themselves, Muslim artists nonetheless avoid this musical point of no return so as not to marginalize the spoken word. For all these artists, reconciling Islam with hip hop means focusing on the spoken art form by emphasizing the voice and words. Thus, British Islamic hip hop is stylistically related to spoken-word poetry, which frequently critiques the camouflaging of hip-hop lyrics behind beats (see Jouili 2012).[9]

When it comes to the performing arts, such as theater or stand-up comedy, the question of form is mainly discussed in terms of the bodily conduct of actors and comedians. In theater, this relates notably to the way in which actors interact with each other, and especially how actors of the opposite sex interact so as to respect the requirements of modesty and chastity. In this way, directors need to reflect thoroughly on how best to portray these interactions. Luqman Ali, the artistic director of the critically acclaimed *Al-Khayaal* theater company, an Islamic-inspired theater ensemble from London (and the only professional Muslim theater ensemble in Europe), provided me with several accounts of how his theater directed its actors and arranged scenes and movements on stage so that they corresponded with Islamic standards of modesty. He mentioned one specific example:

> In one production, we had a mother, an actress playing a mother and an actor playing the son, and the son was about to go away on a long journey, and obviously a son and a mother would normally hug: we couldn't do that onstage, so what we did is that they had a mime hug, they were hugging themselves, but the way they were standing and facing each other, they gave the same emotional feeling as if they were hugging each other.

---

9   In France, hip hop that is reflective of an Islamic identity does not constitute a distinct scene as such. Religious Muslim hip-hop artists, such as Médine, Kerry James and others, are part of the larger, commercially successful and politically conscious French rap scene; they do not perform, as is the case for British Islamic hip hop, mainly in front of a Muslim audience. Nonetheless, these rappers have been criticized by some French-based imams for the illegitimacy of their musical practices and have individually and in different ways, and at various moments of their careers, tried to solve the tensions between their art and certain religious interpretations (e.g. Kerry James produced an album without string and wind instruments). On Muslims in French rap, see Swedenburg 2001; Amghar 2003; Jouili forthcoming.

Another example worth mentioning is the Islamic musical *Etoile Brillante* performed by a group of Muslim women who live in the Paris region. This musical from Syria portrays the life of the Islamic Prophet and the women in his entourage, and was performed by female actors for a solely female audience. Meticulously copied from a musical circulating in the Damascene Islamic revival scene, the play consisted of religious chants, pious texts and choreography in traditional costume, neatly embodying Islamic standards of female modesty. Given that dance is often considered to be antithetical to the requirements of chastity and modesty, the choreography employed slow, soft, rhythmic movements rather than explicit dance movements, as has been the case in modern Islamic dance theaters (Stellar 2011).

This concern with appropriate bodily conduct impacts and delimits the form that Islamic-inspired performing arts take in very specific ways (whether theater, musicals, pantomimes, etc.). It also determines how Islamic musicians or spoken-word artists perform on stage. Islamic hip-hop artists, for instance, discuss how they consciously avoid moving too expressively to the music, something that is not easy for them, given that their music often inspires them to move. For female performers, especially veiled ones, this is even more critical. There are many ambivalent or even outright unfavorable opinions within the Islamic scriptural traditions regarding female performers. Rabia and Sakina, two sisters of Afro-Caribbean descent who form the *nasheed* and R&B duo Pearls of Islam, explain, for instance, that they prefer to perform in a seated position in front of mixed audiences so that they are not tempted to move to their own music. Samia Oresmane, a French-Tunisian stand-up comedian who has established herself as a popular figure in the Muslim community, also acknowledges the difficulties she has experienced in this respect:

> Unfortunately, I have this temperament, I am very exuberant, with too many gestures; I make too much noise. Sometimes, people tell me, you should be more discreet. I don't really feel like this, I love too much being on stage, having people look at me. But I want to link both [religion and pleasure]. The laws of God are most important to me; the priority is what God demands from you. Even if arts and the theater burn inside of me, it does not hinder me to know, within myself, inside of me, why I am there. So I try to stay modest.

Only a minority of female singers I encountered restrict their performances to female-only audiences, following a stricter interpretation which forbids the performance of female voices in front of a mixed-gender audience.

Arts as Ethical Technology versus Artistic Freedom

Even if the "halal arts" project is one that allows for improvization, divergence and multiple approaches, for contestation and negotiation, it is nonetheless a normative project, which is moral-pedagogical in nature. Therefore, it is centrally concerned with taboos, limits and a conscious practice of ethical self-restraint. As such, of course, it refuses Kantian-inspired ideals of pure aesthetics and the autonomous artist, as condensed in the modernist mantra "art for art's sake," to which many of my interlocutors oppose "art for Allah's sake."[10] To be sure, the ideal of the autonomy of the arts has been consistently questioned and contested. On a normative level, autonomy and its concomitant disinterestedness have been critiqued since their inception, and the idea of ethics as a criterion for aesthetics has been defended; however, these ethics have been articulated mainly around humanist values (including autonomy) rather than religious norms (see, for instance, Carroll 1998; Nussbaum 2000).[11] On an analytical level, this ideal has been questioned not only because of the various disciplinary constraints and modes of training to which artists are subject, but also because of the myriad ways in which arts and cultural practices operate in a variety of regimes of power (the art market, the state, etc.) and because they are increasingly subjugated under specific modes of governmentality in the era of neoliberalism (e.g. Marcus and Myers 1995; Bennett 2000; Yúdice 2004).[12] Nonetheless, the ideal of the autonomy of the arts continues to serve as a powerful model, especially when promoted in opposition to social and religious constraints, in particular with regard to Islam's supposed incapacity to celebrate aesthetic freedom. Islamic artists' explicit and conscious acknowledgment of operating within ethical norms and religious disciplines, which involve practicing self-restraint and respecting limits, is therefore regarded with skepticism. From such a perspective, halal art might appear as the negation of "proper" art and as a violation of the right to free artistic expression. Indeed, the artistic projects developed in this scene have been criticized in these terms, as many of its practitioners have told me.

However, for other pious Muslim art practitioners I talked to, the idea of the autonomy of aesthetics did not make sense. Their work reflects an approach to art where aesthetics does not stand as a "pure" entity conceivable as separate from ethics. Beauty is defined through what is "good." In pious Muslim art circles, one is often reminded of the *hadith*: "God is beautiful and He loves beauty." In this

---

10   Pious Muslim art practitioners in the Arabic-speaking world have coined the term "purposeful art" (*al-fann al-hadif*). See, for instance, Nieuwkerk 2008; Winegar 2008a.

11   And, according to Bourdieu (1984), this principle still defines the conventional understanding of what makes up high arts as opposed to popular arts.

12   These authors, of course, do not oppose these modes of power to an idealized notion of freedom. Following the Foucaultian understanding of the intrinsic relation of subjects with power, they acknowledge that modern discourses of freedom are always about "the inculcation of particular kinds of relations that the human being has with himself" (Rose 1999: 42). Thus, specific self-understandings of autonomy and freedom are not understood as merely reflecting authentic autonomous and free individuals, but as fashioned by a specific regime of freedom. See also Brown 1995. As Bennett (2000) shows, governing through the employment of arts converges precisely with the liberal concern of shaping subjects' conduct by respecting their liberty and autonomy.

sense, not respecting Islamic ethics within one's art would amount to an aesthetic defect.[13] To live up to these norms in the performing arts is a welcome challenge for these artists, for whom Islamic ethics increase, rather than circumscribe, creativity. As Luqman Ali explains:

> Obviously, as Muslims, our understanding of art is very different. Art for us is about celebrating and expressing the beauty of the divine, whatever form it takes, and that as an ethos governs our heart ... Even within the grammars with which we are working, imagination can be used to say the same thing in a way which is not in contradiction to the beliefs and sensibilities.

If one takes seriously the notion of *embodied ethics* that practitioners as well as event organizers and the public stress as a central element in the evaluation of the artistic form, then one can approach the matter from a different perspective. The Aristotelian tradition, on which the Islamic ethical tradition builds and expands, has defined ethics as embodied practices rather than in terms of abstract moral reason, as the Kantian tradition would have it. As demonstrated by recent work that makes this earlier, Aristotelian approach fruitful for a study of religious practices – especially by reviewing it through a Foucaultian perspective (Mahmood 2005; Hirschkind 2006) – ethics are a set of material disciplinary practices that "endow the self with certain kind[s] of capacities that provide the substance from which the world is acted upon" (Mahmood 2012). While I do not want to argue that this model of ethics is able to account for all the ethical practices in which religious (and secular) subjects engage, notably when it comes to practices and modes of reasoning that do not lend themselves to habitual enactment, it nonetheless provides a powerful analytical grid through which to make sense of the ways in which Muslim art practitioners I talked to, as well as their publics, understand the requirements for artistic practices.

Halal arts here become something akin to a technology for the self, for the practitioners as well as for their pious audiences. Given the strong pedagogical nature of this understanding of the arts, which is a project for fashioning the subject, these artistic practices are structurally linked to other contemporary *da'wa* practices that are central to the revival project. In its most classical sense, *da'wa* is an "ethical mode of speech and action" aimed at improving the moral conduct of the community (Hirschkind 2006: 116). It is about cultivating pious sensibilities and emotions that strengthen specific virtues, such as consciousness of God, guide audiences toward appropriate moral conduct and orient their practical reasoning. While *da'wa* in a contemporary Western context refers to a much larger sphere of pedagogical moral action because it responds constantly to a context that is seen as rendering

---

13   In this specific respect, my Muslim interlocutors formulate arguments similar to those voiced in contemporary art debates by the moralist humanist approaches (see, for instance, Carroll 1998).

an Islamic lifestyle difficult, it continues its vocational impetus.[14] Performing and singing, but also listening and watching, with their sensory and visceral qualities, are understood as ethical practices that contribute to shaping and sustaining the pious self by inculcating specific emotional states which enable a person to live as a pious individual or which, at least, do not jeopardize that endeavor.

Because the artists conceive of their artistic project as an ethical venture, or a mode of self-cultivation linked to an Islamic ethos, they pay a good deal of attention to their own inner attitude, which they bring to their artistic activity. This is why all the artists I spoke to conceive of their work as requiring a constant dose of vigilance and self-criticism. One of the first things that artists mention is the danger of the ego (*nafs*), which can endanger the legitimacy of their project. Luqman Ali consciously sets apart an Islamic perspective of art or, more generally, what he calls sacred art versus secular art:

> Within the art sector here, everyone says, oh we are against censorship. So I said to them, part of my art is consciously censoring myself, because for me, my art is not about my ego, so I have to censor my ego. This is quite at odds with their way of thinking and, you know, you need to censor out interference coming from your lower self. Self-censorship is very much a part of sacred art in general.

The art practitioners I talked to often openly recognize that as artists, they use their body as a mode of expression and thus tend to have more extroverted personalities and enjoy their presence onstage, public applause and admiration. But at the same time, they are aware that once their ego takes over, their good intentions will be lost. Not only would such conduct make their art illicit from an Islamic perspective, but it would also make it lose its moral-pedagogical quality of promoting piety and a Muslim lifestyle, since they consider this humble approach as the condition for the very success of their project. As one member of the female Pearls of Islam duo put it:

> If we don't do it for the sake of Allah, then there is not a distinction between secular art and our art, because we are going up there to feel good about ourselves and get people to idolize us, and that is not our intention, *insha'allah*, because we try to keep our intention with Allah, doing it for the sake of *rasul Allah, sallah lahu alayhi wa sallam*, and Allah, and that is what I feel, *insha'Allah*, will distinguish us. Because we are only human, and we do have egos, and that is something that needs constantly, constantly rechecking, each time we go on

---

14 Interestingly, the invocation of *da'wa* is also one of the most common explanations Muslim artists use to *justify* their artistic work. Given that Islamic legal sources are very ambivalent about the status of music and the performing arts, and many interpretations are rather negative when it comes to the admissibility of female performers, these artists feel in need of "justification." Invoking the message they want to disseminate and phrasing it in Islamic terms through the notion of *da'wa* is one way to accomplish this.

stage, keep on checking, each time people say, oh, you're brilliant man, check back, you know.

By Way of Conclusion

It goes without saying that once an Islamically licit artistic practice is performed, things are far more messy and tricky. The project is pervaded by tension and contradictions that complicate its very "normativity." First of all, the Islamic artistic scene is not coherent, but highly fragmented: some artists do not even consider themselves as part of this scene, even while aspiring to produce "legitimate" and meaningful art. I have already mentioned that there exist very different understandings of what counts as "licit": what for some is "halal" is for others "*haram*," as one can easily see in the ongoing debates around the legitimacy of music among Muslim musicians, their audiences and religious scholars. The same holds true for "pious" or "modest" conduct: what for some is a controlled and restraint body movement amounts for others to indecent dancing. At times, conscious self-restraint is altogether forgotten and gives way to situations that will be heavily criticized in the Islamic scene afterwards. These raise questions that are important not only for performers but for their audiences as well: what is an appropriate mode of listening and watching? How much can a listener be swayed by music? How loud can she laugh? How much can she applaud the artist? All these questions are relevant precisely because Muslim observers of these performances so often witness the limits of proper conduct being transgressed.

Even more tensions emerge when the artists step out of the "safe" zones that constitute an all-Muslim "counter-public." Most artists have in mind a larger non-Muslim public as well, and this objective is, once again, made with reference to *da'wa*. When addressed to a non-Muslim public, *da'wa*, as used by the art practitioners I talked to, does not primarily denote an effort at conversion, but rather an attempt to rectify the negative representations of Islam prevalent in the West. Pious Muslim artists pursue this objective by defending a positive, peaceful and modern image of Islam. Performing in front of a non-Muslim public requires performing in a context that does not necessarily guarantee the conditions for doctrinal legitimacy (for example, clubs or concert halls where alcohol is served). Particularly when it comes to musical events, it does not guarantee an audience guided by Islamic etiquette. These different settings provide the potential for additional conflicts and tensions that can render the disciplinary practices to which the artist subjects herself even more difficult.

The tensions to which I can only briefly allude in the scope of this chapter should not, however, be understood as an argument that seeks to question the ethical obligations that the artists I worked with feel committed to, nor does it question the project of halal arts. The fact that ethical projects are pervaded by tension and contradictions does not call into question the projects themselves, as this messiness is a part of human practices in general. What is important here is to underscore that what appears as the highly normative, and therefore restrictive, nature of this artistic project has to be read as an ethical practice inspired by specific understandings of how to enact Islamic tradition in contexts where ideas about the social role of the arts as well as the modern culture industry have profoundly shaped young Muslim practitioners.

References

Al Faruqi, L-I. 1985. "Music, Musicians and Muslim Law," *Asian Music*, 17(1), 3–36.

Amghar, S. 2003. "*Rap* et *islam*: quand le rappeur devient imam," *Hommes et Migrations*, 1243, 78–95.

Bennett, T. 2000. "Acting on the Social: Art, Culture, and Government," *American Behavioral Scientist*, 43(9), 1412–28.

Boubekeur, A. 2007. "Islam militant et nouvelles formes de mobilisation culturelle," *Archives des Sciences Sociales des Religions*, 139, 119–38.

Bourdieu, P. 1984. *Distinction: A Social Critique of the Judgment of Taste*, Richard Nice (trans.). Cambridge, MA: Harvard University Press.

Brown, W. 1995. *States of Injury: Power and Freedom in Late Modernity*. Princeton, NJ: Princeton University Press.

Carroll, N. 1998. "Art, Narrative, and Moral Understanding," in J. Levinson (ed.), *Aesthetics and Ethics: Essays at the Intersection*. Cambridge: Cambridge University Press, 126–60.

During, J. 1997. "Hearing and Understanding in Islamic Gnosis," *The World of Music*, 3(2), 127–37.

El-Asri, F. 2009. "L'expression musicale de musulmans européens. Création de sonorités et normativité religieuse," *Revue européenne des migrations internationales*, 25(2), 35–50.

Flood, F.B. 2007. "From the Prophet to Postmodernism? New World Orders and the End of Islamic Art," in E. Mansfield (ed.), *Making Art History: A Changing Discipline and its Institutions*. London: Routledge, 31–51.

Haenni, P. 2002. "Au-delà du repli identitaire … les nouveaux prêcheurs égyptiens et la modernisation paradoxale de l'islam," *Religioscope*, December. Available at: http://www.religioscope.com/pdf/precheurs.pdf.

Hirschkind, C. 2006. *The Ethical Soundscape: Cassette Sermons and Islamic Counterpublics*. New York: Columbia University Press.

Jouili, J-S. 2012. "British Muslim Hip Hop and Ethical Listening Practices," *Sounding Out!* http://soundstudiesblog.com/tag/beautification.

Jouili, J-S. forthcoming. "Rapping the Republic: Utopia: Critique and Muslim Role Models in Secular France," *French Politics, Culture & Society*.

LeVine, M. 2008. *Heavy Metal Islam: Rock, Resistance, and the Struggle for the Soul of Islam*. New York: Three Rivers Press.

Mahmood, S. 2005. *Politics of Piety. The Islamic Revival and the Feminist Subject*. Princeton, NJ: Princeton University Press.

Mahmood, S. 2012. "Ethics and Piety," in D. Fassin (ed.), *A Companion to Moral Anthropology*. Somerset, NJ: Wiley, 223–41.

Marcus, G.E. and Myers, F.R. (eds) 1995. *The Traffic in Culture: Refiguring Anthropology and Art*. Berkeley: University of California Press, 1995.

Nelson, K. 1982. "Reciter and Listener: Some Factors Shaping the Mujawwad Style of Qur'anic Reciting," *Ethnomusicology*, 26(1), 41–7.

Nussbaum, M-C. 2000. "Literature and Ethical Theory: Allies or Adversaries?" *Yale Journal of Ethics*, 9, 5–16.

Rose, N. 1999. *Powers of Freedom: Reframing Political Thought*. Cambridge: Cambridge University Press.

Roy, O. 2004. *Globalized Islam: The Search for a New Ummah*. New York: Columbia University Press.

Shiloah, A. 1995. *Music in the World of Islam: A Socio-Cultural Study*. Detroit, MI: Wayne State University Press.

Stellar, Z. 2011. "From 'Evil-Inciting Dance to Chaste 'Rhythmic Movements': A Genealogy of Modern Islamic Dance-Theater in Iran," in K. van Nieuwkerk (ed.), *Muslim Rap, Halal Soaps, and Revolutionary Theatre: Artistic Developments in the Muslim World*. Austin: University of Texas Press, 231–56.

Swedenburg T. 2001. "Islamic Hip-Hop versus Islamophobia," in T. Mitchell (ed.), *Global Noise: Rap and Hip-Hop Outside the USA*. Middletown, CT: Wesleyan University Press, 57–85.

Swedenburg T. 2004. "The 'Arab Wave' in World Music after 9/11," *Anthropologica*, 46(2), 177–88.

Van Nieuwkerk, K. 2008. "Creating an Islamic Cultural Sphere: Contested Notions of Art, Leisure and Entertainment. An Introduction," *Contemporary Islam*, 2(3), 169–76.

Van Nieuwkerk, K. (ed.) 2011. *Muslim Rap, Halal Soaps, and Revolutionary Theater Artistic Developments in the Muslim World*. Austin: University of Texas Press.

Winegar, J. 2008a. "Purposeful Art between Television Preachers and the State," *ISIM Review* (International Institute for the Study of Islam in the Modern World), 22, 28–9.

Winegar, J. 2008b. "The Humanity Game: Art, Islam, and the War on Terror," *Anthropological Quarterly*, 81(3), 651–81.

Yúdice, G. 2004. *The Expediency of Culture: Uses of Culture in the Global Era*. Durham, NC: Duke University Press.

PART IV
Halal, Sharia and Secular Law:
Competing Sources of Normativity

Chapter 12

The British Debate over Sharia Councils: A French-Style Controversy?

Jean Philippe Bras

The French and British legal models are generally seen as being antithetical. The former, "continental" model is based on the Roman tradition of civil law and codification in which the expression of the general will is the principal source of law and which relies on the notion of public order to protect society's values. The republican model is legislation-centered (*légicentrist*) and the subjects of its laws – the nation, the people, the Republic – are the sources of norms that govern society. The law applies to everyone, and the contract is framed purely in terms of public norms. According to Portalis' famous phrase, the judge is "the mouth of the law" (Portalis 1801). On the contrary, the Anglo-Saxon model of common law rests primarily upon the contract, the expression of the autonomy of free will. In a contract, individuals forge the law for themselves. At the same time, case law plays an important role in the regulation of contractual disputes and the judge establishes legal norms by using two types of approaches: that of common law, resting upon precedent and customary rule, and that of *equity*, rallying around the principles of justice and fairness.

Within these contrasting legal landscapes, the methods for settling disputes differ. In France, controversies swiftly reach a national level, as the law, and thus Parliament, is involved in resolving disputes. In controversies surrounding Islamic normativity in the French public space, we see remarkable examples of this in the 2004 and 2010 laws concerning the "Islamic headscarf." The different features of the controversy are governed by this highly centralized method of conflict resolution in which legislators respond by submitting to demands for new laws. Numerous examples of similar attempts can be cited: legislation on mosques (for example, the Swiss referendum on minarets), cemeteries and confessional mortuary spaces, the sale of halal food, dress codes, public services, Islamic finance and questions of matrimony as they pertain to Muslims. But these attempts to settle disputes by law do not always succeed (and, in fact, succeed less often as time goes on), suggesting the contemporary limits of the legislation-centric model in France. In the UK, the established culture of compromise continues to impose structures of negotiation, privileging arbitration and mediation. We are witnessing the construction of a decentralized politics, where the terms of agreement vary according to the place, time and interlocutors involved. Political debates and judicial procedures are localized; in the case of litigation, the judge (and not the law) is the arbiter, and not all litigation ends with a promulgation of law. From a more political point of view, governments do not hesitate to rely on communities, whether religious or ethnic, for the implementation of public policies. Shrinking public budgets have strengthened this trend towards seeking intermediaries in civil society. In France, the republican tradition has crystallized the distrust of intermediary bodies, all the more so when they are religious. *Laïcité* leads public authorities to consider the minimal relationships they can maintain with religious institutions. When the state is in contact with them, it tries to impose its own logic of action on the mode of centralization within a religious community, hence the French government's attempt to create a standard representation of Muslims in the French Council for the Muslim Faith (*Conseil Français du Culte Musulman*: CFCM). This attempt has met with very limited success, since Islam is pluralistic, particularly when it is diasporic, while Catholicism established its own centrality before that of the state.

In light of these differences, it is often argued that common law legal systems facilitate the integration of migrant populations and their legal traditions into different cultures more effectively than does continental Europe's civil law. By giving the autonomy of free will greater importance through legal minimalism and the invocation of public order, these systems open windows of opportunity for the implementation of Islamic normativity itself and for relationships between individuals because individual and community norms occupy the same space. On the contrary, under continental law, access to Islamic normativity is severely restricted by the supremacy of law and the imperative of public order, which rigorously frame contractual liberty – a trait that is even more marked in France due to its traditions of *laïcité* and centralization. And, indeed, the British community model, producer of a kind of legal pluralism, has developed in relative tranquility in contrast to the voluntarist, integrationist and even assimilationist French republican model, whose implementation is a source of regular tension and convulsion.

However, recent developments tend to blur the lines on both sides of the Channel: legal models of reference seem to lose their consistency, or even their ground, when confronting demands to implement Islamic normativity at the very heart of Western legal systems – a fact that potentially supports the theory of "Islamic exceptionalism" in the trajectories of the contemporary state. In a previous work, I argued that in its treatment of a matrimonial question referring to Islamic normativity, the French controversy over "the marriage in Lille" indicates a current weakening of the foundations of the *laïque*, republican model (Bras 2011).[1] The discussion that follows concerns a British controversy over the institution of Sharia councils (Bowen 2009; Bras 2010). The Sharia councils are both a testament to the

---

1   The controversy concerns a court in Lille in 2008 accepting a husband's argument that his marriage should be annulled on the grounds that his wife had lied about her virginity. The parties were Muslims: a convert and a French Muslim woman of Moroccan background. And the court, disregarding the national civil code, decided on the specificity of the case and considered virginity as "an essential quality of the person."

possibility of establishing structures for community regulations in a common law legal system and emblematic, by the opposition that these councils incite, of the temptation for a treatment *à la française* of such a legal question.

Sharia Councils: An Object of Controversy

What are Sharia councils? They emerge as religious institutions in the service of the Muslim community:

- exercising an advisory function on legal issues involving Islamic law;
- contributing to the establishment and authentication of legal acts of Islamic law (marriage, divorce, commercial acts);
- resolving disputes between Muslims, primarily concerning family law: questions relating to divorce, child support and child custody. They also resolve disputes relating to inheritance, domestic violence and commercial concerns.

What is the nature of their functions and how exactly do we qualify these councils? Do they have a mere consultative function, simply offering opinions? Or do they represent legal authorities for implementing the law, authenticating legal acts and exercising a jurisdictional function in pronouncing judgments on the disputes before them? And are their decisions binding for those involved?

In other words, are Sharia councils and Sharia courts composed of judges? Semantic challenges represent a defining element of this controversy. A distinction must be made between Sharia councils that fall under the Arbitration Act of 1996 (alternative dispute resolution) and those that do not. There are seven of the former, registered in 2007, located, among other places, in London, Birmingham, Bradford and Manchester. This network of Muslim Arbitration Tribunals (MATs) is headed by Faïz Saddiqi, the son of a prestigious Pakistani Sufi lawyer who works in the field of commercial law. The MAT arbitrates civil and commercial disputes. Ordinary courts can register the MAT's binding decisions, but the parties at trial are always entitled to appeal to those same ordinary courts. The second category, informal Sharia councils, was established in the 1980s within mosques. They proceed via "judgments," agreements on questions primarily concerning family law, which often take place in the presence of a solicitor who records the agreement as a legal act. This council notably pronounces (Muslim) divorces, which have (legal?) validity within the community. Some of them also belong to networks; for example, about a dozen Muslim Sharia councils set the price for divorces at £100 for men and £250 for women. The elevated rate for women is ascribed to the more complex procedure that is required for them.[2]

---

2   This information can be found on the website of the Sharia Councils UK: http://shariahcouncil.org.

The MAT first sparked controversy in an indirect and delayed manner. The trigger came from where it was least expected: not from secularists or Muslims, but from the public remarks of the Archbishop of Canterbury, Rowan Williams, who in a speech on 7 February 2008 noted the "unavoidable" character of the adoption of Islamic law in the UK. He expressed the need to find a "constructive accommodation" with some aspects of Muslim law, as British authorities already do with some other religious laws. Support for this position within the state was found in none other than the Lord Chief Justice, Lord Phillips, considered the head of the judiciary, who, on 3 July 2008, declared: "There is no reason why Sharia principles, or any other religious code, should not be the basis for mediation or other forms of alternative dispute resolution." These remarks, which would be unthinkable in the public sphere in France, gave rise to violent polemics in the press. Protests were organized. In December 2008, an opinion campaign with the slogan "One law for all" was launched, denouncing the discriminatory, arbitrary nature of the Sharia councils and calling for a ban on all religious tribunals. Suddenly, a French-style controversy had erupted. The government distanced itself from the declarations of Williams and Phillips, and the then Prime Minister, Gordon Brown, remarked that only "British law should apply in this country, based on British values."

The controversy was reopened in 2009 with the publication of a very critical report by the thinktank Civitas entitled "Sharia Law in Britain: A Threat to One Law for All."[3] It was widely cited by the press, effectively stirring up a hornet's nest. The report highlighted the expansion of Sharia councils to an estimated 85 in Britain, analyzing and denouncing their discriminatory practices towards women – practices seen as the logical consequences of the application of Islamic law and leading to a dualistic community alongside that of British law.

The current of opposition to Sharia councils very quickly found political spokespeople, notably within the Conservative Party.[4] Thus, during the period of pre-election campaigning, the Conservative Manifesto called for a future Tory government to exclude Sharia councils from the British legal system. But objections also came from the Labour Party and from MPs such as Jim Fitzpatrick whose electoral constituencies are predominantly Muslim. Even more radically, the political veteran Lord Tebbit referred to members of Sharia councils as a "band of gangsters."

In 2011, this issue rose to the top of the political agenda, accompanied by a strong media campaign. For example, an article in the August 7 issue of the *Daily Telegraph* entitled "Sharia: A Law Unto Itself" reported that Suhaib Hasan, one of the judges on the Leyton Sharia Council, was in favor of introducing a penal law in Britain for the stoning of female adulterers, a position that incited the fury and vehement denials of Muslim organizations. The article also mentioned another episode in which posters declaring "Sharia-controlled zones" were hung in London suburbs (Wynne-Jones 2011).

---

3 See www.onelawforall.org.uk.

4 This can be found, for example, on the blog of Conservative MP Mark Pritchards.

The Source of the Controversy

The principal arguments of the opponents of Sharia councils are as follows. First, Sharia law, as it is implemented, is profoundly non-egalitarian and detrimental to women as regards marriage, divorce, child custody and testimony. Likewise, Sharia law is a vehicle for inequality and to call for its application is to promote this inequality. It is enough to consider the legal regimes of Muslim countries to establish this inequity. This vision of Islamic law is substantive: it rejects the arguments of reformist, modernist Muslims, considering Islamic law itself, and not only its interpretation, as discriminatory. Another argument of the defending party can also be ruled out: if women constitute the majority of those using the Sharia councils to obtain divorces, this is not evidence of their virtuous protection of these women; it is simply that men have no need for this recourse, because they have at their disposal the unilateral method of divorce by repudiation.

Second, concerning the alleged voluntary and liberal nature of recourse to Sharia councils – a notion that is at the heart of the arbitration process – it appears in fact that the autonomy of free will does not exist. The community exerts full pressure, notably on women, to settle disputes within its framework. Upon arriving from her village in Pakistan, a woman may be ignorant of her rights in the UK. Intimidation is a common practice, with the Muslim community considering it a crime for Muslims to contact British courts to settle internal disputes (according to the report published by Civitas).

Third, the decisions of the Sharia councils have discriminatory leanings. This is the case regarding the forced marriage of minors, which is deemed to be compliant with Islamic law; the question of domestic violence against wives, who are encouraged – at their peril – to return to their husbands; and even the modalities of registering marriages. On the last point, mosques have the option of employing the Marriage (Registration of Buildings) Act of 1990. This legislation permits the simultaneous performance of civil and religious ceremonies within the building of worship. Yet mosques rarely use this power, and the number of solely religious marriages, lacking civil registration, is constantly on the rise. However, these undeclared marriages have dramatic consequences for wives if the husband takes a second wife or decides to divorce them. The practice continues as it is hard to dispel the myth of the *common law wife* or the belief that in a common law country, religious marriage has legal value (Hasan 2011). This myth is often used by the husband in order to avoid civil registration and instead rely on religious law alone for marriage and divorce, which contributes to a process of rampant legal dualism. Moreover, the sole possibility afforded to the wife to dissolve religious marriage is to go before a religious judge (that is, a Sharia council), before whom she can obtain a divorce and restitution only if the man wants it, because the decision of the religious judge has no bearing before the civil courts in the case of non-execution. The situation is different before the MATs, whose decisions can be submitted to the civil courts, but in a procedure that requires the consent of the husband. Meanwhile, studies show that different Sharia councils have different conservative leanings; for example, the Birmingham Sharia Council has a reputation for being liberal and favorable towards women.

Fourth, the Sharia councils are also reproached for going out of their jurisdiction and presenting themselves as true courts, discouraging women from going before ordinary courts to settle disputes. Opponents of these courts point out that the proceedings are not public and the rationale for their decisions are opaque, except in the case of the MAT. In addition, Sharia councils make dangerous intrusions into the field of penal law regarding issues of rape and domestic violence, notably by encouraging women not to file charges or to withdraw them based on the argument that marriage must be given a second chance. In this sphere, there is collaboration between the MAT and the Crown Prosecution Service, but this is also criticized, because it amounts to a *de facto* recognition of the involvement of Sharia councils in this type of litigation.

Lastly, Sharia councils pose serious threats to the unity of the UK's legal order. Their development introduces a substantial contradiction between the order decreed by the principle of equality (the rule of law) and an order based on the principle of inequality, which obstructs integration and promotes the withdrawal of the community. Hence, in the face of this threat of a double dualization of legal and jurisdictional order, the slogan "One Law for All" has emerged, proclaiming the futility of a project which imagines the coexistence of two legal systems.

Attempts to Defuse the Controversy, or the Arguments of the Defense

The first argument in defense of Sharia councils concerns the law. Sharia councils are institutions that conform to the major principles of British law. British Muslims live in a free country where people can make free choices in their private relationships; the choice to appeal to Sharia law to settle family affairs is an expression of that liberty. In addition, the procedures of Sharia councils are formalized, offering the guarantee of a smooth process, which is similar to what ordinary courts provide. Procedures are led by judges who are experts in Islamic law, having received training to that end. Before the MAT, they are accompanied by a solicitor or a barrister. In addition, these institutions are under the control of civil judges, who can refuse to register their decisions or to set in motion their execution if they are contrary to the principles or laws of the British legal system. From this point of view, there is no risk of legal dualism.

On a more practical level, Sharia councils offer procedures that are simple, rapid and inexpensive in comparison to those in use by the civil courts, so much so that non-Muslims do not hesitate to use Sharia councils for their own disputes. They also provide strong ties to the community thanks to the judges' familiarity with Islamic law schools and the native languages of the claimants (which is often Urdu). They seem to facilitate the integration process of Muslim communities and protect Muslim women, as evidenced by the fact women submit 80 percent of their cases to these councils for judgment. This protection extends to the women's countries of origin, where legal authorities and administrations are more inclined to recognize the validity of the decisions of the Sharia councils than those of the British civil courts.

Finally, from a judicial standpoint, Sharia councils also contribute to the integration process of Muslims in the UK by promoting evolution within Islamic law, bringing it into line with Western legal standards. For example, in 2008, the Muslim Institute in South London initiated a type of Muslim marriage contract adapted to meet the requirements of UK law, notably regarding the principle of equality between spouses (Rahman 2008). In relation to Tariq Ramadan's position on the anchoring of Islam in the West and based on the Pakistani Hanafi rite, Ghayasuddin Siddiqi proposes a type of marriage where matrimonial guardianship is optional, which protects the material interests of the spouse, discourages polygamy and confers full weight to the testimony of women and non-Muslims. In the spirit of the same concern for equality, the *talaq* (unilateral divorce) is transferred by delegation to the female spouse in divorce procedures as well. The wife is also protected from the husband's verbal, physical or sexual abuse. Although the measure is supported by multiple Muslim organizations, it has been met with hostility from the UK Islamic Sharia Council due to its Salafi ideology. It should be noted that such a standardization of Muslim marriage results from a *légicentrist* approach and, within the community, from an increasingly prescriptive process that limits contractual liberty.

Upsetting the Agenda

The intensity of the controversy surrounding Sharia law has had the effect of upsetting the agenda by not keeping with British tradition with regard to civil cases, which have been highly politicized. Notably, this controversy has sparked demands for the safeguarding of law and public order, which more closely resemble the parlance of the French rather than the British system. Is the UK, in short, becoming continental?

The public was mobilized in 2011 via a government survey conducted by the Ministry of Justice on the activity of Sharia councils. This was to be an exploratory study on the compliance of their activities to current family law. However, the limited nature and insufficiency of the results obtained led the minister to prevent their publication in August 2011, noting the absence of input from Sharia councils in the survey. For their part, Sharia councils cite a lack of manpower and the importance of their other activities as reasons for their unavailability, and express their defiance of the stereotypes applied to them, particularly by the media.

The turn towards Parliament and the call for new laws manifested itself at the start of June 2011, when Caroline Cox (independent) introduced a bill proposal into the House of Lords entitled "The Arbitration and Mediation Services Equality Bill," which proposes general rules on mediation without explicitly targeting Islamic law. The text notably introduces a punishment of five years in prison for anyone who falsely claims that Sharia councils (or any other such form of mediation) have legal jurisdiction in regard to penal or family law. It does not, however, prohibit their activity as community councils, which would run contrary to religious liberty. Another measure provides for the protection of women against the discriminatory uses of Sharia, obliging these caucuses to respect the principle of equality, a value which is "at the heart of English justice." Moreover, the text proposes the explicit elimination of the capacity of these caucuses to arbitrate family law (divorce, child custody) or penal law, appealing to the Canadian precedent set in Ontario that halted the activity of Sharia councils. Finally, it calls for information about English law to be made available to women. The Islamic Sharia Council commented on the draft bill by noting that "Ms. Cox has made no attempt to understand the workings of Sharia councils." At the same time, a debate on Sharia councils was held June 28 at the House of Commons, giving rise to particularly powerful and virulent interventions (Namazie 2011).

The evolution in the tone of the controversies over the place of Islamic normativity within Western legal systems clearly marks a confluence of the different responses to this "challenge," with the boundaries between contrary legal paradigms seeming to weaken as they confront these convergences. The factors underlying this reconciliation are political and ethical, marking a return to society's core values, as well as structural and legal, drawing the legal systems of the Western world closer together.

References

Bowen, J-R. 2009. "Private Arrangements: 'Recognizing Sharia' in England," *Boston Review*, March–April, 15–18.

Bras, J-P. 2010. "La shari'a comme droit : cas de figure de la combinaison entre normativité juridique et normativité islamique," in P. Gandolfi and G. Levi (eds), *Entre théologie et politique*. Venice: Cafoscarina, 85–96.

Bras, J-P. 2011. "La controverse autour du mariage de Lille. Quel compromis sur la virginité des femmes," in M. Nachi (ed.), *Les figures du compromis dans les sociétés islamiques*. Paris: IISMM-Karthala, 159–76.

Hasan, K. 2011. "The Islamic Shariah Council," *Per Incuriam of the Cambridge University Law Society*.

Namazie, M. 2001. "Houses of Parliament, Sharia Law Debate," http://www.onelawforall.org.uk/28-june-2011-houses-of-parliament-sharia-law-debate.

Portalis, J-E-M. 1801. *Discours préliminaire du premier projet de Code civil*. Available at http://classiques.uqac.ca/collection_documents/portalis/discours_1er_code_civil/discours_1er_code_civil.pdf.

Rahman, S. 2008. "Changing the Face of Muslim Family Life," *The Guardian*, August 8, http://www.guardian.co.uk/commentisfree/2008/aug/08/religion.islam.

Wynne-Jones, J. 2011. "Sharia: A Law Unto Itself? *Daily Telegraph*, August 7, http://www.telegraph.co.uk/news/uknews/law-and-order/8686504/Sharia-a-law-unto-itself.html.

Chapter 13

Ethics and Affects in British Sharia Councils: "A Simple Way of Getting to Paradise"

Julie Billaud

> I remember a very touching question I was asked once. It was some young woman
> who rang, she said: "Can you just give me a simple way of getting to paradise?"
> Usama Hasan, imam and former presenter of *Journey Through the Koran*,
> a Q&A weekly TV programme about Islamic law broadcast on Islam channel.
> (Personal communication, February 2011)

In February 2008, a speech given by the Archbishop of Canterbury, Rowan Williams, at the Temple Church in London sparked the beginning of a long controversy that suddenly put Sharia councils, which had operated informally since the 1980s, in the spotlight of the media. In his speech, he declared that "the integration of some elements of Sharia law within the British legal system is inevitable" (Williams 2008). A moral panic immediately ensued, with journalists and politicians signaling the threat of social disintegration and Muslim secessionism. The debate over the nature of the interaction between Muslims and the British legal system represented a clash of a given set of values, identities and claims of interest by state law and the Muslim community. This occurred in the context of increased suspicion regarding British Muslims' loyalty toward the state post-7/7 and a broader questioning of the values of liberalism and multiculturalism as a framework for integrating cultural diversity (Lentin and Titley 2011; Triandafyllidou et al. 2011; Bowen 2012). If this debate was particularly intense in the UK, it gradually reached other European countries such as the Netherlands (Berger 2009), Austria (EuropeNews 2010) and, more recently, Germany (Spiegel Online 2012), where opinion polls and journalists' reports warned against increasing demands for a vaguely defined notion of Sharia among European Muslims. Similar debates had taken place a few years earlier in the province of Ontario in Canada (CBCNews 2005).

In the Western imagination, the word "Sharia" triggers images of brutal corporal punishments such as stoning, limb cutting, public lashing and, more generally, systematic discrimination against women. The recent Arab revolutions and the calls for Sharia that Islamic parties have put at the center of their political agenda have been interpreted in the West as major threats to democracy-building. The word "Sharia" has therefore become associated with a sense of clash that is noticeable in the reiteration of narratives about the "Islamization of Europe" and the "failure of multiculturalism" in which demands for accommodation of "Sharia law" are used as the ultimate evidence. This distorted representation obscures the smooth and quiet ways in which Sharia is routinely practiced and used in European contexts.

In this chapter, I attempt to define the nature of these practices by giving an empirically grounded account of everyday interactions in various British Sharia councils. Based on ethnographic fieldwork conducted in 2009[1] and 2011, I study the ethics and values that inform Muslims seeking Islamic justice, as well as the methods used by the British Ulema to guide their clients. By doing so, I aim to provide a more complex analysis of the ways in which Islamic agency asserts itself through ethical disciplining. As one imam told me, Sharia councils "care for the soul," whereas mainstream justice is perceived as procedural, confrontational and somewhat distant from Muslims' ethical concerns. Muslims making use of Sharia councils therefore seek to cultivate an ethical self by actively engaging with the values, norms and codes of conduct they perceive as essential to the nurturing of their faith. They strive to take part in a moral universe in which Islam is the discursive terrain upon which believers collectively struggle to define alternative conceptions of "the good."

More specifically, this chapter examines the issues of authority and knowledge in contemporary Islamic legal practice. Moving away from the methodological individualism that dominates debates on multiculturalism (Cowan, Dembour and Wilson 2001), it explores zones of tension and interpenetration (Göle 2005) between secular justice and Islamic law, as well as the power of emotions in Islamic legal practices in Britain. I show how these dynamics contribute to the making of a unique form of Islamic justice in Europe, which Werner Menski (2000) has called "Sharia Angrezi" or the British law of Islam.

Locating Sharia Councils

In a small room in the Birmingham Central Mosque, lit by narrow windows overlooking the highway, the Sharia Council has gathered for its monthly hearings. The couples who have been called on this day have been through a three-month reconciliation process, and today the Council will give its final verdict: either their marriage will be dissolved or the couples will be asked to persevere a little longer, until the Council has collected all the information it needs to render a fair decision. Behind a desk, Amra Bone, a mother of two children and a doctoral candidate in Islamic Studies at the University of Birmingham (one of the rare women appointed to sit in a Sharia council in Britain), and Dr Naseem Mohammed, a medical doctor, and the mosque's director, are going through the different cases they will review. I am told that the imam usually sits in the Council

1   My fieldwork in 2009 was partially realized as part of the EuroPublicIslam Project directed by Nilüfer Göle (EHESS) and funded by the European Research Council under the European Community's Seventh Framework Programme (FP7/2007–2013)/Grant Agreement n° 230244.

as well, but that he is busy with other matters today. Two women are also present in the room: Dr Sayeda Wageha, a retired pediatrician with a Master's degree in Islamic Studies from the University of Birmingham who runs the mosque's reconciliation clinic, together with sister Saba Butt, a divorcee with two teenage children who is responsible for preparing the agenda and briefing the councilors. While they do not intervene in the Council's decisions, their detailed knowledge of each case makes their input highly valuable. I am sitting in the corner of the room, right next to Dr Sayeda.

The first woman to enter is a half-British, self-employed children's caretaker with five children who has been married to her disabled Yemeni husband for 25 years. The couple have been separated for two years. The woman's husband now lives in a separate house and does not provide her with any child support. Their families have attempted to help with their reconciliation, without success. She thinks that the constant arguments between her and her husband affect her children's wellbeing: she wants closure and asks the Council to dissolve her marriage. Dr Sayeda explains that the husband is very dismissive of the Council and believes his permission is needed for his wife to obtain a divorce. He has not come to the meeting, but has sent his eldest son to defend his version of the story.

The second case is a Pakistani woman who does not speak English. She came to the UK to be the third wife of an older man who wanted to have more children. They married under Islamic law, but their marriage has not been officially registered. Because her marriage is not recognized under British law, the only way for her to obtain a divorce is to go through the Sharia council. The young woman has deserted her husband's house and now lives in a women's refuge. She comes accompanied by a social worker who wants to know more about this institution.

The third case is a British Egyptian woman married to a British Somali man. The couple have been separated for two years, after the husband pronounced "talaq" on numerous occasions. The husband has not replied to any of the letters addressed to him by the Council and has never shown up at the reconciliation clinic. As a result, the woman's file is composed of only her words. She feels that her situation should be clarified as she does not know whether she is married or not, which she thinks is both confusing and sinful.

These are but some of the issues that arise at the Birmingham Sharia Council. Established in the 1980s by the Birmingham Muslim community in response to a perceived demand for mediation in family disputes, it remains immensely popular today and is frequented by people from all walks of life, as demonstrated by the steady stream of people – most of whom are women – who enter the Council from the moment it opens at 10:30 am until after it closes at 6 pm. Observations conducted in other Sharia councils confirm the growing success of these alternative and informal dispute resolution mechanisms among British Muslims, to the extent that councils struggle to find the human and financial resources to meet this increasing demand. In a study she conducted in 2003 in four British Sharia councils, Samia Bano found that the frequentation of Sharia councils increased by 15.62 percent between 2002 and 2003 (Bano 2004: 136).

The Emergence of Sharia in the UK

The creation of Sharia councils reflects the development of Islamic religious practices in Britain. Indeed, mosques were the first institutions that Muslim immigrants to the UK created upon their arrival. As Werbner points out, the establishment of mosques was driven by the need of migrants to "sacralise an alien cityscape – the 'land of the Infidels' – and reconstitute this land as moral space" (Werbner 1996: 310). From the initial stage of prayer halls to the appointment of imams and the construction of mosques, Sharia councils illustrate the cultural and religious norms that underlie these developments. In particular, it is the close relationship to mosques that has shaped the type of Sharia councils that we see emerging in Britain (Bano 2004). British mosques cater to the needs of Muslims of various ethnic backgrounds including Punjabis, Mirpuris, Pathans, Bangladeshis, Yemenis, Somalis and Gujaratis. In larger communities, mosques are not only based on ethnic differences but are also split along doctrinal teachings. The different Islamic schools of thought that have been identified in Britain are Barelwi, Deobandi, Jama'at-i-Islami, Ahl-i-Hadith, Shi'a and Ahamadiyya (Lewis 2002). Most Pakistanis belong to the Barelwi tradition and consequently mosques are closely aligned to the sectarian affiliation of the local community.

However, over the years, Sharia has not only been displaced from one cultural area (i.e. Muslim countries) to another (i.e. England), but has also moved outside the premises commonly identified as "religious." Indeed, Sharia in Britain has gained public visibility by physically moving outside of the confined space of the mosque where it initially developed. Prior to the establishment of Sharia councils, imams provided all spiritual and religious guidance to Muslims in local mosques, including settling marital disputes and issuing divorce certificates. However, imams found this work to be time-consuming, taking them away from their traditional duties of providing spiritual guidance and sermons for Friday prayers (Bunt 1998). As a result, Sharia councils developed as separate institutions, and were responsible for dealing with family disputes and divorce requests. For example, the Islamic Sharia Council UK in East London has recently been relocated to a reconverted sweet shop. The Muslim Law Sharia Council UK (MLSC) in West London is based within the premises of the Muslim College, an institution that trains new generations of British imams.

Whereas the first generation of South Asian immigrants to the UK defined themselves primarily along ethnic lines, the new generations who were born in Britain identify most systematically with Islam and the larger *umma*. This shift was initiated by the Salman Rushdie affair (Modood 1990), when Muslims' protests against *The Satanic Verses* and the fatwa issued by Ayatollah Khomeini boosted widespread Islamophobia and the public vilification of Muslims, who were depicted in the press as backward fundamentalists. This experience added to the economic tensions that followed the neoliberal turn in politics in the 1980s as well as the rampant cultural racism (i.e. the general contempt displayed towards Muslim values) that became so poignant during the Salman Rushdie affair had the effect of reinforcing Muslims' attachment to and identification with their faith.

The vitality of the internal debates on the place and role of Sharia law that have emerged among Muslims in the UK reflects the Islamic Revival that is taking place both within and outside Europe today. Some aspects of this Revival as they developed in Egypt have been studied by Saba Mahmood (2005) and Charles Hirschkind (2006). Their respective works have been particularly attentive to underlining the relationships between the power of Islamic ideals of morality and piety, the connections between everyday religiosity and religious knowledge, as well as the interconnections and tensions between Islamic practices of piety and the architecture of secular power. The concepts of "tradition," "self-discipline" and "personal ethics" that these scholars have explored have shown the necessity of revisiting the binary associations that oppose "reason" and "rationalism" to Islam in light of the post-colonial dynamics that give this Revival its unique cultural shape. However, the focus on "piety" made this work somewhat irrelevant in explaining the new cultural "assemblages" and "interpenetrations" that have taken shape in European societies as a result of the increased visibility of Islam (Göle 2005; 2010). This is where the work of Nilüfer Göle on Islam in Europe and her specific interest in "multiple modernities" can give us analytical keys for understanding Islamic legal practices in secular Western societies. Indeed, the legal practices that I will further describe in this chapter highlight not a quest for purity, but a desire to find the right balance in order to produce a new cultural expression while remaining faithful to Islam and the sacred texts. While Islam has become the discursive field upon which British Muslims are trying to define alternative versions of their identity, the practices I observed within Sharia councils highlight an attempt at reconciling "the tension between the cultivation of pious subjectivity in tune with the temporalities of the global Islamic Revival and the perceived necessity to integrate Muslims into local European contexts" (Caeiro 2010: 435).

Authority Decentered

In the British context, the authority of Ulema is the object of constant contestation, not only from the outside (clients of Sharia councils sometimes mobilize sheikhs located abroad in order to challenge the decisions of British councilors) but also from within, as fatwa-seekers use their own knowledge and interpretation to influence Ulema's judgments. The multiplication of sources of authority has forced Ulema to develop important pedagogic skills in order to guide Islamic justice-seekers on their path towards an ethical life.

During the monthly hearings of the Birmingham Sharia Council and also in the correspondence of the MLSC, I noticed the carefulness with which councilors explained the methods through which they came to their decisions. One was a case I mentioned earlier of a woman who had come to the Birmingham Sharia Council to seek divorce from her disabled husband from whom she had been separated for two years. She argued that the constant arguments she had with her husband as well as his violent attitude had caused an unbearable amount of stress for her and her children, and that the chance of reconciliation had vanished as a result. Unable to attend the meeting, the husband had sent his eldest son to defend his version of events. According to him, the real reason for his mother's request was motivated by her desire to lead the life of a "single woman." In his opinion, the Council's decision to issue a divorce would have the effect of encouraging her to acquire more freedom and to abandon her responsibilities as a mother. The loosening of her "modesty" following her separation from his father was given as evidence for his mother's "hidden agenda." After carefully listening to the young man's opinion, Amra Bone explained that remaining in an unhappy marriage could in some instances be more sinful than being divorced. She reminded him that the purpose of marriage was "love and compassion" and that his mother felt her marriage did not fulfill these essential needs. If divorce was the most "reprehensible of all permitted acts" (*makruh*), it was still preferable to a greater sin, like adultery, which all schools of fiqh consider as forbidden (*haram*). Recounting the story of the slander against Aisha in Surat An-Noor, she reminded the young man of the importance of "good faith" in forming opinions of others. She eventually concluded:

> So taking into account what you said, all we can do is try to speak to her and – once the case does come to the Council, it is our duty to make sure that more injustice is not done within that marriage – there is no reason why your parents couldn't get married again because it's not a final divorce or anything. It's your mum who is the one who initiated the process. So if this marriage is dissolved, there is no reason why the two parties can't come together again and be married again. Perhaps she may feel that she has now more independence and she feels that she can form the contract on her terms perhaps. It just gives that flexibility to people. Now of course, there's obviously the possibility that she might not want to do that, but Islam takes both parties as independent individuals, having certain responsibilities toward each other and giving them their right and the duty not to harm each other. Ideally, it's better to stay together, but situations like this arise because one party is not being satisfied. But if the situation is allowed to carry on the way it is, it's not helpful. It's harmful. Do you understand? … You see when two people are married, then they have to give each other their physical rights. They have to give whatever emotional rights to each other. When that's not happening, that's actually harming. Get it?

This conversation illustrates that while trying to maintain the boundaries of the permissible within Islam, councilors are also concerned with educating not only their clients, but also their relatives whom they consider as legitimate stakeholders in family disputes. Therefore, the arguments mobilized by the young man, who was anxious about maintaining the honor and reputation of his family by controlling the modesty of his mother, are counterbalanced by arguments stressing the responsibility of the Council in avoiding greater harm. The councilor also emphasized values that according to Islam are at the center of the marriage contract: love and compassion. In the councilors' opinion, the cases that they routinely consider should not only concern the two parties in conflict but should also include the opinions and feelings of the larger family. The relationship that they strive to establish with them relies on co-responsibility and on a shared understanding of the values and ethics promoted in Islam. The Council, whose primary concern is to foster living in peace first with oneself and then with the wider community, offers a space for multiple voices and perspectives to be heard, and for sharing knowledge and developing a common appreciation of the purpose and meaning of Islamic prescriptions. Contrary to secular law that is based on an individualist vision of justice, Sharia councils endeavor to maintain family and community values as well as the rights and duties that Muslims have towards each other.

In a conversation between a social worker and two councilors from the Birmingham Sharia Council, Amra Bone and Dr Naseem explained their working methods in order to clarify what they perceived as a common misconception among British Muslims that considers Sharia law and British law as two totally separate legal systems. This exchange highlights the councilors' desire to be perceived as knowledgeable facilitators of people's affairs instead of coercive arbitrators applying an inflexible version of the Sharia. While using an Islamic framework to guide their clients towards the "good," their discourses are also concerned with deconstructing arguments that place the Sharia in a moral sphere totally separated from the mainstream justice system:

> Naseem: The law of the land applies to Muslims, wherever they live … So we make it very clear to people who apply for an annulment of marriage if the case is in the court, because according to the Sharia they're not required to get an Islamic divorce, but we do it if they insist.

> Amra: Allah does not want us to have conflict in our minds. If they've already got a divorce from the civil courts, then we have to give [a] divorce because they can't be married in one and divorced in the other. Some people are playing with this, which is totally wrong. We can't be single in one form and writing married in another … This is cheating.

The pedagogic skills that councilors deploy in their everyday practice demonstrate that the purpose of the councils is less to pronounce the correct doctrine than to reconcile Muslims' relationships to Islam and British law. While mobilizing common Islamic ethical principles as illustrated by the life of the Prophet and the models of good actions he provided to his followers, councilors also feel it is their duty, as British citizens, to encourage women to have their marriage registered under British law. They generally refuse to issue a divorce until the civil divorce has been pronounced. In doing so, they strive to promote Islam as an accommodating 'civil religion' (Caeiro 2010: 437).

Affective Performance

The authority of Sharia councils does not rely on doctrinal coercion, but rather on the capacity of councilors to accompany their clients in their journey toward an ethical way of life. As one imam told me, Sharia councils "care for the soul," while British courts are more concerned with procedures and the application of the law. As the legal historian Wael Hallaq puts it:

> the state permits and forbids, and when it does the latter, it punishes severely upon infraction. It is not in the least interested in what individuals do outside of its spheres of influence and concern. Islamic law, on the other hand, has an all-encompassing interest in human acts. It organises them into various categories ranging from the moral to the legal, without however making conscious distinctions between the moral and the legal. (Hallaq 2009: 19)

I noticed on numerous occasions the attention with which councilors listened to their clients, avoided interrupting them and let them express their emotions and go into the very intimate details of their marital relationships. At the MLSC, Maulana Raza, the chairman, explained in the following terms the difference in nature between an "affidavit" written in the context of civil divorce proceedings and the statements clients wrote to the Sharia council:

> In most cases we insist that we will not accept their civil divorce petition as their statement for Islamic divorce ... Because those petitions are mainly prepared by the solicitors. They may not take into account the *personal situation of their client*. They design it in a way which is more conducive to the legal requirement of the country so it may not reflect fully the *real personal emotions* and reasons for that. So we don't wanna base things upon these petitions which are designed particularly for the purpose of the courts here ... We leave it to the applicant. It could be very brief. We do not dig into it; we do not wish to open their wounds. It's up to them if they want to give us a five-page statement ... but we never put any condition ... We never do that, it's up to them but a personal statement seems to us a bit of a reflection or a representation of the situation or of the nature of a dispute. (Maulana Shahid Raza, March 2012)

In contrast to the space of the court, where emotions and clients' grievances are filtered through the expert language of a solicitor, the councils offer a space deprived of such disciplinary techniques. Most importantly, the fact that clients express feelings and emotions is considered proof of their good faith. On numerous occasions, I witnessed councilors who, when faced with similar cases, sometimes took different decisions, depending on their own evaluation of the psychological condition of their clients. In one instance, the Birmingham Sharia Council had received divorce requests from two women who presented very similar grievances: they had both lived separately from their husbands for two years and all attempts at reconciliation had failed. Their husbands had not been particularly collaborative with the Council, refusing to attend the meetings set up at the reconciliation clinic. In one instance, the Council decided that Jamila (not her real name) could persevere a bit longer and suggested that she wait for the next meeting of the Sharia Council the following month to give her husband another chance to come and give his side of the story. The reason the councilors gave for this decision was that there was no rush in pronouncing the divorce, since Jamila's husband had a police injunction not to enter her house and so he could not harm her anymore. Jamila looked "okay," psychologically, they agreed. Her performance in front of the Council did not give them the impression that it was an emergency. In the case of Sabrina, however, the Council decided to dissolve the marriage on the day of her hearing. The reason for not delaying this decision any longer was that "she looked quite upset, exhausted and depressed. She does not seem to be able to put up with more waiting."

Discussions taking place in Sharia councils involve perhaps as much psychology and counseling skills as Islamic legal knowledge. One imam mentioned to me that a third of the time, he answered "I don't know" to the questions he was asked. He explained this was a strategy he used in order to make people speak about their problems in more personal and specific terms:

> All the good muftis have already understood that in Islam, law and spirit are intertwined and that's why you can't give a fatwa that is the same in every situation. It's all in the end for people's cases, you're helping them with their spirituality or trying to help them in the path to God and therefore there will be these variations and you have to take the context into account. You know, Sheikh Abdullah bin Bayyah has written a lot on this. So, for example, he quoted Al Ghazali who said giving fatwa or fiqh jurisprudence, only 10 percent of it is about knowing the text, the other 90 percent is knowing the situation of the people. (Usama Hassan, February 2012)

Emotions play an important role in determining the Council's decisions. Therefore, the setting provided by the Council does not attempt to neutralize them. Councilors even appeal to the emotions of their clients when in doubt of their good faith. In one instance, Imam Mamadou of the MLSC told me the story of a man who had accused his wife of adultery. The man was invited to come to the Council to take an oath on the Koran and swear that his wife was guilty. The wife was invited to do the same in order to deny his accusation. The fact that the husband did not show up at the appointment and the woman did was considered as a proof of the husband's "fear of God" and his realization of the gravity of his accusation. The Council eventually considered that this represented a clear case of *Li'an* (cursing) involving elements of *dihar* (harm) and that the marriage had to be dissolved immediately. The symbolic power of the ceremony worked as a booster of the believer's consciousness of God (*taqwa*), of the metaphysical realities of Islam (*iman*) and of the necessity of fearing Allah's final verdict on Judgment Day.

Another example of the power of emotion in Sharia practices was revealed to me when Sheikh Khalifa Ezzat, the chief imam of the Regent Park's Mosque, told me that he sometimes sent his clients to other Sharia councils. He had done this recently with a man who repeatedly pronounced "talaq" to his wife and who constantly used his anger as an excuse. Somewhat surprised by this revelation, I asked him whether he did this because he was uncertain of the right advice to give. He answered:

> No, not at all! I just wanted to make it harder for him. Because this person was joking and playing with divorce all the time, so I wanted to give him a lesson. Otherwise, he will keep on doing the same thing over and over again. He is playing with divorce all the time and divorce is a serious thing. That was not the first time he came here and I had warned him already. So I referred him to Leyton [another Sharia council in East London], warning him that he may well be divorced to [sic] his wife this time.

By doing this, Sheykh Ezzat wanted to teach his client the virtue of patience and forbearance in marital relationships and make him aware of the gravity of his actions. Indeed, councilors rarely came with a ready-made answer to a specific problem: for each of their clients, they strived to design the most pedagogic advice, tailoring their responses to the specific needs of the believers who seek their guidance.

In addition to arbitrating family disputes and divorces, the councilors' practice is often similar to that of a personal counselor. Once, a man came unannounced to the monthly hearings of the Birmingham Sharia Council. He entered the room, looking angry and depressed, and threw a pile of photographs on the councilors' desk. The pictures had been extracted from his ex-wife's mobile phone: she appeared on them with someone he called "her new boyfriend." The Council had recently dissolved his marriage, after his wife had received a decree absolute from the civil court. The man accused his ex-wife of lying about her true intentions when she had first approached the Council. He also reproached the Council for having pronounced a divorce without seeking his agreement first. To soothe his anger, Amra explained to him that the Council had no other choice but to pronounce a divorce, since his wife had already obtained a decree absolute. She also made him aware of his responsibility, as a Muslim, not to spread rumors about his wife. She said: "If you think the worst of people, that's not good for your own character. If you think the best of people, then that's the best for your character because then you're not being judgmental." She went on to advise him to spend more time evaluating the character of a woman before getting married for a second time:

> When you meet somebody out in town, you don't know their background, you don't know who they are, what they have done. They may show a lot of love and all that, but the best way to meet is through families, through friends, in wholesome environment[s]. Then you can find out from the people they know, whether they have a really good character, a good personality. When you meet

somebody out in town, you don't know, they could be drug dealers, they could have a really bad character and you don't know, but it's difficult to find out. I'm regularly being asked, "Oh can you find me a good brother?" These girls can find people themselves, but they don't because they want a good person, but they want it through a group of people that they feel may know a commendable person. And then you still have the opportunity to meet and evaluate whether you have things in common.

The advice Amra gave the young man was very similar to what an expert in "personal development" might say, but with an Islamic touch to it. She encouraged him to "Trust Allah," remove the bitterness in his heart and sign up for one of the "marriage events" that took place at the mosque once a month: these were an opportunity to meet potential brides in a perfectly "halal" and safe environment.

One should not consider Sharia councils merely as instances to deliver Islamic justice, but rather as community spaces that Muslims can consider their own because of the common language and shared moral universe that allow them to be fully understood. Embedded in the social landscape where they developed concern for people's spiritual and social wellbeing, Sharia councils cater to the needs of a wide range of Muslims: from first-generation migrants to re-Islamized youths and converts. The discursive tradition that they seek to cultivate and the interactive nature of their deliberations make Sharia councils spaces where Muslims can nurture and interpret values and norms important to them. However, the importance given to emotions makes them different from liberal public spheres, where the emphasis is put on rational discursive exchanges. Their dual character as spaces for withdrawal as well as "training grounds" for activities that challenge the norms and values of dominant publics underlines the subaltern character of these spaces. Michael Warner's conceptualization of counterpublics as performative and affective spaces is well suited to an understanding of the nature of Sharia councils. In his view, the cultural horizon against which a counterpublic marks itself off is not just a general or wider public, but a dominant one. The conflict extends not only to ideas but also to the genres of speech and modes of address that constitute the public. This friction against the dominant public forces the poetic-expressive character of counterpublic discourse to become salient to consciousness. Participation in counterpublics is one of the ways in which its members' identities are formed and transformed. A counterpublic is a "world-making project" which fashions subjectivities. It is a space of circulation in which it is hoped that "the poesis of scene-making will be transformative, not merely replicative" (Warner 2002).

Conclusion

The creation of Sharia councils in the UK is emblematic of the global Islamic Revival and of the ethico-normative project that guides this movement. However, the development of such practices in Western countries should not be interpreted as an indicator of "radicalization" or "fundamentalism." Indeed, the practices that I have described in this chapter highlight Ulema's desire to present Islam as a civil religion. Sharia councils are not meant to cater to the needs of specific ethnic groups, but rather to serve the entire Muslim community. The recent transformations of Sharia councils with a trend towards greater diversity and inclusiveness as well as the constant internal and external challenges to their authority indicate their translocal anchorage (Mandaville 1999), i.e. their belonging to a movement that disrupts, transforms and reinforces the normative basis of Islam.

It is therefore necessary to comprehend this phenomenon within a post-migration framework, since the actors who participate in the making of Islamic justice in Britain are bearers of values, norms and ideas that reach beyond national borders and that are not clearly tied to a Muslim country "of origin." Indeed, the unique position of British Muslims as a religious minority that carries the memorial and experiential baggage of the post-colonial past and present explains in large part the development of different interpretations of their living environment and scope of action. As bearers of imaginary and collective memory that differ from the British mainstream, Muslims have created "counterpublic spaces" where they discursively and collectively shape alternative representations of their identity. The sense of ethical agency that Sharia councils strive to promote by preserving values and codes of conduct important to Muslims (the protection of the most vulnerable – the elderly, children, women – the recognition of the wisdom that comes with age, the practice of *adab*, the prescribed Islamic etiquette that values refinement, morals and decency) indicates a new moral economy (Fassin 2009) through which a counterhegemonic definition of British Muslims' identity is discursively shaped.

The various dimensions of Islamic legal practices that I have emphasized in this chapter, including the pedagogy of Islamic guidance, the shared responsibility of Islamic justice-seekers and the Ulema who advise them, the quest for keeping a balance between *haram* and *makruh* acts while remaining within the boundaries imposed by the "law of the land," indicate Ulema's concern for helping Muslims on their path to an ethical Muslim life. The central role played by emotions and affect places their practices on the border between the legal, the spiritual and the psychological. I believe it is this emphasis on the embodied form of morality that imposes itself not through doctrinal enforcement, but rather as a new form of "care of the Self" (Agrama 2010) that explains the growing success of Islamic justice in the UK.

References

Agrama, H.A. 2010. "Ethics, Tradition, Authority: Toward an Anthropology of the Fatwa," *American Ethnologist*, 37(1), 2–18.

Bano, S. 2004. "Complexity, Difference and 'Muslim Personal law': Rethinking the Relationship between Shariah Councils and South Asian Muslim Women in Britain," available at: http://wrap.warwick.ac.uk/1205.

Berger, M. 2009. "Let Muslims Have Their Sharia Courts," *nrc handelsblad*. Available at: http://www.nrc.nl/international/opinion/article2296919.ece/Let_them_have_their_sharia_courts.

Bowen, J.R., 2012. *Blaming Islam*. Cambridge, MA: MIT Press.

Bunt, G. 1998. "Decision Making Concerns in British Islamic Environments," *Islam and Christian–Muslim Relations*, 9(1), 103–13.

Caeiro, A. 2010. "The Power of European Fatwas: The Minority Fiqh Project and the Making of an Islamic Counterpublic," *International Journal of Middle East Studies*, 42(3), 435–449.

CBCNews, 2005. "Ontario Premier Rejects Use of Shariah law – Canada – CBC News," available at: http://www.cbc.ca/news/canada/story/2005/09/09/sharia-protests-20050909.html.

Cowan, J-K. Dembour, M.-B. and Wilson, R. 2001. *Culture and Rights*. Cambridge: Cambridge University Press.

EuropeNews. 2010. "Austria: Majority of Turks Want Sharia Personal Law Incorporated into Legal System," *EuropeNews*, available at: http://europenews.dk/en/node/29130.

Fassin, D. 2009. "Les économies morales revisitées," *Annales Histoire, Sciences Sociales*, 64(6), 1237–66.

Göle, N. 2005. *Interpénétrations: L'Islam et l'Europe*. Paris: Galaade.

Göle, N. 2010. "The Civilizational, Spatial and Sexual Powers of the Secular," in J. Vanatwerper and G. Calhoun (eds), *Varieties of Secularism in a Secular Age*. Cambridge, MA: Harvard University Press, 243–64.

Hallaq, W.B. 2009. *An Introduction to Islamic Law*. Cambridge: Cambridge University Press.

Hirschkind, C., 2006. *The Ethical Soundscape: Cassette Sermons and Islamic Counterpublics*. New York: Columbia University Press.

Lentin, A. and Titley, G. 2011. *The Crises of Multiculturalism: Racism in a Neoliberal Age*. London: Zed Books.

Lewis, P. 2002. *Islamic Britain: Religion, Politics and Identity among British Muslims*. London I.B.Tauris.

Mahmood, S. 2005. *Politics of Piety: The Islamic Revival and the Feminist Subject*. Princeton, NJ: Princeton University Press.

Mandaville, P.G. 1999. "Territory and Translocality: Discrepant Idioms of Political Identity," *Millennium – Journal of International Studies*, 28(3), 653–73.

Menski, W. 2000. "Muslim Law in Britain," in M. Koga, M. Naito and T. Hamaguchi (eds), *From Migrant to Citizen: South Asian Communities Overseas*. Tokyo: Institute for the Study of Languages and Cultures of Asia and Africa, 294–318.

Modood, T. 1990. "British Asian and Muslims and the Rushdie Affair," *Political Quarterly*, 61(2), 143–60.

Spiegel Online. 2012. "Politician Blasted for Support of Islamic Law," available at: http://www.spiegel.de/international/germany/0,1518,813148,00.html.

Triandafyllidou, A. et al. 2011. *European Multiculturalisms: Cultural, Religious and Ethnic Challenges*. Edinburgh: Edinburgh University Press.

Warner, M. 2002. "Publics and Counterpublics," *Public Culture*, 14(1), 49–90.
Werbner, P. 1996. "Stamping the Earth with the Name of Allah: Zikr and the Sacralizing of Space among British Muslims," *Cultural Anthropology*, 11(3), 309–38.
Williams, R. 2008. "Archbishop's Lecture – Civil and Religious Law in England: A Religious Perspective," available at: http://rowanwilliams.arch bishopofcanterbury.org/articles.php/1137/archbishops-lecture-civil-and-religious-law-in-england-a-religious-perspective.

Chapter 14

The Eclectic Usage of Halal and Conflicts of Authority[1]

Rachid Id Yassine

The word "halal"[2] is now part of the common vocabulary, and its Gallicization – or, more precisely, its Europeanization – is being imposed progressively by the public debate on the Muslim presence in Europe. The variety of its forms of social significance is apparent in the simple observation that this usage is as heterogeneous as the actors employing it. CEOs, investment bankers, ordinary consumers, religious lawyers, activists, policy makers, young lovers, painters and so on: not all are so obviously Muslim. And what else can we note about the public usage of this term? That it touches every aspect of social and cultural life: eating[3] and dressing habits,[4] hygiene[5] and upkeep,[6] emotional[7] and sexual relationships,[8] art[9] and leisure,[10] finance[11] and politics, and even infrastructure.[12] Everything can be halal – well, almost everything!

---

1   The research leading to the results in this chapter has been partially financed by the EuroPublicIslam Project directed by Nilüfer Göle (EHESS) and funded by the European Research Council under the European Community's Seventh Framework Programme (FP7/2007–2013)/Grant Agreement n° 230244.

2   I distinguish the word "halal," a sort of vulgarized form of the original Arabic word *halâl*, meaning licit as opposed to *harâm*, meaning illicit.

3   Pork products, fast food, frozen foods, candy, beer, eggs, water, cat food, dry dog food, etc.

4   Fashion, lingerie (the G-string and the jilbaab rub shoulders on HijabGlam.com).

5   Toothpaste, shampoo, cosmetics, etc.

6   Dish soap, deodorant, etc.

7   Friendship, sympathy or antipathy with Muslims or non-Muslims, with the opposite or same sex.

8   Couples who desire "to make it *halal*": flirting, condoms or sex-shops. See http://elasira.com/intro (Blass 2010). Or, more recently, the opening in Casablanca of a "halal sex-shop," called "Eros."

9   Theatre, music, painting, sculpture, etc.

10   Swimsuits, swimming pools, fitness centers, soap operas and films, clubs, camps, etc.

11   Banks, Sharia-compatible financial services, etc.

12   Notably ports, such as that of Marseille in France and of Zeebrugge in Belgium, the only two ports in Europe to be labeled "halal" by the Halal Food Council International (HCFI), an international entity of halal certification with its headquarters in the US.

One is certainly led to question the limits of halal. But, more sociologically, this chapter is interested above all in the processes and dynamics that the use of this term carries with it. How can we understand its spread to so many different activities? Why do these actors all use the same word "halal"? Do they share one identical and accepted meaning, justifying this common usage? Or, on the contrary, is it that the semantic flexibility of this term invites conflicting positions to converge around its use? Is it because halal is a controversial issue in Islam that it is also the object of controversy in Europe?

To provide some answers to these questions, I will begin with the emergence of this term in the public sphere where it is mobilized with such exuberance by a diverse array of actors. This production of halal as a public category is confirmed in the political aspect that has imprinted on it a connotation of identity. Next, I will show how the secular suspends the religious by desacralizing halal; on the one hand, as the logical consequence of sociocultural conditions in European societies and, on the other hand, as the consequence of systems specific to Islam. The encounter between European secular values and Islamic religious norms is negotiated in such a way that it also necessarily becomes the site of at times insoluble conflicts of authority. In light of these observations, I will conclude with a reflexive return to the notional predispositions of halal that I believe help to explain such a success.

Halal as a Public Category: From Communal to Public Space

It is undoubtedly due to the initiative of Muslim populations that we owe the emergence of the term "halal" in European public debate. Indeed, for several decades, these populations have been formulating multiple claims in relation to Islamic normativity. I suggest that these claims should be clarified according to the three spaces identified by Dominique Wolton, namely "the communal space, the public space, and the political space." According to him, "the communal space concerns circulation and expression; the public space, discussion; and the political space, decision" (Wolton 2012).

In a more or less coordinated fashion, the claims of Muslims in Europe obviously concern worship.[13] It can be noted, as shown through this first type of claim, that if the visibility of Islam was confined to the communal space, there would be no public controversy: intercommunity polemics would be sufficient for the social regulation of the Muslim presence. Within the framework of secular societies, Islam is not *publicly* legitimate as a religion in the institutional sense of the term, and in that case, its circulation and its expression are hardly controversial in structuring the public space. European societies do not consider banning Muslims from practicing their faith as long as the accommodating division between the public and private spheres is respected. The production of halal as

---

13   As in the construction of mosques and religious schools or the establishment of cemeteries.

a public category is confirmed by the political powers that have imprinted on it a connotation of identity.

Having said that, some claims extend beyond the common space by conveying aspirations for social recognition and political affirmation. These enable the Muslim presence to enter the political space and, sometimes with little regard for social developments, to force "difference." The radicalism of certain behaviors, whether individual or communitarian, translates into an exacerbation of identity that is a vehicle for the young and urban popular classes, or into an assimilationist cultural inferiority complex among the majority of social elites. More concretely, the creation of special courts takes over decision making in response to such claims. Sometimes, in order to be heard, these claims go so far as resorting to illegitimate violence and terror. The marginality of such claims, springing from charismatic personalities or small antisocial groups, reduces the possibility of these controversies engaging society as a whole. The Islamic identity as formulated in the political space is subject to a democratic consensus that is quite compelling among the majority of Muslims in Western societies who assert their rights as citizens. Consequently, we can understand why these claims of exceptionalism, which are registered in the political space, make no significant use of the word "halal," preferring instead the word *harâm*, meaning illicit.

On the other hand, there is another type of claim that makes frequent use of the term "halal," namely the claims calling for the right to demonstrate one's religiosity in the public space, thus extending beyond the communal space such as the wearing of the "Islamic headscarf" at school or in the workplace, at the country club or at political party events. Other examples are the arrangement of flexible working hours around prayer times and the demand for halal meals in big-box stores and restaurants as well as in schools,[14] hospitals and business cafeterias (Lamghari 2012: 54). There they are made public and thus result in controversial discussions about practices that are not necessarily inherently religious. It is precisely this situation that continues to feed the controversies around Islam in Europe. This passing of communitarian claims to social claims is the prelude to entering the political space where society makes its decisions. "The public space is obviously the first step towards the political space" (Wolton 2012), which is why we distrust any religious expression that by claiming "public opinion" can bring about political decisions or even simply influence them.

The Standardization of Halal Commerce

During the 1980s and 1990s, we saw an initial usage of the word "halal" that was rather narrative and about identity, with associations now giving way, since the

---

14   For example, the city of Villeurbanne in the Rhône department in France opted in its 24 school cafeterias for a system of colored tokens that would make parental choices regarding pork or vegetarian menu options more anonymous.

start of the 2000s, to more practical nuances which reflect the term's progressive integration into capitalist societies. New promoters of halal are emerging, notably among the younger generations. In accordance with the liberal context of post-industrial societies, Muslim patterns of consumption in Europe tend towards progressive uniformity with that of the rest of the population (Amalou 2005). Recent studies[15] have shown this evolution by proving that younger generations are diversifying and broadening the demand for halal across all product categories, not just in their consumption of meat products, as was the case with previous generations. Associations, shops, companies and multiple initiatives will be created in order to offer goods and services capable of responding to this demand for "all things halal." These organizations will wrest halal from its initial religious template and will impose on it an economic aspect. This marks the development of "a world of Islamic-business that circumvents traditional religious authorities as well as States in the current context of liberalization and globalization" (Roy 2003: 94).

The term is being transformed into a commercial label and a reference point, insomuch as it represents a specific market: "the halal market." Rather than religious experts and ideologists, a body of specialists, technicians and sales personnel – more or less legitimized in reference to Islam – will contribute to the distribution of halal and ensure its insertion into conventional markets. In this new framework, the word "halal" is not only integrated into market institutions but is also infused with mercantilist culture: marketing, management, investment, profitability, performance … in a word, *efficiency*.

Halal's significance loses its original force as an expression of identity and instead aims not at the complete opposite, but at carving out a niche in a liberal capitalist economy. Consequently, halal becomes acceptable, including for non-Muslims, who are even among the most active in this market, like Antoine Bonnel[16] and Gérard Deslandes,[17] respective leaders of two major professional trade fairs of halal business in Europe.

Muslims are not slow in responding, as modestly illustrated by the opening of purely halal supermarkets.[18] Faced with an onslaught in the food industry, big-box stores[19] and fast-food shops,[20] polemics multiplied around halal certification, as in the case of halal labels for Herta sausages proven to contain pork (Foucaud 2011).

15　See, among others, Brouard and Tiberj 2005; Bergeaud-Blackler and Bernard 2010; Bowen 2011.

16　Director of Paris Halal Expo; see notably http://2012.parishalalexpo.com.

17　Director of Euro Halal Market; see http://eurohalalmarket.eu.

18　Such as Hal'shop and its two locations in Nanterre and Paris, "the first certified 100% halal supermarket." For further information, see http://halshop.fr/fr; Euro Primeurs in Creil in the Oise department; Sunny Market in Fèves in north Metz, presented as "the first organic halal supermarket in Europe"; or Baker Market in Saint-Herblain on the outskirts of Nantes. See http://bakermarket.com.

19　Everyone has its "radius of halal," or even its brand such as Carrefour Halal and Casino-Wassila.

20　KFC, Quick, etc.

Frauds are regularly denounced and requirements raised and multiplied, leading to the emergence of Muslim consumer associations.[21] In this way, people are calling of course for more honesty and transparency, but also for fewer health risks and less greed, more respect and care for animals, for the environment and for the poor. These ethical demands couple halal with the organic, the environmentally friendly and fair trade. In a word, halal comes to mean *authenticity*. Architects of efficiency respond to this with traceability and the certification of halal meat.

This is in fact the main advantage of Muslim entrepreneurs active in the halal market. A wide range of halal meat regulatory organizations exist and, as such, constitute a "halal certification market," with more than roughly 100 such bodies in Europe, of which nearly half operate in France alone. They are not all the same, using very different methods and following different specifications. While the French Council for the Muslim Faith (*Conseil Français du Culte Musulman*: CFCM) has not yet managed to ratify its own "charter of halal hygiene and quality" among its members, abandoning this issue for an indeterminate "reflection period," the *Association française de normalisation* (AFNOR) has succeeded in presenting its findings at the November 2011 European meeting[22] on the feasibility of a European standard on halal. The outcome was to be announced for March 2012, but still nothing is published.

Ultimately, religious and economic actors continue to disagree because each camp sticks to its respective requirements for authenticity and efficiency. "If halal as applied to consumer products is not just purely religious or purely economic, who gets [the] final say in deciding the standard? The issue is more than just the trust of Muslim consumers. What is at stake is the right of all consumers (including those who do not consume ritual products) to information" (Bergeaud-Blackler and Bernard 2010: 155).

From Political Islam to Populist Europe

This then is the moment when political actors, animated by very diverse motivations, insistently make their appearance. In 2011, Daniel Goldberg, the socialist deputy of Seine-Saint-Denis, a Parisian suburb, repeatedly called on the government to act, believing that "the State is entitled to intervene in this debate concerning Muslims and notably in terms of its role in consumer protection." In addition to the argument of consumer health or animal cruelty, it is above all about the right to information that is at the heart of the French controversy over halal

---

21   As in, for example, *l'Union Française des Consommateurs Musulmans* (UFCM): http://ufcm.fr; and *l'Association de Sensibilisation, d'Information et de Défense de Consommateurs Musulmans* (Asidcom): http://asidcom.org.

22   Held on November 21–22, 2012 in Brussels: "The task of the Working Group (CEN/BT WG 212) is to analyse the feasibility of a European Standard regulating the requirements for halal food."

meat. For some columnists, the fact that "the French eat halal without realizing it ... is not merely anecdotal but rather a sort of national scandal" (Giesbert 2012). Opponents to what they call "halalization" attack, with varying degrees of force, the religious archaism, economic greed, and duplicity of politicians. To remedy this, the more reckless even suggest "the creation of a 'Guaranteed non-halal meat' French label" (Heurtebise 2012).

We can thus assume that the pursuit of a European standard could foster the spread of the French controversy over halal meat to other European countries where, as in France, public controversies over halal are initiated by the far-right populist parties (Lyon 2012). In reality, when biting into an apple, the French and all Europeans eat halal. Now, it is interesting to note that if a strong desire for Islamic identity originally led to the public emergence of the term "halal," the "standardization" of halal by economic actors ends up shifting the problem of identity to Europe itself. As characteristic of public controversies over Islam in Europe, this shift seems to be particularly indicative of a reconfiguration of the European public space by Islam.[23] Similarly to the headscarf (full-veiling or otherwise), minarets and, more recently, circumcision, halal acts here as a catalyst of an identity crisis that is probably more European than Islamic.

Indeed, we must question the conditions surrounding the emergence of this French controversy, which paradoxically spreads to the European level in keeping with the political agenda of nationalist and *souverainiste* parties. To understand this, we must remember that, with a self-proclaimed sales pitch as "the guardians of Europe," these populist offensives are reactionary. Their expressions of Euroskepticism does not prevent them from pretending to defend a specific, singular European identity from the particularistic demands of Muslims that would further the multiculturalism of European institutions (Kastoryano 2000). Hence, Marine Le Pen, the leader of the National Front party in France, opposes both Islam and Europe. She had already unleashed the controversy over the "halal Quicks," only to reiterate it two years later during the most recent presidential campaign in Lille on 19 February 2012, when she declared that "all the butchers in the Paris region sell halal, without exception – only halal!"[24] As with French secularism (*laïcité*), Europe would be menaced and to protect it, she denounces the dangers of an "Islamization of Europe," as the project of a European Halal Standard supposedly illustrates. Euphemizing the ethnoracial repertoire of the traditional far-right, she substitutes it for a religious (*laïcité*) and cultural (Europe) inventory, which no doubt owes much to the famous "demonization of the National Front."

If halal first emerged at the initiative of Muslims to manage the supply of meat within neighborhood butchers, the term was then "misappropriated" by more non-

---

23   See the website of the EuroPublicIslam Project: http://europublicislam.hypotheses.org.

24   The Vice-President of the Paris Reigon Livestock Farming Association, Jean-Baptiste Galloo, joined the debate and declared: "Of the four slaughterhouses that remain in the Paris region ... all practice ritual slaughter, either halal or kosher, almost exclusively" (Launay and Legouté 2012).

specialist actors who stretched its usage in commerce well beyond meat products. The search for authenticity by some and for efficiency by others makes it difficult to establish a halal standard that can satisfy such disparate demands. The success of those searching for authenticity is subject to many uncertainties, while, similarly, those searching for efficiency have had to acquiesce at least partly in the meat industry to the rules of *dhabiha* (ritual slaughtering). The relatively widespread use of halal meat has in fact provoked a public controversy, obliging policy makers to place the issue under the umbrella of "ritual slaughter."[25] All competent local and national public institutions have gotten involved both upstream and downstream of the controversy, by regulating certain professional practices such as slaughtering that affected by the religious prescriptions in question. But the controversy is above all a well-primed opportunity to assert identity claims. And for good reason.

Halal as a Secular Category: European Cultural Integration

The public usage of the term halal relates to all aspects of cultural and social life, not just meat or even the entire food industry. If diet is implicitly prominent in the use of this epithet, the fact remains that Muslims in Europe use it to qualify an extreme variety of their consumerist desires ranging from champagne to the G-string, from finance to sport, art and all kinds of products. With this instrumental character of symbolic legitimization, the widespread usage of the word "halal" is a tacit admission that these activities do not belong with certainty to the world of Islamic piety, which "normally" commends the exercise of self-control over one's urges. In any case, the group of activities that Muslims designate halal hardly relates to a strict observation of the Islamic faith. But, as cultural practices, they reflect the cultural integration of Muslim religiosity in a secular context.

If for Jocelyne Cesari (2004: 70), secularization "also and above all designates the decline of the social influence of the religious" – and, in that case, the US is not at all a secular nation, but rather the exact opposite – Olivier Roy (2008: 17) notes that "secularism creates the religious." In fact, it is not so much the weak social influence of the religious that secularizes society, but rather the loss of its social prominence. This process applies to all religions, and the Christian identity of secular societies in Europe also appears to become less evident: we are not *obviously* Christian because we are French, English or Italian, just as we are not *obviously* Muslim because we are Tunisian, Senegalese or Indonesian. This situation creates a kind of aesthetic destabilization and blurs the markers of identity, creating the need to reaffirm certain obvious facts supposedly constituent of national identities or

25 Marine Le Pen's campaign themes precipitated the decree of 28 December 2011, requiring authorization from the Prefect of Police to practice ritual slaughter in French slaughterhouses, initially slated for 1 July 2012, to take effect on 8 March 2012.

of European identity. It is this context that enables certain surprising alliances between militant Christians and militant secularists (Baubérot 2006) from the far-right to the far-left. Islam is perceived less as an irreverent religion by the secular order than as a threat to the relative cultural homogeneity of Europe.

If, as I recommend, we consent to a rigorous distinction between culture and religion, "Islamic culture" as such is imaginary, as there is no objectively Islamic cuisine, articles of clothing, sexuality or music. Islam is not a culture, and the epithet of "Islamic" – which we can easily replace with "halal" – points to conformity with Islamic religious norms. However, as we avoid the naïve confusion between culture and religion, we must also not superimpose them. As Nilfüfer Göle (2005: 128) points out: "Culture and religion are not always superimposed. It is perhaps just this difficulty in establishing the separation and recognizing the gap between them that, today, has again become the major challenge for humanity – and for Europe in particular." This insight is especially convincing, since the Muslims of Europe not only seek to respect Islamic religious norms but also to win over European cultural norms.

This reading of the "halalization" of ordinary activities may be sufficient, thus explaining the phenomenon through proven processes of internalization of dominant cultural norms and their social reproduction. It is undeniable that these same systems of socialization are indeed at work in the daily practices of the Muslim populations of Europe. I have previously explained these dynamics by demonstrating how they are the result of an established secularization, which separates the religious from the cultural (Id Yassine 2012a: 122). This European cultural integration of Muslim religiosity is only possible with the assistance of what Danièle Hervieu-Léger (2006) calls "a religious hollowing out of European culture." But that is only half the story.

An Islamic Desacralization

Along with this "Europeanization" of Islamic identity, the Islamic religion is contributing to a redefinition of European cultural identity, which is clearly visible in public controversies. Through its association with cultural rather than religious practices, halal is established as a secular category. Some see the "halalization" of worldly affairs as an attempt at a pervasive sanctification of social life and concrete proof of the encompassing and conquering nature of Islam. According to the followers of this "Islamization," this sanctification is simply the result of Islam's expansionist tendencies. When refusing to renounce the conception of *shumûliyya* (globality) that characterizes Sharia, Islam is supposedly incompatible with the secularism of the Western world. Focusing his work on this divide, Bernard Lewis (1993: 374) dogmatically confirms "the Islamic religion concerns life as a whole, with unlimited, global jurisdiction." Others, such as Henri Mendras, do not hesitate to fall back on this injunction. According to the author of *L'Europe des Européens*: "Islam does not recognize the separation between religious and political power that is so fundamental in the West ... Muslims can practice their religion but must renounce its political, legal, and theological syncretism" (Mendras 1997: 304–10).

But it is not a question of the kind of *syncretism* with which we too often deny in the *legal* field the distinction between the *political* and *theological*, secular and religious spheres. Rather, it is a kind of eclecticism that requires strict maintenance of a distinction that some Muslims neglect and some Europeans find hard to acknowledge. The principal difficulty lies in accepting that modernity is not more European than Islamic. Many studies of Islam in Europe continue to be dependent on the religious experience of historically Christian societies. They refrain notably from seeing, in the discrepancies of the excessive and confused use of the halal designation, a paradoxical desacralization of daily life. Through the mediation of ethics, this phenomenon is nothing other than the expression, sometimes unfulfilled or unsatisfied, of an outdated modernity. Incidentally, the elimination of cultural boundaries is made possible by the supremacy of the individual, who sets out to formulate for himself or herself the norms that are imposed upon them only by an ethicization of the world. "A name, an ideal brings together souls and reanimates the heart of Western democracies ...: ethics. Far from being directly opposed to postmoralist individualistic culture, the effect of ethics is one of its complimentary manifestations" (Lipovetsky 2000: 11).

To take up Max Weber's distinction, Europe is dedicated to "member socialization" and Islam to "communitarian socialization." Muslims actually consent to a double socialization: that which society requires as well as that which is at work within the community. That is why Islamic identity is indisputably experienced as an affective mode. We then understand better what Mohammed Benkheira (1997: 6) notes – even if "the role of mufti has always been important ... its importance undoubtedly increases as society goes through the process of modernization." Modernity is in force in the eclectic usage of "halal" not only because secular European societies exercise their socializing prerogatives over the cultural identity of the Muslims who live within them, but also because in all likelihood "the dichotomy between the secular and the religious ... is a foreign problematic within Islamic thought" (Boulaabi 2005: 65).

However, the unsure absence of such a dichotomy must not conceal the sure presence of crosstalk between the religious and the secular in Islamic law. Thus, there is nothing surprising in the fact that, ignoring the stigma of an obvious anachronism, some see "secular" thinking at work among the Muslim lawyers of the first Hijri centuries. Hesna Cailliau (2003: 210) reckons in fact that "the Hanafi school developed a secular jurisprudence before the word [revelation]." Louis Massignon suggests that, for him, Islam is defined as a "secular theocracy," as André Brottier, alias Louis Gardet, likes to remind us (Gardet 1981: 48; Bouamrane and Gardet 1984: 185; Gardet 1999: 74–5). That said, the *usuliyyun*[26] were actually quick to differentiate legal rules according to whether they applied to the religious (*ibadah*) or secular (*mu'amalât*) domains. The relationship to the texts was determined according to whether the problem to be resolved raised religious issues – where nothing was permitted except for what had been prescribed – or cultural issues – where everything was permitted save what had been forbidden. In other words, with regard to a secular usage of "halal," authority was conferred to human deliberation.

Consequently, religious, economic, political and civil actors are empowered to define halal. Posing truthfully few limitations,[27] the liberal spirit of the Revelation even allows transgressions if Reason deems it appropriate.[28] In accordance with the presuppositions of Islam as an anticlerical religion, this leaves the human being in full responsibility of its liberty. Indeed, as Mohammed Benkheira (2000: 14) reminds us, "one of the principal characteristics of Islam is the absence of normative codification."

Banning is Banned

Continuing in the consideration of the Islamic point of view, I would like to note that halal is above all a secondary legal category, imposed only via contemporary Islamic discourse. From the point of view of classic Muslim law, acts are evaluated according to one of five available legal statuses: *wajib* or *fard* (obligatory); *mustahabb*, *mandub* or *Sunnah* (recommended); *mubah* (permitted); *makruh* (censured); and *harâm* (forbidden). Halal is not covered explicitly, but it emerges only in joining together with the first four statuses of this classification in contrast to the fifth. Even legally, halal lends itself to controversy, varying from obligation to censure and including recommendation and permission with regard to horsemeat, pork gelatin, women's hard-rock, figurative art, masturbation and oral sex. Halal is a soft notion that is elastic and transversal. It does not have as many moral connotations as *harâm* does, offering up to personal judgment in a positive way a wide and inclusive range of human activities. Again, everyone is free to choose their own recourse.

Moreover, the Arab etymology of the word *halâl* conveys the idea of liberty, which has a bearing in the abundant use of this term among the Muslim populations

---

26   Muslim lawyers specializing in the basis of law (*usûl al-fiqh*), which is associated, but is not to be confused with, religious principles in the stricter sense (*usûl ad-dîn*) that are fundamentally spiritual or ethical and usually dogmatic and moral. The latter formulates the truths of the Muslim faith (arkân al-imân) as well as the practical modality of their lived experience (*arkân al-islâm*) and could thus be likened to a philosophy of law.

27   Basically consuming pork, alcohol, *imago Dei*, idolatry, fornication and sodomy.

28   The notion of *darûra* (of duress, of necessity) is often invoked to justify a parsimonious transgression of divine laws, with the permission of God Himself (Koran 2: 173).

of liberal societies. The word in fact comes from the term *hall*, which is the act of disentangling, of unknotting, of untying, of undoing, in short of freeing in one way or another. This performative etymological aspect thus suggests the freedom to perform a particular act. With a legal status for all thought of action,[29] such liberty transforms into authorization, locating halal entirely within the normative concept of lawfulness.

And yet the legalism characteristic of Muslim religion (Id Yassine 2012b: 90) introduces a necessary opposition between the lawful and the unlawful. As I have said, this leads to the homogenization of halal by distinguishing it from its opposite: *harâm*. If this reification prohibits thoughts of halal without *harâm*, the sociological approach makes it possible to avoid subjection to this binary logic, because the usage of the halal category is eclectic, refusing to respond systematically to the Islamic normativity that wants what is not *harâm* to be necessarily halal and vice versa. *Harâm* itself is not as precisely established as one might think, and actors play with the leeway that is created by this lack of indisputable authority.

But designating something as halal is also and above all to say that it is *Islamic*. And yet there are three levels of interpretation to be distinguished of what Islam is: consequently, the definition of halal depends on each of them. In addition to 1) the founding texts and 2) the interpretation of them produced for centuries by the doctors of Islamic theology, Islam can be defined as 3) the enactment of this scholarly discourse via social practice, either popular or elitist, even when offset or inconsistent with the formulations of it in the texts or by the learned. Indeed, to speak of halal mobilizes different cognitive systems, and it is this disparity that is at the heart of the many ambiguities and equivocations.

We sense therefore what about halal makes it more predisposed to create controversy than *harâm*. As the moralistic connotation of this word could easily suggest, it is not really *harâm* that is the focus of European controversies over Islam. Despite its legal liberality, it is over the term "halal" that a latent consensus is formed between different actors engaged in the public controversies over Islam in Europe. While *harâm* seemingly intrudes into the public space of societies of the Muslim world,[30] the Muslims of Europe use and abuse halal as they are imbued with European secular values and liberalization, the mores of which, if only surreptitiously, ban them from banning.

---

29 In fact, action is first the consequence of a supposedly free agent, inserted into objective reality, implying a relation to truth and ordained to a transitive end (Laupies 2007).

30 Consider the public debates of these societies: the controversies are more over opposition to something *harâm* than claims for *halâl*; for example, idolatry or fetishism (the royal hand kiss or sorcery in Morocco); condemnations of brothels (in Tunisia) and homosexuality (in Egypt); ostentatious displays of femininity (nail polish in Saudi Arabia); atheism or religious irreverence (such as the allegations of blasphemy against the Turkish pianist Fazil Say); religious otherness (Christians in Nigeria) or heterodoxy (Ahmadiyya in Pakistan); subversive or eccentric art (Lady Gaga's concert in Indonesia), etc.

Conclusion

I have sought to establish the processes that have enabled halal to be set up as a public category. First, the *claims* of religious actors passed from the common space to the public space. This then enabled economic actors to enact a standard *commercialization* of halal. Finally, the divergent interests of these two institutional actors led to the intervention of political actors, which brought about a polarization, shifting the problematic around identity from the politics of Islam to that of populist Europe. The controversies surrounding halal amalgamate cultural and religious identities, ignoring both European *acculturation* and Islamic *ethicization*. Desacralized and modern, halal gets established as a secular category, a testament to the liberalization of lived Islam.

As I have shown, the usage of "halal" should not be reduced to the commerce that it carries with it, and the polemics of which it is the object cannot be isolated from the rest of the public controversies surrounding Islam in Europe. The actors of halal commerce shape their interactions according to differentiated strategies, one according to the primacy of quantity and the other to the primacy of quality. This tension is situated in the wake of the opposition between secular interests and religious concerns. I propose that we read the difficulties that the institutional actors experience in attempting to regulate halal commerce through the laborious reconciliation of the search for efficiency (secular and modern) and the demand for authenticity (religious and traditional). We can then better delimit the paradox in which the more widespread halal becomes among consumer products, the less religious relevance it has and the more notoriety it has in terms of economic and commercial value. Certainly, "the establishment of a veritable economics of quality in France (and in Europe) will, then, ensure genuine transparency in the sale of halal meat" (Zemmour 2006: 101). But institutional, economic, religious and political actors should incorporate into their agenda the underlying dynamics that, in a democratic context, make individuals agents of authority. Whether customer, worshiper or voter, European citizens of the Muslim faith influence these dynamics and participate in them as civil actors. The attitude of civil society is decisive in this respect.

If the EU is passing through the most serious crisis in its history, the principal change in the post-Maastricht era is the shift towards an indifferent and indecisive attitude, not towards an attitude of rejection or opposition to the European project. The indifference and indecision of ordinary citizens are mass phenomena that, however, seem to be little studied (van Ingelgom 2012). Resurgence in nationalism and the development of protectionist ideas are objectively dependent on current difficult economic circumstances, fed by a discourse of decline around European identity and culturalist reaffirmation. It is in this general context that Islam in Europe acts as a catalyst of sociopolitical tensions and presents itself as an easy means of establishing a frontline between pro-Europeans and Euroskeptics of all kinds. In that sense, Islam is very much involved in a reconfiguration of the European public space.

References

Amalou, F. 2005. "La nourriture halal attire de plus en plus les jeunes musulmans," *Le Monde*, June 13.

Baubérot, J. 2006. *L'intégrisme républicain contre la laïcité*. Paris: Éditions de l'Aube.

Ben-Rhouma, H. 2011. "Halal européen: les conclusions rendues en mars 2012," *Saphirnews*, November 30.

Benkheira, M-H. 1997. *L'amour de la Loi. Essai sur la normativité en islâm*. Paris: Puf.

Benkheira, M-H. 2000. *Islam et interdits alimentaires. Juguler l'animalité*. Paris: Puf.

Bergeaud-Blackler, F. and Bernard, B. 2010. *Comprendre le halal*. Liège: Edipro.

Blass, M. 2010. "Halal sex website – no contradiction," *Radio Netherlands Worldwide*, April 2.

Boulaabi, A. 2005. *Islam et pouvoir. Les finalités de la Charia et la légitimité du pouvoir*. Paris: L'Harmattan.

Bounrane, C. and Gardet, L. 1984. *Panorama de la pensée islamique*. Paris: Sindbad.

Bowen, J-R. 2011. *L'islam à la française*. Paris: Steinkis.

Brouard, S. and Tiberj, V. 2005. *Français comme les autres? Enquête sur les citoyens d'origine maghrébine, africaine et turque*. Paris: Presses de Sciences Po.

Cailliau, H. 2003. *L'esprit des religions. Connaître les religions pour mieux comprendre les hommes*. Paris: Milan.

Cesari, J. 2004. *L'islam à l'épreuve de l'Occident*. Paris: La Découverte.

De Foucaud, I. 2011. "Nestlé suspend la production de ses saucisses halal Herta," *Le Figaro*, February 1.

Gardet, L. 1981. *La Cité musulmane. Vie sociale et politique*. Paris: Vrin.

Gardet, L. 1999. *Les hommes de l'Islam. Approche des mentalités*. Brussels: Complexe.

Giesbert, F-O. 2012. "Halalisation française," *Le Point*, March 8.

Goldbert, D. 2011. "Lettre à Claude Guéant," *Al-Kanz*, August 23.

Göle, N. 2005. *Interpénétrations. L'Islam et l'Europe*. Paris: Galaade.

Hervieu-Léger, D. 2006. "The role of religion in establishing social cohesion," in K. Michalski (ed.), *Conditions of European Solidarity, vol. II: Religion in the New Europe*. Budapest/New York: Central European University Press.

Heurtebise, R. 2012. "Halalisation forcée et sournoise: grâce à vous, la peur change de camp!" *Riposte Laïque*, May 20.

Id Yassine, R. 2012a. *L'Islam d'Occident ? Introduction à l'étude des musulmans des sociétés occidentales*. Perpignan: Editions Halfa.

Id Yassine, R. 2012b. "Comment l'islam a-t-il pu devenir occidental?" in F. Kaoues et al. (eds), *Religions et frontières*. Paris: CNRS Éditions.

Kastoryano, R. 2000. "Des multiculturalismes en Europe au multiculturalisme européen," *Politique étrangère* 1.

Lamghari, Y. 2012. *L'Islam en entreprise*. Louvain-la-Neuve: Harmattan, Academia.

Launay, G. and Legouté, D. 2012. "Marine Le Pen sème la confusion sur le halal," *Libération*, February 21.

Laupies, F. 2007. *L'action. Premières leçons*. Paris: PUF.

Lewis, B. 1993. *Le Retour de l'islam*. Paris: Gallimard.

Lipovetsky, G. 2000. *Le Crépuscule du devoir. L'éthique indolore des nouveaux temps démocratiques*. Paris: Gallimard.

Lyon, C. 2012. "La polémique sur le halal s'exporte bien, hélas," *Courrier International*, March 28.

Mendras, H. 1997. *L'Europe des Européens. Sociologie de l'Europe occidentale*. Paris: Gallimard.

Roy, O. 2003. *L'islam mondialisé*. Paris: Seuil.

Roy, O. 2008. *La sainte ignorance. Le temps de la religion sans culture*. Paris: Seuil.

Van Ingelgom, V. 2012. "Mesurer l'indifférence. Intégration européenne et attitudes des citoyens," *Sociologie* 1.

Wolton, D. 2012. "Espace public," available at http://www.wolton.cnrs.fr/spip.php?article67.

Zemmour, S. 2006. *Le marché de la viande halal : évolutions, enjeux et perspectives*. Paris: L'Harmattan.

Chapter 15

Animal Rights Movements and Ritual Slaughtering: Autopsy of a Moribund Campaign

Florence Bergeaud-Blackler

A poster campaign endorsed by a number of associations for the protection of animals denounced a "generalization of ritual slaughter" in French slaughterhouses. The excessive nature of the messages and the pictures displayed on the posters was attributed to one of the associations that had underwritten the campaign, the Brigitte Bardot Foundation, presided over by the former actress who was known for her sympathy for the National Front and, for this very reason, was shunned by the media. The impact of the campaign was therefore limited. Yet the Bardot Foundation had not initiated this campaign alone; other animal welfare groups, not suspected of sympathy for the far-right, had also approved the text and signed the posters. How could such a change of attitude be accounted for? Can a radicalization of the debate about ritual slaughter be observed and, if so, how can it be explained; what can have triggered it? I try to show that, far from proving a systematic alignment of animal welfare advocates on the Islamophobic stances of far-right political parties, this radicalization signals a new approach, animal welfare organizations having switched from a passive compassionate strategy to an aggressive "unveiling" strategy. I shall question the effectiveness of this new approach, which could well turn an economic problem into a cultural one.

Shock Campaign

In November 2010, a group of animal welfare associations[1] was preparing to launch a campaign they hoped would shock the public in order to combat the abusive practice of slaughtering without stunning animals whose meat was not destined for the religious markets. This campaign consisted of displaying two posters, side by side, on gigantic boards propped up along thoroughfares at the entrance of towns. One showed a young calf whose throat was about to be cut ritually, "live, in excruciating pain," and the other showing a young girl, "Laura,"

---

1   I employ the expression "animal protection associations or groups" interchangeably with "animal welfare associations or groups."

fair-haired, who looked as if she did not belong to the religious groups to whom the consumption of those ritual meats is "imposed." Underneath the portraits, against a red, bloodstained banner, one could read the following captions: "Halal and kosher sacrifices must not become the norm in France" and "60% of the animals slaughtered ritually, without being stunned and in great pain, find their way to our shops without any particular mention on the label."

These posters were examined by the ARPP (the authority for the professional regulation of advertising),[2] which refused to approve their being displayed in the streets. Electronic versions were then posted on the Internet, mainly via and on far-right groups' websites.

A few months later, in January 2011, a revised version was approved by the ARPP, was displayed on 2,266 billboards in the main cities of France and was replicated on a dedicated website.[3]

Gone is the picture of the fair-haired child. But the first poster remains, with the young calf on top of the same red banner – whose bloodstains have been removed. The phrase "Let's stop that butchery!" has been replaced with an excerpt from a position paper of the official Federation of European Veterinaries. It is a technical explanation: "From the standpoint of the protection of animals and out of respect for the animal, insofar as it is a sensitive being, the practice consisting of slaughtering animals without prior stunning is unacceptable, whatever the circumstances."

The first campaign conveyed two messages: the refusal to generalize "kosher" and "halal" (explicitly named) slaughtering on the one hand, and the demand that ritual meats be labeled so as to inform the consumer of the slaughtering method used for the product on the other. In the second campaign, ritual slaughtering, the "cause of great suffering for the animal," is described as disrespectful. At first sight, given the polemic character of the first campaign, one might think it is more hostile to ritual slaughtering than the second. As a matter of fact, what is rejected in the first campaign is the systematization of ritual slaughtering and its use for religious consumption, whereas the second campaign condemns the very principle of ritual slaughtering. The message is therefore more radical in the latter, but it is more implicit, the words "halal" and "kosher" are not mentioned, and it no longer seems to impact a part of the population.[4]

The second campaign suffered from the fiasco of the first one, which had quickly been denounced as "a smear campaign against the Jews and the Muslims."

---

2   Created on 11 November 2010.

3   www.abattagerituel.com, designed by the PMAF on behalf of the associations who had signed the campaign: Oeuvre d'Assistance aux Bêtes d'Abattoirs (OABA), Confédération Nationale des Sociétés Protectrices des Animaux (SPA) de France (CNSPA), Conseil National de la Protection Animale (CNPA), Fondation Assistance aux Animaux, Protection Mondiale des Animaux de la Ferme (PMAF), Société Nationale pour la Défense des Animaux (SNDA) and Association Stéphane Lamart.

4   Jews and Muslims. This was the reason why the ARPP refused to approve the first campaign.

The media suspected the former actress Brigitte Bardot, president of the eponymous foundation and known for her racist slip-ups,[5] her unashamed Islamophobia[6] and her support to the National Front, to have had a hand in it. There were a few skirmishes in cyberspace between the Muslim media and bloggers on the one hand and activist secularists on the other. On 9 March 2011, in a paper entitled "Love of the Animals or Hatred of the Muslims?" the website *Oumma.com* thus denounced the Islamophobia and the anti-Semitism of the campaign.[7] Identitarian lay groups such as *Resistance Républicaine, Ripostes Laïques* or *Bloc Identitaire* refused the "censorship" of the ARPP and, using reverse victimizing rhetoric, blamed the administration of a republic which had "sold" itself to Islam for "double standard" decisions favoring Muslims. Comparing the posters in question with similarly oversized posters advertising the brand Isladélice, on which appeared a rooster looking "proud" to be halal, Christine Tasin quoted a letter to the "dhimmi" Dominique Baudis, the President of ARPP: "Have the 'Proudly halal' posters been banned? No, of course not. This is yet another example of the 'double standards' that have become the norm in France … Why do you refuse that the truth be told about ritual slaughtering? Why do you insist on misleading people?" The campaign timely reinforced the theory according to which France was Islamized – a theory that was supported by a few groups who had just organized an anti-Islamization rally in Paris[8] attended by several hundred people, bringing together an amazingly disparate crowd, from far-right public figures to left-wing advocates of sovereignty, members of the far-left and feminists.[9] The meeting happened to have been planned just after the success of "*Apéro Saucisson-Pinard*" on 18 June 2010, a pseudo-festive Islamophobic event which, according to one of its organizers, "enabled people to speak out freely on the subject of the Islamization of France" (Robert 2011).

The animal welfare campaign proved less successful than its authors had hoped. It nonetheless raises a few questions. How could animal protection groups,

---

5   Brigitte Bardot was found guilty of "inciting racial hatred" because of her comments about Muslims. In a letter published in December 2006 by the newsletter of her Foundation, she wrote: "We are sick and tired of being abused by those populations that destroy us and our country by imposing their acts."

6   "I am against the islamization of France! The compulsory allegiance that forces submission disgusts me," she wrote in her book (Bardot 2003).

7   He quoted Tahin Party, the publisher of antispecist authors like Peter Singer, who dissociate themselves from the campaign: "the media offer numerous analyses in which commentators show that in the ideological changes undergone by the European far-right, the Muslim has replaced the Jew as a foreign body, barbarous and hostile to the nation." The signatories of this campaign blend the most classical anti-Semitism and the most modern Islamophobia.

8   Espace Charenton, Paris, 12th Arrondissement, 18 December 2010.

9   This event caused a counter-demonstration led by various groups such as the NPA, the left-wing party, SOS Racisme, the Ligue des droits de l'homme (LDH: Human Rights League) and Attac.

most of whom are usually very discreet and consensual organizations, participate in such a frontal campaign on a subject (animal slaughtering) about which they normally communicate very little? How could they end up supporting a poster campaign that sounds hostile to religious minorities?

The Radicalization of Animal Welfare Groups

Not all the groups who signed those posters had affinities or links with far-right groups or their ideology; far from it. The campaign was approved by the most important French animal welfare groups.[10] Contrary to a commonly held view that it belongs mostly to the far-right of the political spectrum, animal advocacy is politically heterogeneous.[11] One of the most prominent signatories of the campaign, the OABA (Assistance for Animals in Slaughterhouses), founded by Jacqueline Gilardoni in 1961 with the support of the Ministry of Agriculture and the Veterinary Academy, is recognized as useful to the public and is regularly solicited for its expertise by governments, be they right-wing or left-wing. It is endorsed by personalities of the cultural and scientific world.[12] Presided over by Jean-Pierre Kieffer, officer and Knight of the Order of the Agricultural Merit, it has always kept radical animal welfare groups at arm's length. Notwithstanding the heartfelt passion of its members in their steadfast fight for "humanitarian" slaughtering, its communication has always been moderate. The French confederation of Societies for the Protection of Animals, mainly known to the public for its campaigns against the abandonment of pets during holiday seasons, signed this campaign, along with other traditionally "reformist" groups, thus joining forces with organizations considered more radical that they traditionally keep away from, such as "L214" or the Brigitte Bardot Foundation.

In recent years, the way in which the highest echelons of the state have handled the question of ritual slaughtering has caused immense disappointment among animal welfare advocates, who had steadfastly denounced the generalization of slaughtering without stunning. The OABA, which had inspired the 1964 decree making it compulsory to stun ruminants before bleeding them,[13] argued against

---

10   The OABA, the CNSPA, the CNPA, the PMAF, the SNDA and the Association Stéphane Lamart. Eurogroup for Animals, a European organization, quietly supported this national initiative.

11   "For the past two centuries, efforts undertaken to reform human behaviors towards animals have always been the result of a number of very different motives. Neither exclusively right-wing, left-wing or center, nor totally reactionary or progressive, the cause of animal welfare find supporters in all political traditions" (Traïni 2011: 219).

12   Including the biologist Etienne Wolf, the writer Marguerite Yourcenar, the physicist Alfred Kastler and the explorer and philosopher Théodore Monod (source: OABA).

13   The organization won the privilege of being recognized as the main advocate of the animal welfare movement after J. Gilardoni, its founder, succeeded in 1964 in making stunning before slaughtering compulsory, except in the case of ritual slaughtering.

the fact that slaughterhouses now tended to avail themselves of a derogation to produce ritually slaughtered meat that was then sold in conventional markets and not specifically in halal or kosher outlets. The OABA, the only non-governmental organization (NGO) empowered to investigate this practice in slaughterhouses, actively contributed to the investigation conducted by an inter-ministerial inspection committee. The figures published by the Office of International Agriculturists, disclosed in the committee report entitled "A Survey on the Scope of Halal Meat," revealed a fact that had remained little known up to that moment: in French slaughterhouses, 80 percent of sheep, 20 percent of cattle and 20 percent of poultry were slaughtered according to the ritual method. These percentages far exceeded the religious needs in the country, bearing in mind that according to a very rough estimation, Jews and Muslims did not account for more than seven percent of the French population.[14] The slip backwards of the "minimal" advance in stunning animals prior to their actual slaughtering (as compared to the more successful advances in promoting the renouncing of eating meat products) has always been regarded as unacceptable by OABA activists, for whom this seminal combat justifies all the others. In the wake of inter-ministerial inspection committee report, the French Veterinary Academy commissioned a study in order to try and identify reversible stunning techniques and the government announced consultations on the subject.

In 2008, Nicolas Sarkozy, the then French President, asked Michel Barnier, Minister of Agriculture and Fishing, to launch a series of meetings to which, for the first time, local MPs and other elected officials, delegates of the various meat channels and related industries, NGOs, scientists and public servants would jointly participate to reflect on the protection of animals. These "Animals and Society Meetings," which aimed at better defining and protecting the status of animals bred for human consumption, raised immense hopes amongst activists. Indeed, Nicolas Sarkozy had clearly committed himself to the generalization of stunning livestock before slaughtering. "I want animals to suffer as little as possible during their slaughtering. I want to generalize stunning before slaughtering as much as possible. I want halal slaughterhouses to commit themselves right now to the generalization of prior stunning."[15] In January 2007, as the Minister of the Interior in charge of religions, Sarkozy had even considered having Muslims write a chart of halal good practices, including a reversible painkilling technique. The chart was, in effect, written three years later, but the text included no compulsory stunning; on the contrary, it demanded permission to waive this rule. The CFCM (French Council for the Muslim Faith), instead of embracing the positions of other authorities of the Muslim world who had declared themselves in favor of non-lethal measures aimed at easing the death of livestock – a stance on which Dalil Boubaker, then rector of the Paris Mosque, had based his arguments 10 years earlier when he had written his

---

14   Questions related to religious allegiance or feelings of belonging to religious groups are not included in French census questionnaires.

15   Letter signed by Nicolas Sarkozy, 22 December 2006.

chart governing halal slaughtering (Bergeaud-Blackler 2001) – chose instead to agree with French rabbis, who fiercely objected to this provision. French rabbis were all the more determined as Michèle Alliot-Marie had solemnly expressed her renewed support.[16] The Ministry of Agriculture then suggested a post-mortem stunning, in other words performed not just before the actual slaughtering, but seconds *after* it, so as to exclude any possibility that the animal might die before its throat was slit according to the rite.[17] The OABA, considering this compromise as the lesser of two evils, reluctantly accepted it, thus risking a split between animal welfare associations. But Jewish and Muslim religious authorities joined in, categorically refusing any form of stunning. So, despite prior hopes and notwithstanding the last resort concession of animal welfare movement, the meetings produced no concrete outcome whatsoever. The debate was left as it was. In a letter dated 4 November 2008 to President Sarkozy, Jean-Pierre Kieffer, President of the OABA, voiced his disappointment and his concern: "I wish to express my profound disappointment. After several ministers had made promises, after some religious leaders had committed themselves, after scientists had expressed opinions which had led us to hope ritual slaughtering methods would evolve, the 'Animals and Society Meetings' have ended up with causing a regression of the question of ritual slaughtering." Indeed, Muslim representatives, who had previously been divided about the issue, now seemed to agree on the most uncompromising view. This failure was painfully felt by animal welfare groups as a major setback in their multisecular struggle against slaughtering "fully conscious" animals.

At the European Commission level, lobbying efforts led by Eurogroup for Animals – an umbrella organization for European animal welfare groups – and by Federations of European Veterinaries in order to include stunning in the new rule about the protection of animals at the time of their slaughtering[18] had not proved more successful. The Council and the European Parliament both reaffirmed the principle of subsidiarity on the issue such as it was in the directive it was replacing: each Member State, and not the European Union, was to decide whether to accept the derogation or not.

Since negotiations behind closed doors brought no result, some of the associations – the OABA, the Brigitte Bardot Foundation, the Society for the

---

16   Michèle Alliot-Marie, then Minister of Interior Affairs, told a group of representatives of the European Congress of Rabbis which paid her a visit at the ministry that she had pleaded with the President of the European Council and the President of the European Commission to convince them that the draft of the rule regarding the protection of animals during the course of their slaughtering must not interfere with religious prescriptions. See *Le Nouvel Observateur*, March 5, 2009.

17   It is the lethal effect, deliberate or not, of the stunning that is the basis of the refusal for Muslims.

18   Rule (EC) 1099/2009 by the Council on September 24, 2009, on the protection of animals at the time of their slaughtering, replacing Directive 93/119/EC, by the Council on December 22, 1993. This rule applies as of January 1, 2013.

Defense of Animals and the Stéphane Lamart Association – decided to publicize the debate and to turn it into a consumer issue. They commissioned an IFOP (French Institute of Public Opinion) opinion poll about stunning and the attitude of consumers regarding meats produced by ritual slaughtering. A total of 1,015 people over the age of 18, considered as representative of the French population by means of the quota method (sex, age, occupation) after regional and type of town stratification, were interviewed.[19] The first question was worded as follows: "Since 1974, the European regulation makes it compulsory to stun animals before slaughtering them. However, a special dispensation is granted in the case of animals killed in the framework of ritual slaughtering, whose throat is cut while they are fully conscious, without having been stunned. Do you approve or disapprove of this dispensation – the fact that animals are not stunned before being slaughtered?" A total of 72 percent of the respondents expressed disapproval. Broken down according to political sensitivity, the results showed the problem was rather clearly politicized, since 69 percent of left-wing respondents disapproved of it, as opposed to 81 percent of those considered as right-wing and even 90 percent in the case of the far-right. Paradoxically, right-wing respondents declared themselves less attached to "religious freedom," as opposed to animal welfare, than left-wing respondents.[20] When asked the more pragmatic question "Would you accept to eat meat knowing the animal had been slaughtered without stunning?" 43 percent answered they preferred not to, as opposed to 24 percent who said they would not object. Political differences tended to be blurred on this precise issue, giving way to a more traditional divide according to genre, with only 17 percent of women declaring that they would accept eating this type of meat.

At the time, the facts that the questions were biased and that the issue aroused little interest in the public at large left room for doubt.[21] But these are not the only reasons why the media chose not to mention the results of the survey. The presence of the Brigitte Bardot Foundation among the groups which had commissioned it cast a doubt regarding its real motivations, even though, as far as the actress was concerned, the cause was precisely a repeat of what had led her to commit herself to the animal welfare cause in the first place.[22] The magazine *Charlie Hebdo*, well

---

19   Online IFOP survey, 8–10 December 2009.

20   Ritual slaughtering: "You object to it because you think it is not necessary to make animals suffer" (55 percent left-wing respondents, 68 percent right-wing respondents) versus "You do not object to it because you think it is necessary to respect each person's religious practice" (34 percent left-wing respondents, 24 percent right-wing respondents).

21   On the other hand, it did arouse obvious interest during the presidential campaign, halal meat remaining a prominent theme for several weeks.

22   In January 1962, she had arranged to appear on the one TV channel then operating to demand that special guns be used to stun animals before they were slaughtered and, taking advantage of her celebrity, she addressed government officials, advocating the cause of the newly created OABA.

known for its anti-religious opinions and whom nobody could suspect of far-right sympathies, was the only one to support the campaign unambiguously, citing only the OABA (Lapin 2010).

In an effort to drive their message home and draw attention to their cause, animal welfare groups opened their circle even wider and wrote an open letter to President Sarkozy, disclosing the findings of the IFOP survey. The letter also warned that a national campaign would be organized if nothing was done to "modify the modalities of ritual slaughtering in order to put an end to animal suffering and to improve the opaque distribution system of the meats produced in that manner." Very few papers, among them *Le Monde* and *Le Figaro*, printed extracts of that letter. And the President did not bother to answer it. Animal welfare activists then decided to change their strategy, as they had said they would. The OABA was not the last to follow suit, thanks to the support of a new, firmer generation of activists led by Frédéric Freund, a man with a legal background who had been promoted to the position of Director of the OABA shortly after joining it.

The "Unveiling" Strategy

According to Christophe Traïni (2011), a sociologist who teaches political sciences and wrote a book on the animal cause, for the past 200 years, animal welfare groups have mainly resorted to three "emotional" levers to build their awareness campaigns. The oldest – no longer used by today's activists – is all about denouncing the barbaric behavior of the people who mistreat animals. The campaign then consists of lecturing, re-educating, punishing and rewarding. The second lever appeals to people's compassion towards animals, perceived as being sensitive and having a heart. The third lever of the unveiling consists of exhibiting the hidden suffering of animals, provoking dread, contempt and anger regarding the "deviants" who mistreat animals. French organizations have traditionally played simultaneously on these two levers, the latter being more telegenic but less popular. In France, the more systematic resort to the unveiling strategy dates back to the 1970s, notably with Brigitte Bardot's campaigns against the killers of baby seals and all those who are involved in their exploitation, including women who wear the fur. Campaigns against Aid el Kebir (the Muslim holiday when animals are sacrificed) also belong to that finger-pointing strain, which is supposed to arouse anger and revolt against the "deviants," those Muslims alleged to reject modernity. However, since the media has never made them a public issue, alluding to them only to ridicule their instigator, rallying efforts based on this strategy have never proved very efficient in France.

The November 2010 campaign was obviously more an effort to unveil hidden horrors than to elicit compassion; moreover, it brought together virtually all the parties involved in the French animal welfare movement. Should this change be interpreted as a populist drift of animal welfare advocates?

The reformist tradition of French animal welfare groups rests on their close relationship with the elites and the state. In exchange for their acceptable behavior and their discretion, some organizations are regularly consulted by the central government, which lends them a kind ear. The OABA in particular has always been careful to maintain its "nice" image and is systematically consulted by the Ministry of Agriculture whenever decisions must be made about animal slaughtering. Veterinaries and former high-ranking civil servants sit on its board. Thanks to these discreet exchanges, the OABA is in a position to know and see everything. The doors of slaughtering houses, highly guarded places, are always open to it. But its influence is steadily declining, for the "understanding" strategy no longer works. Under the growing pressure of industrials, in a context of unemployment, which is especially acute for the French meat industry, political promises are not always kept, including at the highest level.

Moreover, the one-to-one, behind-closed-doors relationship between understanding activists and a benevolent state is no longer relevant now that decisions are made at the European level. Other observers from EU Member States have gained access to slaughterhouses. They carry out unexpected investigations then write reports in English, which are subsequently posted on the EU website, in full compliance with regulations regarding the transparency of reports and documents.[23] The figures summing up the findings of the OABA survey on ritual slaughtering have accordingly been shared with a consortium of consultants commissioned by the Health and Protection of Consumers Directory in order to study stunning practices.[24] Scientists, experts and journalists can therefore access these figures and make them known. No longer tainted by the far-right allegiance suspicion which had hitherto blocked their publication, they can now be openly released by the media.

As we have seen, the fact that the ARPP disapproved of it has not prevented the widespread dissemination of a less polemic but still highly critical message regarding ritual slaughtering. The means used by activists have changed now that Europe is more open, each of the EU Member States being subject to the control of others. Animal welfare activists hope that this will help bring about an alignment improving the way in which animals are handled and they support European initiatives aimed at turning animal welfare into a bankable food characteristic, an added value for the food industry. But the effectiveness of the approach in terms of fulfilling its goals remains doubtful.

---

23   Regulation (EC) 1049/2001 of the European Parliament and of the Council of May 30, 2001 regarding public access to European Parliament, Council and Commission Documents: http://eur-lex.europa.eu/LexUriServ/LexUriServ.do?uri=CELEX:32001R1049:en:HTML.

24   Study on the stunning/killing practices in slaughterhouses and their economic, social and environmental consequences. Framework Contract for evaluation and evaluation related services – Lot 3: Food Chain (awarded through tender no 2004/S243-208899), http://www.civic-consulting.de/reports/slaughter_study_part2.pdf.

Food and Civilization

In the aftermath of the Bovine Spongiform Encephalopathy (BSE) crises, traceability and identification schemes were put in place in order to reassure consumers, not directly on the sanitary quality of the meat but indirectly via information about its geographic origin. The idea that what is produced locally tends to be healthier was reinforced by messages like those of French Beef Association or the branding of species and *terroirs* (limousine, blonde d'Aquitaine and bazadaise, to name but a few). As a matter of fact, this strategy uses the same identity lever which, at least in part, maintains the kosher route and increases halal consumption. These messages have reinforced the implicit link that the consumer could establish between safety and proximity. For the European Commission, the issue of animal welfare was to be a marker of EU-made products. In the same way as Mediterranean food has become a symbol of health, the fact that animals were well treated, along with environmental friendliness, had to create value: the meat had to sell outside Europe as a natural product of our European civilization.

True enough, as far as the visitors from the Brussels institutions are concerned, significant advances have been made, especially in terms of communication. A visit to the Animal Protection Bureau website illustrates the EU efforts to promote the farming model of the old continent and set it as a worldwide exemplar of economically competitive *and* ethically sustainable agriculture. The European citizen may not exist in a political entity, but he is built upon the lifestyle to which he is supposed to be traditionally attached. From the Finnish fjords to the Portuguese hills, he is deemed to care equally for his environment, his wellbeing and well-eating, the continuation of traditional skills being regarded as key to good food as well as good health. The European identity, polymorph and multicultural, is perhaps epitomized by this responsible *art de vivre*, resisting genetically modified organisms (GMOs) and hormone-treated beef for the sake of tasty and authentic foods. The food producing model and the way in which animals are handled thus contribute to the building of a "Europeanness" of *terroirs*.

Behind the animal welfare campaign lurks another. The rosy picture hides the downside of European agricultural policies. Caught in the trap of hyperproduction, the actors of the food industry and agricultural trade unions find it hard to match this image (which is supposed to make them more competitive), since they have to apply intensive production methods whose negative impact on society and the environment is well known. There is a growing gap between the food industry and big-box retail on the one hand and the much-vaunted European model on the other. This is increasingly obvious in the meat industry, where working conditions have seriously deteriorated. In the meat industry (whose actors talk of "ore" to designate animal flesh), it is still the economic returns that dictate the main development choices while simultaneously, but quite disconnected, a *terroir* rhetoric flatters national identities.

When "Culture" is a Cover-Up for Economic Failure

The public campaign lays the blame of animal suffering on "ritual slaughtering," but the problems it reveals have more to do with the industrialization of breeding and slaughtering practices. Animal welfare groups like the OABA, the PMAF or the Bardot Foundation are obviously aware of this fact. Indeed, there is a significant discrepancy between the theme of the campaign and the expertise exhibited in documents that are meant to be read by insiders or public agencies. In the latter, the OABA signals the problems inherent in increasingly mass slaughtering, in particular slaughtering without stunning, on chains that have not been designed for this purpose. They denounce a "regression" in the industrial handling of the animals about to be slaughtered and complain that the government has given up, no longer doing what it takes to ensure that the public interest (the good treatment of animals) takes precedence over the private interests of retailers. The OABA considers that the generalization of stunning will take several decades to achieve. In times of economic crises, in particular, advances regarding animal welfare are quickly lost again. The legislation remains, of course, but its implementation is made difficult, either because relevant technologies are not used as they should be, the machines no longer work well, their operators are absent or because people find loopholes that enable them to bypass the regulations.

So far, the OABA has chosen a strategy that has enabled it to make the most of its expertise, for a number of reasons. To begin with, there is the specific difficulty of discussing animal death in public: it is easier to campaign and raise awareness against abandoned pets during the summer holidays than against practices that do not photograph well and about which steak eaters feel powerless, like slaughtering methods. Moreover, the strategy of showcasing its expertise had proved rather successful for this old association, since it had secured the financial and logistic support of public authorities. Finally, the OABA had thus cultivated a good image, leaving the "dirty job" to the Bardot Foundation. It has thus been able to enjoy the returns of its efforts, without giving rise to suspicions of anti-Semitic and racist intentions.

However, an alternative strategy was becoming necessary in the face of a slaughtering industry as opaque as the army can be. Not only is the industry in question dumb, it is blind as well. Slaughtering areas are accessible to scientists and journalists only if they have obtained the approval of the slaughtering house director, who grants it on a discretionary basis, without bothering to provide reasons for his decisions. In a system within which the principle of transparency has become the norm as a reassuring strategy, such behavior can easily give rise to suspicions and open the way to unveiling strategies.

The campaign put together by animal welfare associations denounces the effects (animal suffering) of ritual slaughtering, but never mentions its source (the industrialization of slaughtering). Even if their expertise has enabled them time and again to observe that the slaughterers simply do what the industrialist tell them to do according to his own orders, it is the ritual itself they attack, highlighting its alien characteristics, pitting *them* (Jews and Muslims) against *us* (the identifying figure of Laura), the mainstream being carefully stripped of its Jewish and Muslim components. They resort to an ancient and rather common anthropological archetype, the ruthless executioner being presented as a stranger, which is one of the many ways to obscure animal death.[25] Carried out by others, the slaughtering is close enough to be condemned, but also far enough so as not to be unbearable. Is the battle against ritual slaughtering merely an instrument aimed at stigmatizing foreigners? Or is it used as a searchlight meant to reveal *all* the abuses committed in slaughterhouses?

The Artifact

Governments legislate to protect racial, cultural and religious minorities. However, they do not always take action to protect their heritage or, if they do so, they do it in a selective way. The state contributes to the restoration of monuments, pieces of furniture and works of art as part of its heritage maintenance policy, but it does not protect religious symbols. This disengagement regarding "religion" permits others to be free to act and advertise. The state could not possibly bring a religious denomination to the attention of the public, but the market does it unhampered, such as when entrepreneurs register their halal brand at the National Industrial Property Institute.

Ritual slaughtering along with halal meat is regarded as a "religious" practice and not as a market matter. As a result, even if the act is not carried out or controlled by religious institutions, it is considered to be beyond the scope of public control. Halal ritual slaughtering does not comply with the legal obligation to stun animals before the actual killing. But who solicited the exemption and on what grounds? Why are only three mosques authorized to approve priests?[26] There are no religious answers to these questions. The French government automatically extended the Islamic faith the same rights as those already granted to the Jewish faith, but at the time that this authorization was granted, Islamic officials had not asked for it, since they had found no clear theological grounds to ban stunning.[27]

---

25 From Roman times to the nineteenth century, butchers had a bad reputation in Europe. They were supposed to be cruel, violent and unruly. In traditional societies, butchers, along with executioners, often have a foreigner status, whether or not they come from a different tribe, or have a special relationship with the supernatural.

26 Priests responsible for the slaughtering must be authorized by the religious organizations that are officially recognized by the Ministry of Agriculture: the Great Mosque of Paris and the Lyon and Evry Mosques.

27 "Ulemas demonstrate some flexibility," wrote Benkheira (1995: 39), "the only meat they declare illicit is that which is imported from communist countries. Besides, they never mention the concept of a Muslim butchery. They reaffirm the constant stance of Sunnite jurists, who regard scriptural immolation as licit."

In a sense, halal slaughtering was made "sacred" by means of a semantic change, the Muslim slaughterer being referred to as a "priest" in the French law, a term unknown among Muslim exegetes. As a consequence, the actual act of performing the slaughter being regarded as "sacred," the veterinaries that inspect slaughterhouses claim to not have a precise notion of the limits of what they are supposed to control. For the sake of religious neutrality, they consider that they do not have to control "religious" products. Then, in order to clarify the situation, the Ministry of Agriculture has chosen to hand out flyers listing the details of "the Islamic ritual," a kind of fatwa (religious opinion) that we expect from an Islamic country, but not from a secular state.

In order to avoid playing into the hands of the National Front, the veterinary services acting under the authority of the prefects are told to turn a blind eye to the imperfections within the halal market, for fear that it would "stigmatize the Muslim community." The margin for interpretation is such that, *in fine*, the conditions of halal ritual slaughtering are established by the most powerful force in a slaughterhouse apart from legal constraints: productivity. This, in turn, is justified by a philanthropic concern for Muslim families who must have access to a meat-based diet even though their financial means are modest. In the same vein, it is to avoid "discrimination risks" that the industry declares itself to be hostile to the disclosure of the slaughtering method on meat labels.[28] In the end, the overproduction of ritual meat (killing more animals by ritual slaughtering than is necessary to cater for religious groups), the presence of workers slaughtering without having received a proper training, the non-compliance with contention methods, which is compulsory in the case of slaughtering without stunning, as well as the non-compliance with production times calculated so that the animal has time to die before its carcass is cut up are all tolerated. In the end, the word "religious" is an artifact which enables the slaughtering industry to avoid complying with the legal obligations that a context of open-border competition has made burdensome.

Conclusion

In France, animal welfare organizations have recently decided upon a change of strategy regarding slaughtering. The traditional lobbying behind closed doors, so far better adapted to advocate the cause of livestock in a predominantly carnivorous population, has become ineffective in a context of European community

---

28   To the amazement of consumer associations, Douzain, of the Fédération Nationale de l'Industrie et des Commerces en Gros des Viandes, made himself the spokesman of religious communities when he reminded the audience during the Animals and Society Meetings that "religious communities [were] against mentioning the slaughtering method on meat labels, the reasons being that meats issued from ritual killing might end up with being discriminated against." Verbatim # 4, meeting of May 4, 2008, available at: http://www.animaletsociete.fr/verbatims/Verbatim-Groupe3-Reunion4.pdf.

transparency. The move towards a strategy of unveiling, based on emotional anger against "deviants," is, however, highly dangerous for animal welfare associations. By assigning to a cultural and religious specificity what, in fact, has much more to do with the difficulties of the meat industry in a context of increased competition and privatizations, they might end up with putting the blame on a religion (Islam). As I have demonstrated, far from being desired by the very wide political spectrum of animal welfare groups, the stigmatizing effect is largely taken up and used by a new Islamophobic trend which combats what it calls the "Islamization" of nations across many European countries. The polemic around the "100% halal in Paris region," launched by the far-right candidate in the 2012 presidential elections which claimed that the inhabitants of Paris and its suburbs consumed "only halal meat"[29] has shown the catastrophic limits of such a strategy. The rhetoric used to describe the way in which animals are treated reflects the logic of "identity" supply and demand, which appears to be not only counterproductive in terms of animal protection, but also likely to arouse xenophobic feelings.

References

Bardot, B. 2003. *Un cri dans le silence*. Paris: Editions du Rocher.

Benkheira M-H. 1995. "La nourriture carnée comme frontière rituelle," *Archives des sciences sociales des religions*, 92, 67–88.

Bergeaud-Blackler, F. 2001. "La viande halal peut-elle financer le culte musulman?" *Journal des anthropologues*, 84, 145–71.

Lapin, L. 2010. "Viande halal, vous en mangez tous! [Halal Meat: You All Eat It!]" *Charlie Hebdo*, November 17.

Robert, F. 2011. "Assises contre l'islamisation: Act II de la résistance," *Bloc Identitaire*, April 1.

Traïni, C. 2011. *La cause animale (1820–1980): Essai de sociologie historique*. Paris: PUF.

---

29   Marine Le Pen, the presidential candidate of the far-right, claimed at a meeting held on February 19, 2012 that all the meat sold in Paris region was halal, thus triggering an outcry far beyond the members of the National Front and her sympathizers. She based her declaration on the comments (which she later altered) of a reporter during the *Envoyé Spécial* TV program, which had been broadcast a few days earlier on France 2. This program had declared that slaughterhouses in the Paris region carried out all of their slaughtering ritually. However, the production of these slaughterhouses only accounts for a very small part of the meat consumed in the region. The exact percentage of halal meat, which depends on the species involved, is not known.

Chapter 16

Halal Circle: Intimacy and Friendship among the Young Muslims of Europe[1]

Simone Maddanu

A Shared Space

Today, we are witnessing a period of growing participation by Muslims in European civil life. The exercise of citizenship raises new questions in European democracies, sometimes eliciting protectionist reactions which test the limits of the notions of equality and difference. Young generations in particular are the protagonists and actors in the civil space at the local, national and transnational levels (Allievi 1993; Dassetto 2000; Frisina 2005). Their need and desire to participate is inscribed in a subjective process and shows how much these new citizens want to be recognized in the public space and convey their Muslim way of being citizens "without banality" (Ramadan 2003). When they are not confined to urban ghettos as victims of the economic and social depression that characterizes "rejects" (Khosrokhavar 1997), these young Muslims, unlike those of the previous generation, have a better knowledge of the rules of communication and are capable of using this knowledge to act and make themselves heard, displaying an inventiveness that encourages hybridization. This generation often participates in religious, cultural, secular and political organizations, and engages with alter-globalism and a number of different cultural movements (Farro 2006; McDonald 2006). They occupy a new position by intervening in the criticism of globalization and the capitalist and imperialist system from the standpoint of their religious specificity, as activists or via their ecological and egalitarian practices in their daily lives. Though not without spurring internal debates, they are opening up an oppositional and critical space previously held by leftist and Third-World movements on the environment, war, democratic participation and the reform of financial capital.

Constantly linked to different groups, these young people engage with "autochthonous" non-Muslims from different backgrounds in the physical space of

1 The research leading to the results in this chapter has been partially financed by the EuroPublicIslam Project directed by Nilüfer Göle (EHESS) and funded by the European Research Council under the European Community's Seventh Framework Programme (FP7/2007–2013)/Grant Agreement n° 230244.

the city as well as in virtual spaces created on the Internet. It is important to note that these two spaces are distinguished from each other because they are not regulated by the same rules of conduct. In particular, diversity has different characteristics and meanings in these two spaces. The possibilities for participation and openness as well as the individual and collective practices of conduct are diverse. As Hugon affirms, "the originality of the social phenomena we observe leads us to consider that places and social spaces are central, not just tools or means" (Hugon 2010: 102). As we will see, this distinction allows us to understand the different ways of being in space and examine the range of Muslims' feelings and actions among themselves and with others.

The public space constitutes a major stake in the representation of difference and its recognition (Walzer 1993; Hall 1997; Fraser 2005; Göle 2005). It is also a space of *mise-en-scène* (Goffman 1973) where individuals participate in the "social game" (Maffesoli 1993). Confrontation, imitation and phenomena of the reproduction of practices and values spread to the private and emotional space as well. For Appadurai, this is even more notable among young people who want to seem normal "among their neighbors and peers" (Appadurai 2001: 82). Karl Mannheim underscores the power of interpretation and absorption of which new generations are capable, historically and anthropologically, dynamics of change which occur just as transformations are taking place (Mannheim 2008: 61). At the same time, we must take into consideration Inglehart's socialization hypothesis in which he asks: "are these values sufficiently rooted in the minds of the adult population to resist fluctuations in the socio-economic environment?" (Inglehart 1993: 98).[2]

In this chapter, I try to analyze the issues of intimacy and friendship within the circle of halal, based on empirical research that I have done in France and Italy between 2005 and 2012 at different Muslim organizations such as Young Muslims of Italy (GMI), Muslims of the Parti des Indigènes de la République in France and the Global Movement of Non-Violent Resistance. The questions on love and friendship are part of a discussion on the practices of Muslim actors, which came up in the qualitative interviews conducted. Some are the object of internal micro-controversies, evaluated in terms of confrontation or intergenerational relationships.

Kissing and Forms of Address

Examining the range of Islamic behavior and religious symbols in the public space changes the perceptions of Muslims and autochthons as well as those within the Muslim community itself, where varying interpretations and intergenerational relationships face off. Young campaigners for European organizations face internal micro-controversies that modify their role within the group, as well as when they

---

2   This hypothesis also implies that "it is equally necessary to consider the long-term effects of the cohort. The values of a given generation tend to reflect the conditions which existed during the pre-adult phase" (ibid.: 98).

imagine and project their role outside of it, perceiving themselves in a broader public space as individuals, independent from their communities. In this way, the new generation retraces the contemporary meaning of the *Umma*. Here, it is not a regulatory entity that defines the believer's path. Although young people defend the *Umma* – especially when Islam and Muslims are perceived as "under attack," targets for the media and for new forms of religious discrimination – young people prefer to be judged according to their own acts and daily lives, refusing to be reduced to the images put forward by the media. The young generation's way of being, of participating in space and of believing (Babès 1997) are different from their parents' in terms of their capabilities and intentions, the doubt with which they counter certainties, and especially in their ambitions and desire to define their path and their lives in an autonomous way. The changes they embody and their role as protagonists are the expression of an interpenetration (Göle 2005), and are developed by their ways of living at the local level, though they belong to transnational networks. It is within this framework that controversies around young peoples' different practices and ways of being break out in the group, community and organization (especially those in which they mix with adult participants). Diversity, their relationships to their bodies and more generally gender relations push the limits and interpretations of Muslim actors' conduct.

The casualness of physical contact between men and women that we see every day in the West is a source of constant questioning for young Muslims, caught between a pursuit of pious behavior and the quest for normality. Forms of greeting doubly call into question Muslim practices where the relationship to the body, the value of modesty and Islamic prescriptions concerning physical contacts between men and women are central. On the one hand, there is the specificity of "Middle Eastern" customs and modes of relating to the opposite sex; on the other, there is the normalization of more Westernized customs which are apparent in the choice of clothing, where justifications are found to accept diversity and forms of greeting that are seen as relaxed or "without ulterior motives." In the workplace, school or university, an explanation is needed to clarify why they won't kiss on both cheeks, a problem that is easier to discuss among women. At work, the unwritten rules of relationships between colleagues weigh heavily on Muslims, who sometimes prefer to adapt to the forms of greetings practiced by others so as not to "trouble the group's wellbeing" (Y, male, Paris). On other occasions, for public figures, accepting to kiss a (non-Muslim) woman on both cheeks, even at a local level, can be a cause for criticism by Muslim brothers and sisters:

> One of my close friends is a national political figure and he is known to be too outgoing … When he hugs and kisses a woman on both cheeks in public I have to answer for that to brothers who consider this behavior to be un-Islamic. But I couldn't be that rude! (O, male, Rome)

Modesty has controversial connotations in daily public space in forms of address which are "granted or denied," whether they are among Muslims or between

Muslims and others. Shaking hands remains a discretionary practice and is largely observed between Muslims and non-Muslims. We observe this formal gesture among the pious as a cordial act to which young women assign little importance: women will quickly extend their hand, without squeezing, showing the absence of any intention other than responding to a greeting. This accommodation through the "dead hand" confirms the woman's modesty:

> Among ourselves, we don't shake hands in order to avoid any embarrassment … we know it and I don't do it. With others [non-Muslims], personally I shake hands, no problem. (A, female, Milan)

These young people's experience as activists leads them to confront the demands of mobility and the familiarity with collaborative and open confrontational spaces with Muslims and non-Muslims. The transnational character of these movements and the platforms they adopt often lead them to travel in Europe and abroad. This raises the question, especially for young women, of traveling alone or in the company of other male and female activists. The strictest interpretation of Islamic rules forbids women from traveling alone without a *mahram*, a close male relative, and can become a barrier to action if their relatives do not consent. But "how do you grow if you can't travel?" as one of my interviewees shouted (S, female, Paris). Involvement in religious, cultural and political organizations is seen as a valuable justification for overstepping these boundaries, even within their own familial circles or groups. The need to be present and to act in these "noble" and important causes concerning the place of Muslims in Europe allows a relaxing of rules and permits active Muslim women to take leadership roles in European organizations. They thus claim an autonomy of judgment, a capacity and a will to empower themselves without the accompaniment or "protection" of male figures. This has both short- and long-term effects on the forms of representing Islam and its practices in the public space (Ali 2012). These women's roles transgress traditional boundaries linked to the patriarchy. On the one hand, the internal micro-controversies they cause shift intergenerational positions, while on the other hand, it shows the public affirmation of new and dynamic Muslims, capable of intervening in various fronts with their specificity by occupying spaces that were considered closed to them.

What Friendship, What Love?

Young Muslims in Europe live in secular spaces of confrontation and exchange (Göle 2003, 2005). Their revolutionary power for change is inscribed in a contemporaneity, in a here and now that is all-inclusive. In this way, their feelings are part of a dynamic space, capable of changing others' image of them, of the community and even of Islamic practices. As this young man claims, the major questions adolescents ask in

Muslim organizations in Europe concern the male/female relationship: "What we have learned from the West is friendship between young men and women."

Though not acting in a religious way, they engage in practices and ways of being in space "through" religion. The Muslim being, this Islamity, is pieced together. Young people know they must remain consistent, framing their practices in morality and Islamic values. They also do so in order to see themselves in equilibrium in the confrontation between their religiosity and Western ways of life; in other words, they aim to act without excluding the reality of their daily experiences.

Muslim male-female friendships begin in organizations and movements among colleagues who know how to distinguish between friendship and flirting, that ambiguous territory between unspoken feelings and seduction. In the case of sincere feelings, the purity of conversation and the "dispositions of the heart" are made apparent in order to avoid any misunderstandings or judgments by others. Coming together to learn about religion or to act as citizens on local and transnational objectives is necessary for their participation and provides an alibi for their practices. Their own Islamity and pious behavior are thus combined with active participation in different communal and civic spaces as actors. The definition of "brothers and sisters" in Islam thus becomes "colleagues" and, finally, "friends." The friendships that develop through different kinds of participation and daily interactions are not confined to Muslims. Friendship with "autochthones" is often seen as the reflection of an openness and reciprocity, and has the advantage of avoiding the ambiguity of relationships between Muslim men and women, since in this case "there are no ulterior motives."

The distinctive Muslim identity on the theme and practices of love and the mixing of men and women is also a way of affirming differences with others of the same age group or with the larger majority society. Sometimes, the latter's romantic behavior is criticized as debauched, risqué and superficial. In the case of "Islamic" love, a more noble, serious, profound and reflective stance is taken. There is a personal responsibility in the choice of the partner and the control of feelings and desires which are seen as signs of maturity. Thus, questioning these feelings becomes a kind of stage in the passage to adult life:

> When you talk to me about love, I'm tempted to say that love is universal. But if I think about romantic actions … I've heard impossible stories … One day, a girlfriend of mine said that she was madly in love with this guy, and the next she didn't love him anymore. What is that? … Me, I'll only get married to someone who can make me happy, someone who shares my perspective on life. He has to respect me. If, after we are married, he doesn't make me happy, he doesn't take care of me, or he wants to be with other women, then I'll divorce him. In Islam, I can do that. (N, female, Milan)

Organizations of young Muslims in Europe, assembled on the international level by FEMYSO,[3] officially support the campaign against forced marriage. The necessity of choosing one's own spouse is seen from the bottom up as a desire to break with certain traditional practices. Often, young Muslims get married "amongst themselves," among the young people they meet in their activist work, or in the same organizations (Amiraux 2000; Saint-Blancat 2004). Jocelyne Cesari notes that "young women are as demanding as young men, especially when they have cultural capital" (Cesari 2000: 96). Young people get to know each other better in religious and secular organizations and sometimes continue to pursue each other on the phone (calls or texts) or on the Internet.

The "weakness" ascribed to adolescents facing the role models from European societies is perceived as an intrinsic characteristic of this age group, whether or not they are Muslim. Mastering good behavior is thus a value and at times is seen as a way of reinforcing their relationship to Islam. Changing attitudes about male/female relationships can, as Cesari has shown (2000: 96), be a way of controlling individuals, leading them to an "early marriage" and preventing "illicit sexual practices."

Alongside the largely moralistic forms present among closed groups and their strict codes of behavior, a more nuanced type of discourse can be found among youths who experience the questions that interpellate them constantly in European contexts as open issues that require constant dialogue, and an interrogation "with no taboos" (Chaouki 2005). Turning to the Islamic advice offered by adults is not always satisfactory for young people, especially when they feel ashamed or when these relationships are characterized by silencing certain topics. In this case, confrontation occurs among young people or in their personal recourse to Islamic texts. Marongiu reminds us that these Muslims, even if they have some autonomous knowledge of religion and are not content with what their relations tell them, do not have a "learned" perspective of Islam (Marongiu 2002). They may turn to the Internet, to chatrooms or websites with legal advice for answers (Caeiro 2011) or to a space where they can at least speak and share their own doubts and questions. This is why Fatema Mernissi refers to al-Qaradawi as the "digital imam as paternal authority" (Mernissi 2004: 179–89). Questions and doubts about the kind of behavior to adopt in relation to issues of sexuality and relationships between men and women are even more controversial for young Muslims living in Europe.

Bausani reminds us of the difference between "real love" and "metaphoric love" in Islam: the first is reserved for God, while the second refers to the love for women in modern times (Bausani 1994: 78–85). The opposition between love for/of God and the sentimental, carnal love between men and women reached its height in the Middle Ages in Arabic poetry and literature and its semantic shifts in meaning around the terms for love, beloved, lover and the "preoccupation with

---

3   The Forum of European Muslim Youth and Student Organizations.

how to sing the *muhabba*" (Arazi 1990: 35–49).[4] Ibn 'Arabî's "Treaty of Love" (1986, an excerpt from "The Spiritual Conquest of Mecca") exalts the act of singing "the love of Love" (Arazi 1990: 35–6). In this well-known treaty, there is a passage on the love for God (himself the essence of love) and the exaltation of the man who succeeds in experiencing this supreme sentiment. The totality of love thus supersedes the real relationship between two bodies and two intellects: "the love of love (*hubb al-hubb*) consists in being so preoccupied by love as to forget the object that caused it" (Arazi 1990: 53). Later on, Ibn 'Arabî explains this further in verse:

> 'I am the one you ask for, I am the one you desire, I am your beloved, I am the renewal of your being, I am Leyla!' Qays turned towards her, exclaiming: 'Leave my sight, for the love I have for you calls me so deeply that I neglect you!'. (Arazi 1990: 53)

In more philosophical terms, Ibn 'Arabî underscores the affirmative, voluntary character of love in its "concrete appearance" (Arazi 1990: 62). This "will (*irâda*)" appears when the distinction is drawn between the love between man and woman and the love "for and of" God by young Muslims. We can imagine that neither of these two experiences has yet been clearly articulated in the experiences of young European Muslims. Their access to Arab-Islamic poetry is limited by their knowledge of classical languages; nevertheless, a number of translations are available. The link between the rhetorical aspects of romantic relationships in Islam and the construction of a "conviction" of love among young Muslims in Europe must not, however, exclude the common feelings they experience in the open space among other Muslims' experiences, as well as those of the non-Muslim majority. Young people of the same age at school, work and in the media exchange words, feelings and symbols of "rhetorical" romantic experiences, sometimes by expressing its more "platonic" form. Nilüfer Göle reminds us that the space inscribed in male/female intimacy represents the resistance to forbidden boundaries in the Islamic public space and that love "constitutes a resistance to the suppression of male-female subjectivities and to the puritanization of the public sphere" (Göle 2000: 108).

The elucubration of the concept of love, as love for an imaginary, distant being or for a close acquaintance, makes it possible to respect religious limits – except, perhaps, in secret. This also allows romantic experiences and acts of desire, as long as they are controlled and oriented by personal spirituality and as a practical way of being Muslim in contemporaneity:

> It's love that makes me say you are beautiful. You are beautiful because I love you; you are intelligent because I love you, etc. It's not an objective judgment everyone shares, but it's my love that makes her that way ... There are all kinds

---

4   The term *muhabba* or *mahabba* is also translated as "constant friendship."

of things that I include in it [in the idea of love]: my religion's fundamental values, the rationality of a stable plan for the future. (S, male, Paris)

In sum, a pragmatic vision of love is created, especially for married people who hope to show their relationships as following both religious and emotional criteria. This choice shows their wisdom and a commitment of the "heart," but never blind love. The "heart" that is central in this choice is not a place for irrational feelings, nor is it a deep well of desires and hopes where "anything is possible," or a direct reflection of their soul. On the contrary, the heart is seen here as a site of sincerity and respect of "privacy," and their choice goes beyond society's judgments and relationships: a Simmelian secret with the "ornamental" function that Nisbet mentions (Nisbet 1984: 137). It is also a site of complicity between the two people who share this "secret world," different from the outside world and its lack of mystery (Simmel 1989: 291–345). Their choice in love is rational: a persuasive, intimate and thought-out will. It is "voluntary" love that, in their eyes, can only reside in the heart, since it rejects utilitarian aims and an objective view of people and things. On the contrary, this last characteristic is the source of reproach in the Middle Eastern conception of the love life, at least in a stereotyped and often widespread imagination.

Love in Western culture is characterized by its acceptance of "desire for the beloved" (Schopenhauer) or his absence (Socrates, or the ennui experienced by Kierkegaard's Don Juan), carnal possession (as in Christology) or, in the sacrificial figure of the Virgin Mary, a figure also present in Muslim culture (Dousse 2005). What would literature, the arts and cinema be without love? Poetry would be empty. How much "rhetorical love" has it been able to inspire? Lovers, both experienced and inexperienced, nourish themselves with this literary romanticism in poetic speech, prose and songs. In this same way, these rhetorical figures are present among young Muslims in Europe: they ponder the meaning of Valentine's Day,[5] the depths of spurned love in religion and in Giacomo Leopardi's "cosmic pessimism" or Young Werther's doubts and hopes, the romantic plotlines of "elective affinities" in soap operas and songs. These same images nourish a tragic view of love, as in Shakespeare's *Romeo and Juliet*. OS told us his own love story:

I want to tell a personal story that might interest you based on what you were talking about before [love in the West and love among practicing Muslims]: I had a girlfriend; we had a pretty serious relationship that, for reasons outside our control, ended badly ... because our parents forbade us from seeing each other and getting married.

---

5   This celebration dedicated to lovers is not confined to Europe. Aymon Kreil describes at length this phenomenon in Cairo as a transnational and transcultural celebration. It is re-adapted and reformulated as timeless, universal and cosmopolitan (Kreil 2011: 77).

Me: You didn't stand up to your parents? You wanted to marry her, right?

OS: Yeah, but this fight lasted three years. After a while, we gave up.

Me: Does love mean the same thing for practicing Muslims and Westerners?

OS: When you put it like that, it's too ambiguous. For us, it was something romantic. We even went to Verona, where Romeo and Juliet came from. We went to the house, stood under the balcony. It was romantic and we both believed it. Her parents, I think, made the biggest mistake of their lives. And all for traditional reasons. Real religion has nothing to do with that.

Questions of love and friendship, along with all topics relating to feelings and emotions, are central in any society that tries to control morals, values and practices as they are defined by the dominant culture (Foucault 1984). According to Mernissi, it is through love that the Muslim world can meet the West (Mernissi 2009). The choice of a spouse and the "untranslatable" complexity of young love open up internal micro-controversies where the adult generation comes into conflict with youth. Familial reasons or negotiations in which both sides concede in small ways help avoid generational disputes and allow a partial resolution of controversies. Nonetheless, young people necessarily outstep these generational positions because they constantly renew the meaning of religion here and now and embody modernity.

The "Western" mode of friendship is a pressing issue within the Muslim community and in general, a marker of the generation that was born and raised in Europe. Marriages between different communities and the limits firmly established by Islam – the clear distinction between possibilities of interfaith marriages as a distinguishing factor in Muslim woman's choices – are restrictions on the "triumph" of love as the "*statu nascenti*" (Alberoni 1981), a revolutionary moment of transformation and change (Göle 2005: 17), and limit new encounters. The renunciation of "impossible love" for a non-Muslim is often mentioned in online forums, except in the case of the man's conversion, which is sometimes judged within the community itself as dishonest and unfair. Love among believers finds other rhetorical paths: the definition of the possible love between men and women cannot obscure Muslim values or the Muslim "qualities" that a potential partner must possess. Often, the "practical difference" between "Western" and "Islamic" types of love centers on physical contact and a generally unconcealed or manifest intimacy in the male/female relationship. If deep feelings characterize both conceptions of love, a distinction can be found in this answer: "love in Islam begins after marriage" (Z, female, Bologna). This is not "capricious," mad or adventurous love and passion that is at once ephemeral and eternal. It is a calm love, chosen voluntarily, framed in mutual respect and a respect for religion. At the same time, some women claim a right to pleasure and sexuality in an Islamic framework that allows for the full development of the person. Sometimes, they publicly claim a normal, even a rich sexual life by wearing sexy lingerie or engaging in other rhetoric of sensuality within the walls of the domestic space.

On the question of polygamy, women seem to tend towards a personal refusal that does not question Islamic tradition or the historical reasons for this choice. The exceptionality of love is always imagined as monogamous and exclusive (Alberoni 1981: 19–20). The exclusivity of amorous experience remains a dominant image, a destiny, although it must be compared to the range of real-life experiences and religious conditions surrounding the individual as well as collectively within the group.

Online Dating: The Ephemeral and the Eternal

Love has become an object of consumption in society. The cultural consumption of love (as distinct from sexuality and the sex trade) responds to a need for new socialization. Romantic encounters occur outside the context of daily life, work and intrapersonal communication that orders the urban space and Goffmanian frameworks for relationships. The slogan of the dating site Meetic's TV advertisement, "Meeting great people happens everywhere, but especially elsewhere," shows how desires for socialization, both friendly and romantic, can happen in a virtual way online. This market specializes in targeting new consumers' demands in their search for something they cannot find in their daily lives. The idea of meeting someone of the opposite sex no longer corresponds with the expectations of the individuals, their romantic dreams or demands for a relationship. Online dating sites have become successful by proposing a specific target ("a dating site for demanding singles" is the tagline for attractiveworld.net), including for Muslims. This is the strategy of Muslima.com,[6] an international marriage site with no intermediaries. This multilingual site (English, French, Italian, Norwegian, Swedish, German and Arabic) also links to dating sites for other communities (brazilcupid, chineselovelinks, SouthAfricanCupid, etc.).[7] Converts can also find opportunities to meet other Muslims for romance or simple friendship. Here, knowing the future partner's religion is the central criterion. One interviewee confided that she tried this tack, but came away disappointed:

> When they see my picture and see that I'm blonde, not Arab, I get lots of messages but only to meet right away. I need to talk, to exchange ideas before

---

6 This is also true for Mektoube, a dating site for Muslims and Maghrebis which is widely used in France and advertises widely on Facebook.

7 http://www.muslima.com/French/?ovchn=GGL&ovcpn=French+France+New+Muslim+Dating&ovcrn=site+de+rencontre+musulman+exact&ovtac=PPC&gclid=CILmzMSHxq8CFYQMfAod_GLvcQ.

I can meet someone. Lots of people who contact me don't write very well and they don't seem to want to take the time. I don't want things to go that quickly … Maybe I should wear a headscarf … Even the fact that I am not Arab must be a problem. I'm starting to wonder about it. (B, female, Paris)

These sites offer a wide variety of paid and unpaid services without intermediaries. The Internet user can directly establish contact via email and continue the encounter through other media by sharing pictures, videos, chatting on a webcam or more if they choose.[8] The website Inchallah.com ("Marriage, Allah willing")[9] has been mentioned in the French media (including the newspapers *Libération* and *Le Parisien* and on the television channels France2, France3 and BFM television). These websites allow individuals to make transnational connections to people who are linked by their similar dating requirements. The difficulty in finding the "right person" in real space while respecting, for example, the Islamic preference for gender segregation finds a useful loophole online. However, the potential ambiguities of communication hidden in *html* codes, despite the guarantees of physical distance, remain. Nonetheless, as one of our interview subjects reminds us, "Islam also has a place in the bathroom," in personal, secret, or hidden spaces: thus, young Muslims rely on their own personal evaluations and judgments rather than resorting to the control of the community and the surveillance of relatives or adults. Affinities are not "elective," but dialogical and discursive: they are organized in terms of convention and reciprocity, leading to a virtual relationship that can be casual or become a lifelong commitment. This holds true for everyone, Muslim or not.

The anonymity that the Internet guarantees and the flexible rules this communication provides represent a new space of openness where experience and expression can occur in a new way. Nonetheless, it is in the real, daily space that confrontations with the "totality of the body" through personal, expressive practices occur. Participation in organizations or simply personal affirmations in daily life increase the need for young Muslims to engage with one another on affective topics, finding a path where they can combine their Islamity and their present, formed and shaped by socialization. Once again, it is in the search for new spaces in parallel to, yet intertwined with, traditional spaces that the expectations and hopes of Muslims will be expressed in the strength and universality of their feelings.

---

8 The site offers free membership that allows the user create a profile and see other members' profiles; this allows them to get inviting "glances" which they can only see in the second, paid phase of membership. Becoming a "gold member" or "platinum member" allows them to have discussions and multiple exchanges with several people directly and use a number of the site's interactive media, giving them a wider selection of virtual partners.

9 http://www.inchallah.com/bie4n-rencontre-musulmane.html.

References

Alberoni, F. 1981. *Le choc amoureux*. Paris: Ed. Ramsay.

Ali, Z. (ed.) 2012. *Féminismes islamiques*. Toulouse: La Fabrique.

Allievi, S. 1993. "I giovani musulmani in Europa: tra identità tradizionale e mutamento culturale," in L. Tomasi (ed.), *I giovani e le religioni in Europa*. Trento: Reverdito, 81–93.

Amiraux, V. 2000. "Jeunes musulmanes turques d'Allemagne. Voix et voies de l'individuation," in F. Dassetto (ed.), *Paroles d'islam. Individus, sociétés et discours dans l'islam européen contemporain*. Paris: Maisonneuve & Larose, 101–23.

Appadurai, A. 2001. *Après le colonialisme. Les conséquences culturelles de la globalisation*. Paris: Payot.

Arazi, A. 1990. *Amour divin et amour profane dans l'islam médiéval. A travers le Diwan de Kalid Al-Katib*. Paris: Maisonneuve et Larose.

Babès, L. 1997. *L'islam positif. La religion des jeunes musulmans de France*. Paris: Les Editions de l'Atelier.

Bausani, A. 1994. "Amore e culture. Ritualizzazione dell'Eros," in *Atti del VI Covegno internazionale di studi antropologici*, 78–85.

Caeiro, A. 2011. "The Making of the Fatwa: The Production of Islamic Legal Expertise in Europe," *Archive des Sciences Sociales des Religions*, 155, 81–100.

Cesari, J. 2000. "La querelle des anciens et des modernes: le discours islamique en France," in F. Dassetto (ed.), *Paroles d'islam. Individus, sociétés et discours dans l'islam européen contemporain*. Paris: Maisonneuve et Larose, 86–100.

Chaouki, K. 2005. *Salaam Italia*. Rome: Aliberti.

Couchard, F. 1994. *Le fantasme de séduction dans la culture musulmane. Mythes et représentations sociales*. Paris: PUF.

Dassetto, F. 1995. *L'islam in Europa*. Turin: Edizioni della Fondazione Giovanni Agnelli.

Dassetto, F. (ed.) 2000. *Paroles d'islam. Individus, sociétés et discours dans l'islam européen contemporain*. Paris: Maisonneuve & Larose.

Dhaoui, H. 2001. *L'amour en Islam*. Paris: L'Harmattan.

Dousse, M. 2005. *Marie la musulmane*. Paris: Albin Michel.

Farro, A.L. (ed.) 2006. *Italia alterglobal. Movimento, culture e spazi di vita di altre globalizzazioni*. Milan: Franco Angeli Edizioni.

Foucault, M. 1984. *L'Usage des plaisirs. Histoire de la sexualité*. Paris: Gallimard.

Fraser, N. 2005. *Qu'est-ce que la justice sociale ? Reconnaissance et redistribution*. Paris: La Découverte.

Frisina, A. 2005. "Musulmani e italiani, tra le altre cose. Tattiche e strategie identitarie di giovani figli di immigrati," in A. Pacini and J. Cesari (eds), *Giovani musulmani in Europa*. Turin: Centro Agnelli, 161–87.

Goffman, E. 1973. *La mise en scène de la vie quotidienne*, volume 2, *Les relations en public*. Paris: Les Editions de Minuit.

Göle, N. 2000. "Snapshots of Islamic modernities, *Daedalus*, 129(1), 91–117.

Göle, N. 2003 [1991]. *Musulmanes et modernes*. Paris: La Découverte.

Göle, N. 2005. *Interpénétration. L'islam et l'Europe*. Paris: Galaade Editions.

Hall, S. 1997. *Representation: Cultural Representations and Signifying Practices*. London: SAGE Publications.

Hugon, S. 2010. *Circumnavigations. L'imaginaire du voyage dans l'expérience Internet*. Paris: CNRS Editions.

Ibn 'Arabî. 1986. *Traité de l'Amour*. Paris: Albin Michel.

Ibn Azm. 1992. *De l'amour et des amants, collier de la colombe sur l'amour et les amants*. Paris: Gabriel Martinez-Gros.

Inglehart, R. 1993. *La transition culturelle dans les sociétés industrielles avancées*. Paris: Economica.

Khosrokhavar, F. 1997. *L'islam des jeunes*. Paris: Flammarion.

Kreil, A. 2011. "La Saint-valentin au pays d'al-Azhar: éléments d'ethnographie et de l'amour et du sentiment amoureux au Caire." in M. Gross, S. Mathieu and S. Nizard (eds), *Sacrées familles! Changement familiaux, changements religieux*. Toulouse: Erès, 71–83.

Maffesoli, M. 1993. *La contemplation du monde*. Paris: Grasset.

Mannheim, K. 2008. *Le generazioni*. Bologna: Il Mulino.

Marongiu, O. 2002. "L'islam au pluriel. Etude du rapport au religieux chez les jeunes musulmans," Ph.D. thesis, Université de Lille.

McDonald, K. 2006. *Global Movements: Action and Culture*. Oxford: Blackwell.

Mernissi, F. 2009. *L'amour dans les pays musulmans*. Paris: Albin Michel.

Nisbet, R.A. 1984 [1966]. *La tradition sociologique*. Paris: PUF.

Ramadan, T. 2003. *Les musulmans d'Occident et l'avenir de l'islam*. Arles: Actes Sud.

Saint-Blancat, C. 2004. "La transmission de l'islam auprès de nouvelles générations de la diaspora," *Social Compass*, 51, 235–47.

Simmel, G. 1989. *Sociologia*. Milan: Edizioni di Comunità.

Taylor, C. 1992. *Multiculuralisme, différence et démocratie*. Paris: Aubier.

Taylor, C. 2003. *La diversité de l'expérience religieuse aujourd'hui*. Quebec: Bellarmin.

Walzer, M. 1997 [1983]. *Sphères de justice. Une défense du pluralisme et de l'égalité*. Paris: Seuil.

PART V
European Genealogies of Islam and Politics of Memory

PART
Environmental Monitoring
and Disaster Manageme

Chapter 17

Medieval Spain and the Integration of Memory (On the Unfinished Project of Pre-Modernity)

Gil Anidjar

A peculiar divide marks the figure of medieval Spain, whether it is deployed in collective memory or explored in sober and meticulous historical accounts. From al-Andalus to the Spanish Inquisition, from the Golden Age of *Convivencia* to 1492, Spain is at once positive and negative, dark and light, exemplary and exceptional. It constitutes, in other words, a perfect illustration, a vector of reference, and a propitious occasion for sustained reflection on "pluralism, integration, and identity" – an indicator of sorts for the promise, and the threat, that are inherent to these terms. The same divide famously affects 1492. That most emblematic of dates parts discursive universes across oceans of time and space, between the taint of cruel and arbitrary expulsions in the Old World and the glory of discovery and adventure in the New. Such characteristic features do not necessarily constitute a paradox or a contradiction (one evident, for instance, in the title of David Nirenberg's celebrated book *Communities of Violence*) (Nirenberg 1998). Dialectical and supple, the divisions of medieval Spain can be, and often have been, harmonized, narrativized and historicized. They are, as it were, easily integrated. One simple, but not necessarily simplified, version of this processual tale runs thus: first, it was good (when Muslims, Jews and Christians lived together); then, it was bad (when the Almoravids and the Almohads destroyed it, or when the Christian kings put an end to it all). As the recent French debates around "The Greeks, the Arabs, and Us" demonstrates, none of this is uncontroversial, of course, or undisputed (Rosier-Catach et al. 2009), but the enduring force of medieval Spain in the contemporary imagination does seem to emerge from an internal oscillation or tension (between "culture, conflict, and coexistence" as the subtitle of a notable volume has it) (Collins and Goodman 2002), as well as from the measure of wistful longing one feels authorized to express (or condemn) in its wake, while always insisting on the decisive end or termination that befell it.

Increasingly now, the figure of medieval Spain, which has engaged scholars and occupied the Western public sphere across a wide-ranging spectrum, would also be telling us something about Islam and its historical resources (Doubleday and Coleman 2008). Here the matter of exceptionality stands out in a striking manner, insofar as Islam's ability to coexist with others is scrutinized in the light of its past and distant achievements. As Harold Bloom phrased it in the preface to a book dedicated to the elevation of Islamic Spain in our collective memory, "there are no Muslim Andalusians visible anywhere in the world today" (Bloom 2002: xv).

One might grant the meticulous, philologically and demographically informed research that has no doubt been performed to reach this conclusion, while nonetheless noting, here and elsewhere, the hint conveyed with regard to the demonstration of past achievements, namely that it still requires a particularly strenuous kind of rhetorical and persuasive exertion. And so, not surprisingly, the question is repeatedly asked in a number of ways. Can Muslims do it again? Did they in fact do it? Can they coexist in and with Europe as they did, if they did, in the Middle Ages? Can they now, perhaps for the first time, be integrated?

It seems strange to have to point out, if only for the benefit of a more integrated memory, what a diminutively expanded perspective would make easily apparent, namely that when it comes to the coexistence of Jews, Muslims and Christians, there is, as a matter of world historical fact, nothing exceptional. One can debate the precise nature of that existence, of course, and the quality of life involved. But one cannot deny that throughout the Mediterranean and beyond (that is, southward and eastward), Jews, Christians and Muslims have lived together for centuries. From Baghdad to Marrakech and Timbuktu, from Sarajevo to Alexandria, Sanaa and Cochin, Jews, Christians and Muslims have lived together. They have done so more or less well, more or less peacefully and more or less productively, but they did live (which, of course, is also to say that they died, unfortunately: see Nandy 2001). They lived in a multifarious togetherness, under diverse political and legal arrangements, at distinctive levels of economic or cultural autonomy, and of course with varying degrees of asymmetric violence (Baron 1973; Alcalay 1993; Cohen 1994). Most importantly, they accomplished this togetherness unexceptionally.

Underscoring the banality of these facts, we may add that they could only become exceptional – indeed, they have only become exceptional – in (Western) Europe and within a European (and specifically Eurocentric) perspective. It is, after all, Europe that celebrates medieval Spain (and assigns great importance to 1492). And it is Europe that, over the centuries since 1492, invented a range of regimes and technologies that were predicated on unparalleled forms of legal and linguistic, religious and political exclusivity. It is in this precise context that one could come to speak, and with great pertinence, of *integrity*, the very concept that ultimately sustains and nourishes any discussion of *integration*, and the institutional practices that characterize the Western, Christian or post-Christian polity. This, again, is to recall that Europe's integrity was manufactured and produced in a manner and form unequaled anywhere else, and accompanied by a philosophical, theological and scientific set of claims and justifications that otherwise constitute the very pride of Western thought and culture. The most famous among these forms is reluctantly associated with the Inquisition, which inherited the sophistication and achievements of what Harold Berman and others have called the "legal revolution" of the twelfth century (Berman 1983;

Peters 1989; Caldwell-Ames 2009). The forerunner of modern homogenization, of the modern state in its systematicity, the Inquisition constitutes the under-recognized backbone of a long-standing and still current policy of mass expulsion in population management. Less divided than it seemed at first, 1492 rightly marks, in fact, the expulsion of both Jews and Muslims, and the brutal conquest of America. It prefigures the development of security services the world over and articulates, finally, the enduring choices for "emancipation" offered to Jews and others: "You who are so unlike us, either become like us, or get out." I will return to this, but for now let me reiterate that the fact of Jewish, Christian and Muslim coexistence can only be considered exceptional in Europe, insofar as it happened on European soil. And, indeed, such exceptionality is openly presented as such in Western historiography and memory, and precisely by way of a conjuration of sorts, the ritualized invocation of the figure of medieval Spain.

The inner divisions, or paradoxes, that are associated with medieval Spain may thus be treated as historical fact, but they can also be recognized for what they constitute just as well, namely psychological mechanisms and political symptoms (on "political psychology," see Nandy 1998). One could hardly speak of a repressive hypothesis, here, à la Foucault. Recalling Aimé Césaire, one would have to suggest instead that this time no chickens come home to roost. No practice is imported or exported, and it would be more accurate, therefore, to speak of a reversed paralepsis, in which instead of saying by not saying, one is actively *occluding by telling*. Or, to continue along these rhetorical lines, the figure of medieval Spain can be understood as a synecdoche of a peculiar sort, where the part stands for the whole (one instance for myriad cases of coexistence), but the whole is denied as such (as if there were no other case of coexistence). Its elevation to the status of exception or to that of a wishful but futile exemplar turns out to be a conceit of sorts, the site of a certain deceit and deception, and particularly because it marks the beginning of world conquest and the end of coexistence everywhere. What is otherwise the perfect banality of coexistence, negotiated and arbitrated under multiple skies and regimes, is at any rate concealed under the hyperbolic vision of a singular exception. Then and there – *only* then and there – would Jews, Christians and Muslims have been living in (relative – always relative) harmony. And then there was enlightenment.

Pluralism, integration and identities, then, and the alignments or realignments of liberalism. This is where, in relation to the figure of medieval Spain, I would want to argue that it is of particularly momentous importance in the integrated construction of memory and of modernity, in the self-understanding of liberalism that actively carries and deploys its Andalusian memories. There are other ways than reiteration to make the hyperbolically consensual, and self-serving, argument that we live at the pinnacle of progress and of universal advance and improvement, not to mention ethical and political understanding, worthy of being spread and taught to others. Still, let me insist and assert that the figure of medieval Spain does hold a measure of significance, which is, minimally, of symptomatic value. If engaged in this perspective and evaluated as positive, medieval Spain is concisely grasped along lines such as: "it would be good if it had lasted." If deemed wanting, however ("there was no real coexistence, only the nostalgic fiction of an idyllic past"), medieval Spain can still be made to serve as the privileged figure of an earlier, and darker, period, the escape from which is sufficient ground for our eternal, albeit modern and emancipated (even emancipating), gratitude. I speak again of the Inquisition, of course, but more generally of "the Black Legend," and I merely extend thereby Maria de Guzman's (2005: xii) claim that "the construction of Anglo-American identity as 'American' has been dependent on figures of Spain" (see also de Guzmán 2007). Spain might yet function as another kind of placeholder, a figure this time for everything that goes under the heading of "liberalism and empire," such as was explored by Uday Mehta (1999), Jennifer Pitts (2005) and Karuna Mantena (2006), and the "intolerance" against which, as Wendy Brown (2008) has shown, "enlightened tolerance" was articulated. It is not for nothing after all that Jules Ferry, to recall one Mediterranean example among many, was at once the prophet of *laïcité* and the main architect of French colonial expansion, that other unfinished project of modernity.

Be that as it may, the figure of medieval Spain has served its purpose very well, convincing us that the dark side of modern imperialism, the truly bloody empire, was a Catholic empire, and not the relentless series of Protestant empires, from the Dutch to the American. Denegation here grows to embrace even the quasi-inexistent notion of a German empire, the embodiment (albeit hypothetical) of what Edward Said (1978) strangely confessed to having omitted under the heading of "German Orientalism" (see also Pollock 1993; Zantop 1997; Raz-Krakotzkin 1998). Can one really and fully distinguish after all between Orientalism and Nazism? Let us not forget that the most sophisticated among Orientalist philological inventions was the division between Aryan and Semite, that *Lebensraum* translates *espace vital*, and that neither the Reformation nor the Industrial Revolution can be considered independently of 1492. Therefore, 1492 does not constitute their dark and historically distant opposite. It is, again, no exception, but must rather be understood as the initialization of that same famous (once infamous) principle, which had been earlier rehearsed with the expulsion of the Jews from every major Christian kingdom in Western Europe. As Foreign Affairs summarized the gist of this dynamic period of European history:

> Massacre and expulsion were the most common methods of religious cleansing, which tended to target Jews, the only sizable minority in most countries. Jews were thus expelled from England (1290), France (1306), Hungary (1349–1360), Provence (1394 and 1490), Austria (1421), Lithuania (1445), Cracow (1494), Portugal (1497) and numerous German principalities at various times. Spain was unique among European countries because of its sizable Muslim population. (Bell-Fialkoff 1993: 112)

This principle was later instituted by way of state apparatuses and it remains very much alive today. It is a neat, practical principle that resonates through Said's analyses, or earlier in Hannah Arendt's *The Origins of Totalitarianism*. As I have already suggested, it could be called the *integrity principle*, and it goes something like this: "you who are so unlike us, either become like us, or get out." And then came indirect rule and the *valuation* of cultural difference, also known as the clash of racializations, and the "question" of integration.

The Israeli historian Amnon Raz-Krakotzkin recently pointed out that the formula adopted by the Christian kings, "either become Christians like us, or face expulsion" (personal conversation; see also Raz-Krakotzkin 2007b), is shockingly proximate to the modern formulation of emancipation: "become citizens like us, or face deportation"; Karl Marx (1992) notably recognized what was meant here as well: "become Christians like us." Hardly harking back to a dark, medieval past, 1492 instead prefigured and instituted that most notorious form of integrated polity, the modern nation state. As Arendt (1958) showed long ago, it is after all the establishment and enforced dissemination of this now universally accepted juridico-political form which gave rise to exhaustive, and structural, projects of educational homogenization and linguistic eradication (see e.g. Mitchell 1991; Nandy 2003), legal unification (the exportation of Western law and particularly of the *code civil* and mercantile law: Hallaq 2009; Mantena 2010), territorial partitions (often drawn with impeccably straight rulers and other sophisticated technologies: Pandey 1990; Makdisi 2000), ethnic cleansing and systematic genocide (Mamdani 2001).

What I want to underscore, therefore, is the particularly powerful manner in which a potent figure partakes of and sustains an historical, political and psychological mechanism, whereby an alleged virtue of the West (its having resolved and transcended the problem of war and conflict by rising – if noticeably often and with remarkable recurrence – from the ashes of religious, civil and racial wars) comes incarnate and is, as it were, differentially injected into varied loci, both past and present, in order to serve as a comparative term or an evaluating standard. Thus, with medieval Spain, we persist in thinking of Europe as an exemplary, and exceptional, site of peaceful coexistence, although we know very well about other chapters in its gruesome history. We might also know today of the horrendous treatment to which the Roma people are still subjected in overcrowded camps and elsewhere (the camp is the *nomos* of this modern), the proliferating erection of walls and "security fences," the brutal policing of the Schengen borders, the targeting of immigration (and now "Islam") as the alarming issue of choice in the reigning culture of fear, and the management of social conflict contemporaneous with economic and social (not to mention financial) policies of devastating proportions. We know much more than that, I think. We know about "peasants into Frenchmen" and the role played by colonial rule in the advent of communalism (and later partition), sectarianism (and later civil war), tribalism (and later genocide) and even *communautarisme* (and the competing value assigned to anti-Semitism and Islamophobia). And we might go over the history of bombing and discuss how cold the Cold War was in Africa, or in Asia from East to West (see Lindqvist 2001). Have we not observed for some time the devastating effects of earlier European exports and impositions, the *Tanzimat*, such as they were deployed in the Ottoman Empire in Lebanon and in Turkey? Or the arresting intricacies of "la France musulmane" in sub-Saharan Africa and what Timothy Mitchell (2009) compellingly described recently as "Carbon Democracy"? We have begun to learn about the other 1492, the extermination of native Americans, and the modernity (and modernization) of transatlantic slavery; we should know all about the "making of the English working class," the development of biological racism and the "scramble for Africa," and we are learning more about the intricacies of settler colonialism, direct and indirect rule; we are familiar with "discipline and punish," in other words, and are growing increasingly aware of the history of eugenics in the US and elsewhere, of segregation and apartheid rule there and elsewhere. We know the radical and violent reshaping of populations in the modern state, the enormous atrocities that took place within or outside of the European continent over the course of the long, all-too long, twentieth century. We are beginning to hear, finally, of the current state of the planet of slums (Davis 2006). We are gaining knowledge about all this and still we ask, in the name of Equal Opportunity Criticism: are *they* capable of coexistence? Can they be integrated? How do we protect ourselves – ourselves and our identities? How do we maintain our integrity as we confront *their* lack of "pluralism," the absence (or alleged absence) of "cosmopolitanism" and religious tolerance in Islamic countries, customs and manners?

The divided figure of medieval Spain is thus split along rigorously recognizable lines that correspond strictly to the paraleptic and synecdochic logic I alluded to earlier. It is constituted as the strategic division, a series of erected walls, between philosophy and history, the old and the new world, colonialism and liberalism, the Enlightenment and the Dark Ages, the West and the rest. As I conclude, therefore, I wish to remain with that figure, in order to take some distance from its European construction, to invoke a different kind of integration, one that does not merely assume the fact of coexistence, but acknowledges the constitutive violence thereby involved, while also providing the means to examine, and even verify, the nature of such coexistence yesterday and today. For there is a different figure for medieval Spain, one where divisions and paradoxes are on display while coming undone, and where the question of integration presumes nothing less than integrity. It should be recalled that, in Israel/Palestine as well, the "peace process" has been about maintaining separation between and among Jews and Arabs *in the name of coexistence*. Instead of separation, then, the Palestinian poet Mahmoud Darwish proposes a sense of exile that is shared, that refuses the rule of property as a model for belonging. "Soon," the poet says, "soon we will seek what has been our history around your history in the distant lands." It is of course impossible to do justice to Darwish's intricate and complex poem, which inscribes its own multiple chronology, at once al-Andalus and Palestine, documenting the dates and times of 1492, 1948, 1967, 1992 and beyond. But it is possible to recognize here what Raz-Krakotzkin (2007a) identifies as the essential import of a "binational perspective."

To put it in the terms that have guided me in this chapter, the question, if we follow Darwish, is not whether al-Andalus was ever an exception, but whether we can still imagine and establish an al-Andalus as a place and time in common:

> On the last evening on this earth, we cut off our days
> From our shrubs, and we count the ribs that we will carry with us
> And the ribs that we will leave behind, there … on the last evening
> We bid farewell to nothing, and we do not find the time for our end
> Everything remains as it is, the place changes our dreams
> And changes its visitors. Suddenly, we are no longer capable of irony
> And the place is ready to host our nothingness … here on the last evening
> We fill ourselves with the mountains surrounded by the clouds: conquest and reconquest
> An ancient time grants to this new time the keys of our doors
> Come on in, O conquerors, enter our homes, and drink the wine
> Of our complacent muwashshaha. For we are the night when it splits in two,
> No horse rider arriving from the last prayer call to deliver the dawn …
> Our green hot tea – drink it! Our fresh pistachio nuts – eat them!
> These beds are green made of cedar wood – surrender to drowsiness!
> After this lengthy siege, sleep on the feathers of our dreams
> The sheets are ready, the scents are at the door, and the mirrors are many
> Enter them so that we can come out! Soon we will seek what
> Has been our history around your history in the distant lands
> And we will ask ourselves in the end: was al-Andalus
> Here or there? On the earth … or in the poem?
> (Darwish 1992: 9–10, my translation)

References

Alcalay, A. 1993. *After Jews and Arabs: Remaking Levantine Culture*. Minneapolis: University of Minnesota Press.

Ani, F. 2008. "The Archeology of Conquest: Calisthenics, Ideology," M.A. Thesis, Department of History and Classics, Edmonton, Alberta.

Arendt, H. 1958. *The Origins of Totalitarianism*. Cleveland, OH: Meridian Books.

Baron, S-W. 1973. "Ghetto and Emancipation," in L. Schwartz (ed.), *The Menorah Treasury*, Philadelphia, PA: Jewish Publication Society of America, 50–63.

Bell-Fialkoff, A. 1993. "A Brief History of Ethnic Cleansing," *Foreign Affairs*, 72(3), 112.

Berman, H-J. 1983. *Law and Revolution: The Formation of the Western Legal Tradition*. Cambridge, MA: Harvard University Press.

Bloom, H. 2002. "Preface," in M-R. Menocal (ed.), *The Ornament of the World: How Muslims, Jews, and Christians Created a Culture of Tolerance in Medieval Spain*. Boston, MA: Little, Brown, and Co.

Brown, W. 2008. *Regulating Aversion: Tolerance in the Age of Identity and Empire*. Princeton, NJ: Princeton University Press.

Caldwell-Ames, C. 2009. *Righteous Persecution: Inquisition, Dominicans, and Christianity in the Middle Ages*. Philadelphia: University of Pennsylvania Press.

Cohen, M-C. 1994. *Under Crescent and Cross: The Jews in the Middle Ages*. Princeton, NJ: Princeton University Press.

Collins, R. and Goodman, A. (eds) 2002. *Medieval Spain: Culture, Conflict, and Coexistence, Studies in Honour of Angus MacKay*. New York: Palgrave.

Darwish, M. 1992. *Ahada 'ashara kawkab* [*Eleven Planets*]. Beirut: Dar al-Jadid.

Davis, M. 2006. *Planet of Slums*. London: Verso.

De Guzmán, M. 2005. *Spain's Long Shadow: The Black Legend, Off-Whiteness, and Anglo-American Empire*. Minneapolis: University of Minnesota Press.

Doubleday, S-R. and Coleman, D. (eds) 2008. *In the Light of Medieval Spain: Islam, the West, and the Relevance of the Past*. New York: Palgrave Macmillan.

Gourevitch, P. 1998.*We Wish to Inform You That Tomorrow We Will be Killed With Our Families: Stories from Rwanda*. New York: Picador.

Greer, M-R., Quilligan, M. and Mignolo, W-D. (eds) 2007. *Rereading the Black Legend: The Discourses of Religious and Racial Difference in the Renaissance Empires*. Chicago, IL: University of Chicago Press.

Hallaq, W. 2009. *Shari'a: Theory, Practice, Transformations*. Cambridge: Cambridge University Press.

Lindqvist, S. 2001. *A History of Bombing*, trans. Linda Haverty Rugg. New York: The New Press.

Makdisi, U. 2000. *The Culture of Sectarianism: Community, History, and Violence in Nineteenth-Century Ottoman Lebanon*. Berkeley: University of California Press.

Mamdani, M. 2001. *When Victims Become Killers: Colonialism, Nativism, and the Genocide in Rwanda*. Princeton, NJ: Princeton University Press.

Mantena, K. 2010. *Alibis of Empire: Henry Maine and the Ends of Liberal Imperialism*. Princeton, NJ: Princeton University Press.

Marx, K. 1992. "On the Jewish Question," trans. Rodney Livingstone and Gregor Benton, in *Marx, Early Writings*. New York: Penguin Books and the New Left Review.

Mehta, S-U. 1999. *Liberalism and Empire: A Study in Nineteenth Century British Liberal Thought*. Chicago, IL: University of Chicago Press.

Menocal, M.R. 2000. "Culture in the Time of Tolerance: Al-Andalus as a Model for Our Time," *Yale Law School Occasional Papers*.

Mitchell, T. 1991. *Colonizing Egypt*. Berkeley: University of California Press.

Mitchell, T. 2009. "Carbon Democracy," *Economy and Society*, 38(3), 399–432.

Nandy, A. 1998. *Exiled at Home*. Delhi: Oxford University Press.

Nandy, A. 2001. *An Ambiguous Journey to the City: The Village and Other Odd Ruins of the Self in the Indian Imagination*. New Delhi: Oxford University Press.

Nandy, A. 2003. *The Romance of the State and the Fate of Dissent in the Tropics*. New Delhi: Oxford University Press.

Nirenberg, D. 1998. *Communities of Violence: Persecution of Minorities in the Middle Ages*. Princeton, NJ: Princeton University Press.

Pandey, G. 1990. *The Construction of Communalism in Colonial North India*. New Delhi: Oxford University Press.

Peters, E. 1989. *Inquisition*. Berkeley: University of California Press.

Pitts, J. 2005. *A Turn to Empire: The Rise of Imperial Liberalism in Britain and France*. Princeton, NJ: Princeton University Press.

Pollock, S. 1993. "Deep Orientalism? Notes on Sanskrit and Power Beyond the Raj," in C-A. Breckenridge and P. van der Veer (eds), *Orientalism and the Postcolonial Predicament*. Philadelphia: University of Pennsylvania Press, 80–96.

Raz-Krakotzkin, A. 1998. "A Few Comments on Orientalism, Jewish Studies, and Israeli Society," *Jama'a*, 3, 34–61.

Raz-Krakotzkin, A. 2007a. *Exil et souveraineté: Judaïsme, sionisme et pensée binationale*, trans. Joelle Marelli. Paris: La Fabrique.

Raz-Krakotzkin, A. 2007b. *The Censor, the Editor, and the Text: The Catholic Church and the Shaping of the Jewish Canon in the Sixteenth Century*, trans. Jackie Feldman. Philadelphia: University of Pennsylvania Press.

Rosier-Catach, I. et al. (eds) 2009. *Les Grecs, les Arabes, et nous. Enquête sur l'islamophobie savante*, Paris: Fayard.

Said, E-W. 1978. *Orientalism*. New York: Vintage.

Soifer, M. 2009. "Beyond Convivencia: Critical Reflections on the Historiography of Interfaith Relations in Christian Spain," *Journal of Medieval Iberian Studies*, 1(1), 19–35.

Zantop, S. 1997. *Colonial Fantasies: Conquest, Family, and Nation in Precolonial Germany, 1770–1870*. Durham, NC: Duke University Press.

Chapter 18

The Contemporary Afterlife of Moorish Spain

Charles Hirschkind

I

In 2003, the Spanish government of then-President José Maria Aznar agreed, in the face of immense popular opposition, to send a contingent of Spanish troops to join in the US-led invasion of Iraq. In preparation for the mission, the Spanish military produced a new badge for the soldiers emblazoned with the emblem of Santiago Matamoros, St. James the Moor-Killer. With its sword-point tip and brilliant red color, the cross has long served as a symbol within Spain for the defeat and elimination of the Moors by the Christian armies in the fifteenth century. Spanish troops, now armed with this symbol, were sent off to Iraq to patrol the city of al-Najaf – one of the holiest cities in Shi'a Islam.

The choice of the Moor-Killer emblem was not incongruous with Aznar's strident anti-Muslim rhetoric or with his historical sensibilities. In a talk on "global threats" that he gave in Washington in 2006, Aznar drew the connection between the fight against Muslim radicals and what is known as the *Reconquista*: "It's them or us. The West did not attack Islam, it was they who attacked us … We are constantly under attack and we must defend ourselves. I support Ferdinand and Isabella" (cited in Gulfnews 2006). At the same event, while defending Pope Benedict's controversial claim that Islam was an inherently violent religion, Aznar suggested that Muslims should apologize for having invaded Spain in the eighth century.

Aznar's tenure in power ended with the general election of March 2004 (he later joined the right-wing think-tank the American Enterprise Institute and then moved on to join Rupert Murdoch's News Corporation). Despite a significant lead in the polls just weeks before the elections, his government's response to the March 11 train bombings in Madrid, particularly the widespread perception that government officials had continued to place the blame on the Basque separatist movement ETA despite evidence that Muslim radicals were involved, provoked immense popular condemnation and produced a decisive defeat three days later. Upon assuming the presidency, the victor, José Luis Rodríguez Zapatero of the Socialist Party, immediately instituted a recall of Spain's troops from Iraq. In addition, he quickly produced and presented an initiative to the United Nations for what he called an "Alliance of Civilizations," its purpose being to "deepen political, cultural, and education relations between those who represent the so-called Western world and, in this historic moment, the area of Arab and Muslim Countries" (BBC News Online 2004). As with his predecessor, Zapatero also invoked Spain's Islamic past in presenting his initiative, not, however, as one more campaign in a long-standing war between the West and Islam, but rather in terms of a legacy of *Convivencia*, the practice of mutual tolerance and respect that, according to some scholars, characterized relations between the Muslims, Christians and Jews of al-Andalus.[1]

Across much of the nation's history, Spanish political elites have engaged some of the most pressing questions of the day through a detour into the Moorish era, those aligned with liberal currents often invoking the romantic image of interconfessional harmony, while those linked to conservative Catholic Monarchism depicting the period as a brutal interruption of Spain's pious Christian soul.[2] Contemporary debates on immigration, on Spain's role within the EU or on the War on Terror frequently come to pivot upon discordant interpretations of the Andalusian legacy. Since the development of Spanish nationalism in the nineteenth century, much of the Spanish historiography of the Moorish period has itself been highly conflictual, never too distant from ideological struggles over the definition of Spanish identity, struggles fed by long-standing anxieties over the nation's peripheral status in relation to Europe (at least until recently, and perhaps now again with unemployment well over 20 percent).

These tensions within the historiography of al-Andalus are not exceptional within Europe but are characteristic of a more general phenomenon: the ideological appropriation and deployment of the distant past by nationalists of all types. This phenomenon is particularly evident today in the context of contemporary micronationalist movements throughout Europe, with Spain being no exception (Payne 1991; Stolcke 1995; Borneman and Fowler 1997). While Catalonian and Basque nationalisms represent the strongest regionalist movements in the country, the southern province of Andalusia has also been the site of long-standing efforts to secure greater independence *vis-à-vis* the Spanish state. In order to do so, the Andalusian state and other regional entities have sought to cultivate and promote a distinct historical identity through an emphasis on its "Moorish legacy" and its multicultural and multireligious past – a project that testifies to the economic importance of local heritage industry (Aidi 2006; Rogozen-Soltar 2007). I will return to the Andalusian context a little later on.

My concern in this chapter, however, is not about the distortions introduced into historical accounts by political pressures, such as the subordination of the Spanish historiographical tradition to nationalist imperatives. Rather, I want to explore a tradition of inquiry that focuses on Spain's medieval history as means to pose questions in the present about the conceptual and moral boundaries of Europe. Since the late nineteenth century, the question of Spain's relationship to

---

1   American President Barack Obama also invoked Spain's legacy of *Convivencia* in his speech at Cairo University in 2009. For an analysis of this speech, see Hirschkind 2009.

2   Hishaam Aidi (2006) provides an excellent overview of contemporary ideological struggles in Spain to define the meaning of the country's Moorish past.

centuries of Islamic presence in Iberia has repeatedly come to the fore of public discourse in moments of national crisis, including the devastating defeat of 1898 and the Civil War of the 1930s, as if such critical moments produced a fracture in the nationalist narrative of Spain's Catholic career through which other histories momentarily exacted a claim. In other words, for a variety of thinkers, the problems posed by such national crises demanded a reflection on the nation's Muslim and Jewish past, as if the path forward and beyond the current predicament could only be found via an acknowledgment of that legacy. For a number of these thinkers, as I explore below, this act of acknowledgment was not to be simply a belated recognition of a distant debt, but the animation of a political sensibility they saw as grounded in layers of historical experience, woven into the social, aesthetic and moral fabric of Spanish life. This sensibility was present yet trapped within the ideological erasure of the nation's non-Catholic self, an erasure most dramatically affected by the institution of the Inquisition, but also in an all-pervasive fiction of Spain as an eternal Catholic crusade (for which Aznar may stand as an example). To disinter these underground resources of historical inheritance, to right Spain's distorted relation to its existential career, would open up possibilities of action and reflection necessary for overcoming the crises of the moment. What was at stake, in other words, in the tradition of Spanish historiography I explore here was not Islam and Judaism's contribution to medieval Europe, but rather how the ongoing reverberations of these Spanish traditions might act as a dynamic force within the political present.

The question I am raising here, of course, concerns not simply Spain but Europe on a whole. As Edward Said (1994) has famously argued, the idea of Europe as a civilizational unity was constructed in way that was dependent on a principle of differentiation opposing a Muslim Orient to a Christian Europe. Today, the project of securing this boundary has received new impetus due to increasing anxieties around European identity occasioned by the growing presence of Muslim immigrants within the continent. The demand to include a reference to Europe's Christian character within the 2003 Draft Treaty establishing a Constitution for Europe, a position strongly championed by Aznar, is one symptom of this project, though it is also evident in claims that Europe's secular traditions are an extension of its own forms of Christianity. Thus, for Marcel Gauchet (1999), it is Christianity alone among religious traditions that has the theological resources to achieve its own self-overcoming and thus set in motion the processes that lead to secular modernity and the autonomous subject of modern democratic political life. Accounts of this sort introduce religion into the conceptual vocabulary of modern political life in a way that simultaneously naturalizes one particular religious tradition (Christianity) and secures the civilizational boundaries of modern Europe. Most importantly, for my analysis here, such accounts identify the conceptual edifice of European modernity in a way that forecloses a consideration of Europe's long-standing entwinement with the Middle East.

I want to begin this discussion by examining how Spain's Moorish past has been taken up as a problem and affirmed as an inheritance by a few different thinkers responding to conditions of social and political crisis. Within the dominant currents of Spanish historiography, the final defeat of Spain's Muslim rulers in the fifteenth century and the subsequent expulsion of the Muslim and Jewish populations from its territories stand as the founding events of the Spanish nation. Yet, despite a vigorous and sustained attempt within Spanish historiography to erase Islam and Judaism from Spain (coupled with systematic attempts to purify the language of Arabic influences, the land of Arabic architectural forms and so on), a counter-history of the lasting imprint left on Spanish life by 800 years of Muslim presence has repeatedly emerged onto the stage of national public dialogue. Until the late nineteenth century, this counter-history of Muslim influence was most developed in aesthetic arenas, particularly in the fields of literature, language and music. It is with the approach of the twentieth century, however, that we see the emergence of a historiographical literature, tied to liberal political currents, aimed at affirming and documenting the heterogeneity of Spain's historical origins and the contribution of Islam to Spanish national culture and identity. In addressing this literature, I aim to highlight the historical sensibilities, attitudes and practices that ambivalently link the Spanish nation to its Muslim past and that have found expression in a range of contemporary social and political movements.

In the second part of this chapter, I turn to some of these contemporary movements that incorporate a lived relation to the Islamic past as a condition of ethical agency. In doing so, I want to question the tendency to dismiss these movements as founded upon a fictional or distorted image of the past. Rather, I focus on how the forms of historical memory discussed in relation to Spanish historiographical literature continue to inform social and political practices of both Muslims and non-Muslims in southern Spain, conditioning and enabling a variety of contemporary political projects in the region. By exploring some of the fissures within contemporary narratives of Europe's Judeo-Christian identity, I hope to contribute to current scholarly conversations on religious pluralism within Western societies, and particularly to debates on the place of Muslim minorities within Europe.

II

The most provocative and influential interpretation of the Moorish contribution to the formation of Spain written during the twentieth century is that of Americo Castro.[3] Writing from exile in the US in the early years of the Franco regime, Castro came to formulate an understanding of Spanish history which saw "the enthronement of mental ineptitude and paralysis," exemplified by the Franco dictatorship, as a direct consequence of the Inquisition, the cult of pure blood, and

---

3   While Castro wrote many works on Spanish literary traditions, the most important statement of his broader vision of the Moorish and Jewish contributions to Spain is found in his *Espana en su Historia*, first published in 1948.

the historiographic operation by which a Spanish essence was secured through
a compulsive denial of the constitutive role of Jewish and Muslim traditions in
shaping Spanish life. Castro rejected a long tradition of Spanish historiography
that posited the origins of the nation in the Visigothic state, and viewed the 800
years of Muslim presence as a national parenthesis, finally to be overcome by the
Reconquista and the return to religious and territorial unity, and to its essentially
Western identity. Rather, he argued, the uniqueness of Spanish identity was the
product of a creative symbiosis among Muslims, Jews and Christians set in motion
by the occupation of Spain by the Moors in 711. As he summarizes: "that which
made possible such great works as the Celestina and the Quijote, and hence the
European novel and drama, was a certain vision of man in which were woven – as
in an ideal and precious tapestry – the Islamic, Christian, and Judaic conceptions
of man" (Castro 1961: 13, my translation). Castro was not an historian by training,
but rather a literary scholar, and his romantic and existentialist vision of history
took language and literary works as its primary material. Through a brilliant and
original reading of medieval and early modern Spanish literary forms, he sought to
elucidate how this conjunction of the three "castes" (*castas*) had produced a unique
form of life, or what, in his existentialist vocabulary, he termed a *morada vital*,
a dwelling place of life; namely, a weave of moral, aesthetic and religious values
that conjoined to form a distinctly Spanish way of reflexively inhabiting a specific
context of possibilities and obstacles. His inquiries gave particular attention not
only to grammatical and semantic hybrids, but also to the way in which Spanish
literary expression had incorporated a vision of human life – of love, joy, pain and
death – directly from Muslim and Jewish traditions.

Influenced by German Romanticism, Castro understood the task of the
historian to revivify the dynamic relation between past and present, and thereby
release the creative potential of historical events from their temporal prison.[4] In
this, he saw himself as the inheritor of a long lineage of liberal and Romantic
thinkers – historians, Arabists and literary scholars – going back at least as far
as the mid-nineteenth century.[5] It was in this period, one marked by a growing
rift between liberal and conservative political currents, that the notion of Spain's
inferiority and decadence in relation to the rest of Europe acquired considerable
force both outside the country and within it. In this context of dissatisfaction
and frustration, many of the leading intellectuals grew disillusioned with the
continuous attempts to Europeanize, and began to promote, in response, an anti-
historicism emphasizing Spain's unique spiritual foundations as embodied in its
ancient traditions. One product of this romantic reassessment of the distinctness
of Spain's historical vocation was a body of scholarship demonstrating the

---

4   For some useful essays on the intellectual currents that influenced Castro's thought,
see Lain-Entralgo 1971.

5   The Spanish Orientalist tradition has been explored with great insight and depth
by James Monroe (1970). The Spanish scholar Bernabe Lopez-Garcia (1990) has also
provided a useful assessment of the tradition.

multiplicity of ways in which Arabic and Jewish cultural forms had left their imprint on European knowledges and institutions (Monroe 1970: 151–2). For at least some of the scholars of this generation, notably the Arabists Julian Ribera y Tarrago and Miguel Asin Palacios, this exhumation of a buried and fragmented Moorish past was seen as necessary to the revitalization of Spanish cultural and educational institutions, much as Americo Castro would argue half a century later.

The encounter of cultural and historical horizons articulated in a variety of forms by nineteenth-century scholars was conditioned by the orientalization of Southern Europe that began a century earlier. As European Orientalism was reaching its apogee in the mid-eighteenth century, a new logic of European self-definition emerged in which the Oriental other was internalized, translated and relocated into Europe's own south.[6] Europe's antithesis was now incorporated within its own heterogeneous topography. In Hegel's formulation, Europe is the site where all of the civilizational principles unite within a single unfolding, "the continent where the infinite process of civilization can be traced" (cited in Dainotto 2000: 380). As literary scholar Roberto Dainotto observes:

> The "infinite process of civilization" – the teleological movement from what was to what is now – institutes then a geographical past of Europe, an "origin" that is no longer elsewhere – in the wilderness of Africa or in the flatlands of Asia – but right in the middle of the "liquid" and "centerless" *mare nostrum*. Europe, in order to become a totality, invents its own south, the place, namely, where the "other" civilizations are translated into, and internalized as, a past moment in the giddy progress of Europe. (Dainotto 2000: 380–81)

Not surprisingly, it is precisely at this historical juncture that the question of Moorish roots emerges as a problem within Spanish historiography.

Forced to inhabit the role of the nobly savage past within the total system that consolidates Europe's identity, Spaniards react in two directions. One, evident in most historical writing up to the present day, is to insist on its essential Europeanness, often through the erasure or denigration – almost as a ritual act, the textual embodiment of the Christians and Moors ritual – of its own African and Middle Eastern genealogy. A second direction, however, personified in Castro and his nineteenth-century predecessors, has been to exploit the gaps opened up within Spain's historical experience by its very peripheralization so as to articulate a unique role for Spain within the story of modern Europe, one constituted, in part, by the imprint of al-Andalus explored across a variety of expressive media, language, literature, architecture, art and so on. It is worth remembering here that German Romanticism, a movement that powerfully shaped the sensibilities of Spanish historians from the nineteenth century onward, was not concerned with

---

6   Roberto Dainotto has written insightfully about the impact of this orientalization of Spain on Spanish intellectual life (2000, 2006, 2007).

recovering past practices or with inventing an imaginary tradition where none existed, as critics of Castro and his contemporary followers often assert. In other words, the sense of belonging articulated by the Romantics was not understood as something simply given; it was both real and imaginary, built upon a dynamic and creative engagement with the past. The historian Charles Larmore brilliantly captures this aspect of Romanticism in the following quote: "the Romantic imagination in general aims to be creative and responsive at once, attuned to experience as it also enriches it. So it may well be true that the Romantic sense of belonging is inescapably an act of the imagination, transfiguring as it does its favored traditions in a traditionalist spirit that they themselves did not have before. But this does not mean that such forms of life do not really exist. And where they do exist and move our being, our imaginative identification of them can count as an expression of reason" (Larmore 1996: 63). It is this imaginative act, both creative and responsive, by which forms of sedimented historical experience relegated to the margins of Spanish public life are animated and deployed within contexts of political action that characterizes the historiographical tradition to which Castro contributed.

The style of inquiry pioneered by Spanish Arabists continues to shape contemporary investigations into the country's Moorish past. I provide one relevant example. Barbara Fuchs, in a recent article, explores the highly ambivalent relationship that sixteenth-century Spaniards had with the Moorish culture they so vehemently attempted to negate. On ceremonial occasions, she notes, it was common that participants would adorn themselves in Moorish attire. This still takes place today, notably in the mock-battles between Christians and Moors enacted in many parts of the country. As opposed to contemporary festivals that celebrate the defeat of a mortal enemy, in many sixteenth-century festival occasions, all celebrants wore Moorish garb. Such usages of Moorish style, she suggests, could be and have been interpreted as "ethnic cross-dressing" – a practice of staging otherness as a means to fabricate, by counter-position, a Spanish national identity. However, while this is clearly one feature of the practice, the identification with Moorishness is far more contradictory than this suggests. This is because in many instances, Fuchs observes, Moorish style was not fetishized or marked as "other" in any way, but was simply made to represent Spanishness. In other words, it was through such a self-orientalizing gesture that, paradoxically, Spain constructed certain elements of its own identity in the sixteenth century. As Fuchs concludes, "whether embraced or stigmatized, Moorishness becomes an essential component in the construction of national identity. The process is not one of simple othering but a more complex negotiation between past and present, intra- and extra-European pressures, and fictive identities crafted both at home and abroad" (Fuchs 2007: 97). This double gesture by which Moorishness is both denigrated and celebrated, both expunged and embodied, points to a far more complicated relationship than that which we see today in the simultaneous enthusiasm for the Noble Moor coupled with an often racist discourse on the Arab immigrant.

III

I have attempted so far to sketch out the rudiments of a Spanish tradition geared towards creatively interrogating the past as a practice of ethical and political self-fashioning, a task oriented towards a present of determinant demands and possibilities. I now want to shift focus to look at some of the contemporary practices and movements that this tradition animates. To do so, I will focus on some facets of the contemporary regionalist movement in Andalusia.

Although the Andalucista movement has its origins back in the early years of the twentieth century, it is not until the late 1970s, with the end of the Franco era, that the movement acquired particular momentum.[7] Many of the men and women who gravitated towards *Andalucismo* in these years were intellectuals and political activists who, disillusioned with the social and political transformations that accompanied post-Franco Spain's integration into the global economy, came to embrace a regionalist model of politics centering on the renewal of local histories and traditions. This movement has since generated a vast proliferation of associations and advocacy groups emphasizing the contemporary importance of Andalusia's Moorish and Jewish heritage and organized around a wide variety of social and political causes.

A number of the activists involved in the formation of this movement eventually converted to Islam, and today Andalusia has the most rapidly growing community of converts in all of Europe.[8] Many of these converts have played an active role in tying the movement for regional autonomy to a cultural politics aimed at establishing connections to the Muslim world. They have also frequently lobbied for legal protections on behalf of Muslim migrants. This group represents a dynamic and well-organized force within the political scene, especially in Granada, where they have been instrumental in securing official representation for Muslim celebrations, in extending greater protections to Muslim historical sites and in organizing the construction of a large mosque, despite a highly organized movement to oppose the project.

As many scholars have noted, the project of producing a unified Europe has, paradoxically, led to a reassertion of regional identities and the proliferation of numerous subnational movements pressing claims for greater autonomy (Payne 1991; Stolcke 1995). Seen in this light, Spain's convert movement has been interpreted as one face of the contemporary politics of identity, attractive to frustrated elites dissatisfied with more New Age options and allured by Islam's current counter-hegemonic aura. While I do not want to entirely discard this view,

---

7   On the history of the Andalucista movement, see Cortes and Luis 1994; Sanchez-Mantero 2001; Moreno 2008.

8   A vast body of scholarly writings on conversion to Islam in Spain has appeared during the last decade. See in particular Bahrami 1998; Stallaert 1999; Olmo 2000. Javier Rosón-Lorente's (2000) ethnographic study of relations between Muslim converts and Spanish Christians is particularly useful on this topic.

I do want to briefly point to some aspects of the conversion phenomenon that challenge the adequacy of such a framing.

One association formed by the early wave of converts to Islam founded a University of Islamic Studies in Cordoba. The University's own founding narrative echoes a set of tropes common within convert circles:

> The revival of Islam in Andalus, Spain, has been a cherished ideal of the Muslims since the fall of Grenada in 1492. The Holocaust coming in the wake of the down-fall of the Muslims was unprecedented in the annals of human history. The Inquisition carried out by the Spanish church in the name of religion undoubtedly tarnished the image of Christianity in the eyes of the impartial observers and students of history … In spite of this bleak period hundreds of thousands of Muslims retained their religious commitment and strived hard to impart some sentiments of Islamicity to their forth-coming generation … There has always been a feeling in the educated class of the Andalusians that their real identity was different from the Northern Spaniards who denied this right to their Southern compatriots. This long feeling found expression in the conversion process started soon after the ending of General Franco's dictatorship. Several thousands of people embraced Islam within a short span of time. (Ibn Rushd, University website)

Many converts experience their turn to Islam as the gradual liberation of that barely perceptible trace left dormant across the generations.

Karim Viudes, now in his late seventies, is an historian and architect affiliated with the recently built Mezquita de Granada. His conversion story is not unlike that of many others Spanish converts: "I was living in Paris in 1968, in exile from the dictatorship of Franco. It was there that I read Ignacio Olague's book on the Islamic Roots of Spain, which prompted me to take an interest both in Spanish history as well as in Islam. A few years later, an occasion came for me to travel to New York where I had the possibility of studying with a Sufi Shaykh from Iraq. It was that way that after a few years I became convinced of the truths I encountered in the religion, and I decided to convert."

Olague's book is a commonplace in many Spanish conversion stories, despite the fact that its central claim – that there was no occupation of Southern Iberia by Muslims from North Africa and the Middle East in the eighth century, but rather a mass conversion by the local community – has been shown to rest on numerous historical errors.[9] However, it is not the accuracy of Olague's text that is crucial, but the processes of historical exploration and self-transformation that it serves

---

9   Despite his enthusiastic reception by Andalusian activists and converts, Olague was in no way a moorophile, nor did he have any interest in the Arabic language or the Middle East. Rather, as Maribel Fierro (2010) has recently examined, he was first and foremost a Spanish nationalist, and one, moreover, with strong links to certain Spanish fascist intellectuals.

to set in motion. Viudes links his personal trajectory with his place of birth, the city of Murcia, established in the ninth century by Abd al-Rahman II, the Emir of al-Andalus, and then called *Medinat Mursiya*: "I am a witness to history without wishing to be so, by my family origin, which extends as far back as the 13th century, a descendent of a family present at the colonization of al-Andalus after the fall of Granada, and by my personal experience of having observed the time we live in for three quarters of a century, with acuity and depth" (Viudes 2005). Viudes weaves himself into the past genealogically, but also through his "acute and deep" engagement with the present. In this regard, a motto frequently cited by Spanish converts states: "Somos moros viejos y musulmanes nuevos" ("We are old Moors and new Muslims").

Viudes played an important role in the establishment of the Mezquita de Granada, completed in 2003 after a 20-year struggle against local and national opposition, designing the interior. In preparing for the task, he spent many years studying Moorish architectural and decorative styles, and also traveled throughout the Middle East, visiting Islam's greatest architectural accomplishments. The mosque that resulted from his inquiry and designing skills is extraordinary, fusing stylistic elements from some of the most outstanding examples of Islamic architecture within an overarching aesthetic form derived from Andalusian traditions. Thus, the *mihrab*, or prayer niche, is a replica of the one found in the Red Mosque in Cordoba; colored marble panels repeat a pattern found in the al-Aqsa mosque in Jerusalem; some of the stained-glass windows reproduce those of the Blue Mosque in Istanbul. The mosaics lining the patio and prayer hall were made by craftsmen in Fez who had preserved traditions of design and techniques of production used in al-Andalus. For Viudes, the construction of the mosque, the first in Granada in 500 years, is not about the return of al-Andalus, as others sometimes describe it. "Al-Andalus is gone," he says, "but from its ruins we are creating something new, that is spreading throughout Europe." Viudes' mosque, a frequent site stop for Muslim dignitaries traveling to Europe, inhabits an imaginative geography that fits uncomfortably within the conceptual and material contours of Europe.

Another Spanish convert to Islam, Mansur Abdulsalem Escudero, a long-standing advocate for Muslims in Spain and the founder of a vast Internet archive of contemporary and historical writings on issues of concern to Muslims, views the rebuilding of Islamic institutions in southern Spain by converts and Muslim immigrants within an eschatological frame:

> al-Andalus will continue to be al-Andalus, for all Muslims at all times. This is given; we didn't create it. Here we have our dead, who still live on, waiting for the Day of Resurrection. Today, on the spiritual plane, saints from all Muslim regions reunite here in al-Andalus, as they have always been reuniting. The Islamic presence has always existed, without interruption, in spite of the fact that we were apparently expelled in the 17th century. We are not few,

but rather multitudes, but there are those who see this and those who don't. (Escudero 1999)

Al-Andalus for Escudero has escaped historical time, as if a place held in the mind of God (along with its dead) until the Last Day. Who are the multitudes only apparently expelled by the Christian armies? The dead themselves, ever passing through on a spiritual plane? The present-day inheritors, some of whom are now awakening to this fact and returning to Islam? The final clause – about those who see and those who do not – echoes the Koranic verses concerning the two categories of people: those who see and hear the truth of God's word and those who cannot. It is only within eschatological time that the events of Andalusian history – past and present – achieve their true dimensions and significance.

Let me finally turn to a second activist movement that also has its roots in *Andalucismo* and that includes both Muslims and non-Muslims alike. The movement I am referring to centers on a campaign to replace the Catholic-nationalist festivals celebrated (seemingly without pause) throughout southern Spain with festival forms emphasizing Andalusia's pluralist and liberal traditions – the *Convivencia* of Jews, Muslims and Christians during the Moorish period, but also the liberal martyrs of the nineteenth and twentieth centuries, from Mariana Pineda to Federico Garcia Lorca, themselves inheritors of the life-blood of this tradition (as Lorca certainly recognized). For its organizers, this campaign is a vehicle for promoting and creating an open, tolerant, multicultural society in southern Spain, and many of the group's activities focus on the policies and politics of immigration.

Paco Vigueras is one of the primary coordinators for this group, sometimes known as the "Collective of the 2nd of January Manifesto." Like Karim Viudes, Vigueras' first encounter with a different Spain was through Olague's work, though he has since read Castro and many other historians of Moorish Spain, as well as the works of Blas Infante, the intellectual and political father of the Andalucista movement back in the 1920s and 1930s. For close to 15 years, he has worked tirelessly to counter the xenophobia and intolerance he considers inherent in contemporary Andalusian cultural forms and public life, through an ongoing effort to give public recognition to the region's rich cultural legacy. In a statement criticizing the *Dia de la Toma*, the annual celebration of the conquest of Granada in 1492 that marked the end of the Moors in Spain, he observes:

The poet-king *al-Mutamid* was as Sevillian as Antonio Machado; the philosopher Averroes, as much a son of Cordoba as Seneca; and King Boabdil (the last Moorish ruler, who surrendered to the Spanish), no less Granadan than our Federico Garcia Lorca ... In these times, when xenophobia has returned to the old continent, it is useful to remember that Andalucia was much more than beaches, sun, bulls, and subsidies; that while Europe wrapped itself in shadows, and agitated itself with the phantom of the Inquisition, al-Andalus knew how to share, to exchange, to create.

IV

For many residents of Granada, the "2nd of January Manifesto" and other such efforts are based on a fictitious past. "They don't want to acknowledge the real history of Spain," as one woman told me, though what counts as "real" in such comments, that which Juan Goytisolo has called a "clean-shaven Hispanic civilization" – a Spain free of Islamic and Jewish influence – clearly owes its force to a vast endeavor of historical fiction. It has become common today for Spaniards to hold together the two rather contradictory ideas that the Moors, in some fashion, left a permanent imprint on Iberian soil *and* that the real history of Spain is to be found in an ideal that crystallized with Ferdinand and Isabella. The same gesture by which Islamic and Jewish roots are posited is also that which prophylactically consigns them to an irrelevant past.

While I was in Granada a few years ago, a story appeared in the newspaper *El País* indicating that recent archaeological work suggested that San Isidro, the Patron Saint of Madrid, had most likely been a Morisco, a Muslim forcibly converted to Christianity in the sixteenth century. A very popular comedic television program called *el Intermedio*, Spain's answer to Jon Stewart, reported the findings, spinning them into a series of skits set up by the host's question: what if the Moors had never been defeated? Lots of headscarves, turbans, beards and orientalist paraphernalia were then dutifully donned and paraded about in some role reversal fantasy, a fetishization of the exotic Muslim "other" in response to an anxiety produced by San Isidro's Muslim genealogy. But that anxiety can lead in two directions.

I have attempted here to outline, in a tentative fashion, what might be seen as a tradition whose advocates and adherents seek to adjust their lives to a different geopolitical imaginary, understood by many as an ethical response to the xenophobia and racism they see around them. While often relegated to the margins of Spanish public memory, this tradition nonetheless has repeatedly found expression in literary and aesthetic domains, as well as within political life. It is worth noting here that over the course of the last 25 years, Spain has gone further than most other European states in recognizing and responding to the demands of its religious minorities, especially Muslims. A key moment in this evolution is the Cooperation Agreement of 1992 between the Spanish state and the Islamic Commission of Spain, an agreement that makes explicit reference to the historical contribution of Islamic traditions to Spanish identity. This agreement is exceptional in the European context for the variety of rights it extends to recognized Muslim communities in Spain, among them the right of Muslim children to receive Islamic religious training in public schools, the right to be exempted from work on Friday at the time of prayer and the right to halal food in public institutions such as schools and the military. Moreover, the previous government of Spain under the socialist Zapatero passed a measure that granted amnesty to as many as one million Muslim immigrants who were in the country illegally, a step strongly at odds with the policies of other EU nations. Admittedly, many of these measures have yet to be implemented and continue to be viewed by many as a dangerous accommodation to an undeserving religious minority, as well as a betrayal of Spain's Catholic identity. However, what is interesting in these debates is the way they have reintroduced into public discourse the question of Spain's Islamic heritage in relation to contemporary deliberations over issues of Muslim immigration. The legacy of Castro and his predecessors remains a vital point of reflection for Spaniards, and Europeans more generally, concerned with the place that Muslims will occupy within European social, political and religious spaces.

References

Aidi, H.D. 2006. "The Interference of al-Andalus: Spain, Islam, and the West," *Social Text* 87, 24(2), 67–88.

Bahrami, B. 1998. "A Door to Paradise: Converts, the New Age, Islam, and the Past in Granada," *City and Society*, 10(1), 121–32.

BBC News Online. 2004. "Spain Proposes Cultural Alliance." September 22, http://news.bbc.co.uk/2/hi/europe/3679336.stm.

Borneman, J. and Fowler, N. 1997. "Europeanization," *Annual Review of Anthropology*, 26, 487–514.

Castro, A. 1948. *Espana en su Historia: Christianos, Moros, y Judios*. Buenos Aires: Losada.

Castro, A. 1961. *De la Edad Conflictiva*. Madrid: Editorial Taurus.

Cortes, P. and Luis, A. 1994. "El Ultimo NAcionalismo: Andalucia y su Historia," *Manuscits: Revista de Historia Moderna*, 12, 213–43.

Dainotto, R. 2000. "A South with a View: Europe and its Others," *Nepantla: Views form the South*, 1(2), 375–90.

Dainotto, R. 2006. "The Discreet Charm of the Arab Thesis: Juan Andrés, Historicism, and the De-Centering of Montesquieu's Europe," *European History Quarterly*, 36(1), 7–29.

Dainotto, R. 2007. *Europe (In Theory)*. Raleigh, NC: Duke University Press.

Escudero, M. 1999. "A Fondo con Mansur Abdussalam Escudero," *WebIslam*, September 16, http://www.webislam.com/noticias/41375a_fondo_con_mansur_abdussalam_escudero.html.

Fierro, M. 2009. "Al-Andalus en el Pensamiento Fascista Espanol: La Revolucion Islamic en Occidente de Ignacio Olague," in M. Marin (ed.), *Al-Andalus/Espana. Historiogrfia en Contraste: Siglos XVII–XXI*. Madrid: Casa de Velasquez.

Fuchs, B. 2007. "The Spanish Race," in M. Greer et al. (eds), *Rereading the Black Legend: The Discourses of Racism in the Renaissance Empires*. Chicago, IL: University of Chicago Press, 88–98.

Gauchet, M. 1999. *The Disenchantment of the World: A Political History of Religion*. Princeton, NJ: Princeton University Press.

Gulfnews. 2006. "Aznar Defends Pope's Remarks," September 25, http://gulfnews.com/news/world/other-world/aznar-defends-pope-s-remarks-1.256520.

Hirschkind, C. 2009. "Obama on Palestine: What New Beginning?" *The Immanent Frame*, http://blogs.ssrc.org/tif/2009/06/09/obama-on-palestine-what-new-beginning.

Lain-Entralgo, P. (ed.) 1971. *Estudios sobre la obra de Américo Castro*. London: I.B. Taurus.

Larmore, C. 1996. *The Romantic Legacy*. New York: Columbia University Press.

Lopez-Garcia, B. 1990. "Arabismo y Orientalismo en Espana: Radiografia y Diagnostia de un Gremio Escaso y Apartadizo," *Awraq, anejo al volumen*, XI, 35–69.

Monroe, J. 1970. *Islam and the Arabs in Spanish Scholarship (Sixteenth Century to the Present)*. Leiden: E.J. Brill.

Moreno, I. 2008. *La Identidad Cultural de Andalucia*. Seville: Junta de Andalucia.

Olmo, M. del. 2000. "Los conversos espanoles al Islam: de mayoria a minoria por la llamada de Dios," *Anales del Museo Nacional de Antropologia*, 7, 15–40.

Payne, S-G. 1991. "Nationalism, Regionalism, and Micronationalism in Spain," *Journal of Contemporary History*, 26(3/4): 479–91.

Rogozen-Soltar, M. 2007 "Al-Andalus in Andalusia: Negotiating Moorish History and Regional Identity in Southern Spain," *Anthropological Quarterly*, 80(3), 863–86.

Rosón-Lorente, F-J. 2000. *"El retorno de Tariq" Las comunidades musulmanas en la ciudad de Granada*. Granada: Laboratorio de Estudios Interculturales.

Said, E. 1994. *Orientalism*. New York: Vintage Books.

Sánchez-Mantero, R. 2001. *Historia breve de Andalucia*. Madrid: Sílex.

Stalleart, C. 1999. "El movimiento Neomusulman y el Intento de (Re)construccion de una identidad Andalusa/Andalusi," in S. Rodriguez Becerra (ed.), *Religion y Cultura*. Seville: Junta de Andalucia/Fundacion Machado, 189–97.

Stolcke, V. 1995. "Talking Culture: New Boundaries, New Rhetorics of Exclusion in Europe," *Current Anthropology*, 36, 1–24.

Viudes, K. 2005. "La alianza de civilizaciones, el punto de vista de los musulmanes," Mezquita de Granada website, http://www.mezquitadegranada.com/index.php?id=lacomunidadmusulmanadegran02.

Chapter 19

Fugitive or Cosmopolitan: The Bosniaks' Desire for Europe and Trouble with the Ottoman Past[1]

Halide Velioğlu

I

The non-sovereignty of Bosnian Muslims (Bosniaks), a historically conditioned survival skill, has been severely challenged after the violent break-up of Yugoslavia. Since the 1992–95 war, the Bosniaks have been facing the urgent need to carve out a political space for Muslim-only subjectivity with cosmopolitan and/or nationalist accents. Nevertheless, the contemporary question of the Bosniaks' political and cultural survival cannot be understood without taking into consideration their connections with the broader Muslim community at home and across the border, and the way in which they reconfigure their Muslim identity within Europe. In this framework, the Ottoman past emerges as one of the major issues that the Bosniaks need to address in the process of reconfiguring their identity and a plausible political space for it at home, in Europe and in the wider Islamic community.

In her seminal work *Imagining the Balkans* (1997), Maria Todorova describes one of the common features of nineteenth-century nationalist revivalisms in the Balkan states as a total negation of the Ottoman past. According to her, this negating act, which is more radical than simply making a break with the past, envisioned the Ottoman Empire as a "religiously, socially, and institutionally alien imposition on autochthonous Christian medieval societies" and was deeply ingrained in the belief that Christianity and Islam are incompatible in Europe. Expanding on Todorova's work, Hajdarpašić (2008) elaborates on the intellectual framework in which the Ottoman past is addressed in post-war Bosnia. According to his account, this framework mimics the nineteenth-century nationalist gesture of their Slavic and Greek neighbors so as to relegate the "legacy" to the absolute past, while also cherishing it as a "golden age" during which the "essential accomplishments of the Bosnian Muslim people" took place. Hajdarpašić underlines the rigid nature

1   I am thankful to Nilüfer Göle for her constructive remarks at the EuroPublicIslam Colloquium at which I presented the first version of this chapter in Paris in May 2012. This chapter would not have been possible without Zehra Cunillera's invaluable intellectual and editorial support.

of this plot that provides Bosnian Muslim intellectuals with a "fixed position from which to speak" at the expense of reifying identity.

The Ottoman past, however, is a deeply ingrained and broad phenomenon, the lingering effects of which compel the existing regimes of representations. Moreover, increasing rapprochement between the Turks and the Bosniaks during and after the recent war, accompanied by a growing desire for and interest in Turkish things among the Bosniaks, necessitate the re-evaluation of the analytical frames in which this past can be understood with recourse to intellectual frames neglecting the anthropology of present times. In this chapter, I critically examine Hajdarpašić's cogent account of the intellectual frameworks of the "Ottoman legacy" in post-war Bosnia from the perspective of two alternative and complementary lines of inquiry. The first is the particular way in which the religious leader of the Bosniaks, the Reis-ul-ulema Mustafa Cerić, whose role as a public figure goes far beyond his position as the head of the Islamic community (*Islamska Zajednica*) in Bosnia, addresses the Ottoman past. On the other hand, mundane and intimate registers of the Ottoman past from the perspective of the recent rapprochement between the Turks and the Bosniaks constitute a second complementary line of inquiry. Broadly informed by two years of ethnographic work on the aesthetic, habitual and sentimental registers of the daily lives of Bosniaks in post-war Sarajevo,[2] I aim to give a sense of the psychic topographies on which the entangled sensibilities of Bosniak cosmopolitanism, nationalism and Islamism are potentiated. I argue that the age-old, deeply ingrained survival skills of the Bosniaks as a non-sovereign community within larger political entities conditions their cosmopolitan, exilic and assimilationist predispositions, and constitutes the mercurial ground on which newly rising nationalist and Islamic sensibilities are articulated.

The national question among Bosniaks, namely, their difficulties in carving out a national identification from religious and cultural identifications, has been scrutinized in relation to the consequences of the incommensurabilities of the Ottoman Millet system with the nineteenth-century Western taxonomy of a nation state (Donia 1981; Pinson 1996; Gagnon 2004), the gravity of their territorial attachments and the primacy of the peculiarities of Bosnianness that cut across ethnic and religious identifications (Todorova 1997), their strong attachment to the ethos of Yugoslavism (Banac 1996; Djokić 2003) and, finally, their fluid identities (Buturović 2002) as the culmination of all these historically conditioned structural phenomena. Moreover, Pinson (1996) points to the lack of a golden age or a prototypical state in the history of the Bosniaks to provide them with an object of collective identification, as is the case with other Slavs in the country. In this sense, Hajdarpašić's elaboration on Bosniak intellectual frameworks suggesting that the Ottoman past is a congealed plot that is radically severed from the present and cherished as the "cultural heyday" of Bosnia informs us about the tenets of the formation of new Bosniak subjectivity following the war.

---

2   This ethnographic research was part of my doctoral work in anthropology, as a result of which I wrote a dissertation (Velioğlu 2011).

Today, ethnic homogenization of the territory and the territorialization of ethnic-cum-religious identities envisioned by the war and confirmed by the Dayton Peace Accords (1995) have compelled their own regime of legibility, knowledge and production of truth as well as structures of feeling in Bosnia. Sixteen years after the war's end in 1995, and despite the partial achievements of internationally governed efforts to rebuild the state, return refugees and cultivate peace, mutual trust among communities, the existence of a common Bosnian public and optimism about the future of Bosnia are still questionable issues.

The majority of Serbs and a strong minority of Croats still prefer the idea of secession from Bosnia. While Bosnian Croats and Serbs enjoy the security of protectorate status from the states of Serbia and Croatia, Bosniaks, unlike other constituencies, have a higher stake in collaborating with the Western international community's agenda of maintaining the ethnic-cum-religiously divided tripartite political landscape of the country as designed and implemented by the Dayton Peace Accords. A deeply ingrained belief in the weak plausibility of a national sovereignty of their own within Europe (due to its perceived reluctance to permit a Muslim state within its own territory) is commonly articulated in reference to Europe's anxiety towards Islam and Muslim populations within its confines. Mundane talks are inundated with complaints about Europe's and the international community's unwillingness to grant the Bosniaks a state of their own, anger against "corrupted" politics and politicians and self-deprecating humor about the Bosniaks' lethargy, laid-back attitude and non-sovereign survival skills. Their prickly relationship with a national imagination and its burdensome protocols is one of the biggest "public secrets" (Taussig 1999: 2) among Bosniaks today. Expressing a desire to have a state of their own constitutes one of the mundane complaints among Bosniaks; however, this state is seen as something that needs to be "granted" to them.

The stakes for the Bosniaks have always been in representing a small segment of a larger political entity and limiting their representation through their recognition as a distinct social group marked by their religious identity. Their political history can be read as an account of shifting alliances with other Slavs in the region and compliance with the large political entities (the Ottoman and Austro-Hungarian Empires and the various forms of Yugoslavia) ruling the country. The Bosniaks were the primary figures in the Austro-Hungarian policy of promoting *Bošnjaštvo* (Bosnianhood)[3] at the end of the nineteenth century and

---

3   During the period of Austro-Hungarian rule (1878–1918), the Habsburg governor Benjamin Kállay introduced the idea of *Bošnjaštvo* (Bosnianhood) as an attempt to secularize Bosnia and divide Bosnians into three religious groups with equal rights: Serbs, Croats and Muslims. Substitution of religion for national identity among Bosnian Muslims urged some secular Bosnian Muslims to develop pro-Serb or pro-Croat affiliations. Friedman (1996) explains Muslims' overall compliance with the new Austro-Hungarian regime as a matter of maintaining their socioeconomic privileges and way of life, which accompanied the Austro-Hungarians' policy of balancing Serbs' and Croats' political will over Bosnia and curbing their nationalistic and irredentist agendas. According to Gagnon (2004: 15),

Yugoslav syncretic nationalism until recently. Moreover, the residual sensibilities of the supranational ethos of Yugoslavism and the fluid and regional multiethnic and multi-religious identity of Bosnianness are still vibrant signs of belonging among Bosniaks today. Therefore, any work that attends to the political life of Bosniaks at the level of representation without taking into account the political significance of their habitual and learned stakes in being politically ineligible while watchfully guarding the intactness of their multilayered reality is extremely limited and misguiding.

Islamization in Bosnia has been regarded as the most salient aspect of the political agenda since the recent war (Velikonja 2003; Bougarel 2008; Helms 2008). The accumulation of Islamic sensibilities and social and cultural capital have burgeoned with the impact of newly generated Islamic networks across Near and Middle Eastern countries and Europe. Definitions, revisions and the plausibility and urgency of protecting Bosnian Islam against outside (especially Arabic) influences constitute one of the current major issues in public debates in Bosnia. Nevertheless, the issue of the Bosniaks' involvement with global Islamic networks cannot be understood without taking into account serious questions such as "What if the day of judgment comes again?" and "who is ready to die in Bosnia if not for Bosnia?" In this sense, the cumbersome question of whether or not to grant citizenship to former Wahhabi warriors, for instance, is not only about protecting the local form of Islam against outside influence, as the dominant frame of discussion suggests, but also and even primarily concerns the unspeakable existential anxiety that the Bosniaks have felt due to the lack of a protectorate state.

It is important to keep in mind that a sense of confusion, disorientation and lethargy as well as a lack of interest and a hatred of politics are not only collectively held positions that are commonly regarded as being of secondary importance to politics, but are major forces that tightly delineate the mundane life of any political agenda and blur the referentiality of any political representation. Accordingly, the juxtapositions and displacements that some of the grand mufti Cerić's public addresses portray, and which I will discuss in more detail, are not merely his own idiosyncratic expressions or those of the institution he heads, nor are they the tangible evidence that he is a "homo duplex," as some have asserted in order to underline the ambivalence of his statements. Rather, this "duplicity" is the most tangible manifestation of the mercurial grounds of Bosniak existence that would imbue any kind of neat political expression or agenda today.

---

the Habsburg legacy is the major historical force that introduced "political homogeneity" in spatial terms. Territorializing politics in terms of linguistically and ethnically homogenous units, he claims, was an imposition on the existing complexity of the Ottoman polity in which identities were not spatialized.

II

The role played by Cerić at the local and international levels far exceeds the religious affairs of Bosnian Muslims.[4] The political significance of the grand mufti of Bosnia has increased because of the post-war political vacuum in state sovereignty, the cumbersome position of the Bosniaks in the national order (their ethnic and religious identity being conflated), their growing connections with the Islamic community abroad (due to refugee experiences during the war and the influence of charities from Muslim countries since the war) and the recent increase in the saliency of the Muslim question in Europe. At the local level, Ceric has become one of the most prominent figures articulating the nationalist position that Bosnia needs to be a nation state governed by the Muslim majority, whereas his "Declaration of European Muslims" has become one of the most elaborate articulations not only of the present controversies concerning the Muslim question in Europe, but also of the contingent contours of the political space that the increasing deterritorialization of Islam creates in the West. Moreover, Cerić's training and vocational practice that stretches across continents (encompassing Egypt, Malaysia and the US) has added much to his prowess and charisma; he is entitled to be called a "world citizen" (*svjetski covjek*) or a cosmopolitan in all possible senses of the word among Bosnian Muslims today.[5] His skill in making public addresses is widely recognized even among secular Muslims and his detractors.

However, Cerić has been criticized for playing a double game concerning the central issues facing the country. His attitude towards the Wahhabi presence, for instance, is often a matter of debate: is he critical of their extended stay and their receiving Bosnian citizenship (mostly through marriage with local women) following the war and their conspicuous intervention in local practices of Islam or is he supporting them and/or turning a blind eye? Likewise, concerning his relationship with Arabic countries: is he more than welcoming in inviting them to support Bosnian Muslims, invest in the construction of mosques and thereby forming alternative nodes for Islamic sensibilities, practices and interpretations within the country, or is he just connecting Bosnian Muslims with the *umma*,

---

4   In his book *Mi, Građani Etnopolisa* [*We, the Citizens of Ethnopolis*], Asim Mujkić (2007: 12) extensively quotes the criticism of *Rešid Hafizović*, the professor at the Sarajevo Faculty of Islamic Studies, of politicians sounding like religious figures, whereas religious figures take the floor on political issues in Bosnia (Hafizović 2005: 149–50).

5   *Biti svjetsi covjek* (being a citizen of the world) has become a popular phrase, especially after the recent war. The phrase covers all the dire conditions and maltreatment that Bosnians may have experienced as refugees. Those who returned to Bosnia brought with them residual sensibilities, habits, languages, professional skills and diplomas (degrees from Malaysia, Austria, Germany, the Netherlands and Turkey) from the countries in which they took refuge and, no less importantly, an urgent and vital sense that cultural capital might help them survive anywhere in the world. *Svjetski covjek* claims to belong nowhere and everywhere.

as might be expected by someone in his position? Is he complying with the protocols of the tripartite structure of Bosnia[6] as it is or is he propagating the idea of a Bosnian state under the patronage of the Muslim majority, or a Muslim community in Europe with a legal status of its own? Is he a moderate Muslim or an Islamist? He condemns anti-Semitism, but what can we make of his siding with the Muslim Brotherhood, which is known for its anti-Semitism? The list can be extended to his dubious declarations about Sharia and Muslim education in the country. But is it possible to determine which of his statements reflects his real intentions, a hidden agenda or a deeper truth? What if the political implications of his "duplicity" in making ambiguous or contradictory statements far exceed their political content? In other words, what if this "duplicity" itself is an articulation of mundane sentiments that have political valence with a life and generativity of its own? Paying closer attention to Cerić's statements concerning the Muslim presence in Europe and tracking its mundane trajectory will help to illuminate these issues.

III

In the "Declaration of European Muslims," issued by the Zagreb Mosque on 24 February 2006, Cerić covers the principal issues of Muslim presence in Europe, ranging from legal and institutional framework, education, political representation and immigration policy to protection from Islamophobia. Cerić underlines the urgency of creating a "European culture of Islam" that will play a leading role in the unification of Muslims all over the world in tandem with the requirements of the contemporary era of globalization, while warning Muslims not to cling to "ethnic or national expressions of Islam." In the following months, Cerić presented a series of talks abroad that elucidated the basic issues raised in the Declaration. The experience of the Bosniaks of a uniform version of Islam under the auspices of a single institution, *Islamska Zajednica*, (Islamic community), and its distinctive culture of tolerance perfectly in sync with European multicultural values were the primary topics he raised. Historical reference to Islam in Europe was another recurring topic he addressed in these talks, emphasizing the significance of the Andalusian past, whereas he deftly avoided explicit reference to Ottoman heritage.

At this juncture, I draw on Cerić's presentation at the MIT in Boston[7] to illustrate the peculiar ways in which the grand mufti historically situates the Muslim

---

6   The Presidency of Bosnia-Herzegovina consists of three members: one Bosniak and one Croat elected from the Bosnian-Croat Federation and one Serb elected from the Republika Srpska. Together, they serve four years. One member becomes the chairman on the basis of the majority of votes, a position which rotates every eight months.

7   The talk was sponsored by the MIT Muslim Students' Association with support from the Technology and Culture Forum, the Dean of Humanities and Social Sciences, and the Center for International Studies.

presence in Europe. In this presentation, he joins the common European lament of cherishing the distant, absolutely remote Andalusian past as an exemplary case of peaceful coexistence in Europe (see Anidjar, Chapter 17, this volume), while deftly avoiding the Ottoman past as a milestone for the Muslim presence in Bosnia and the Balkans:

> The arrival of Islam in Europe occurred through two main gates: the gate of the Iberian Peninsula in the 8th century and the gate of the Balkan Peninsula in the 14th century. Eight centuries of Islamic presence in Andalusia, Spain, produced a unique culture of religious and cultural tolerance as well as academic freedom, which has greatly helped Europe on its way to Humanism and the Renaissance. Unfortunately, the idea of Andalusian tolerance did not survive European history. By the end of the 15th century, the Jews and Muslims were forced to leave the Iberian Peninsula for good. About seventy thousand Sephardic Jews of Andalusia migrated to Sarajevo with their unique manuscript of *Haggadah*, which is today an important symbol of Jewish-Bosnian history. (Cerić 2006)

The striking feature of this brief quote from Cerić's speech is his mention of the "arrival of Islam to Europe" as a matter primarily of time and place. Limiting his references to the eighth-century Iberian and the fourteenth-century Balkan peninsulas makes the presence of Islam in Europe sound like a natural phenomenon peculiar to peninsulas. What he dexterously avoids is the cumbersome question of the Ottoman past in Europe or the "Ottoman legacy." The following quote is from the question and answer session following his talk. An audience states that many mosques have been built with money coming from Saudi Arabia and asks why this money is not channeled into building schools, roads and investing in cultural projects. Cerić's answer is as follows:

> I know what you are saying. First, let me tell [you], we have this Ottoman culture which is very much influenced by the Byzantine architecture. Those who study architecture know very well and now ... unfortunately these mosques have been destroyed. We were not able to protect them. Ferhadija Mosque in Banja Luka,[8] and *Aladža* Mosque in Foča.[9] *Those ... the grandchildren of the Ottomans are not, now, interested to protect these mosques, let's say ...* And Saudis came to us in 1993–94 and offered us to build some mosques in the areas that there were no mosques before, because the communists did not allow building mosques in some urban area. Saudis built these mosques but they are under our control. (Ceric 2006, emphasis added)

---

8   The second largest city in Bosnia-Herzegovina and today the administrative capital of the Republika Srpska.

9   A town in the south-east of Bosnia-Herzegovina within the territory of the Republika Srpska.

Cerić not only distances the Ottoman past and its contemporary Turkish inheritors but also complicates the issue by casting a suspicious eye on the provenance of the architectural styles of the mosques. Interjecting the continuity of the Ottoman Empire with Byzantium, he implies the difficulty of drawing neat boundaries between different cultural traditions that occupied the same spaces or succeeded each other. Moreover, his cursory remark on the country's socialist past is significant not only in terms of the prohibition of building mosques in urban areas, but also for reminding the audience of the multilayered texture of Bosnian identity. His deft performance thereby juxtaposes and destabilizes any attempt to fix identity on solid ground and evokes strangeness as an inalienable part of belonging. Another important point about his words is their reference to Bosniaks having survived two empires and two Yugoslavias as a non-sovereign community. He emphasizes the institutional know-how of the Bosniaks as the primary grounds for legitimacy in articulating an urgent demand for a legal framework for Muslims in Europe. In a way, his statement is a tacit articulation of the age-old non-sovereign survival skills of the Bosniaks. His words suggest a (historically approved) guarantee of abstinence from political agency in return for the guarantee of a legal framework for the existence of the Bosniaks and other Muslims within the confines of Europe.

Cerić's distance from the Ottoman past is also manifested at the level of the linguistic devices he utilizes. He makes fleeting statements that destabilize the meaning conveyed by main clauses of the speech. For instance, "Let's say" at the end of the statement concerning the demolished mosques belonging to the Ottoman cultural heritage in the country intervenes in the referential meaning conveyed by the main clause or casts doubt on the validity of a final meaning in the existing vocabulary. These interjections intervene in the referential meaning conveyed by the main clause or cast doubt on the validity of a final meaning in the existing vocabulary. Cerić's interjection suggests to the audience to be aware of the weak referentiality of the statement as well as the convergence of its making and unmaking at the same time. This is similar to the tools of parody, in the sense of maintaining both the main reference as well as its destruction. His statement denotes both the contemporary saliency of the Ottoman heritage in Bosnia as well as its consignment to the absolute past with no hint of its appropriation as a zenith of cultural achievement. It also, evasively, touches upon the relationship between Bosnians and Turks (the "grandchildren of Ottomans") that brings us to a very significant issue in Bosnia today: the growing Turkish presence and the specific ways in which the developing relationship between Bosnian Muslims and Turks articulate the infamous "Ottoman legacy."

IV

The "Ottoman legacy" has attracted significant scholarly attention because it sets the foundations for controversies that condition the political space today, not only for Bosnian Muslims, but for all of Europe. Todorova (1997) shows how one of the common features of nineteenth-century nationalist revivalisms in the Balkan states was to negate the Ottoman past altogether, a more radical gesture than simply breaking it. This negating act portrayed the Ottoman Empire as a "religiously, socially, and institutionally alien imposition on autochthonous Christian medieval societies," deeply ingrained in the belief in the "incompatibility between Christianity and Islam" (Todorova 1997: 162). Expanding on Todorova's work, Hajdarpašić (2008) elaborates the peculiarities of the "Ottoman legacy" in Bosnian history and the significance it gained as a point of comparison since the recent war. In his work, he tracks the neglected register of the Ottoman past, stating that Bosnian Muslims embraced the Ottoman past precisely when Serb and Croat nationalists demarcated and abandoned it in the nineteenth century. According to him, Bosnian Muslims did not reproduce the Serb and Croat nationalists' distancing gesture, but acknowledged Ottoman times and began to refer to the Ottoman heritage as a "glorious heyday of cultural achievement that should be retrieved and cherished as 'essential' accomplishments of 'the Bosnian Muslim people'" (2008: 725). Moreover, in his account, the post-war celebration of the "Ottoman legacy" works like a tired plot, a kind of *mal nécessaire* that provides Bosnian Muslim intellectuals with a "position from which to speak" at the expense of reifying identity, which he explains with recourse to Stuart Hall: "a kind of fixed point in thought and being, a ground of action, a still point in the returning world" (2008: 726).

From the perspective of intellectual frameworks, Hajdarpašić's historical account is a layered and cogent analysis of the Bosniaks' share of the "Ottoman legacy" in the Balkans (see Rieff 1993; Brown 1996; Bougarel 2008; Lockwood 2009). However, the mundaneness of life is full of surprising juxtapositions, instances and scenes which provide us with rich insight and detail into the existing representational frameworks. Drawing on my two years of ethnographic fieldwork in Sarajevo on the Bosniaks' mundane sentiments, I argue that content-centered attention to the linguistic phenomena that does not grant an analytical and expressive space to the shift between speech and performative events or the emotional modality of their concrete use provide us with limited insights concerning the psychic topographies on which identities are articulated and disarticulated. The intellectual modality of engagement with the Ottoman past might itself appear as a congealed plot, but the "structure of feelings" that regulates the relationship of the Bosniaks with the "Ottoman legacy" is far from reified or constitutive of a "fixed point in thought and being."

V

The question of origins[10] is one of the most widely discussed public issues in Bosnia. One often hears a prominent historian or public intellectual explain where the Bosniaks came from. Cerić is also one of the public figures who addresses this

---

10   Adanır (2002) gives a very comprehensive historical account of this issue.

cumbersome question. For instance, in 2008, during the Turkish Prime Minister Erdogan's visit to Bosnia at the Muslim foundation *Merhamet*, Cerić declared that "Turkey is the mother to Bosniaks. It has always been and will always be so." This statement was criticized not only by non-Muslims but also by segments of the Muslim population in Bosnia.[11] Nevertheless, for most Bosnians, who are used to the discordant "political statements' of the Reis-ul-ulema, it was not much of an issue. Or, rather, it was not more controversial than countless instances of its kind, reflective of the mercurial ground on which attachment and detachment to the Ottoman past is reflected.

Poturice (Turkified) is a pejorative term the ultra-nationalist Serbs frequently use to address Slavic Muslims of Bosnia (Velikonja 2003). In Mahmutćehajić's words, the "specter of Bosnia is overlaid with the specter of the Turk in Europe (Velikonja 2003: 1). During the recent war, Bosnian Muslims were forced to declare their "real" origin – Croat or Serb – and were threatened with expulsion or extermination. Following the war, Bosnian Muslims then accepted the invitation to found a nation – not Serb or Croat, but "Bosniak." Since then, as part of an attempt to participate in the dominant grammar of nationhood, they have persistently worked to establish a "legitimate and continuous history" (Bringa 1995: 36) and connect their version of Islam with the heretical Christianity practiced in medieval Bosnia. In terms of drawing on the *long durée* in order to substantiate primordial claims to the country, their historical claim rhymes with those of Bosnian Serbs and Croats. Nevertheless, the Bosniaks' most urgent issue embedded in this claim to history is that Bosnia should never be part of Serbia or Croatia.

The dominant explanatory framework that has wide public purchase in Bosnia today underlines the medieval Bosnian church and Bogumili sect (Lopašić 1979; Pinson 1996; Fine 2007) that were neither Catholic nor Orthodox, and stresses that it was convenient for those Bosnians to switch to Islam gradually due to the pressure from both Christian churches. Their explanations underline consent, convenience and gradual initiation that leave space for individual choice. Nevertheless, it is important to add that this Bogumili reference acts as a rigid plot in its ordinary trajectory. It is always useful if and when an historical reference to origins needs to be made. It has no residual or excessive qualities, shattering the effects that linger on contemporary sentimental registers of belonging.[12] On the other hand, there are numerous jokes about Serbs' origins that tell us much about the anguish of Bosniaks about the question of their origins, a concern marked by the Ottoman reign in the region. Accordingly, Serb women had to sleep with Ottoman Turks since they did not convert to Islam, and most of the Serbs who claim Slavic purity today are the progeny of these couples. Therefore, the logic follows that the Serbs are biologically contaminated by the Turks, whereas, by

---

11   *Đorđe Latinović (Nezavisne Novine*, July 15, 2012); Fatmir Alispahić (*Bošnjaci. net*, December 10, 2012)

12   Marian Wenzel's (1993) skeptical examination of Bogomil registers through the curatorial practices in Bosnia resonates well with my observations.

implication, the Bosniaks have kept their biological Slavdom intact by converting to Islam. This half-ironic half-serious scenario has a broad appeal among the Bosniak public. The scenario is interesting not only in claiming true Slavdom, but also in revealing the cumbersome and obscene dimensions of relationships with the Ottoman Turks. In this account, the Serbs and the Turks share the same valence of trouble *vis-à-vis* the Bosniaks. This story skillfully reverses all claims and insults about their origins, charging Serbs with conversion while saving the Slavdom of the Bosniaks.

VI

New spaces for Muslims from Near and Middle East countries have been opened up by the re-Islamization of life in Bosnia in the heat of the war, followed by the fragile peace and dire conditions of subsistence in the post-war period, as well as the rapprochement between the political and religious actors in Bosnia, namely the *Islamska Zajednica* and the SDA (*Stranka Demokratska Akcija*: Party of Democratic Action) after the 1990s. However, many Bosnian Muslims, both those with a strong or explicit secular orientation as well as those with a more religious orientation (but with an emphasis on the necessity of watching over the traditional Bosnian form of Islam), are anxious about the growing presence of the international Muslim community in the country. This anxiety *vis-à-vis* foreign Islamic influence is profoundly manifested in their sentiments towards Wahhabis, which range from ambivalence to outright hostility. Wahhabis are the former Islamic fighters who extended their stay in the country and claim to play a significant role in the Islamization of Bosnia. Because of their vocation, Cerić, along with the wartime leader of the Bosnian Muslims, Alija Izetbegović, has been blamed for allowing these *mujahideen* to come and stay in Bosnia. Bosnian Muslims' ambivalence and anxiety is not only about which Islamic texts, teachings, philosophies or political and institutional frameworks would best serve their interests and aptly fit their traditions; rather, it is a matter of daily contact and encounters. For instance, for Bosnian Muslims, the Wahhabis are not just "conspicuous, lunatic, and dangerous fundamentalists" who spread their version of Islam with coercive techniques such as preaching in public about the proper way of being a good Muslim or raiding mosques in protest of local religious rituals that they deem pagan (as they did in June 2010, during the annual Muslim pilgrimage of Ajvaz Dedo),[13] or "indoctrinating jobless and hopeless Bosniak youth in return for daily subsistence." Wahhabis are also postmen, taxi-drivers, carpet cleaners and husbands of distant cousins that one encounters every now and then. Every single Bosnian Muslim who survived the war knows deep down that if and when the "day of judgment" comes again, they will need everybody around them, and especially the Wahhabis. Therefore, Cerić's answer, "We were not able to protect

---

13   A spiritual leader who is believed to have introduced Islam to Bosnia 500 years ago.

mosques," communicates the basic urge and limited capacity of not only cultural but also biological survival during wartime.

The growing Turkish presence in Bosnia(Solberg 2007; Karčić 2010; Türbedar 2011; Somun 2011; Bechev 2012) does not share the same dramatic urgency as is the case with the Wahhabi influence in the country. The official rhetoric of "historical and cultural proximity" between Turkey and Bosnia is not only a common expression, but has its reciprocity in the daily life of the Bosniaks. There is a growing desire for increasingly available Turkish things such as clothes, Islamic paraphernalia and kitsch, food, household appliances, ornaments, words, expressions, codes and mannerisms, popular music and laments, singers, serials, translated books, a TV channel, language courses and travel packages. However, the modality of engagement with Turkish cultural and Islamic forms, things and people is not monolithic, but layered in the occasional use of the parental metaphor used by the grand mufti of Bosnia. For the purposes of this chapter, I analytically differentiate and describe two major modalities of attachment to Turks and Turkish things. The first is to experience it as one of the features, if not requirements, of being a Sarajevan, Bosnian or Muslim cosmopolitan. The other is to experience it as the accumulation of cultural, symbolic and social capital that might be vital in the case of a temporary or permanent migration. However, it is important to understand that these two modalities of engagement are analytical constructions lacking neatly delineated boundaries between them. Moreover, switching from one mode of engagement to the other does not create excitement in a mundane plane of expressivity.

In the cosmopolitan modality of engagement with Turks and Turkish things, the Bosniaks, like some of their non-Muslim fellow countrymen, enjoy multiple repertoires of identity as one of the gifts that the history of their country has provided them with. Just like the weak referentiality of some of the grand mufti's statements mentioned above, this cosmopolitan gesture retains both the resonance of what I call the "imperial aura" of the Turkish things they are commonly related with and their unmaking at the same time. The psychic space that enables such an accumulated and deeply ingrained act of distancing comes from having been the citizens of two Yugoslavias and the Austro-Hungarian Empire, the Europeanness of which are commonly less questionable than that of the Ottoman Empire and its Turkish continuum. No wonder that some of the Turkish missionaries and professionals who I met and befriended during my fieldwork in Bosnia communicated, in their occasional confessional mood, "a kind of difficulty to name" sense of condescension by the very Bosniaks whose neediness and fragility was out of question for them.

The other modality of engagement with Turks and Turkish things is organized primarily by the deep sense of likelihood of having to leave Bosnia one day. According to this mindset and psyche (or perhaps "mood"), Turkey appears to be the most proximate and probable first destination. Some Bosniaks already have family members and friends in Turkey and, through their mutual visits, they have gained some familiarity with the ways and lifestyle in Turkey. In this, which I call the "fugitive modality of attachment," Bosniaks behave like future citizens in the making or, behaving well, as malleable subjects in front of their possible protector state as embodied in the person of a Turkish missionary and/or a friend.[14] Their deeply ingrained survival skills as non-sovereign citizens in their own country enable them to adjust comfortably to the infantilizing protocols of learning things in Turkish. A famous saying, not used without irony, *gde svi Turci, tu i mali Mujo* (wherever all the Turks are, the little Mujo is also there), best summarizes this mode of relationality. This old saying, which still enjoys wide popularity in Bosnia, is not used primarily or particularly in terms of their relationship with the Turks, but to express their historically conditioned, structurally mediated non-sovereign survival skills within a larger political entity.

It is important to note that this "fugitive modality of attachment" does not enjoy the same space of choice and distance as that of its cosmopolitan version. Nevertheless, it is worth remembering that in situations where survival is the essential frame of existence, as is the case in Bosnia, boundaries between choice and necessity are porous. Therefore, the distinction between these two modalities of attachment loses its explanatory power. Most Bosniaks oscillate between these two primary frames of engagement while also trying to attune themselves with the Islamization of their identity under the idiom of cosmopolitanism or Muslim nationalism.

Conclusion

In Bosnia, relating with Turks at home and contemporary Turkey and with the Ottoman past follows an irregular pattern of convergence and divergence, with no linear or easily narrated plot. It is also important to remember that Turkey's relationship with its Ottoman past is anything but monolithic. However, the growing rapprochement between the Bosniaks and the Turks is a promising field of inquiry for understanding the specific ways in which both ex-Ottoman communities reconfigure their Ottoman past in distinct and mutual ways. In the post-war period, the educational and philanthropic activities of religious groups from Turkey have been followed by growing interest in tourism and commercial activities. Turkey's recent initiative in the form of establishing a tripartite consultation mechanism engaging the Ministers of Foreign Affairs and Presidents of Serbia, Bosnia and Turkey (2009) to enhance political and social stability in the region and speed up the integration of the Western Balkans into the EU has made Turkey's claim to play a significant role in the country and region even

---

14 The secular or Islamic accent of this pedagogy depends on the situation and the Turks with whom Bosniaks engage. Although the secular/Islamic distinctions are incomparably more porous among the Bosniaks than among the Turks, Turkish-Bosniak communities of Muslim fraternity and sorority is a broadly neglected area of research that promises to offer rich insight into the formation of new Muslim subjectivities on both sides.

more salient. However, I observe that the Bosniaks juggle very complex feelings towards the growing Turkish presence in their country on the one hand and the cumbersome after-effects of the Ottoman legacy on the other. To be a "European Muslim," a widely held self-acclaimed identity among the Bosniaks since the war, is a discourse that has multiple voices, one of which is to underline the distinctive features of Bosnian Islam that cannot be explained simply through an Ottoman past. In this configuration, understanding the Bosniaks' relationship with the Turkish Islamic community is pivotal, since it intimately nurtures and intervenes in their desire to be "European Muslims."

References

Adanır, F. 2002. "The Formation of a 'Muslim' Nation in Bosnia-Herzegovina: A Historiography Discussion," in F. Adanır and S. Faroqhi (eds), *The Ottomans and the Balkans: A Discussion of Historiography*. Leiden: Brill, 267–304.

Banac, I. 1996. "Bosnian Muslims: From Religious Community to Socialist Nationhood and Postcommunist Statehood, 1918–1992," in M. Pinson (ed.), *The Muslims of Bosnia-Herzegovina: Their Historic Development from the Middle Ages to the Dissolution of Yugoslavia*. Cambridge, MA: Harvard University Press, 84–128.

Bechev, D. 2012. "Turkey in the Balkans: Taking a Broader View," *Insight Turkey*, 14(1), 131–46.

Bougarel, X. 2008. "Farewell to the Ottoman Legacy? Islamic Reformism and Revivalism in Inter-war Bosnia-Herzegovina," in N. Clayer and E. German (eds), *Islam in Inter-war Europe*. London: Hurst & Company, 313–43.

Bringa, T. 1995. *Being Muslim in a Bosnian Way: Identity and Community in a Central Bosnian Village*. Princeton, NJ: Princeton University Press.

Brown, L-C. (ed.) 1996. *Imperial Legacy: Ottoman Imprint on the Balkans and the Middle East*. New York: Columbia University Press.

Buturović, A. 2002. *Stone Speaker: Medieval Tombs, Landscape, and Bosnian Identity in the Poetry of Mak Dizdar*. New York: Palgrave.

Cerić, M. 2006. "European Muslim Identity in the New Millennium," speech given at the MIT, Boston, available at http://pagginusic.com/mp3/Mustafa+Ceric%3A+European+Muslim+Identity+in+the+New+Millennium-song-667994.html.

Djokić, D. 2003. "Yugoslavism: Histories, Myths, Concepts," in D. Djokić (ed.), *Yugoslavism: Histories of a Failed Idea, 1918–1992*. London: Hurst & Company, 1–10.

Donia, R-J. 1981. *Islam under the Double Eagle: The Muslims of Bosnia and Herzegovina, 1878–1914*. New York: Columbia University Press.

Fine, J-V-A. 2007. *The Bosnian Church: Its Place in State and Society from the Thirteenth to the Fifteenth Century*. London: Saqi Books.

Friedman, F. 1996. *The Bosnian Muslims: Denial of a Nation*. Boulder, CO: Westview Press.

Fuchs, B. 2007. "The Spanish Race," in M. Greer et al. (eds), *Rereading the Black Legend: The Discourses of Racism in the Renaissance Empires*. Chicago, IL: University of Chicago Press, 88–98.

Gagnon Jr., V-P. 2004. *The Myth of Ethnic War: Serbia and Croatia in the 1990s*. Ithaca, NY: Cornell University Press.

Hafizović, R. 2005. "Domestifikacija Nicejskog sindroma-'svadbenog veza' Države I Crkve," *Zeničke Sveske*, 1, 147–51.

Hajdarpašić, E. 2008. "Out of the Ruins of the Ottoman Empire: Reflections on the Ottoman Legacy in South-Eastern Europe," *Middle Eastern Studies*, 44(5), 715–34.

Helms, E. 2008. "East and West Kiss: Gender, Orientalism, and Balkanism in Muslim-Majority Bosnia-Herzegovina," *Slavic Review*, 67(1), 88–119.

Karčić, H. 2010. "Islamic Revival in Post-Socialist Bosnia and Herzegovina: International Actors and Activities," *Journal of Muslim Minority Affairs*, 30(4), 513–34.

Lockwood, W.-G. 2009. "Living Legacy of the Ottoman Empire: The Serbo-Croatian Speaking Moslems of Bosnia-Herzegovina," *Spirit of Bosnia*, 4(4), 1–13.

Lopašić, A. 1979. "Islamization of the Balkans: Some General Consideration," in J-M. Scarce (ed.), *Islam in the Balkans*. Edinburgh: Royal Scottish Museum, 50–51.

Ivan, L. 2001. *Bosnia: A Cultural History*. New York: New York University Press.

Mahmutćehajić, R. 2012. "Harmonia Abrahamica: The Spectre of Bosnia and those it Haunts," *Spirit of Bosnia*, 7(3), available at http://www.spiritofbosnia.org/volume-7-no-3-2012-july/harmonia-abrahamica-the-spectre-of-bosnia-and-those-it-haunts/?output=pdf.

McDonald, D-B. 2012. "Imperial Legacies and Neo-Ottomanism: Eastern Europe and Turkey," *Insight Turkey*, 14(4), 101–20.

Mujkić, A. 2007. *Mi, Građani Etnopolisa*. Sarajevo: Šahinpašić.

Pinson, M. 1996. "The Muslims of Bosnia-Herzegovina under Austro-Hungarian Rule, 1878–1918," in M. Pinson (ed.), *The Muslims of Bosnia-Herzegovina: Their Historic Development from the Middle Ages to the Dissolution of Yugoslavia*. Cambridge, MA: Harvard University Press, 84–128.

Rieff, D. 1993. "Notes on the Ottoman Legacy Written in a Time of War," *Salmagundi*, 100, 3–15.

Solberg, A.-R. 2007. "The Role of Turkish Islamic Networks in the Western Balkans," *Sudosteuropa*, 55(4), 429–462.

Somun, H. 2011. "Turkish Foreign Policy in the Balkans and 'Neo-Ottomanism': A Personal Account," *Insight Turkey*, 13(3), 33–41.

Taussig, M. 1999. *Defacement: Public Secrecy and the Labor of the Negative*. Stanford, CA: Stanford University Press.

Todorova, M. 1997. *Imagining the Balkans*. Oxford: Oxford University Press.

Türbedar, E. 2011. "Turkey's New Activism in the Balkans: Ambitions and Obstacles," *Insight Turkey*, 13(3), 139–58.

Velikonja, M. 2003. *Religious Separation and Political Intolerance in Bosnia-Herzegovina*. College Station: Texas A&M University Press
Velioğlu, H. 2011. "Bosniak Sentiments: Poetic and Mundane Life of Impossible Longings," unpublished Ph.D. dissertation, University of Texas at Austin.
Wenzel, M. 1993. "Bosnian History and Austro-Hungarian Policy: The Zemaljski Muzej, Sarajevo, and the Bogomil Romance," *Museum Management and Curatorship*, 12(2), 127–42.

Index

Ceric, Mustafa 242, 254; *see also* Reis-
    ul-ulema
Cesari, Jocelyne 18, 57, 179, 206
CFCM 152, 177, 191; *see also* French
    Council for the Muslim Faith
Chahine, Youssef 109
Charlie Hebdo 193, 200
chronopolitics 11
City of God 58
City of Man 58
citizenry 12, 15
civility 12, 22, 23, 123, 125–35
civility claims 125, 133, 134, 135
Civitas 154, 155
Classicism 27
clash of images 11, 101
Cologne Mosque 62, 65
common law 151, 152, 153, 155
communitarianism 42
common sense 9, 17, 21, 28, 31–4, 35, 93
Confucius 117, 118, 121
Constantinople 66, 67, 72, 103
contemporaneity 11, 23–5, 29–33, 204, 207
contemporaneous 221
controversy (as a theoretical notion) 8–13,
    16, 21–24, 26–34
convert movement 234
Convivencia 16, 217, 225, 228, 237
co-penetrations 17
corporality 53
cosmopolis 37
cosmopolitanism 18, 31, 37, 40–41, 222,
    242, 253
cosmo-political 38
counterpublics 169
counterpublic spaces 170
Cox, Caroline 157–8

darura 106, 182
Darwish, Mahmoud 222–3
da'wa 144–5, 146
Dayton Peace Accords (1995) 243
Declaration of European Muslims 245, 246
decolonialization 60
desacralization 71, 180–1
Descombes, Vincent 24–5, 29–30
Dia de la Toma 237
différend 8, 9, 13, 32, 41

disputatio 22, 23
disruptive effect 9–13, 17
dissensus 8, 9, 13, 32–3
dissimilar 13, 31,
dwelling place of life 231 ; *see morada
    vital*

embodied ethics 144
embodied practices 48, 53, 144
Emigrant, The 109; *see also* al-Muhajir
    and Chahine, Youssef
Enlightenment 15, 43, 53, 59, 117, 219,
    222
Enzensberger, Hans-Magnus 26
Escudero, Mansur Abdulsalem 236–7
ethology 71; *see also* sociobiology
Etoile Brillante 142; *see* Islamic musical
Eurocentric 41, 218
European city, the 15, 57–61, 63–4, 66
European Commission 51, 192, 196
European Muslims 6, 51–2, 61, 159, 207,
    245–6, 254
Europeanness 15, 196, 232, 252
European Parliament 192, 195
exceptionalism 15, 40, 74, 152, 175

Fabian, Johannes 11
face-veil 9, 83–4, 87–9, 92, 94–96
faith-based publicness 10; *see also* reason-
    based publicness
fard 182
FEMYSO 206
Ferhadija Mosque 247
Foucaultian perspective 144
FPÖ 79
Frampton, Kenneth 58
freedom of expression 12, 48, 131
freedom of religion 76
freedom of speech 101
freedom of worship 69
French Council for the Muslim Faith 152,
    177, 191; *see* CFCM
frère ennemi 120
Fuchs, Barbara 233
fugitive modality of attachment 253

Gauchet, Marcel 229
Giordano, Ralph 65